Holiday Ireland

Katie Wood was born [in] [...]
She read Communica[tions ... at]
university, and worked as a freelance journalist
before specializing in travel in 1981. Author of
many guidebooks, she has made a name for herself
both in Britain and internationally for her practical,
down-to-earth approach, and the quality of her
research.

Katie Wood continues to write freelance for,
among others, the *Observer*, the *Independent*, the
Guardian, the *Scotsman*, and several national
magazines. She also regularly contributes to
television and radio travel programmes. She is a
fellow of the Royal Geographical Society, undertakes
specialist travel consultancy work for airlines and
tourist boards, and, acknowledged as an expert
on the impact of travel on the environment, has
recently completed a policy document on green
tourism for the English Tourist Board.

Married with two children, Katie Wood lives
in Perth, Scotland, where she is working with her
husband on a new series of guides aimed at the
environmentally-aware traveller, The Good Tourist
series.

George McDonald was born in Dumfries, Galloway,
and was educated at Fettes College and Edinburgh
University. Since 1981 he has been constantly on
the move, and considers it unusual to be in one
place for more than three weeks at a time. Home,
when he's there, is Guernsey in the Channel Islands.
He now works on various projects, including his
own publishing concern.

Available by the same authors:

Europe by Train
The Round the World Air Guide

Available by Katie Wood:

The Best of British Country House Hotels
European City Breaks
Holiday Scotland
The Cheap Sleep Guide to Europe
The 100 Greatest Holidays in the World
The 1992 Business Traveller Guide
The Good Tourist
The Good Tourist in the UK
The Good Tourist in France

Holiday IRELAND

Katie Wood and George McDonald

Head Researcher: Moira Murray
Editorial Assistant: Wendy Cooper

Fontana
An Imprint of HarperCollins*Publishers*

Fontana
An Imprint of HarperCollins*Publishers*,
77–85 Fulham Palace Road,
Hammersmith, London W6 8JB

Published by Fontana 1992
9 8 7 6 5 4 3 2 1

First published in Great Britain by
Fontana Paperbacks 1989

Copyright © Katie Wood and George McDonald 1989
Copyright © Katie Wood 1991, 1992

The Author asserts the moral right to
be identified as the author of this work

ISBN 0 00 637774 2

Dunluce Castle and Giant's Causeway *Northern Ireland Tourist Board*. All other photographs *The Slide File*.

Set in Linotron Plantin

Printed in Great Britain by HarperCollins Manufacturing, Glasgow

All rights reserved. No part of this publication may be reproduced, stored in a retrieval system, or transmitted, in any form or by any means, electronic, mechanical, photocopying, recording or otherwise, without the prior permission of the publishers.

This book is sold subject to the condition that it shall not, by way of trade or otherwise, be lent, resold, hired out or otherwise circulated without the publisher's prior consent in any form of binding or cover other than that in which it is published and without a similar condition including this condition being imposed on the subsequent purchaser.

In memory of John Wood

Contents

Acknowledgements xiii

What This Guide is About xiii

Part One – BEFORE YOU GO

Key Facts 3

What to Expect 5

When to Go 9

The Climate 10

Where to Go for What 12
The Sun Worshipper 13   The Sightseer 15
The Socialite 19   Healthy Holidays: The Great Outdoors/
The Sportsperson 22   The Nature Lover 27
The Recluse 29   Family Holidays 31

Practicalities 35
Red Tape 35   Embassy and Consulate Addresses 35
Health Formalities 35   Customs 36   Money 36
Banking 39   Insurance 39   Health 41
Pre-planning and Free Information 42
Budgeting 43

Getting Yourself Organized 46
What to Take with You 46

Part Two – HOW TO GO

Package v. Independent 51

Package Holidays 52
Tour Operators in Britain Offering Packages to Ireland 52
General Tour Operators 57   Who Specializes in What 58
Self-Catering 58   *Cost-Conscious Holidays* 59
Short Breaks 60   *Farmhouse/Town and Country House
Accommodation* 61   *Coach Tours* 61   *Driving Holidays* 63
Activity Holidays 64   *Golf and Fishing Holidays* 64
Walking/Cycling Holidays 66   *Cruising Holidays* 67
Horse-drawn Caravans 67   Summing Up 67   Checklist 69

Independent Means 71
The Options 71   By Air 75   By Ferries 76   By Rail 77
By Bus 78   By Car/Campervan 79   Hitch-Hiking 81

Generally Useful Information 82
Time Differences 82   *Electricity* 82   *Water* 82

Part Three – WHEN YOU'RE THERE

Tourist Information 85   Sightseeing 86   Shopping 87
Food and Drink 88   Nightlife 93   Communications 94
Post Offices 94   *Poste Restante* 95   *Telephones* 95
Moving Around the Country 96   *Car-Hire* 96
Trains 99   *Buses* 99   *Horse-drawn Caravans* 100
Taxis 101   Problems/Emergencies 101   *Medical* 101
Police 101   *Embassies and Consulates* 102
Work 102   Women 102

A Potted History of Ireland 103
Be a Good Tourist 113

Part Four – GUIDE TO THE COUNTRY

DUBLIN AND ENVIRONS
Introduction 117   History 117   How to Get There 119
Communications 120   Tourist Information 121   Climate 121
When to Go 122   Culinary Specialities 122
Where to Go for What 123

DUBLIN 124 Accommodation 124   Sights 126
Museums and Galleries 129   City Tours 131   Shopping 131
Parks and Gardens 132   Where to Eat 133   Pubs 134
Nightlife 136   Excursions 137
NORTH OF DUBLIN 138   Howth 138   Malahide 139
Swords 140   Skerries 141   Balbriggan 141   Bettystown 142
Drogheda 142   Ardee 144   Kells 145   Dundalk 145
SOUTH OF DUBLIN 146   Dun Laoghaire 146   Dalkey 148
Killiney 148   Bray 149   Enniskerry 149   Poulaphouca 153
Aghavannagh 153   Wicklow 153   Clara 155

SOUTH-EAST
Introduction 156   Communications 156   Climate 157
Where to Go for What 157
Arklow 158   Gorey 158   Castletown 159   Blackwater 160
Enniscorthy 161   Killanne 163   WEXFORD 164   Rosslare 166
Bridgetown 168   Carrig-on-Bannow 168   New Ross 168
Ballyhack 169   WATERFORD 171   Dunmore East 178
Tramore 178   Annestown 179   Fenor 179   Dungarvan 180
Kilmacthomas 181   Clonmel 181   Marfield 182
Portlaw 183   Cappoquin 184   Ballyporeen 184   Lismore 184
Ballyduff 186   Tallow 186   Ardmore 186   Grange 187
Gorteen 187   Youghal 187

SOUTH-WEST
Introduction 190   History 190   Practical Information 192
Tourist Information 192   Climate 193
Where to Go for What 193   Forest walks and trails in Cork 194

Midleton 196   Roche's Point 197   Cobh 197   CORK 198
Kinsale 208   Clonakilty 211   Glandore 212   Skibbereen 214
Crookhaven 214   Bantry 215   Macroom 218   Mallow 218
Forest walks and trails in Kerry 219   Kenmare 220
Glanmore 222   KILLARNEY 223   Killorglin 226
Kells Bay 228   Caherdaniel 229   Dingle Peninsula 231
Dingle 231

WEST
Introduction 234   History 234   Communications 235
Tourist Information 236   Climate 236   Where to Go for What 236   Forest walks and trails in West Ireland 237
LIMERICK 239   Annacotty 243   Castleconnell 243   Killaloe 243
Murroe 244   Kilfinane 245   Kilmallock 245   Adare 246
Rathkeale 247   Dromcollogher 247   Portrinard 248   Glin 248
Knockpatrick 248   Foynes 248   Askeaton 248   ENNIS 249
Corofin 251   Tulla 251   Craggaunowen 251   Scariff 252
Killimer 252   Kilrush 252   Kilkee 253   Carrigaholt 253
Lahinch 254   Doolin 254   Kilfenora 255
GALWAY CITY 255   Clarinbridge 257   Kinvara 257
Craughwell 257   Loughrea 257   Woodford 258   Clonfert 258
Ballinasloe 258   Milltown 258   Oughterard 259   Connemara 259
Carraroe 259   Clifden 260   Ballynahinch 260   Cleggan 260
WESTPORT 260   Knock 261   Mayo 262   Fallmore 262
Crossmolina 262   Killala 262   Ballina 263   ROSCOMMON 263
Boyle 264   SLIGO 265   Strandhill 265
Carrowmore 265   Mullaghmore 266   Carrick-on-Shannon 266
Manorhamilton 266   Dromahair 267

NORTH-WEST
Introduction 272   History 272   Communications 273
Tourist Information 274   Climate 274
Where to Go for What 274
Forest walks and trails in the North-west 275
Bundoran 276   Rossnowlagh 277   Ballintra 277   Laghey 277
DONEGAL 277   Mountcharles 278   Killybegs 279   Kilcar 279
Carrick 280   Glencolumbkille 280   Glenties 280
Letterkenny 282   Bunbeg 284   Gortahork 284   Falcarragh 284

Tory Island 284   Dunfanaghy 285   Creeslough 285
Carrigart 286   Kerrykeel 287   Rathmullan 287   Ramelton 288
Kilmacrennan 288   Manorcunningham 289   Buncrana 290
Clonmany 290   Ballyliffin 290   Malin Head 290

MIDLANDS
Introduction 292   History 292   Communications 293
Tourist Information 293   Climate 294
Where to Go for What 294
Monaghan 295   Cavan 297   Longford 299   Westmeath 300
Offaly 302   Kildare 304   Laois 305   Kilkenny 307
Tipperary 302

NORTHERN IRELAND
Introduction 312   History 312   Practical Information 314
Tourist Information 316   Climate 316
Where to Go for What 317
BELFAST 317   Edenderry 325   Larne 325   Carrickfergus 326
Antrim 327   Lisburn 327   Hillsborough 328   Bangor 328
Holywood 328   Newtownards 328   Groomsport 329
Comber 329   Donaghadee 329   Ballyhalbert 330
Portaferry 330   Newcastle 330   Downpatrick 331
Annalong 332   Kilkeel 332   Newry 332   Lurgan 333
Portadown 333   Armagh 334   Markethill 337
Crossmaglen 337   Dungannon 337   Ballygawley 339
Fivemiletown 339   Cookstown 339   Tullahogue 339
Omagh 340   Plumbridge 341   Newtownstewart 341
Strabane 341   Enniskillen 343   Moneymore 345
Draperstown 345   Toomebridge 345   Derry 346
Eglinton 349   Limavady 349   Coleraine 350
Portstewart 351   Portrush 351   Portballintrae 352
Cushendun 354   Cushendall 354   Glenariff 354
Glenarm 354   Ballymoney 355   Ballymena 355

Index 357

ACKNOWLEDGEMENTS

Thanks are owed to Darra Quinn, the itinerant Irishman now residing in Perthshire.

I should also like to thank the Irish Tourist Board in London and Bord Fáilte in Ireland for their support throughout the project and their help with updating.

On the home front, a personal thanks is owed to my mother who 'kept the home fires burning', and allowed me snatched moments of childless peace to get this book written, and, of course, a thank you to my husband without whose practical help and support this would not have been published.

Lastly, to Wendy Cooper and Moira Murray for their 1992 updating.

WHAT THIS GUIDE IS ABOUT

For too long now there has been a gulf in the guidebook market. On the one hand there are the 'heavies' – books which, though good in their way, assume that holidaymakers want a stone-by-stone description of all the ancient remains in the country of their choice, and, what's more, assume that their readership is middle-aged, middle-class and predominantly American with a lot of cash to splash about. At the other end of the scale are the backpacking, student-orientated, 'rough it on £15 a day' guides which assume the traveller wants to cover the maximum amount of ground possible and spend the absolute minimum doing so (even if this does mean surviving on one bowl of vegetable rice a day and no baths for two weeks).

But in the middle of these poles lies the vast majority of tourists: normal, fun-loving people who go on holiday to unwind from a year's toil, and who, though not able to throw cash around indiscriminately, are willing to spend enough to enjoy themselves. Predominantly these people fall into the under-forty age group – the 'young ones' keen to see the countries they visit and have a good time in their own way. This guide is written for this sort of person.

It does not wade into pages of history – it just gives you the basics to enable you to make sense of the monuments and places you'll see while on holiday. It does not pretend to be a specialist guide for one group of people (watersports enthusiasts, golfers, nature lovers) but it does point you in the direction of where to pursue these types of hobbies once you are in the country.

In the following pages you will find information to help you prepare for – and survive – an independent holiday to Ireland. Package holidaymakers are not forgotten either: although there are only around forty or so Irish tour operators, you will find that the range of holidays on offer is quite remarkable. We look in some detail at the various packages and the pros and cons associated with each. All the relevant up-to-date information is in Part One – 'Before You Go'.

We hope this guide will help you to have a rewarding time in Ireland, a country whose diversity and appeal never fail to amaze first-time visitors. As much detail as possible has been included to help ensure that your holiday is an enjoyable one, but if you feel we have missed anything out, let us know. This is a different type of holiday guide: informal and chatty, not academic and definitive. We are not setting ourselves up as *the* authority on Ireland. We know a lot and have travelled there extensively, but our knowledge is more of where the best places for different types of holidays are, than of Irish history. If any of our recommendations fails to come up to the mark, or if you find a super undiscovered beach which you are willing to share, or a new lively night-spot, write and tell us about it. After all, we all want the same in the end – the memory of at least two glorious, fun-filled weeks to sustain us through the long, dark winter nights.

NB All prices mentioned in this guide were correct at the time of going to press.

Part One
BEFORE YOU GO

KEY FACTS

ENTRY REQUIREMENTS: No passports are required by British citizens, travelling from Britain. Visitors from North America and Australia require passports, but not visas.

POPULATION: 5,000,000 (Eire 3,700,000; Northern Ireland 1,300,000)

CAPITAL: Dublin (pop: 920,000)

CURRENCY: Irish pound or *punt* (£1 = IR£1.10)

POLITICAL SYSTEM: Parliamentary democracy

RELIGION: Roman Catholic

LANGUAGES: English (plus some Irish Gaelic)

PUBLIC HOLIDAYS:
1 January	June holiday (first Monday in June)
St Patrick's Day, 17 March	August holiday (first Monday in August)
Good Friday	
Easter Monday	October holiday (last Monday in October)

TELEPHONE CODES FROM WITHIN IRELAND:
Arklow 0402	Dundalk 042
Athlone 0902	Ennis 065
Bandon 023	Enniscorthy 054
Bundoran 072	Galway 091
Castlebar 094	Kilkenny 056
Clonmel 052	Killarney 064
Cork 021	Letterkenny 074
Donegal 073	Limerick 061
Drogheda 041	Longford 043
Dublin 01	Mallow 022

Mullingar 044
Naas 045
Navan 046
Port Laoise 0502
Rathluirc 063
Roscommon 0903
Sligo 071
Tralee 066
Waterford 051
Wexford 053
Wicklow 0404
Youghal 024

followed by telephone number.

If phoning from the UK to Dublin, dial 0001 followed by the private telephone number. To anywhere else from the UK dial 010 353 then the relevant code without a 0 in front, followed by the private telephone number.

What to Expect

Unlike most holiday destinations, Ireland lives up to all expectations. The popular image of an Emerald Isle peopled by friendly folk is not far from the mark, and thousands of people each year are attracted by the promise of peaceful havens and unspoilt scenery in the ancient land of the Celts.

Despite the country's growing popularity, Ireland is obviously not in the same league as Mediterranean countries, whose beaches are swamped yearly by pale Europeans in search of sun, sea 'n' sand. As a result, little is sacrificed on the altar of mass tourism. The positive spin-offs from the more modest proportions of the Irish tourist industry are the lack of execrable concrete tourist villages and the sensitive (and sensible) preservation of Ireland's historical and natural heritage. There are over 400 forest parks distributed throughout the country, as well as three national parks located at Glenveagh in Co. Donegal, Connemara in Co. Galway and Killarney in Co. Kerry. The numerous historical monuments which between them chart the growth of Ireland's religious, social and political identity are carefully preserved by the National Monuments Commission which frequently charges nothing or a minimal fee for viewing.

With a population of around five million, Ireland is one of the most underpopulated countries in Western Europe due to the mass emigration of the early nineteenth century. A better get-away-from-it-all location would be difficult to imagine. An oft-quoted maxim, loved by Americans, is that rush-hour in Ireland is when the cows go for milking! Whilst it's ideal for relaxation, there is nevertheless a surprising diversity of countryside to discover if you have the time and the inclination. In the East, the capital, Dublin, is one of the world's great cities and brings a flavour of internationalism to an essentially provincial country. Days could be spent here, delving into the various Joycean voyages, sampling some world-class theatre or drinking in one of the numerous pubs. Heading out of Dublin, however, the world of small-town Ireland unfolds in the charming traditional seaside resorts along the east coast, culminating in the stretch of coastline which is virtually non-stop sand from Arklow to Wexford.

The southern coast has a different character, with some magnificent cliffs interspersed with small, secluded coves and the occasional large resort, such as Tramore, where the Irish themselves prefer to spend their summer holidays. In the South-west the magnificent scenery of Co. Kerry, exemplified by the traditional Ring of Kerry tourist route, fuses low, blue mountains with a countryside of waterfalls and rugged coastlines. Killarney, the tourist centre of the South-west, is a bustling little town whose attempts to flog traditional souvenirs are always accomplished with good-natured charm. Inland, the landscape is fertile fields interspersed with networks of rivers and lough systems – a paradise for anglers!

Further up the west coast to Co. Clare, Galway, Sligo and Donegal, the holidaymaker moves into the truly traditional Ireland of rainswept peat bogs and isolated communities. Here can be found pockets of Gaelic-speaking communities known as the Gaeltacht who preserve a fragment of the ancient Irish tongue which has long been usurped by English as the common language. Here too can be found Connemara National Park in Co. Galway, with its stark granite countryside sloping up into the magnificent Connemara mountain range, unrivalled by anything else in Ireland for its majesty and gloomy beauty. Co. Donegal is the most northerly part of the Republic of Ireland, and also one of the poorest. Depleted by years of endemic depopulation, the community is predominantly old people and the way of living is strongly traditional, with donkeys, horses and sheep roaming freely over the roads, and thatched cottages punctuating a moorland landscape.

For all the tranquil face of Southern Ireland today, the history of the Republic has been a tumultuous one, with periods of war and strife alternating with extraordinary literary and cultural activity. The first such phase followed the Christianization of the Irish Celts around the fifth century AD, when the rapid building and setting up of monastic communities proceeded for around five centuries, interrupted only by the Viking invasions in the eighth century. These religious communities produced some of the richest medieval art and literature in the Western world, the supreme surviving example being the lavishly illustrated *Book of Kells* on display at Trinity College Library, Dublin. This period of artistic ascendancy was interrupted by the first in a long series of struggles with the English crown. Taking advantage of internal political disarray in Ireland, Henry II of England claimed lordship and thus began the influx of Anglo-Normans occupying the positions of power and prestige in Irish society.

Things worsened after the Reformation and the ascension of William of Orange to the British throne, when Penal Laws were introduced which denied the Catholics – by far the majority of the population – any right of property or education and prohibited them from occupying any position of power. The impoverished state of the Irish poor reached terrifying proportions after the Great Potato Famine affected the staple means of support in the mid-nineteenth century. During this period, many Irish died and many more emigrated, predominantly to the United States, so that by the end of 1849, Ireland had been depleted by two million people. After the atrocities of the Famine, the movement for self-government gained momentum, although it was not until the beginning of the First World War that the British government yielded to pressure and granted a degree of independence in the shape of Home Rule. Things came to a head in Easter 1916 when a band of stalwart republicans staged an insurrection outside the General Post Office in Dublin and proclaimed the Irish Republic – the bullet holes from fighting can still be seen in the stonework today. The famous rebels – Connolly, Pearse and Macdermott among them – were defeated after a week of bloody fighting and eventually executed.

The quashing of the rebellion and the subsequent attempts to unseat the government had little effect on the overwhelming public support for an independent Ireland and in 1921, the British ceded the present Irish Republic, reserving the controversial Northern province for British control. Today, Ireland is a relatively poor nation which has benefited greatly from membership of the EC and from the increasing numbers of tourists who come to Irish shores each year.

Untroubled by the disturbances which the Northern province suffers, there is little in the way of crime outside Dublin. This makes Ireland one of the safest holiday destinations for young(ish!) people engaged in camping, hitching or cycling holidays. But undoubtedly where Ireland really scores is with family holidays. There are a considerable number of holiday towns along the Irish coast which have plenty to occupy energetic kids, with funfairs, clock-golf and so on, whilst having places of historical or natural interest for mums and dads only a short car-drive away. On the budget front, Ireland is undeniably more expensive than Britain (for example, petrol costs nearly twice as much), but getting there, whether by ferry or plane, is much cheaper than a charter flight to your favourite Spanish resort. Overall, the costs of a holiday in Ireland are likely to balance out as roughly equal to a package to one of the Mediterranean destinations.

Touring Ireland by car or campervan is the ideal way to penetrate the most remote areas of the country. Although road standards are considerably lower than in the UK, the volume of traffic is light which makes for enjoyable, stress-free touring. For those who don't have a car or can't afford to hire one, public transport in the shape of trains and buses is comprehensive and reasonably inexpensive (by Irish standards anyway). The rail service has undergone a facelift recently and the trains are now on a par with the French TGVs for efficiency, cleanliness and speed. For those planning to travel extensively, a two-week or one-week Rambler's pass for bus and rail travel is a good way to cut costs and at around £75 for an eight-day pass compares favourably with the cost of petrol for a week's car tour. As far as accommodation goes, Bed and Breakfast is a national institution – and once you've tried the traditional Irish hospitality which is on offer in these places, the impersonal ambience of hotels will never seem the same again. Hotels and guesthouses are plentiful, but nevertheless the premier tourist spots of Killarney, Dublin and Cork still become crowded during July and August so booking ahead is strongly advised.

Most people who come to Ireland travel independently, thus there is less demand for comprehensive package tours. This is an area which is growing, however, and a few of the major tour companies, such as Thomson, now offer some type of package to Ireland. Nevertheless, a substantial number of tour operators with programmes to Ireland are specialists who focus on the premium facilities which Ireland offers to, for example, anglers or golfers (see 'Activity Holidays' on page 64). The largest tour operators, such as **Aer Lingus** or **Ryanair**, also supplement their basic packages with a less-standardized choice of river cruises, angling holidays and so on. This leaves the package holidaymaker in Ireland with an unusually wide and comprehensive range of packages to choose from, depending on his/her interests.

When to Go

All over Ireland, July and August are the warmest and driest months. This is also the time when most people pack their bags and take two weeks off for the annual family holiday. The most popular destinations, such as Dublin, Killarney, Cork and towns in the South are likely to be packed out with other holidaymakers at this time of the year, so if you want to do the traditional tourist sightseeing route (two nights in Dublin, one day for the Ring of Kerry, etc.) be warned – you'll be sharing these delights with hundreds of other pleasure-seekers. Alternatively, if you are only planning on a few days away and concentrating mainly on Dublin and its environs, then there is no reason why you shouldn't consider coming out of season in March, September or even January: the crisp winter certainly gives some impetus to sightseeing tours!

For exploring the countryside, and especially if you are touring by car, the end of May to early September is by far the best time.

Any other time of the year and you risk not being able to see the beauty of the landscape for sheets of rain, fog or even sleet. If you are planning on taking your car by ferry from Britain, remember that booking space is essential during the peak summer months. The same goes for foot passengers. Book ahead and check if you need control cards, bearing in mind that many travel agents don't know or won't volunteer this information unless you ask. Control cards guarantee you a passage on the sailing that you booked, and also ensure that you get dealt with quickly and don't have to spend a lot of time hanging around in queues.

July and August are also the best months for the beach – yes, people *do* sunbathe in Ireland. Average temperatures are around 66°C (19°F) but if you're lucky and have a warm spell, there is nowhere on the Mediterranean that can rival a clean, deserted Irish beach fragrant with the smell of drying peat and pines. Irish resorts, such as Tramore or Ballybunion, come alive in these months as the Irish themselves head to the seaside. Even in mildly warm weather, kids can enjoy the ice-creams, the donkey-rides and above all, the numerous amusement arcades.

The Climate

The verdant hills of Ireland's landscape owe a great deal to the quantities of rain which fall every year. The West is the rainiest part of the country with around 225 days in the year experiencing some kind of rainfall, whilst the East does considerably better with only 135 days of rainfall. In mountainous districts rainfall can exceed 2000mm per year and it is worth bearing this in mind when you are planning to tour the Ring of Kerry. Don't be deceived by brilliant sunshine in Killarney; there is often fog and rain in the higher reaches because of the close concentration of mountain peaks. April is the driest month overall, but July generally is more favourable to the southern parts of Ireland.

Because of the tempering influence of the Gulf Stream, winters in Ireland are wet rather than bitterly cold. The average temperatures for the coldest months of December and January are between 4°C (39°F) and 7°C (44°F). Temperatures rise from March onwards to around the 14–16°C mark (58–62°F) in July and August, although the sunniest months are actually May and June when five and a half hours of sunshine a day are not unusual. Inland, winter temperatures tend to be colder (around 1°C/33°F), whilst the inland loughs warm up more quickly than the sea on sunny days, but lose heat more rapidly at night. There is no appreciable climate gradient between the north and south of the country.

Average daily temperatures, based on Dublin:

	JAN	FEB	MAR	APR	MAY	JUN
°F	41	41	43	47	51	56
°C	5	5	6	8	11	13

	JUL	AUG	SEP	OCT	NOV	DEC
°F	59	59	56	50	45	43
°C	15	15	13	10	7	6

As far as sea temperatures go, the South-west undoubtedly provides the warmest bathing water with temperatures rising to around 15°C (59°F) in late summer, compared with 13°C (56°F) for the same period in the North-west. In winter, temperatures are relatively mild (around 10°C/50°F in the South-west) due to the warming influence of the Gulf Stream, but even these temperatures come nowhere near the warmth of mid-winter Mediterranean waters. No winter holidaying here.

Where to Go for What

People often spend weeks deliberating which country to choose for their holiday destination, then leave the final choice of where they stay within the country to either a photo and a brief, optimistic write-up in a travel brochure, or to the discretion and persuasive talk of a travel agent (many of whom haven't actually visited the country). This lottery results, not surprisingly, in people having a disappointing holiday simply because they got the facts wrong on this crucial decision. If anything, the decision about which part of the country you base yourself is more important than the choice of the country itself, for there are good and bad in every country – Britain, for example, offers the tourist a superb holiday destination, but if the visitor were to opt for two weeks in Sheffield when he really wanted a 'get away from it all' type of break, he would be sadly disappointed. Ireland, like Britain, has a lot to offer the holidaymaker, but if you're a fun-loving socialite, there's little point in ending up in wind-swept Donegal when you could be partying the night away in cosmopolitan Dublin.

In order to match your needs to the most suitable resorts we have divided holidaymakers into certain stereotypes. Doubtless most of you fall into several of the categories, but the idea is to find which resorts crop up under the headings which interest you, and match your needs accordingly.

The following symbols representing the various interests appear throughout this book as an easy guide to the places likely to be of interest to you.

The Sun Worshipper

The Sightseer

The Socialite

The Sportsperson

The Nature Lover

The Recluse

Family Holidays

 THE SUN WORSHIPPER

It has to be said – people generally don't come to Ireland for suntans and sandcastles. But you'd be foolish not to pack your bucket and spade because the South usually enjoys some warm sunny weather in the months of July and August, and there are numerous beautiful beaches to choose from – if the weather is right!

On the east coast can be found the attractive old-style seaside towns, to which the Dublin *petite bourgeoisie* used to flock in days past. **BRAY** is a fine example, with its mile-long stretch of sand and shingle beach. Some of the old charm has gone from the place – largely through the boom in traffic which clogs up the main streets – but along the seafront Bray's fine Victorian esplanade still retains some of the original splendour. This is a convenient location for those trying to escape from the city on a hot day as Bray is on the DART commuter line which connects the small east-coast towns with Dublin's sprawling metropolis. Further down the coast, Brittas Bay is probably one of the best beaches between Dublin and **ARKLOW**, an attractive town at the head of a large sweeping bay which eventually culminates in

ROSSLARE. There are four blue-flag beaches in this area: at Courtown, Curracloe, Rosslare and Duncannon. This major resort has five miles of golden sand as its main attraction, although a good golf course and sundry other entertainments certainly help to pull in Rosslare's thousands of visitors each year.

An abundance of sandy coves hidden behind rocky outcrops are the major characteristics of the southern coastline. There are numerous little villages and sleepy towns along this coast which make excellent bases for touring major places of interest, such as Cork city, Waterford or Blarney, whilst also providing close proximity to good beaches and the warm(ish!) seas of the southern coast.

The unpretentious little towns of **DUNMORE EAST**, **ARDMORE** and **CLONEA** all have exceptionally clean and well-maintained beaches – although there is little off-beach entertainment to keep those with lots of party spirit occupied. As far as main resorts go, **TRAMORE** is *the* place to be, for both on-beach and off-beach activities. Even on tepid days people bravely bare all to sunbathe in indifferent weather and swim in the icy Celtic Sea. Plenty of room to build sandcastles here on the magnificent stretch of golden beach, and if you get bored, there are always the donkey-rides, bars, funfairs, amusement arcades . . . Further along into Co. Cork is **YOUGHAL**. Although rather unprepossessing when first confronted, with its built-up appearance, it does have a good beach and as the town has a surprising wealth of historical interest there's plenty to do should it rain, and the entertainments of Cork city are only a short jaunt away.

In the South-west, **DINGLE BAY** has legendary charm – all deserved! **ROSSBEIGH STRAND** on the southern approach is a four-mile stretch of some of the cleanest sand in Ireland. On the opposite side, the small seaside town of **INCH** is a convenient stopping-off point to reach a sand-spit which, again, has plenty of potential for beach lovers. Further up the coast in Co. Kerry, the resort of **BALLYBUNION** has recently won the coveted EC two-flag rating for the cleanliness of its beaches and standards of upkeep. This is also one of the favoured resorts where the Irish themselves like to holiday.

The further north you go, the more unlikely it is that the sun will continue to shine for more than a few hours on end. This is a pity, because it is undoubtedly the north-western quarter of the country which possesses the most attractive beaches. Or then again, perhaps it is *because* it rains so much that the sand on Donegal's beaches is washed clean to its unusual white, luminous quality. If you are lucky enough to get a respite from the spells of mid-summer rain, then a day on one of the northern beaches simply cannot be beaten. **SALTHILL** is perhaps the most urbanized of the popular beach resorts. As a suburb of Galway town, it has a rather soulless promenade of amusement arcades and fast-food joints, yet it still remains the traditional outlet for Galway folk on a sunny day. In Co. Sligo, **MULLAGHMORE**, **ENNISCRONE** and **ROSSES POINT** have beaches which rate highly, whilst **STRANDHILL** and **EASKEY** provide some excellent surfing conditions. **BUNDORAN**, with its fine golfing facilities and lovely beach, is the last major resort town before the wild countryside of Donegal begins. In the most northerly county in the Republic, the white beaches are distributed sporadically between the rocky headlands. **ARDARA** has a beautiful stretch of sand, although it is somewhat inaccessible – ask at the local post office for directions. Finally, **MULROY BAY** in the very north is a good base for exploring the deserted delights of the sandy coves and beaches of this part of the country.

 ## THE SIGHTSEER

The sightseer's task is made considerably easier in Ireland by the excellent information service offered by local tourist offices. Whatever county you are heading for, stop off first at the tourist office and pick up as much information as possible. If you are touring by car, make a point of buying one of the local touring guides (cost: £1). These small booklets provide an entertaining on-going narrative as you pass through the small and seemingly insignificant hamlets of the county. One typical anecdote can be found in the Wexford guide, where we are told that in the small village of Ferns is the grave of a priest who changed the course of history: as a young man in France, he saved a student from drowning and it turned out later that this lucky chap happened to be called Napoleon Bonaparte!

Wherever you go in Ireland, there is no lack of things to see. At the most basic level, crumbling monasteries and ancient churches are scattered all over the place. Whilst the ruins themselves may be fairly unremarkable, they are frequently set amid picturesque countryside and the major sites have been conscientiously protected from unsightly tourist developments. The ancient **GLENDALOUGH** monastery in the Wicklow mountains is a prime example of this type of conservation. Adequate parking facilities are carefully screened from the road, and there is an interesting visitor centre located at a convenient distance from the main ruins. There are well-laid-out walks along the side of the lough and most importantly, the beautiful view up the lough is unspoilt by any tasteless concrete blocks. Visits to churches and monasteries are usually free, whilst castles and stately homes generally charge admission fees. Entrance costs vary from place to place but as a guide, **BLARNEY CASTLE**, one of the most visited tourist attractions in Ireland, charges around £1.50 for adults and 50p for students/children. When you're visiting stately homes or castles, make sure that you know exactly what you're paying for, as many establishments open only their gardens to the public.

Whilst the countryside is scattered with places of interest, the major towns of **LIMERICK**, **KILLARNEY** and **GALWAY** may on first sight appear to be the usual commercial blend of fast-food joints and clothes-shops. If you dig beneath the surface, however, there is a great deal of historical and folk interest in these towns. Try to pick up the walking-tour leaflets from the local tourist offices: the tours can last anything from two to four hours, depending on how long you linger at individual sights, but by the end, you'll certainly have a comprehensive knowledge of the town and its origins.

The east of the country has the greatest concentration of interesting museums, stately homes and parks to visit. The further north-west you go, man-made attractions are replaced by natural ones (see 'The Nature Lover' on page 27), but here is a selection of the major sights from around the country.

DUBLIN: European City of Culture in 1991, this cosmopolitan capital should be the first stop on any sightseer's itinerary. Packed with character and history, it has plenty to keep even the most avid tourist occupied for at least two full days. The attractions range from Trinity College, which houses the medieval *Book of Kells*, to the James Joyce tours and a drink of Guinness beside the banks of the Liffey. Also not to be missed are a visit to the Central Post Office to see the marks of the bullets from the Easter 1916 rising, a trip to Dean (Jonathan) Swift's cathedral and a visit to the Dail, the Irish Parliament. Even if you manage all the sights suggested here and on page 126, you'll only have scraped the surface of this most fascinating of cities.

IRISH NATIONAL HERITAGE PARK (Co. Wexford): One of the best examples of the many fine, imaginative exhibitions to be found throughout Ireland which bring a new meaning to the word 'history'. The Irish National Heritage Park traces 9000 years of Irish life by bringing it alive with reproductions of ancient fortifications and homesteads located in spacious surroundings so you can wander around at your leisure. If you're attracted by this type of thing, **BUNRATTY CASTLE** (Co. Limerick) has an interesting Folk Park. Although on a less ambitious scale than the Irish National Heritage Park, it successfully recreates the buildings and atmosphere of an old Shannonside community.

WATERFORD CRYSTAL FACTORY (Co. Waterford): Waterford Crystal is famous throughout the world and the opportunity to see the glassmaking process should not be missed. Tours around the factory are free, and the guides have an informative and interesting tale to tell as you are shown around. All parts of the process are demonstrated, from glass-blowing to cutting and polishing, and afterwards you can visit the on-site shop selling the genuine article. It should be noted, children are not permitted on the tour.

RING OF KERRY: This is the most famous scenic tour in Ireland, although with the country's wealth of scenery, it would be difficult to assess whether it is also the best. Many people follow it anyway, starting from **Killarney** passing through **Cahirciveen, Sneem** and **Moll's Gap**. Just as interesting as the scenic beauty is the range of history which the Ring encompasses. As you traverse the route, you'll pass through areas which have associations with the 1916 rising and the early Christian settlements as well as places of folklore and myth. Numerous bus tours and train services specialize in Ring of Kerry trips. At the peak of the summer these become very busy, and you may well have to reserve a place a week in advance. If you're not going to be in Kerry for any length of time, booking ahead is possible through tourist offices. One drawback with advance booking is that it is impossible to anticipate the kind of weather you'll get: mist can frequently come down, cloaking all the best views. On a bad day, there is simply no point in doing the Ring of Kerry as you won't see a thing.

KNOCK SHRINE (Co. Mayo): One aspect of Ireland which is instantly noticeable to the visitor is the number of Marian shrines perched at crossroads and beside lay-bys throughout the country. A deeply Catholic country, Ireland is second only to Portugal in the number of 'miracles' (i.e. moving statues, crying figures, etc.) which happen each year. One miracle, which has been officially recognized by the Vatican, occurred in 1879 when a vision of Mary appeared to a group of Knock labourers and children. Since this event, Knock has become the centre for pilgrims across Ireland as well as abroad. Whether you're devout or simply curious, it's worth a visit if you're in the north of the country.

ARAN ISLANDS (Co. Galway): If you're after Old Ireland, this is the place to go. The ancient Irish tongue is still widely spoken here, although most islanders are bilingual. The traditional Irish costume is still worn by some, particularly on the middle island **Inishmaan**. Most notable of the sights on the islands is the Dun Aengus on **Inishmore**. This is one of the finest prehistoric monuments in Europe, spectacularly located on the west-facing cliffs. As with the Ring of Kerry, trips are full up well in advance, so book ahead. Costs are around £20 for a round trip. Passenger ferries leave from Galway city and Doolin, Co. Clare (Tel: 065 74189 for booking information). There is also a daily air service from Galway. This is operated by Aer Arann Teo, and calls at all three islands.

It's evident from the sights detailed above that Ireland possesses a varied selection of unusual and interesting things to do and see. In the individual sections, you'll find a more comprehensive list of sights in each area, but those listed above represent the 'musts' for those on whistle-stop sightseeing tours.

 ## THE SOCIALITE

The pub is the natural gathering place in Irish society, where news is swapped, friendships are made and business deals solemnized. Perhaps it is the Irish love of the 'blarney' which makes the atmosphere of their pubs different; wherever you go, whether country or town, you won't be alone for long in an Irish pub. Often too, the buildings most unprepossessing from the outside turn out to be the locals' favourites, so don't be put off by appearances. If you're looking for something more special than a pint of Guinness in the local to round off your day, then look out for hotels or restaurants offering Irish Nights. These can be found throughout the country and generally include a bit of fiddle and harp music, Irish dancing and a sing-song. You'll have to pay to get in (around IR£3–£5 per head), but if you only have a few drinks then this is a cheap night's entertainment. As Irish music is very popular both with the locals and visitors, you should make a point of trying to get to at least one Irish Night during your holiday. Tourist offices can help you with locations, or, if you're staying in B&B, ask your landlady. These ladies are usually in a much better position to recommend good local shows and if you're staying in official Tourist Board accommodation, you'll find that the landladies are exceptionally helpful and friendly.

In a country which is predominantly rural, there are few flashy discos – although nightclubs sometimes appear in the most surprising, out-of-the-way places. If it's discos that you're after the cities of **DUBLIN**, **CORK** and **LIMERICK** have the most to offer, with towns like **KILLARNEY** and **GALWAY** also having a reasonable quota. Expect entrance fees in the IR£3–£5 price range, with prices depending on how upmarket the place is.

For more off-beat entertainment, try a medieval banquet or horse-racing. Medieval banquets are available at three of Ireland's stately homes in the Shannon area. **BUNRATTY**, **KNAPPOGUE** and **DUNGUAIRE** castles transport you back to the fifteenth century by means of music, song and a fantastic medieval banquet. A novel way not only to see, but experience life in an authentic medieval castle. Prices aren't cheap however, at around IR£26 per head, but this doesn't seem to deter many people as banquets are often booked up well in advance. If medieval banquets are something of a novelty, then horse-racing rates as a national obsession. This is reflected in the hundreds of meetings which are held each year, with over a hundred alone being held in the months of June, July and August. **GALWAY**, **ROSCOMMON**, **LIMERICK**, **NAVAN** and **LEOPARDSTOWN** all have major racetracks, but the premier course in Ireland is the **CURRAGH**, thirty miles outside Dublin. The Curragh plays host to the great equestrian and social event of the year, the Irish Derby, where the Irish elite come out to see and be seen while the horse-racing acts as a diverting side-show. If you're not in this kind of league (and let's face it, not many of us are) don't despair; there are many smaller events where for the entrance price of a few pounds you can spend an afternoon or evening at the races. Details of annual fixtures can be obtained before you go from the Irish Tourist Board in London.

Theatre is another possibility for night-time entertainment. The theatrical tradition is particularly strong in Ireland and the **Abbey Theatre** in **DUBLIN** has a world-wide reputation for excellence. It concentrates mainly on revivals of established works by Irish writers such as Synge, Yeats or Beckett; the smaller **Peacock Theatre** next door is the forum for experimental work by new writers. **CORK** is the home of the **Irish National Ballet** and has its own Opera House, whilst in **TRALEE**, the **National Folk Theatre** has a high reputation and it's worth making a point of seeing one of its productions.

In September, Tralee is the venue for the country's biggest beauty contest called – wait for it – the 'Rose of Tralee'. At that time, the town fills up with other artistes of the song and dance variety, and a good time is had by all. If you're keen on attending this popular event, book your accommodation well in advance because rooms are very difficult to find if you arrive on spec.

Rounding up the other national events, Easter is the focus for a number of social and sporting fixtures. The **St Patrick's Day Parade**, on 17 March, is a colourful cavalcade which proceeds through the streets of DUBLIN. Go early to stake out a place, as O'Connell Street becomes packed with thousands of people. Held over Easter weekend is the **Circuit of Ireland**, a motor-racing event second only to Monaco. Starting in BELFAST and finishing there a couple of days later, the route changes from year to year – check for local details – but essentially forms a loop of Ireland. The other major sporting event at this time is the **Irish Grand National** meeting, held over two days at FAIRYHOUSE (Co. Meath), about ten miles from Dublin. The **Tour of Ireland**, an important fixture in the international cycling calendar, takes place during the month of July. Major cultural events include the **Pan-Celtic Week** in June, where singers and musicians from other Celtic nations assemble in GALWAY for seven days of performances and competitions; the **Cork International Choral and Folk Dance Festival** in May, and the September season of the **Waterford International Festival of Light Opera**, which acts as a forum for lesser-known operatic pieces and provides some first-class entertainment.

Generally DUBLIN is the best place to be if you've got a lot of party spirit. At dusk, the city comes alive with the centre buzzing with a constant mix of race, age and class. Dublin is also a city of music. In the sixties it was the home for the beat generation and flower-power; now it spawns international stars like U2, along with a whole array of lesser-known musicians. New Dublin bands are constantly breaking on to the music scene and often come up the hard way through the pubs and clubs, so wherever you go at night, try to catch some of the rock, jazz and folk music of Irish musicians. TRAMORE (Co. Waterford), on the other hand, offers less of a cultural experience and more of a 'Benidorm' experience. With funfairs, dances, numerous pubs and amusement arcades, there's plenty for teenage kids to do and also places for mum and dad to escape to. CORK, Ireland's second city, is more provincial than Dublin but still has plenty of pubs, nightclubs, etc. It's also the Irish venue for most of the international rock tours; Michael Jackson, U2 and so on all end up at Cork Stadium, as you'll find out if you're there on the day of a big concert. Cork also holds 'Siomsa Cois Lee' annually, an outdoor rock/country festival; this is also held at Cork Stadium (Páirc Ui Caoibh).

Other places to consider for nightlife are **KILLARNEY**, **LIMERICK** and **GALWAY** in the north. All three are usually swarming with tourists, but good fun to be in on balmy summer evenings. Outside these places, you're really struggling to find a good variety of nightlife, although local tourist offices will invariably have suggestions for the special attractions in their areas.

HEALTHY HOLIDAYS: *the great outdoors/the sportsperson*

For those who enjoy the outdoor life, Ireland offers a wide range of activities. Golfing, fishing and cycling are all very popular and consequently are well provided for. Watersports are increasing in popularity, with canoeing, sailing and windsurfing enthusiasts beginning to take full advantage of Ireland's 3000 miles of coastline and 800 loughs and rivers.

As far as **golfing** goes, top-class facilities can be found throughout the country. At **PORTMARNOCK** (Co. Dublin) can be found Ireland's premier tournament course. It has played host to the Irish Open, the Dunlop Masters and the Canada Cup and attracts players of an international calibre. Other courses attracting important professional and amateur tournaments are **The Royal Dublin Golf Club** and **Cork Golf Club**. The **Waterville Golf Club** (Co. Kerry) beside the tiny village of **WATERVILLE** is located on the western tip of the Ring of Kerry and has attracted high praise from many international golfing stars, whilst the nearby **Killarney Golf Club** offers good playing and magnificent views of the surrounding area. **BALLYBUNION** (Co. Kerry), a major tourist resort on the west coast, has two golf courses, one of which was designed by Robert Trent-Jones, whilst **Tralee Golf Club** (Co. Kerry) has a challenging course located only a few miles from the beautiful Dingle Bay. In the north-west of Ireland, the golf courses command attention for their attractive locations and stunning views. **Westport Golf Club** (Co. Mayo) has a particularly good course overlooking CLEW BAY, and **Galway Golf Club** and **Enniscrone Golf Club** also provide challenging courses in magnificent seaside locations. Green fees at many of the courses in Ireland start around the IR£10 mark and if you are planning to concentrate solely on golf for two weeks, you may consider taking a specialist golf holiday. Tour operators offering these packages generally include top-class golf courses and hotel accommodation at prices which could not be obtained if you were freelancing. See page 64 for more details.

Cycling is something of a national obsession. Some of the top professional cyclists in the world are Irish and wherever you go, you'll see amateur enthusiasts practising and training for races. It's not hard to see why cycling should be so popular in Ireland. There's a dense network of roads criss-crossing the country and even at the height of the summer season, a quiet route through the beautiful countryside can easily be found. The main roads also accommodate cyclists with a buffer lane which, while not reserved exclusively for them, is commonly used as a slow lane for tractors and bicycles. If you are thinking about making a cycle tour of Ireland, then you will probably want to take your own bike over on the ferry. On the major Holyhead–Dublin/Dun Laoghaire route, costs for transportation are around IR£5, although on the Stranraer–Larne route, at the time of writing, bikes travel free of charge. If you simply want to spend a couple of afternoons on leisurely rides through the countryside, hiring is another option. There are local bike-hire firms, and Raleigh Renta-Bike has about 100 agencies throughout Ireland. Ladies', gents' and occasionally children's bikes are available. Rental costs are around IR£6 per day or IR£28 per week and a minimum deposit of IR£30 will also be required. Those hiring from Raleigh should also be covered by a basic insurance policy guarding against accident, accidental damage, theft and public liability, but always check the individual insurance arrangements. Before you rent your bike, make sure that you have a test-run to see that the height and weight of the bike are suitable and above all, check the basic equipment of brakes, lights and reflectors. If any part of the bike looks damaged, make sure you point it out *before* setting off, otherwise you may be held responsible. Even better, tell them you're not happy with what they're offering and ask for a replacement. Remember that a bike that isn't properly maintained has the potential to be just as lethal as a car without brakes. To help you choose a route, the Irish Tourist Board provides a very good leaflet with suggested tours. Otherwise a detailed road map is essential. In Galway and Donegal, the small one-track roads are erratically signposted and frequently not even marked on large-scale maps. It may be worth contacting An Oige, the Irish Youth Hostel Association (Tel: 01 363 111) for Go-As-You-Please cycling holidays. For Gourmet tours or individually-arranged cycling holidays which include bikes, accommodation and meals try Easy Riders, Brecon, Tetrarch Grove, Clonee, Co. Meath (Tel: 01 255 484). One final proviso for would-be cyclists: take waterproofs! In the summer, rain generally only amounts to intermittent showers but some of these can easily drench the unsuspecting and ill-equipped cyclist.

Fishing is another sport for which Ireland is justly famous. Wild Atlantic salmon and brown or sea trout are the main catches, either from one of the numerous inland loughs and rivers, or from the west-facing Atlantic shores. Sea-trout fishing really gets underway from around mid-June until mid-October in many places, whilst the salmon season closes at the end of September. The season for brown trout lasts from mid-February/beginning of March until the end of September/beginning of October. The main area for salmon lakes and sea-trout rivers and lakes is in the western counties of Galway, Mayo and Sligo, although Co. Donegal and Co. Kerry also have potential. Major locations are at **LOUGH CORRIB**, **LOUGH CONN** in Co. Mayo, **LOUGH LEANE** and **WATERVILLE** in Co. Kerry for salmon loughs. **THE ROSSES** and **GLENCOLUMBKILLE** in Co. Donegal, **WATERVILLE** in Kerry and numerous Galway locations including **KYLEMORE**, **CARRAROE** and **LOUISBURGH** for sea trout. Inland locations for brown-trout fishing are scattered fairly uniformly throughout the country; try **ENNISCORTHY** on the River Slaney in Co. Wexford, **CLONMEL** and **CARRICK-ON-SUIR** on the River Suir in Co.

Tipperary or the tributaries of the River Blackwater in Co. Cork. Again, there are a number of fishing specialists offering packages to Ireland. Check page 64 for details.

Walking is becoming increasingly popular in Ireland, and a number of special trails of varying lengths and difficulty have been set up in some of the most scenic areas. One of the most spectacular is the **Kerry Way**, following a route through Killarney, Black Valley and finishing up at Glenbeigh. Some of the best scenery in Ireland can be experienced on this walk, as the path leads you up mountain trails and down through verdant valleys. Among the other routes available are the **Wicklow Way**, leading you through the hills and glens from the Wicklow mountains, the **South Leinster Way** through the tranquil landscape from Co. Carlow to Co. Kilkenny and the **Dingle Way**, traversing the famous Dingle Peninsula. For those who enjoy more leisurely walking, the Forest Service has twelve forest parks well provided with interesting and informative nature-trails where you can catch glimpses of local wildlife, and there are over 400 forest parks which have short walks laid out and picnic sites. **LOUGH KEY** (Co. Roscommon) and **KILLYKEEN** (Co. Cavan) are perhaps the most developed of the forest parks, with restaurants and gift-shops supplementing the forest attractions.

Horse-riding and **watersports** enthusiasts will have no problems in Ireland. As far as horse-riding goes, every county has at least two or three stables. These frequently offer tuition for beginners and some specialize in woodland, beach or even mountain trekking. If you're interested write to the Tourist Board in Ireland for their leaflets MB20 and 16D on equestrian Ireland, which gives a comprehensive list of locations and addresses. Watersports, such as canoeing, windsurfing and sailing, may be pursued on the large inland loughs or at sea in the colder waters of the Atlantic. Unlike most Mediterranean countries, these watersport facilities are not readily laid on at the seafront of holiday resorts, so you'll have to go looking for them. The local tourist office should help you to find the nearest watersport centre. Sailing tuition for one day may cost somewhere in the region of £20, or £110 per week in low season, to £195 in high season, whilst windsurfing may cost around £20–£35 a day or £75–£90 for one week. Rough-water canoeing and sea-kayaking are excellent ways of seeing Ireland if you have experience. A week's canoe hire could set you back around £50–£60, with a refundable deposit of £25 per boat on top of the basic price. Obviously, all these watersports are best undertaken in the summer when the weather is most favourable and the water at its warmest. Centres offering watersports equipment and tuition can be found at COBH (Co. Cork) and DUN LAOGHAIRE (Co. Dublin) and there are many others throughout Ireland. All centres include accommodation on week-long courses, so if you're interested in spending a holiday learning a new activity, the Irish Tourist Board has information about locations and addresses.

Galway and Glenans Irish sailing clubs have schools in Baltimore, west Cork; Bere Island, Bantry; Clew Bay, Co. Mayo. Bunk-type accommodation is available at all bases. Minimum age is seventeen years except for junior courses (Tel: 01 611 481).

Baltimore Sailing School offers a course that is a little less intensive, allowing for very good instruction plus an enjoyable holiday. Evening activities such as fishing, barbecues and visits to local islands are arranged. A windsurfing/sailing package is also available and bunk-type accommodation can be provided. Minimum age is ten years (Tel: 028 20141).

The leaflet MB18 available from the Irish Tourist Board gives information on watersports, yacht chartering companies and bringing your own boat.

Aside from the specialist interests, good locations for families of more general sporting inclinations are ROSSLARE (Co. Wexford) where golfing, swimming pools, yachting and windsurfing are on offer; CLEW BAY (Co. Mayo) with sailing, sea and game fishing and an eighteen-hole golf course at Westport; TRAMORE and neighbouring villages in Co. Waterford with two golf courses, a leisure park and coastal walks in close proximity, and of course DUBLIN and its suburbs with superb golfing, walking and fishing facilities. Inland, the National Parks of **Killarney**, **Connemara** and **Glenveagh** have excellent nature trails for an afternoon's ramble in unspoilt surroundings. Alternatively, LOUGH KEY

(Co. Roscommon) or **LOUGH DERG** (Co. Clare) provide a good cross-section of golfing, fishing and walking activities.

More details about locations and prices of the above sports can be obtained by writing off to the Irish National Tourist Board in London and asking for the relevant information sheets.

THE NATURE LOVER

The Emerald Isle has surprising variations within its green and pleasant land. Each part of the country has its own distinctive landscape: in the East, there are the rolling green slopes of the Wicklow mountains; **GLENDALOUGH**, with its seventh-century monastery nestling among blue hills, is one of the most breathtaking beauty spots in this area. In the South the coast is rocky, alternating with sandy beaches – the **DINGLE PENINSULA** in the South-west is renowned throughout Ireland for its picturesque headlands and villages. Bus services from **TRALEE** run to the peninsula and Irish Railways organizes special rail/bus tours. Inland, the rich countryside of Roscommon, Tipperary and Longford has profuse forests and loughs interspersed with emerald fields, while the fertile land of Co. Kerry is the setting for the **RING OF KERRY** scenic route (see 'The Sightseer' on page 15). In the West, the further north you go the wilder and more remote the countryside becomes. Peat-cutting is in evidence in the north-western counties and the mounds of rich, brown peat are a ubiquitous feature of the landscape. Co. Galway is characterized by barren, rock-strewn land and breathtaking sea views. **CONNEMARA NATIONAL PARK** in the north-west corner of Galway has, without doubt, the most spectacular scenery in Ireland. In a landscape of mountain and sea which is reminiscent of the Norwegian fjords, the narrow coast road is highly recommended for its magnificent views of the unique Connemara coast. In Co. Clare, one of the most unusual natural phenomena in the country is to be found at **The Burren**. This is the name given to a limestone landscape of disappearing streams, caves and some fantastic rock formations. Those interested in botany will find a remarkably colourful display of arctic flora. A visitor centre for The Burren is located at **KILFENORA**, and provides interesting background information to this fascinating landscape. In Co. Donegal, with donkeys, wild horses and sheep wandering over the roads, caution is required of drivers. Those planning to spend some time studying the flora and fauna of either Connemara or Donegal should equip themselves with a good Ordnance Survey map as paths are often inadequately marked on large-scale maps issued by local tourist offices.

The Irish are good conservationists and numerous forest parks and three national parks are evidence of this. Besides Connemara, there are national parks at **GLENVEAGH** in Co. Donegal and **KILLARNEY** in Co. Kerry. All these parks are equipped with information centres which offer an introduction to the flora and fauna of the area. Mountainous slopes and waterfalls characterize the 24,000 acres of Glenveagh National Park, where there is a thriving community of red deer. Killarney has two varieties of deer, both red and the Japanese sika, whilst an abundance of bird-life, including the meadow pipit, stonechat and the occasional peregrine and merlin, can also be glimpsed by visitors. The loughs and rivers provide a habitat for herons, kingfishers and mallards and in the winter, 140 rare Greenland whitefronted geese feed in the valley.

The **John F. Kennedy Park** in Co. Wexford, named after the American President whose family originated in nearby Dunganstown, contains a wide range of tree varieties – many of which came as gifts from countries all over the world. The **Fota Estate Wildlife Park** in Co. Cork, under the auspices of the Royal Zoological Society of Ireland, has a number of indigenous animal species and a community of Australian wallabies. Easy access by road or rail ensures that a visit to Fota Park is a highly enjoyable day out for all the family. For those with ornithological interests, there are opportunities for bird-watching both at the seashore and beside the inland loughs. Among these is the bird sanctuary beside **WEXFORD** for Greenland whitefronted geese, and other sanctuary locations include **BALTIMORE** in Co. Cork and **SRAITH SALACH** in Co. Galway.

Access to areas of great scenic value is generally very good. Amenities such as car parks, restaurants and snack-bars are usually located on or near site without spoiling the natural assets of the area. If you are seeking accommodation, B&Bs are to be found even in the smallest village. The only exception to this is Donegal, where the sparsity of population means that you could go for miles without seeing a suitable stopping-off point. Youth hostels are another option as they are strategically located in the rural areas which the 'great outdoors' types tend to head for. Connemara, Glenveagh and Killarney all have youth hostels, either in or near the national park areas.

THE RECLUSE

Get-away-from-it-all holidays are not much of a problem in Ireland and many people return year after year simply because they love the tranquillity and relaxed pace of life. Away from the main roads and larger conurbations, small hamlets remain largely undisturbed by summertime traffic – and there is certainly none of the endless buzz and hassle of Mediterranean resorts.

The inland counties of Roscommon and Longford and the north-western counties are the places the recluse should concentrate on. Co. Kerry, the southern and eastern coasts tend to get busy – by Irish standards anyway – in the summer months, chiefly because these are the areas where a high proportion of the visiting American tourists base themselves. Throughout the interior and North-west, there is no shortage of small villages or towns to use both as a base for touring and a haven for peace and quiet. The town of **MULLINGAR** in Co. Westmeath is a good location for exploring the inland loughs of Owel, Derravaragh and Lene, where fishing or watersports activities can be pursued. Further north in the counties of Cavan and Monaghan, good fishing is also available in the numerous lakes and rivers, and if you're looking for a quiet location try the town of **CAVAN** itself, which is within easy reach of the loughs of **Killykeen Forest Park,** or **VIRGINIA** (Co. Cavan), attractively located on the shores of Lough Ramor. In the North-west, the way of life remains strongly traditional, and those who really want to get away from it all should head for the remote coastal headlands where there is only one road in – and one road out – to communities of one or two houses. Co. Donegal is the most underpopulated area of the country, so head up to the isolated splendour of **THE ROSSES** cliffs, and follow the coast roads down to the charming village of **ARDARA**, which has a wonderful secluded beach, then down to **GLENCOLUMBKILLE**, where there's a folk village and some early Christian remains; then head back to civilization and the small town of **KILLYBEGS**, centre for the production of the world-famous Donegal tweed. In Galway, despite the splendour of the scenery, many people simply drive right through, finding the gloomy mountains rather unpalatable. **CASHEL BAY** and **ROUNDSTONE** are excellent locations perched right on the seashore. **CLIFDEN** is rather misleadingly called 'the big smoke' by the locals, but in fact is a pleasant, sleepy fishing town located right on the edge of **CONNEMARA NATIONAL PARK**.

The suggestions above only form a small fraction of the hidden hamlets that can be discovered in Ireland – the true recluse will search out his/her own – but essentially if you head out on to the small back-roads, or even better, the roads that go nowhere, you should have no problem finding the kind of peace and seclusion you want.

The best way to discover the remote areas of the country is, of course, by car. If you are touring be prepared for some rough and ready surfaces on the back-roads in the North-west. At best, they can be called basic; at worst the percentage area of pot-holes is higher than that of recognizable road surface. If you are travelling by train, the most northerly destination you can reach is **SLIGO**, although the centre of the country is covered reasonably well by the rail network. If you want to strike out from the major centres, then the best idea is to take one of the local CIE buses. These will take you to most parts of the country, although the services may not necessarily be frequent or suit your own touring timetable. If you're planning to do a great deal of bus and/or rail travel, remember that the eight- or fifteen-day passes offered by Bus Eireann and Irish Railways represent good value for money (see 'Budgeting' on page 43).

For accommodation, B&Bs are the obvious choice and can be found no matter how remote the place. If you want complete seclusion, you may consider self-catering in an Irish cottage or holiday home. There are plenty of tour operators offering very good deals to lovely locations; for those who want to go it alone, the Sunday papers and the Irish Tourist Board are the best bets for the latest information on the self-catering scene in Ireland. Prior booking is essential, whether you're travelling independently or with a tour operator, as demand invariably outstrips availability. Alternatively, youth hostels are often located in remote areas of scenic interest and give a roof over the heads of walkers, climbers and like-minded recluses!

 FAMILY HOLIDAYS

As family holidays are largely concerned with keeping the kids occupied, in Ireland it's essential to head to a place which has more to offer than just sand 'n' sea. The Irish weather is unpredictable and there is nothing worse than rainy days stuck in a caravan with fractious children. Happily there are numerous towns, especially along the south and west coasts, which have plenty to offer on good and bad days. Resorts such as **BALLYBUNION**, **TRAMORE** or **BUNDORAN** are traditional seaside towns, with donkey-rides, ice-creams, amusement arcades and fish 'n' chip shops. Beaches, which are generally sandy and gently sloping, are suitable for even the youngest family member. The exceptions to this are some of the smaller coves on the south coast, where steep descents on untarred paths can be hazardous for toddlers, and on the north-west coast, where exposed headlands and choppy seas feel the influence of Atlantic breezes. Stick to sheltered bays and always pay attention when warning flags are flying. In the larger holiday towns, there is easy access to the seafront and beach, although in the more remote areas of Galway, Sligo or Donegal it may be a bit of a trek to get to some beaches – but it's invariably worth it when you get there.

As for accommodation, most hotels offer baby-sitting facilities but availability of cots depends on the individual establishment, so if you're travelling with a baby write ahead and confirm that a cot will be supplied. Farmhouses, guesthouses and B&Bs are usually family-run and have a more ad-hoc approach to baby-sitting. Ask the landlady if she'll be willing to baby-sit – most places have TV rooms and if your children are old enough, she'll usually be more than happy to keep an eye on them. Babies are a different matter. They require more attention and you may be better off looking for a reasonably priced hotel which offers a professional baby-sitting service – even if you have to pay extra for it. Whatever you opt for, don't assume someone will be looking out for the children if you leave them in the B&B/hotel without telling anyone – that's the way tragic accidents can happen. If you are in any doubt about facilities on offer for children, write to the Irish Tourist Board and ask them for their booklet 'Guest Accommodation'. You'll have to pay for it, but for your two pounds you get an extensive list of hotels, guesthouses and B&Bs with details of amenities accompanying each individual listing. If you stick to the establishments listed in this book, you have some kind of comeback if the facilities don't come up to scratch. Generally, it is the international hotel chains which have most to offer family groups. Crèches or play activities are standard features, as are swimming pools, sporting facilities, etc. If you can afford it, this type of hotel is undoubtedly the best for a family holiday as it takes the onus off mum and dad of providing all the holiday entertainment. Ryans Hotels are an Irish-based hotel chain with locations all over the country. They make up special deals for family groups, and it's well worth checking out their very competitive deals.

Another holiday popular with families is a caravan tour. Roads in Ireland aren't exactly ideal (see 'By Car/Campervan' on page 79) but caravan parks are plentiful on the south and west coasts, and no one seems to mind if you park overnight at the side of the road. There are also over 400 forest parks scattered throughout the country, many of them with picnic tables and reasonable access roads which are ideal for summer lunches *al fresco*. Picnicking is a perfect way to take advantage of any good weather, so don't forget to pack a few items of cutlery, a Thermos flask and a can-opener before you go.

The southern coast is the warmest part of the country during July and August. **TRAMORE**, Ireland's equivalent of Blackpool, has one of the largest beaches in the country and is well equipped with on-beach amenities, such as loos, teashops and places to buy food and drink. There's a fairground in the summer months, as well as a boating park and children's playground strategically located beside the promenade. There are two caravan sites in Tramore itself and numerous B&Bs, although you may find accommodation rather tight in peak periods. Another south-coast location which has a lot to offer families is **TRABOLGAN HOLIDAY CENTRE** in Co. Cork. A self-contained development, this centre has outdoor attractions of golf courses, tennis courts, beaches for fishing, as well as an indoor swimming pool, ten-pin-bowling centre and sports hall. For a quieter location, try **DUNGARVAN** or **BUNMAHON** a few miles along the coast from Tramore; both have beaches and caravan sites. On the east coast **ROSSLARE** is an excellent base for families. Watersports such as windsurfing, yachting and fishing can be pursued here and places of interest nearby include the **Irish National Heritage Park** detailing 9000 years of Irish life, and the **Tacumshane Windmill**, the only surviving mill of its kind in Ireland. On the west coast, **BALLYBUNION** is one of the major holiday resorts. The beach is well maintained and children can swim in the sea without any fear of pollution. There are also caves to explore and two good golf courses for dad to try out. Further up the coast in Co. Galway, **SALTHILL** is the bustling holiday suburb of Galway town. There are surfing and watersports facilities in the area, and a recreational centre and golf course. If the weather is bad there is plenty to do and see in the historic town of Galway, only a short bus-trip away. **BUNDORAN**, in south Co. Donegal, also provides the usual seaside attractions along with some sightseeing trips to the unusual rock formations of the nearby cliff-tops or the famous Benbulben, a few miles down the coast. There are also castles, museums and forest parks to be explored at the nearby Lough Erne.

Inland, **LOUGH KEY FOREST PARK** (Co. Roscommon) has lots to keep the kids occupied. There are boat tours or even boat hire if you fancy rowing for an afternoon. An unusual bog garden will interest gardeners and the forest walks and nature trails will keep the energetic occupied. There's a caravan site, and a restaurant perched attractively on the loughside. Another funpark can be found at **Clara Lara**, near **CLARA** village in Co.

Wicklow. You can try your hand at trout fishing here, or simply let the kids loose on the adventure playground.

As far as costs go, caravanning is one of the cheapest and most popular ways of family travel. As you're completely mobile and have your accommodation in tow, all you have to worry about is finding a suitable site and something to eat. If you don't have your own caravan, you may consider hiring, and the tour operators B&I and Sealink offer an extremely good deal of inclusive ferry travel for car and passengers, plus six days' caravan hire.

Self-catering is another option for family groups. Most of the large tour operators deal in Irish cottages or chalets, although you can usually obtain cheaper mid-summer prices either by dealing direct with the chalet owners or by scouring the Sunday papers (see accommodation options on page 58). As we noted above, large chain hotels have lots to offer family groups but can be quite pricey. Out-of-season, special discounts for family groups often operate, so check what's on offer before you hand over any money. Unlike tour operators working in the Mediterranean field, package tour companies in Ireland have yet to tap the potential of family groups, so there is very little in the way of special deals for children beyond the usual reductions for under-twelves. The picture is constantly changing however, as more tour operators are moving into Ireland, so keep scanning the shelves of your travel agent for the latest deals.

For families with older children, hiring a cruiser or narrow boat to travel along Ireland's waterways could be great fun. Two approved operators are Athlone Cruisers (Tel: 0902 72892) and Celtic Canal Cruisers (Tel: 0502 21861). Further useful information is available on leaflet MB19, from the Irish Tourist Board. There is a small charge for this.

Practicalities

Red Tape

There are few formal requirements when entering Ireland. No visas are required for citizens of Australia, America and Britain. Visitors from countries other than Britain require passports. It is nevertheless a good idea for British travellers to carry passports, in the event that they may be changing traveller's cheques or asked to produce ID. This is particularly applicable if you are planning to travel through the Northern/Southern Ireland border.

Embassy and Consulate Addresses

In the UK – Irish Embassy, 17 Grosvenor Place, London SW1.
In the USA – Irish Embassy, 2234 Massachusetts Avenue, Washington. Consulates at 580 Fifth Avenue, New York; 681 Market Street, San Francisco; Rigley Building, 440 North Michigan Avenue, Chicago.
In Canada – Irish Embassy, 170 Metcalfe Street, Ottawa 4.
In Australia – Irish Embassy, Bank House, Civic Square, Canberra.

Health Formalities

No vaccinations are required for visitors from the United Kingdom, North America or continental Europe.

Customs

There are no real problems with customs in Ireland, although those leaving or entering from Northern Ireland will find customs officers and army officials especially vigilant. Tighter security could mean delays, so be prepared to wait a bit longer than usual. Here are the customs allowances you are allowed to take out of Ireland.

UK citizens – 200 cigarettes or 50 cigars, 1 litre of spirits, 2 litres of wine, 50 grammes of perfume and ¼ litre of toilet water. Other dutiable goods to the value of IR£31 per person.

American citizens – 200 cigarettes and 100 cigars, 1 litre of spirits and wine.

Australian citizens – same as American, except that 250 grammes of cigars are allowed only as an alternative to cigarettes.

Canadian citizens – cigarettes and cigars same as UK, and 1.1 litres each of spirits and wine.

Customs allowances when entering Ireland operate on different levels according to the country of origin. Non-EC citizens are allowed 400 cigarettes or 100 cigars, 1 litre of spirits, 2 litres of wine, 50 grammes of perfume. Residents of EC countries with goods *not* bought in duty-free shops are entitled to 300 cigarettes, 75 cigars, 1.5 litres of spirits, 5 litres of wine and 75 grammes of perfume. EC citizens with goods bought in duty-free shops are allowed 200 cigarettes, 1 litre of spirits, 2 litres of wine and 50 cigars. Until recently you must have been outside the Republic of Ireland at least forty-eight hours before you qualified for duty-free allowances; this has now been changed to bring Ireland into accord with EC rulings for free trade.

Money

For British travellers, there is no limit to the amount of either foreign currency or Irish *punts* which can be taken into or out of the country at any one time. Visitors from other countries may not leave Ireland with more money in either foreign currency or

Irish *punts* than was taken in, and not more than IR£100 may be taken out.

The monetary unit of Eire is the *punt* or Irish pound which is composed of 100 pence. The currency symbol is the pound sign (£). Notes and coins are issued in the following denominations:

Coins: 1, 2, 5, 10, 20, 50 pence (p); £1.
Notes: £5, 10, 20, 50, 100.

HOW TO TAKE YOUR MONEY

Undoubtedly the safest ways of carrying your money on holiday are Eurocheques (plus card) or traveller's cheques. If you are the unfortunate victim of a theft, you may simply cancel your Eurocheques or get your traveller's cheques reimbursed (see below). If you are carrying all your holiday supplies in the form of ready cash, the chances are that the thieves will have already spent it when (and if) the police catch up with them. It's not possible to obtain traveller's cheques in Irish pounds. Sterling or dollar cheques may be obtained from your local bank or building society. In many places, you no longer need to order traveller's cheques in advance. Go for the internationally recognized names, such as Bank of England, Thomas Cook or American Express, which are widely accepted throughout Ireland. Once you've bought them, keep a note of each individual cheque number somewhere separate from your cheques. It is also important to keep your receipt. You will need both if you are to be reimbursed for stolen cheques.

Eurocheques plus card are becoming more and more popular among holidaymakers. These you can cash abroad, just as you would your ordinary cheques at home. As with conventional cheques, you must produce your card every time you use them. Although some countries have been slow to adapt to the Eurocheque system, Ireland is not one of them: they are accepted universally and are more convenient to use than traveller's cheques. You can pay by Eurocheques without having to go to a bank or bureau de change, although if you do run into problems you can simply cash a cheque at the local bank. If you intend to take Eurocheques, order them from your bank well in advance, as they may take a few days to come through.

All major credit cards (Visa, Access, Diners Club, American Express, etc.) are widely accepted and are a useful back-up to traveller's cheques or Eurocheques. Don't rely on your credit cards as a main source of cash however, as restaurants and shops in the further-flung parts may simply not accept cards. Remember also, if you're planning on staying in B&B, that many houses do not take credit cards. When you first arrive in the country some ready cash is useful to tide you over until you get to a bank. Banks at home will supply Irish currency, if you order a few days in advance, and large travel agents such as Thomas Cook will issue it on the spot. Most banks and airports have cash machines that take UK bank cash cards. It is a good idea to check which banks in Ireland take your card and pin number. A lot of them deal with Visa and Access as well. Shopkeepers are often happy to exchange pounds and *punts* – but usually at a poor rate!

WHERE TO EXCHANGE

Both commission fees and the exchange rate vary depending on where you change your money. Invariably, the *banks* are the best bet as they offer competitive rates and reasonable commission fees. The larger *bureaux de change* also offer favourable rates, although watch out for the so-called 'official' bureaux de change advertising their services in remote areas. These seem to operate on the principle that if you're changing your money in the middle of nowhere, you're desperate enough to accept mediocre exchange rates and high commission charges, so avoid them if possible. If you're in any doubt about what's an official bureau and what's not, local tourist offices issue lists of recognized exchange offices in their county. *Tourist offices* will also change money and have the added advantage of extended opening hours. Again, rates are not favourable and if you're in a place that is big enough to have a tourist office, the chances are that there will be a local bank offering better rates. Larger restaurants and hotels are another option, but only as a last resort: commission fees can often be between 5 and 10 per cent. Most banks and reputable bureaux de change charge a fixed commission in the region of IR£1–£1.50.

If you are running short of Irish money just before you leave the country, it is worth remembering that many shops in Ireland will accept British coins. Until recently the British and Irish currencies were interchangeable on either side of the border, but now only the fifty-pence and ten-pence coins are widely accepted. Try to get rid of most of your Irish pounds before you leave Ireland: you will invariably lose by changing from Irish to British currency.

Most people opt for a combination of these methods when travelling abroad. In Ireland, Eurocheques (plus a Eurocheque card) with a credit card as back-up and a small sum of Irish currency should provide you with the security and flexibility you want, whether you are planning on staying in one holiday centre or touring extensively.

Banking

Opening hours are 1000–1230 and 1330–1500 (Mon–Fri). In Dublin and major cities, banks are open until 1700 on Thursdays. For other towns, see locally.

Insurance

It really is foolhardy to cut back on holiday insurance, yet each year thousands of people make this false economy and live to regret it. Increasingly if you're taking a package holiday you'll have no say in the matter and insurance will be added to your final bill, whether you like it or not. While this at least makes sure you get some sort of cover, remember you are not obliged to take this policy.

Note, then, that you are under no obligation to accept the insurance policy offered by your travel agent. In some instances these are not as detailed as policies bought from large reputable companies, and all too often the package policies mean long delays in the settlement of claims as they're snowed under at the peak of the tourist season. On the plus side however, the rep at your resort will have been trained in handling claims and this will take some of the strain off you. Tour companies also represent a formidable force in the insurance market and their buying power means that they can usually offer a cheaper insurance policy than you could buy on your own. The secret is to read the small print of the policies carefully. Don't assume that because it has the backing of a big insurance company it is necessarily the right policy for you.

If you consider the inclusive package inadequate for your needs, it is best to go to an insurance broker, tell him what you're taking (remembering photographic equipment, etc.), what you envisage doing (e.g. if you plan spending a lot of time doing watersports) and how long you'll be away. This is a particularly good idea if you're taking some new, expensive equipment with you (many package policies put a limit of around £200 per item on your valuables), or if your chances of requiring medical treatment are higher than average. Also check out the liability clause for delays if it's important that you get home by the date stipulated.

For most people, the basic insurance policy offered by tour companies will be sufficient. But for those who are looking elsewhere, Lloyds of London are particularly good and will provide travel insurance for people who normally find it difficult, e.g. disabled people and pregnant ladies. Independent travellers especially are advised to arrange a good insurance policy, for if anything goes wrong, they have no one (such as ABTA or a travel agent) to argue their case for them.

As regards medical insurance, most comprehensive travel insurance policies incorporate some kind of coverage for medical costs incurred abroad. The amount which will be reimbursed varies from company to company, but many of the major tour operators offer to cover costs up to £500,000. Reciprocal health agreements exist between Ireland and Britain and, on production of the proper documents (see 'Health' section below), British citizens are entitled to emergency medical treatment free of charge. For more prolonged or serious illnesses, a good insurance policy is essential. If you already have a medical insurance policy in this country, it is worth finding out if this covers you for travel abroad. North American travellers and those from further afield are strongly advised to procure good travel insurance before leaving home. If you intend to bring your own car to drive around Ireland you would be advised to inform your insurance company although there is usually no charge for this cover.

Having said all this, Ireland as a holiday destination does not present more potential problems or threats than any other country popular with holidaymakers. The crime rate is relatively low and the odds are that you will enjoy a trouble-free holiday. No one can predict the unexpected, however, and a good insurance policy can go some way towards recompensing you for a spoilt holiday.

Health

Those travelling from Britain and North America will not find the standards of health vastly different from those in their home countries. Overall, hygiene standards should give no cause for complaint although, as elsewhere, the state of public loos in the big resorts leaves something to be desired. If you're touring around a lot, and especially if you have a young family, a loo-roll and some soap are essential to cope with little emergencies. A rudimentary first-aid kit, with plasters, scissors, antiseptic lotion, etc. should also be packed and if you find you've left anything behind, there are plenty of well-stocked chemists throughout the country to supply you with more major items. For minor ailments, apply first to the local chemist shop where a pharmacist will be on duty to make up prescriptions and the chances are that he or she will be able to suggest appropriate medicines. For anything major contact a doctor or hospital immediately.

British people are entitled to free medical treatment in Ireland. There is a health agreement between the UK and Eire. It should be noted that a lot of health care is private in Ireland.

In the case of more serious or prolonged illness you should take out a medical insurance policy to cover costs. Often this is integral to the basic insurance policy offered by tour operators or insurance companies, but if you want to take out a separate medical insurance policy, then check out the AA, RAC and Lloyds, who all offer good deals. The cheapest medical and personal insurance Britons can get, and probably one of the best, is offered by Europe Assistance Ltd, 252 High Street, Croydon, Surrey CR0 1NF (Tel: 081 680 1234). For a small premium (average £17 per person for six to twelve days) you get on-the-spot cash for emergency services. This insurance also covers the expenses that can arise from a car accident (hiring another car, flying out spare parts, etc.).

Pre-planning and Free Information

The first source of information if you are thinking about holidaying in Ireland is the Irish National Tourist Board (Bord Fáilte). In Britain, they have offices at 150 New Bond Street, London W1 (Tel: 071 493 3201). In the USA and Canada, offices are at 757 Third Avenue, NY 10017, and 10 King Street East, Toronto M5C 1C3. These offices will be able to supply you with all the maps and information you are likely to need in the form of leaflets and books. Most of the literature will be free, but you'll have to pay for some of the more substantial publications, such as the accommodation or county guides. Among the most useful titles they publish are the 'Guest Accommodation' booklet with details of hotels, B&Bs, guesthouses, etc. throughout the country, and the 'Caravan & Camping Parks' guide. Both these guides are indispensable for those touring the country independently. When you write to the Board, make clear exactly what kind of information you're looking for otherwise you'll just get a list of current priced publications, which gives you no idea of the reams of free information leaflets which the Tourist Board have available.

Another source of free information is your local library, which is especially useful if you have a specific interest, such as hill walking, history or literature. As far as literature goes, it is difficult to avoid the fact that this small country has produced some of the best writers and poets of the twentieth century. W. B. Yeats' poetry, George Bernard Shaw's and James Joyce's work will be readily available in any library, and if you're spending any time in Sligo or Dublin (the areas strongly associated with these authors) it's worth dipping into a few volumes to get a flavour of their work. Another aspect of literary Ireland is the strong tradition of Irish fairytales and myths. *Irish Sagas and Folk Tales* (ed. Eileen O'Faolain, Oxford University Press) is equally suitable for adults and children alike, providing a charming key to the numerous references to myth and legend in the Irish landscape.

As far as bought sources are concerned, *The Blue Guide to Ireland* is an honest, well-written guide with special attention paid to the lesser-known areas of the country. *Fodor's Ireland* (Fodor's Travel Publications) is standard stuff, well researched and informative although too American-orientated and middle-aged for young(ish!) holidaymakers in search of a good time. *Frommer's Ireland on $30 a Day* is also geared towards the American share of the market, and like Fodor's, is at the upper end of the price range. The perennial favourite, *Berlitz*, has an offering which is particularly strong on visuals, but you may find it rather scanty on detailed touring information.

And you are, of course, already reading the guide best-suited to your travel needs!

Budgeting

Whatever the undeniable charms of Ireland, the cost of living is not one of them. High inflation and a weak currency have pushed up prices to around the same level as in Scandinavian countries. At present, the Irish rate of inflation is around 3.5 per cent per annum, with the rate of UK£1 = IR£1.08, so that a traditional pint of Guinness can cost between £1.70 and £2! That said, a holiday in Ireland need not cost more than a cheap package to the over-developed and over-crowded coast of Spain. The cost of getting to Ireland is cheaper than an average flight to the Mediterranean, and this offsets the higher prices which are to be found within the country itself. Moreover, because Ireland is a traditional holiday destination, there is a wide range of accommodation and restaurants, one of which is bound to suit your pocket.

Accommodation choices range from cheap B&Bs starting at around £8 a night to top-class hotels at about £80 a night. The bed and breakfast provision in Ireland is very good and undoubtedly represents the cheapest accommodation in the country. Aside from a bed, you also get a hearty Irish breakfast, sufficient to keep hunger at bay until well into the afternoon. For cost-effective holidays, coach tours can't be beaten for their combination of sightseeing, accommodation and transportation. However, for the vast majority of people who enjoy some degree of flexibility, freelancing it in B&B at peak season works out cheaper than taking a self-catering holiday offered by one of the tour operators. Where package holidays really score is on off-season months, when inclusive fares for car ferries and self-catering accommodation work out much cheaper than could be obtained independently. Pay special attention to the motoring holiday deals which many of the ferry companies offer. These sometimes include quality hotel accommodation as well as car-transportation costs, and often represent very good value for money.

Food, drink and night-time entertainment can vary dramatically in price depending on what you're going for. A cup of coffee is around 70p, a soft canned drink 50p and a pint of beer IR£1.60. A three-course meal at an average family restaurant will cost about IR£12. If you're working on a tight budget, look out for the special tourist menu, which costs either IR£6 for a three-course meal or IR£8 for a five-course meal. Takeaway restaurants of the pizza or hamburger variety are everywhere: not exactly traditional fare, but cheap and filling anyway. The cost of nightlife really depends on how much you want to spend and what you want to do. A night in the pub will cost the price of a few drinks, Irish Nights of traditional music and song held in local hotels will cost around IR£3–£5, plus a couple of drinks. Entry to discos in the larger places can cost anything from IR£2 to IR£6, depending on how upmarket the nightclub is and the night of the week. As regards leisure activities, a round of golf on a reasonable course will cost around IR£10, a day's cycle hire IR£5, and a week's windsurfing around IR£80.

Touring Ireland by car undoubtedly involves considerable expense. Expect to pay around £60 for petrol during a week of leisurely driving: remember, petrol is roughly twice as expensive as in Britain. A week's car-hire of a Fiat Uno/Renault 5 hatchback in the summer months (June to September) will set you back around £175 in total. Alternatively, you could take your own car across by ferry: transportation costs for three passengers and a driver (two children = one adult) are about £150 return in mid-summer, although note that extra charges must be paid if all members of your travelling party are not declared at the time of booking. Coach/rail tours of scenic areas are surprisingly good value for money if you stick to one of the larger companies. Bus Eireann and Irish Railways offer particularly competitive prices and run tours to most of the major sights, such as Ring of Kerry, Dingle Bay, etc., for fares under £10.

In fact, one of the cheapest and best ways to get around the country is to use the bus and rail networks. Tickets covering unlimited rail and/or bus travel for an eight- or fifteen-day period are available at extremely competitive rates. The fifteen-day Rambler ticket for bus/rail travel costs around IR£110 per adult and IR£55 for a child. With this ticket, you can reach practically any corner of Ireland, and with the eight-day ticket you can nominate the days you wish to travel within a period of two weeks.

Students also have a particularly good deal in Ireland as the vast majority of museums, castles, etc. give discounts on production of an International Student's Identity Card. Overall, the entrance fees for historical monuments and places of interest are surprisingly low: IR£1.50 is a typical charge, with some national monuments charging nothing at all for entrance. Many of the best sights are free anyway, because they're the hills, mountains and cliffs of Ireland's unspoilt countryside.

When working out your budget, err on the side of caution and take too much money rather than too little. In Ireland it is surprisingly easy to underestimate how much you'll need. A credit card is the ideal stand-by for emergencies, but an extra £100 or so in your current account or in traveller's cheques does not go amiss. If you don't use all your traveller's cheques in Ireland, you can cash them in at face value on return to this country. No commission will be charged if you are exchanging them in a bank or building society where you have an account. Remember that at the end of the holiday you'll have souvenir shopping to do and some of the quality goods, such as linen or glass, can be pricey items. Don't spend all your time looking in the quaint countryside craftshops; visit the larger department stores where the mark-up is less.

Getting Yourself Organized

What to Take with You

Whether you opt for a package holiday or an independent touring holiday, only the minimum of luggage should be taken with you. Think back to previous years when you returned home with half the clothes unused, and remember you'll need to allow a bit of extra room in your luggage for the items you buy over there. If you're going on a family holiday with the car, the kids and the dog, don't succumb to every plea for tennis racquets, deckchairs, sunbreaks, favourite games and indispensable books. You are, after all, going on holiday – not moving house. Think small, and if you have a bit of spare room in the boot afterwards, you can squeeze in a few luxuries. If you're flying over, or going by ferry as a foot passenger, try to pack everything into a hold-all suitable for hand-luggage. Think of the advantages of not having to wait in baggage collection queues wondering if what you checked in will actually reappear. If you are aiming to travel with hand-luggage only on flights, do remember that it will have to be a *small* bag; if you can't fit it in the overhead racks, you will have to sit with it under your feet for the whole journey.

As for clothes, light casual garments in the summer plus a couple of sweaters and some good waterproofs should be all you require. Do pack some sun-tops and shorts for good days, but remember that you're more likely to use a selection of trousers and skirts, with some matching shirts or blouses. Some stout walking shoes would also be helpful, as you'll probably spend some time exploring old castles or clambering hills. Dress is not formal in hotels, so there is no need to pack a suit or evening dress unless you're staying in a five-star Grand Hotel.

If you're planning to tour around a lot, you might consider taking a few extras, such as a travelling alarm clock (for early starts), a Thermos flask for tea-breaks and a small first-aid kit. For those camping or hostelling, it's advisable to take a money belt to keep your valuables in and pack your gear in a rucksack, which is much easier to carry long distances than a bag.

Although the best advice that can be offered to any holiday-maker is to travel light, taking only the essentials, there are a few items which definitely merit packing.

(1) Take with you all photographic equipment you're likely to need, and this includes films for your cameras. Film is much more expensive in Ireland, so it makes sense to buy before you go.

(2) Any medicine which is on prescription should definitely be taken with you. Check before you go that you have enough to last for your holiday and take a note of the name of the drugs in case you lose your supplies.

(3) Loo paper and soap – especially if you have a young family. There really is no substitute for them when you need them, and not every bar or restaurant will be equipped, so keep a few packets of tissues handy.

(4) Good maps. These are absolutely essential if you're touring extensively by car. The Irish Tourist Board does issue a fairly detailed large-scale map of Ireland (costing around £2.50) but it is woefully inadequate if you're heading for the back-roads. Maps of individual areas can be bought when you arrive, but the costs of these can soon mount up. Buy a good map-book which includes the Irish Republic and Northern Ireland. The AA produces comprehensive touring guides – easy to use and uncluttered by extraneous detail: this is one item which definitely merits the expenditure.

(5) Any sporting equipment you're likely to use. This is especially applicable for family groups. If little Johnny is a keen angler, and you've forgotten to pack his rod, the chances are that you'll end up hiring one for the day – or suffer perpetual nagging. If your family are particularly active types, who enjoy walking and boating, wellington boots are a useful addition to the car-load. They save damp socks on rainy days, and are essential for any messing about on the river.

Part Two
HOW TO GO

Package v. Independent

Most people coming from Britain choose to holiday independently rather than take a package. This is partly because the close proximity of the Republic means it isn't really considered a 'foreign' destination suitable for package holidays, but it is also because few of the Irish tour operators do a hard-sell in high-street travel agents. As you will see from the following pages, there are a surprising number of tour operators with programmes to Ireland, but many of these are specialist companies, dealing in popular golf or fishing holidays and not exactly household names!

The outlook for those seeking a different sort of holiday in Ireland is very good. There are companies offering cruising, golfing, walking, caravanning holidays, along with the more general coach or fly/drive tours. Most companies recognize that holidaymakers in Ireland want some degree of flexibility and independence, so there aren't many resort-based holidays, but go-as-you-please driving holidays are a perennial favourite. Coach tours are a popular choice of the older age-group, but the 'yuppie' market is not forgotten either with the luxury weekender breaks to cosmopolitan Dublin.

The advantages of package deals are obvious. You get everything organized for you, and don't have to worry about details like car-transportation or overnight accommodation. For those who want to travel independently, a bit more pre-planning is required. Booking of ferries or flights is essential, and if you're travelling in a family group, prior booking of your first night's accommodation is strongly advised. In general, places to stay are in plentiful supply in Ireland. The choice ranges from simple B&Bs to plush four-star hotels in the big cities. Usually you pay for what you get, but most independent travellers will find that the Republic's excellent B&B network more than fulfils all their travel needs.

As to price, the relative cost-effectiveness of a package or independent holiday depends on the standards that you want. If you prefer staying in hotels, with good service and amenities close at hand, then undoubtedly a package from one of the major companies is your best bet. If you're happy in B&Bs and guesthouses, then it's hard to find a package that can undercut the

IR£10 a night that these places offer. The cost of travelling around is also variable. Generally, if you're in a position to take advantage of a cut-price deal offered on car-hire then the advice is to take it. Major tour operators offer some extremely competitive rates, often cheaper than could be obtained if you were freelancing. Given that the difference in price between a package fly/drive and a car hired through an international car-hire firm can be as much as £50, it's worth scouring the brochures to see what the latest offers include. If you can't afford to hire a car, then train or bus travel is worth considering. Contrary to what the other guidebooks say, a rover ticket in Ireland is cheaper than the British, and many European, equivalents. Moreover, the service offered by Irish Railways definitely has the edge on that offered by BR.

It's entirely up to the individual's preferences and interests then, whether to travel independently in Ireland or take a package. If you don't mind sitting back and letting all the arrangements be made for you, then a package is the ideal option. On the other hand, if you like to be your own boss, and don't want to be one of a crowd, going it alone in Ireland presents no insurmountable problems.

Package Holidays

Tour Operators in Britain Offering Packages to Ireland

There are over forty British tour companies who offer holidays in Ireland. Some of these are specialists, others offer comprehensive packages aimed at holidaymakers travelling in couples or in family groups.

ABBEY GOLF HOLIDAYS
27 Victoria Street, London SW1H 0HD.
(Tel: 071 233 6386)

AER LINGUS HOLIDAYS
Aer Lingus House, 223 Regent Street, London W1.
(Tel: 081 569 4001)

ANGLERS ABROAD
6 Park Street, Wombwell, Barnsley, South Yorkshire
S73 0DJ.
(Tel: 0226 751 704)

ANGLERS WORLD HOLIDAYS
46 Knifesmithgate, Chesterfield, Derbyshire S44 6PN.
(Tel: 0246 221717)

ATLANTIC GOLF
54a Richmond Road, Twickenham, Middx. TW1 3BE.
(Tel: 081 891 6451)

BAKERS DOLPHIN
21 Penn Street, Bristol, Avon BS1 3AU.
(Tel: 0934 636636)

BETTERCLASS ANGLING SERVICES
'Chandleford', Forest Road, Wokingham, Berkshire RG11 5SA.
(Tel: 0344 421 084)

B&I TOURS
Reliance House, Water Street, Liverpool L2 8TP.
(Tel: 051 236 8325)

BLAKES HOLIDAYS LTD
Wroxham, Norwich NR12 8DH.
(Tel: 0603 784131)

BOWENS TRAVEL LTD
101 Cotterills Lane, Alum Rock, Birmingham B8 3SA.
(Tel: 021 327 3543)

54 Holiday Ireland

BRANTA TRAVEL LTD
11 Uxbridge Street, London W8 7TQ.
(Tel: 071 229 7231)

BRYMON BREAKS
Sunward Holidays, PO Box 6, Clyst Honiton, Exeter EX5 2AH.
(Tel: 0392 64215)

CIE TOURS LTD
185 London Road, Croydon CR0 2RJ.
(Tel: 081 667 0011)

CLIFF SMART'S ANGLING HOLIDAYS
29 Bridle Road, Burton Latimar, Northants. NN15 5QP.
(Tel: 0536 724226)

DRIVE IRELAND
516 Tower Building, Water Street, Liverpool L3 1BA.
(Tel: 051 231 1480)

EUROGOLF
156 Hatfield Road, St Albans, Herts. AL1 4JD.
(Tel: 0727 42256)

GAMEFISHER HOLIDAYS
Flowersdown House, Hare Stock Road, Winchester, Hants.
SO22 6NT.
(Tel: 0962 62622)

GO-FISHING
190 Rockingham Street, Sheffield S1 4ED.
(Tel: 0742 756443)

GRAND UK HOLIDAYS LTD (For over 55s)
6 Bethel Street, Norwich NR2 1NR.
(Tel: 0603 619933)

HOOKWAYS HOLIDAYS
Meeth, Okehampton, Devon EX20 3EP.
(Tel: 0837 810257)

INSIGHT INTERNATIONAL
26 Cockspur Street, Trafalgar Square, London SW1Y 5BY.
(Tel: 0800 393393)

IRISH ROAMER
6 George Street, Ferryhill Station, Co. Durham.
(Tel: 0740 653169)

IRISH TOURIST BOARD
150 New Bond Street, London W1Y 0AQ.
(Tel: 071 493 3201)

IRISH TRAVEL BUREAU
49 Old Hall Road, Sale, Manchester M33 2HY.
(Tel: 061 976 3887)

IVY COACHES
5 Upperhead Row, Huddersfield HD1 2JL.
(Tel: 0484 517969)

JMB TRAVEL CONSULTANTS
'Rushwick', Worcester WR2 5SN.
(Tel: 0905 425628)

KINGS ANGLING HOLIDAYS
27 Minster Way, Hornchurch, Essex RM11 3TH.
(Tel: 04024 53043)

LEISURE ANGLING/LEISURE BREAKS
33 Dovedale Road, Liverpool L18 5EP.
(Tel: 051 734 2344/5200)

LONG SHOT GOLF
Meon House, College Street, Petersfield, Hampshire GU32 3JN.
(Tel: 0730 68621)

PAB TRAVEL & COACH TOURS
Central Hall, 3 Ryder Street, Birmingham B4 7NH.
(Tel: 021 233 1252)

ROMAN CITY HOLIDAYS
53 High Street, Thornbury BS12 2AR.
(Tel: 0454 412478)

RYANAIR
Freepost Ryanair, Ireland Holidays, Liverpool L3 3AB.
(Tel: 051 227 1399)

RYANS TOURIST GROUP
200 Earls Court Road, London SW5 9QX.
(Tel: 0800 181143)

SAGA HOLIDAYS LTD
Saga Building, Middleburgh Square, Folkestone, Kent
CT20 1AZ.
(Tel: 0800 300 500)

SEALINK HOLIDAYS
Charter House, Park Street, Ashford, Kent TN24 8EX.
(Tel: 0233 646821)

SHAMROCK GOLF
Leinster House, North Hill Close, Winchester, Hants. SO22 6AG.
(Tel: 0962 62622)

SHEARINGS HOLIDAYS
Miry Lane, Wigan WN3 4AG.
(Tel: 0942 824824)

SUPERBREAK MINI HOLIDAYS
305 Grays Inn Road, London WC1X 8QF.
(Tel: 071 278 0383)

TIME OFF
Chester Close, Chester Street, London SW1X 7BQ.
(Tel: 071 235 8070)

TRAFALGAR TOURS
15 Grosvenor Place, London SW1X 7HH.
(Tel: 071 235 7090)

WALLACE ARNOLD TOURS LTD
Gelderd Road, Leeds LS12 6DH.
(Tel: 0532 634234)

WARNERS FAIRFAX HOLIDAYS
Oldbury Road, Tewkesbury, Glos. GL20 5LR.
(Tel: 0684 850400)

General Tour Operators

Diversity is the essence of the package holiday scene in Ireland. It's very rare to find a company which concentrates only on the standard flights and accommodation set-up prevalent in the Mediterranean market. At the very least, you can expect a combination of coach, car and self-catering holidays in any tour operator's programme – at the most, you have companies like **B&I** who offer a bewildering array of activity holiday packages. To guide you through this jungle, here's a quick round-up of the major operators and the kind of packages to expect from them.

Aer Lingus and **Sealink** run some of the most extensive programmes in Ireland, and their brochures are easily available in high-street travel agents. **Sealink Motoring**, the holiday branch of Sealink Ferries, offers an exceptionally good range, from traditional thatched cottages and charming farmhouse accommodation at one end of the scale, to the grandeur of town and country houses at the other. **Aer Lingus** and **Ryanair** do good deals on go-as-you-please driving holidays, with special budget accommodation packages available, and also offer self-catering breaks at limited locations. If you're looking for something different, Aer Lingus also organizes cruising or golfing holidays. For range of holidays and cost-effectiveness, **B&I** are hard to beat. Among their more unusual packages are special all-inclusive trips to horse-racing fixtures, a caravan-hiring option, and fishing/golfing holidays.

Weekender holiday breaks are also possible with most companies, including **Thomson**, focusing almost exclusively on Dublin. For those who enjoy the freedom of independent travelling, car-hire is an almost universal option and often at very competitive rates. The smaller tour operator **Leisure Breaks** is especially geared towards family holidays. Caravan or horse-drawn caravan holidays can be arranged through them, as can horse-riding and walking holidays. Self-catering accommodation is also available with properties mostly concentrated in the south-western corner of the country. Look out for the special deals that Leisure Breaks offers families on weekend breaks or ferry travel; these often represent very good value indeed. Another company which has some good packages for family groups is **Irish Rail** – strictly for those who enjoy train travel – but if you do, then there are packages to Cork, Galway or Tralee offered at very reasonable prices.

At the top end of the scale, **Time Off** offers accommodation in one-star to five-star hotels in Dublin or Cork. Although this group tends to have slightly more expensive holidays than others, the accommodation is tried and tested and of the highest quality. By way of contrast, **PAB** can organize cost-effective holidays in a variety of accommodation, ranging from town and country homes to four-star hotels. Car/drive and fly/drive are also available, but coach tours are this company's speciality, and whistle-stop tours can be taken to the major sights in the north-west, east and inland areas of the country.

Who Specializes in What

SELF-CATERING

Undoubtedly the biggest selection of self-catering properties comes from **Sealink Motoring**. Traditional thatched cottages and conventional villas are available in some of the most picturesque parts of the country. In return for your money, you get some really charming accommodation, although cars are essential to get to the furthest-flung locations. Look out for good deals for family groups too: in summer 1991, children under fourteen were allowed to travel free. **B&I Holidays** also has an extensive range of holiday homes, based at the prime coastal and inland spots. If your family are fresh-air enthusiasts, you may want to take advantage of B&I's farm holiday cottages, where the modern holiday homes are located next to traditional Irish farms. Like Sealink, B&I offers special discounts for children if you book early.

Blakes has a super range of high-quality cottages in some of the most charming parts of the country whilst **Leisure Breaks** from

Swansea/Cork Ferries has a slightly less sumptuous selection of properties, but can hire out cottages for short stays of two, three or four nights, ideal for groups touring by car. Other companies which have a narrower range of self-catering properties are **Aer Lingus**, with cottages located predominantly in the north-west quarter of the country, and the fishing specialists **Kings Angling Holidays**, **Betterclass Angling Services**, **Anglers World** and **Anglers Abroad**.

COST-CONSCIOUS HOLIDAYS

It pays to shop around for holidays which offer good value for money. Prices may vary dramatically from operator to operator, for packages which are virtually identical. However, the cheapest prices may not always represent the best value for money. Don't be fooled by the cost – check out precisely what is included in the price of your accommodation and what facilities are available at your hotel. Remember, you more or less get what you pay for and an extra £30 or so will often result in a higher quality hotel. The larger tour operators offer a range of accommodation to suit all pockets. Those working on a tight budget, but still looking for something special should look out for the value accommodation included in motoring holidays offered by **B&I** and **Aer Lingus**. **CIE Tours** allow you to choose the accommodation within your own price-range, but with **Aer Lingus** you stay in inexpensive farmhouses or town and country homes and with **B&I** you can choose from a decent range of small hotels.

Among the most cost-conscious deals available are the packages based on coach tours (see 'Coach Tours', page 61). However, the cheapest option of all is a caravan-hire holiday. **B&I** offers caravans or mobile homes from around £150–£175 per person for a week in peak season, whilst **Sealink**'s package is slightly more expensive at approximately £175–£200. Alternatively, **Leisure Breaks** offers a very good deal for family groups: standard caravans or mobile homes are available, with children under sixteen travelling free.

Another way to reduce costs is to holiday out of season and take advantage of the price cuts and freebies which companies offer to attract customers. The Easter period, in particular, often has surprisingly sunny spring weather and holidays at this time can be up to £20 per person cheaper. Usually, the earlier you can book the greater the discounts you'll get. Otherwise look out for the special low-cost deals that tour operators offer at the end of the season: it's often possible to pick up weekend breaks to Dublin for around £70 per person. Finally, remember that it usually works out cheaper to choose packages which incorporate ferry travel in your own car. Flying is more expensive, as you'll have to hire a car on top of the price of the basic package.

SHORT BREAKS

Short-break holidays are a thing of the nineties. With more money and high-pressure lifestyles, weekends away are not only an option, but a necessity for many people. To get the most out of your weekend, cities are the best locations. Plenty to do and see, with just enough strangeness to make you feel that you really are abroad.

Dublin is one of the great capitals of Europe: a veritable treasure-house of arts, literature and history, it's not fossilized in its colourful past. The city is essentially a huge meeting-place with bars, clubs and theatres in which to let your hair down and socialize. It is ideal for the seriously-minded art seeker or the fun-loving younger set, and only an hour's flying time from Britain – perfect for a weekend break.

The established company **Thomson Citybreaks** does a good deal, with departures from Glasgow, Manchester and Birmingham as well as London airports, whilst **Ryanair** and **CIE Tours** have a wide selection of accommodation ranging from guesthouses to hotels. **Superbreaks**, a tour operator which specializes in short-stay holidays, offers quality accommodation at very reasonable prices whilst the ferry company **B&I** also does special deals on short stays in Dublin which are not restricted to weekends.

Short breaks to other destinations in Ireland are also available. **Ryan Irish Holidays** offers three/four-day breaks in their hotels in Westport, Galway, Killarney, Cork or Dublin. Alternatively, if you prefer to travel by rail, there are plenty of excellent short sightseeing or based tours arranged by **Irish Rail**.

FARMHOUSE/TOWN AND COUNTRY HOUSE ACCOMMODATION

Farmhouse or town and country house accommodation are popular choices among holidaymakers wanting to get away from the impersonal atmosphere of hotels. It's easy to book these places yourself if you apply to the Tourist Board in advance for addresses. However, if you want somebody else to have all the organizational hassles, a number of tour companies are only too happy to arrange bookings for you.

Don't rely on town or country houses always being old, traditional buildings: some are modern bungalows or terraced houses. Accommodation tends to be classified according to facilities on offer, rather than external appearances – but whatever you end up with you'll find that extra touch of luxury and personal service in recommended town and country houses.

Companies which offer farmhouse and town and country accommodation are **Aer Lingus, B&I Line, Leisure Breaks** and **Sealink Motoring**.

COACH TOURS

Companies specializing in coach tours represent the largest slice of the Irish tour operators' scene. It's not hard to see why. Not only are coach tours invariably cheaper than other types of package holidays, but the compactness of the Irish Republic means that there are no great distances to be covered in sightseeing tours. Moreover, as Ireland is only a short trip away from Britain, there are no lengthy journeys to be endured before you reach your final destination.

The range of tours available to Ireland is quite exceptional. Most of the larger companies deal exclusively with seven-day whistle-stop tours of Ireland, taking in the traditional sightseer's itinerary of Ring of Kerry, Galway, Connemara, Waterford and Dublin. **Insight International, Sealink Motoring, CIE, Aer Lingus, Bakers Dolphin** and **B&I** all offer this kind of tour. Of these, B&I has the most promising programme, with a few more stops at points of historical interest and a little more emphasis on detail.

The smaller companies organize tours focusing on specific areas. **PAB Tours** offers the best combination, with the South-east, the South-west and Galway areas covered. This group is a good option for those who want to get off the usual tourist routes, as the tours tend to concentrate on the lesser-known, but equally rewarding sights. However, with their 'singalong dances' in the evenings, it's clear that their market is really the older age-group, so if you're under sixty – think again! **Shearings Holidays** organizes some good (but pricey!) tours of the north and west of the country, whilst **Roman City Holidays** and **Bowens Travel** offer a standard Ring of Kerry itinerary: Roman City also has tours of the Athlone, Shannon and Galway areas. Minitrips are available from **Bakers Dolphin**, for around the £55 mark – but remember that with these types of tour you're only spending one full day in Ireland and a lot of time travelling overnight on ferries.

When you're deciding which coach tour to opt for, consider carefully what you're getting for your money. Some tours begin in Britain, and costs are inclusive of one night's accommodation in this country. Other companies start their tours in Ireland, so you spend a full seven days there. Moreover, some of the smaller companies are based only in the South of England, and their local departure points are not suitable for those outside that area. At the time of writing, the cost of a seven-day whistle-stop tour was around the £250 mark, with variations according to seasonal demand.

DRIVING HOLIDAYS

With its quiet roads and predominantly rural population, Ireland is ideal for car tours. If you're planning to stay for any length of time in the north-west of the country, then you'll find that you simply don't have a choice. The rail network stops at Sligo town, and the country buses are few and far between.

The vast majority of tour operators, whether specialist or general, offer car-hire as part of their programme. Indeed, some companies automatically include the price of a car in their packages. **Atlantic Golf** and **Aer Lingus**'s golfing packages are two examples of this. Whilst it always works out cheaper to take your own car, if you're not in a position to do this, then hiring through your tour operator is the next-best option. Generally, they manage to undercut the large car-hire firms by at least £20. **Ryanair** in particular offers good cut-price hire for its clients.

Of the companies which offer a special service to motorists, once again **B&I** scores top marks for its flexibility and range of choice. You'll have to take your own car, but you can choose a go-as-you-please holiday, whereby you are issued with vouchers to book selected accommodation one night in advance, or you can pre-book the whole tour before departure: alternatively, you can opt for a centred holiday, using one place as a touring base for six days. **B&I**'s new winter brochure offers the alternative of air travel plus car hire on arrival. **Aer Lingus** also has a good range of packages to choose from. With car-hire, you can opt for a budget package, with cheap but comfortable B&B accommodation, or the golden package with its slightly more plush hotel accommodation. At the top of the scale, Aer Lingus also does luxury motoring holidays, with accommodation in some of the best hotels throughout the country. **CIE Tours** also offers a three-tiered price range with bookings in farmhouses, town and country homes or in hotel rooms. Additional bonuses include a useful touring guide and atlas as well as entry in the 'Meet the People' Treasure Hunt! **Brymon Breaks** does a standard fly/drive package, whilst **PAB Travel** has an ad-hoc service, supplying you with car-hire and making any advance reservations where requested.

Drive Ireland are a specialist company in this field offering a wide variety of holidays, with accommodation arranged in everything from a self-catering lodge through hotels and guesthouses to castles and manor houses. Specialist activities, such as golf, fishing and horse-riding are also available, and both B&I and Sealink ferries are used to connect from the UK. Individual itineraries can be compiled, on request.

ACTIVITY HOLIDAYS

If you enjoy the great outdoors, Ireland gives you plenty of opportunity to enjoy the fresh air and keep fit at the same time. If you're reasonably active, but prefer to indulge yourself a bit on holiday, then with some pre-planning you can arrange your sporting itineraries to suit yourself. The Irish Tourist Board issues excellent information sheets about golf, walking and horse-riding in Ireland, which include details of prices, the kind of facilities to expect and the locations of major golf courses, horse-riding centres, etc.

As far as package holidays go, within the obvious climatic restrictions, Irish tour operators have managed to put together a credible range of activity holidays. True, there is very little in the way of idyllic flotilla holidays or exotic balloon tours, but instead there are cruising vacations on the tranquil inland waterways or holidays spent clopping your way round Ireland in a horse-drawn caravan. Alternatively, how about a weekend at the races, two weeks spent golfing or fishing, or a few days walking through the lovely Irish countryside? All these options are available, and more details are given in the relevant sections below.

GOLF AND FISHING HOLIDAYS

If you are a golf or fishing enthusiast, tour operators specializing in these areas are well worth considering. Not only will companies be able to offer you the use of top-class facilities, it will be easier on your pocket too. Combined packages of quality hotel accommodation and all the golfing or fishing you could want are usually cheaper than could be obtained if you were freelancing. One great advantage for golfers in Ireland is that green fees on the smaller courses are approximately half the price of Spanish or Portuguese equivalents, which means that packages aren't excessively expensive.

Golfing packages are offered by **Shamrock Golf** (part of Gamefisher Holidays), **Atlantic Golf**, **Abbey Golf**. Shamrock Golf and Atlantic Golf offer the most cost-effective holidays. Car-hire (if you're travelling by air) is included in their prices, as are green fees and B&B. At the time of writing, **Atlantic Golf** had a wider range of destinations, offering packages to Portmarnock, Rosses Point and Westport, whilst **Shamrock Golf** dealt only with courses in the south-west of Ireland. **Abbey Golf** (in association with British Airways) is more upmarket, with accommodation in expensive hotels. However, as it has the backing of an international travel company, you can be assured that you'll get something special for your money.

A number of the larger general tour operators also arrange golfing packages. **Sealink Motoring** and **Aer Lingus** offer a golf touring holiday, where you select the courses that you want to play and book your hotels one night in advance as you go. This option gives you the maximum of flexibility and is reasonably priced as well. **Aer Lingus** can also arrange weekender golfing breaks. **B&I** offers a centred holiday, which includes six nights' hotel accommodation at Killarney, Ennis, Kilkenny and Castlebar with three days' free golf thrown in. All four locations are popular tourist destinations, so there's plenty to do for non-golfing members of your family.

Anglers are extremely well provided for in Ireland. **Anglers World** are acknowledged experts in the field and promise good fishing in the lakelands, East Ireland, the Shannon and locations in Northern Ireland. **Kings Angling Holidays** also has a wide range of Irish package holidays, offering both sea and inland fishing, with prices varying according to season and availability. **Anglers Abroad** offers packages tailor-made to suit your particular needs and if you don't want to fly or take the ferry, the company offers coach connections to limited locations. **Leisure Angling** has an extensive programme of coarse fishing in Ireland, and its brochures are particularly helpful in outlining the range of options available. **Ryanair** has a reputation for reliable service, and does basic packages in sea, game and coarse fishing, whilst **Gamefisher Holidays** runs a programme to various prime locations at very competitive prices. Finally, **Betterclass Angling Services** is an Irish-based company which specializes in angling and family holidays to Southern Ireland. Special arrangements can be made for disabled people, and there is an excellent back-up service with lots of information for the first-time angler. All accommodation is approved by the Irish Tourist Board, and there's scope for sea, coarse and game fishing; obviously a good option if you're thinking of travelling in a family group.

WALKING/CYCLING HOLIDAYS

Walking or cycling are ideal ways to see and experience Ireland. **English Wanderer** offers a multi-activity tour in the Kerry mountains. In this, you will cycle through the quiet lowlands of Kerry, walk around the National Park area, and on the final days, there'll be canoeing down the glacial valley of Lough Caragh. Instruction will be given, so this exciting tour is open to beginners as well. For the less ambitious, there's a seven-day easy tour of the Kerry coast. **Leisure Breaks** does a very competitively priced cycling holiday, inclusive of youth hostel accommodation, one week's bike-hire and return ferry fare, with special reductions for the under-eighteens. Alternatively, you can try their cycle-as-you-please holidays in conjunction with Raleigh Renta-Bike, when you are provided with accommodation vouchers and thereafter left on your own to cycle where you will.

CRUISING HOLIDAYS

For a 'different' kind of holiday to Ireland, you may consider taking a cruising holiday. Usually you don't need any previous experience to operate the modern cruisers, and as a means of getting away from it all, river cruising is hard to beat. Four-, six- and sometimes eight-berth cruisers are available for hire and the most popular cruising area is undoubtedly the Shannon river. For the angler, a cruising holiday ensures that you're never far from 'messing about on the river' and **Anglers World** offers cruiser-hire, plus angling and water charts/maps. For non-fishers, **B&I**, **Aer Lingus** and **CIE Tours** all offer competitive deals on river cruises on the Shannon.

HORSE-DRAWN CARAVANS

Every year, hundreds of people discover the delights of Ireland from the vantage point of horse-drawn caravans. You won't cover hundreds of miles (expect to travel around five miles a day!) but you'll have a superb chance to relax and meet the locals. **CIE Tours** offers a basic seven-day package, with prices inclusive of return travel. If you fancy a bit more choice, remember that there are a number of independent companies which hire out caravans in Ireland (see 'Healthy Holidays' on page 22). If you are keen on horses, you may consider a weekend at the races. Racing at Phoenix Park, Leopardstown and The Curragh with accommodation in Dublin is available through **B&I**.

Summing Up

Although the package holiday scene in Ireland is certainly not as developed as in the Mediterranean, there is nevertheless a decent range of holidays to choose from. Variations in price do exist, but if you shop around and study the brochures carefully, you'll soon find the one which suits your means best.

Generally speaking, the majority of packages are geared towards couples rather than family groups. However, **Aer Lingus**, **B&I** and **CIE** all offer deals which are suitable for families (caravan-hire, activity centre holidays), and **Irish Railways** have some touring packages which will be of interest to all age-groups. The older travellers are especially well catered for with a large number of coach tours, not to speak of Aer Lingus' and **Saga**'s special over-fifties packages. The younger set are not forgotten, however, and the short breaks offered by established companies such as **Thomson** indicate a direction in which the Irish package scene may yet develop.

For activity holidays, Ireland is one of the best destinations in Europe if you are a golfing or fishing enthusiast. Travelling with a specialist company generally works out more expensive than the standard week-long package holiday, so unless you want non-stop golfing or fishing, think again. If you only want a couple of days out on the river or golf course, remember that it's quite easy to make your own arrangements if you apply to the Irish Tourist Board for information before you go. Again, walking holidays can come free if you write off for some hiking maps before you go, but for those who want something more organized there are two or three groups offering their expertise and advice.

The outlook is also bright for those who want to break out of the standard package-holiday mould. The town and country homes or farmhouse accommodation are attractive options for those who want to see a bit more of the traditional life of Ireland, whilst the fly/ or ferry/drive option combines the freedom of independent travel with the security of a package holiday. Alternatively, a holiday cruising the tranquil byways or a horse-drawn caravan tour are viable options for those who want to get out and meet the locals.

Whichever holiday you choose, remember that most packages to Ireland are based on week-long, rather than two-week, stays. If you want to stay longer, then each day extra is charged individually. This is unfortunate, because it means that holidaymakers in Ireland can't take advantage of the cheaper fortnightly rate which invariably operates for Mediterranean package holidays. The cheapest prices, as always, can be obtained out of season, which makes Ireland an ideal destination to escape to during the Easter or autumn school holidays.

Checklist

A final reminder to anyone taking a package holiday anywhere: check the following points before booking:

(1) Is your travel agent competent? Unfortunately many are not, and all too often it's the large chains of high-street agents who give the worst service and advice. Try to avoid the obvious trainees when you go into the shop, and have a list of questions prepared so that you don't end up having to make several trips when one would do.

(2) Is your travel agent a member of ABTA? If not, think seriously about finding one who is. There are plenty of them, and membership could make a big difference to you if things start to go wrong.

(3) Having chosen your country of destination, do you really know about all the packages available on the market? Many of the smaller tour operators do not get their brochures into the high-street travel agents but that does not mean their holidays aren't reliable or worth checking out. Check against the list on page 52 and phone for a brochure from any likely-looking company.

(4) If the travel agent can't book the holiday you finally selected, don't necessarily accept his/her substitute recommendation. Have your second and third options sorted out beforehand, or if there really is no substitute, forget the whole idea and consider something completely different. Remember that travel agents are in the business of selling holidays for commissions –unscrupulous agents often don't much care what they sell, but they do like to clinch a sale before you leave the shop.

(5) As for the holiday itself, check the following before paying your deposit:

(i) Does the holiday price include all airport or port taxes and security charges (for both the UK and abroad)?
(ii) Does it include meals on the journey?
(iii) Is it extra for a weekend flight or a day-time departure?
(iv) Is transfer between the point of arrival and your hotel included?
(v) Are you clear about supplementary charges made for single rooms/balcony/sea view/private bathrooms etc.?
(vi) Be sure you know on what basis you are booked in at your hotel, i.e. full/half-board/B&B etc.
(vii) What is the cost for children, does it cover all the meals that you want them to have? Irish hotels can charge a surprising amount for children.
(viii) Is the insurance sufficient for you? Does it cover pregnant women/disabled people/people going on sports holidays? Is the limit on personal baggage high enough to cover all you are taking? Does it include a clause on delayed departure for your return journey? What provisions does it make for cancellations? Finally, check you're clear about the procedure in case a theft or loss does occur – often these matters have to be reported within a specified time limit and a police report procured.

(6) And finally, before handing over your money, ask:

(i) What is the position on cancellations (from both parties' point of view)?
(ii) What happens if your holiday needs to be altered significantly? Under the ABTA code you must be told and given the choice of accepting either the new hotel/resort/flight, etc., or a full refund. (Alterations caused by bad weather or industrial disputes will only be covered by your insurance.)

(iii) What's the score on overbooking? Is there a 'disturbance' compensation to be paid (there should be under the ABTA code)? Will the alternative accommodation be of equally high standard (it must under the ABTA code)?

Once you have gone through all these points you should have a clear understanding of the contract you are signing, and your travel agent will undoubtedly be in such awe of your intimate knowledge of the travel industry that you will receive preferential treatment all the way!

If, despite all this good groundwork, you still have cause for complaint, ABTA's address is 55–57 Newman Street, London W1N 4AH. Write to them with full details of your complaint and enclose copies of all your correspondence with the travel agent or tour operator.

Independent Means

The Options

Accommodation prices in Ireland can range from IR£100 a night in a top-class hotel to around IR£10 or less in a simple B&B establishment. Obviously, what you get depends on what you pay for, but by far the vast majority of holidaymakers in Ireland spend some part of their time in **B&B** accommodation. The Irish Tourist Board officially inspects selected B&Bs annually, assessing them on value for money, cleanliness and the amenities which they offer. Those which meet the required standards are awarded the 'green shamrock' sign, and this can be seen wherever you go in the country. If you're planning on staying in B&B, always make these approved establishments your first choice, then if they don't come up to scratch you always have the option of complaining to the Irish Tourist Board; you don't have this come-back in B&Bs which have no recommendation. Generally you'll find that the standards of hygiene, quality of food, etc. are more than adequate but don't expect tasteful decor or four-star service. For a couple of pounds extra, some places offer ensuite bathrooms. You may find it's worth a bit more money – otherwise you'll be sharing a loo with other guests, and have to get up early to be first in the queue for the showers.

Guesthouses providing evening meals are the next step up the accommodation ladder. Like B&Bs they are usually small family-run affairs, and the Irish Tourist Board grades them from A to C according to the amenities available. **Farmhouses** are another option and can be simply a stop-off point in a larger tour, or you can spend a holiday there, enjoying the outdoor life. Some farms (but not all) may allow the children to help out with the livestock. **Town and country houses** are a somewhat more elegant accommodation choice. The town houses are the dwellings of the Dublin middle-classes from days gone by, and the country houses are frequently splendid buildings located in spacious well-kept gardens. Both cost a bit more than guesthouses, but in return, you get a touch of luxury normally associated with top-class hotels. **Hotels** themselves come in five grades, ranging from A★ to C. In an A★ hotel, expect to pay around the IR£40 (or more) mark for B&B; this pricing reflects the effort which has gone into the cuisine, night-time entertainments, comfort of your surroundings, etc. In a C-rated hotel, expect clean and comfortable accommodation – but nothing special in terms of food or service.

Bookings for hotels, guesthouses and B&B can be done through the local tourist office for a small commission fee, which is charged to cover phone costs. Make clear to the staff you're dealing with what price range you're willing to pay, what type of accommodation you would prefer, and how many nights you're planning to stay. In peak season it is always advisable to book ahead, especially if you are travelling in a family group or if you are planning to spend several nights in one place. Dublin,

Killarney, Tipperary and other large tourist centres could provide you with real problems if you haven't reserved accommodation at least a day ahead. If you're touring by car, you'll have more chance of getting a room if you concentrate on the small villages on the outskirts of town. In Dublin, city-centre accommodation is always at a premium and a room in the capital always costs more than elsewhere in the country. Remember that DART, the commuter line, connects the suburbs with the city centre in a matter of minutes, so you don't lose out by choosing places like Blackrock or Dun Laoghaire as your sightseeing base.

Self-catering accommodation is another option. Apartments, chalets and even authentic thatched cottages are available to holidaymakers, some located in the most wild and beautiful parts of the countryside. If you are freelancing, check first with the Irish Tourist Board who have details of properties which may be booked through them. If you don't like what they're offering, the alternative is to scour the Sunday papers for details of apartments and cottages to let by private arrangement. There are more pitfalls if you adopt this course of action, but if you're careful it can be a success; get all the details before you commit yourself, along with a full inventory and recent photograph – that way the risks can be minimized.

As for **camping** and **caravanning**, there are numerous sites scattered around the country and especially along the coastline. There are ninety-one parks officially recognized by the Irish Tourist Board, but many more unofficial sites throughout Ireland. Standards and facilities vary dramatically; some may be merely an empty field to pitch your tent in, others have children's play areas, showers, shops on site and so on. Costs range from IR£8 per unit for the exceptionally well-equipped sites to IR£3 per unit for basic running water and shower facilities. Apart from caravan parks, there are over 400 forest parks countrywide and many of these provide convenient places to stay overnight if you haven't been able to find a site. Although there are no official facilities in these areas, there are large flat spaces and plenty of shelter from road traffic and adverse weather conditions. In some places, you'll see 'No Overnight Parking' signs or alternatively, bars preventing caravans from entering lay-bys. These warnings aren't aimed at holidaymakers in general, but at the gipsies who travel the country, making their base wherever they can find a space. Usually, holidaymakers won't be disturbed if they camp rough. One word of warning: don't head away from main roads, expecting to find a lay-by in quiet, leafy lanes – your 'lay-by' will probably turn out to be the gate where cows go out for morning milking!

Finally, **Youth Hostels** are about the cheapest form of accommodation that you can find anywhere, and don't forget that there is no upper limit on age for admission to the Youth Hostelling Association. Hostels are also frequently found in areas of great scenic interest, such as Connemara or Glenveagh National Parks, so they are ideal accommodation for climbers or hill walkers. An IYHA card is required and costs range from IR£4.90 for seniors in the busy hostels of Cork, Dublin, Killarney and Limerick, to IR£2.50/£3 elsewhere. Whilst the official IYHA hostels at least guarantee some degree of cleanliness, the same cannot be said of the unofficial youth hostels currently cashing in on the numbers of young people coming to Ireland. Some of these are okay – especially the ones that take the trouble to send a mini-bus to the railway station to meet the trains. However, beware of hostels, especially in Dublin, which are advertising bed and breakfast for IR£4 a night. The chances are that these grotty places have bed-bugs and lavatories that haven't been cleaned for a decade. If you're strapped for cash and tempted, *never* pay your money before seeing the sleeping accommodation and checking out the toilets and showers.

The Independent Hostel Owners is a co-operative society with over 70 hostels located all over Ireland. The hostels are independently owned and family run. All offer fully equipped kitchens, hot showers and dormitories, and some also offer private and family rooms, meals and camping. No membership cards are required. Further information can be found at the Dooey Hostel, Glencolumbkille, Co. Donegal (Tel: 073 30130).

Overall, the accommodation scene for the independent traveller is very good. Sleeping accommodation in hotels or guesthouses is nowhere as cheap as can be found on the continent, but for the extra cost you get decent standards of cleanliness and quality of service. Again, do book ahead, especially if you're travelling in a family group – otherwise you might feel the squeeze in busy cities and towns during the peak season.

So much for the independent accommodation scene. Now let's turn our attention to travelling to Ireland.

By Air

Air services between Ireland and Britain are excellent. Not only are there frequent services (up to ten a day) from the London airports to Dublin, but practically every significant provincial airport offers similar flights. Outside London, services to Ireland are run from Birmingham, Bristol, Cardiff, Edinburgh, East Midlands, Glasgow, Liverpool, Isle of Man, Jersey, Manchester and Newcastle. Most services fly only to Dublin or Cork, but there are also frequent flights available to Farranfore, Galway, Knock, Shannon, Sligo, Waterford and Donegal. Shannon deals predominantly with transatlantic flights and services connect with the major cities in the US, such as Atlanta, Boston, Dallas/Fort Worth, New York and Los Angeles, among others.

Ticket prices are kept down due to the number of airlines competing for the Irish travel market. Airlines with scheduled flights to Ireland are Aer Lingus, British Midland, Brymon Airways, Dan Air, Manx Airlines, Ryanair and Loganair. Of these, the Irish companies Ryanair and Aer Lingus have the lion's share of the market. It's always worth shopping around for prices as companies frequently have special offers. Ryanair have a good reputation for cut-price deals and generally can be relied upon to offer something a bit cheaper than their competitors. The only disadvantage is that they fly from Luton and Stansted airports and so may not be suitable for travellers outside the South-east of England. Flight times between London and Dublin are approximately seventy minutes, and Glasgow to Dublin approximately fifty minutes.

A variety of fares is available. The MAXISAVER, at around £60, is the most economical but must be booked a month in advance and includes a weekend stay. SUPER-APEX booked two weeks in advance costs around £79, and a ticket bought on the spot with no prior booking costs around £106. However, both of these involve staying over a weekend; if you are not able to do that prices increase to around £156. The cost of a full fare is £121 for a single or £242 return. It is sometimes possible to find an end-of-season bargain in a travel agent's window, with return tickets sold for as little as £50.

Special low prices can be obtained if you're under twenty-five. Aer Lingus, for example, does a one-way £43 fare from London to Dublin. Students qualify for reduced air travel if they can produce proof of student status. Costs are about £65 return from London to Dublin. More details are obtainable from USIT, London Student Travel, 52 Grosvenor Gardens, London SW1W 1AG (Tel: 071 730 3402), or from a local travel agent.

By Ferries

Unless you fly, a ferry to Ireland will come into your journey one way or other. Ferry travel is expensive – some might say too expensive for the length of journey involved – but once on board, the companies certainly make every effort to make your journey a comfortable one. Spacious lounges, snack-bars and restaurants – even television on some routes – create comfortable surroundings and alleviate the tedium of a journey which can take anything from 2hrs. 20mins. to 10hrs.

These are the main ferry routes connecting the British mainland with Ireland: Stranraer/Larne; Swansea/Cork; Holyhead to Dublin and Dun Laoghaire; Fishguard and Pembroke/Rosslare. Douglas on the Isle of Man also has seasonal sailings to Belfast and Dublin. On the busy routes (Holyhead, Fishguard and Stranraer departures), there are often two or three sailings a day.

Obviously, prices vary from company to company and also depend on the length of the crossing. However, on the popular Dun Laoghaire/Holyhead or Dublin/Holyhead sailing, you can expect to pay around £200 return in peak season for a car and up to four adults (2 children = 1 adult). Foot passengers can expect to pay around £30 return or more, depending on the time of year. Most companies operate a three- or four-tier pricing system which varies from day to day according to seasonal demand. For example, weekends in the peak period of mid-July to beginning of August may rate as grade A, whilst Tuesdays may rate as grade C. If you are able to pick the days of travelling carefully, you can make considerable savings. Caravans usually cost around £100 return whilst bicycles are charged a £4 transportation fee. These prices may seem steep, but some discount fares are occasionally offered on short-stay returns of 60 hours or 120 hours, and sometimes on specific out-of-season periods. The full sailing timetables, plus details of prices and special offers, are readily available in travel agents. Booking is essential during the summer months, particularly if you are planning to take a car/caravan. Casual travellers run the risk of being turned away. Avoid the queues at the port and arrive in good time for your departure.

By Rail

As British Rail provides services to the major ferry ports (Holyhead, Stranraer, Liverpool, etc.), travelling by train is a convenient alternative to relying on the goodwill of friends and relations. You can book tickets in Britain for any destination in Ireland, inclusive of ferry costs. As a guide, the approximate cost of a return fare to Dublin, travelling from London via Holyhead, is £75 second-class or £132 first-class. The journey lasts 9 hours and buffet facilities are available throughout. For those travelling from the North or Scotland, the inclusive ferry/train fare from Glasgow to Belfast is around £49.50 second-class return travelling midweek or £54.50 at weekends, and again the journey lasts around 9 hours. The journeys to and from ports are reasonably efficient, and in the event of delayed sailings, etc., British Rail lays on coaches to meet the boat and take travellers with through tickets to their destinations.

In Ireland itself, the rail service is excellent. The trains are modern, with continental-style electric doors, air-conditioning and impeccable upkeep. As journeys around the country are relatively short, time-keeping is generally very good and delays are uncommon. From Dublin, connections are available to other destinations in the country. The capital has two stations: Heuston to the northern destinations of Westport and Galway, and Connolly for elsewhere. Journeys from Dublin to Cork, Belfast and Galway last approximately three hours. Non-stop trains running at peak time on the busiest routes take an hour less.

As far as discounts go, students have the best deal. Those with young persons' railcards – such as the Eurail Youth Pass for under-twenty-sixes – can obtain cheap fares on the British end of the connection. Eurail cards are eligible for use in Ireland but Interrail cards bought in Britain are not valid although, as in the UK, you get a 50 per cent reduction on fares. Special rover passes can be bought in Ireland from Irish Railways; these cost approximately £55 for an eight-day pass and allow you unlimited rail travel throughout the country.

If you are planning to travel by rail to Ireland, reservations are strongly advised, especially if you are travelling at the weekends during the mid-July/end of August period. On some services from London, a seat reservation system is operational so be sure to enquire *before* you're on the train, otherwise you might find that it's standing room only.

By Bus

Coach travel is undoubtedly the cheapest way to get to Ireland, although it's certainly not the quickest – or the most comfortable. Overnight bus travel must be one of the most harrowing experiences known to man, even though it does leave you with a fascinating insight into human nature!

National Express runs at least one trip a day from London Victoria Station, leaving at approximately 1900 in the evening and travelling overnight via Holyhead to arrive in Dublin at 0745 the next day. The Cork service from London Victoria runs to a similar timetable, crossing from Fishguard to Rosslare and arriving around midday. Costs for a round trip to Dublin are about £57 and Cork £60. Services to regional ferry ports (Stranraer, Liverpool, etc.) are also available – check your nearest depot for details. From Dublin, Bus Eireann, the national service, runs express coaches to other destinations in the country, including Cork, Galway and Killarney. Alternatively, Slattery's Coaches, an Irish coach company, operate an extremely good service from London to almost any major destination in Ireland; costs are competitive at £30 per adult to Dublin and £40 per adult to Cork. Journeys to Wexford, Waterford, Tralee, Limerick and Killarney are also available. Telephone 071 485 2778/071 482 1604 for more details.

By Car/Campervan

Touring by car is undoubtedly the best way to see Ireland, although it may work out rather more expensive than you anticipated: petrol is nearly twice as expensive as in Britain and the cost of transporting the car by ferry must also be budgeted for (see 'Ferries', page 76). Expect to pay £200 in mid-summer for a car with four adults, although remember that you will have to pay extra for any person travelling who was not declared at the time of booking.

Obviously the route you take depends on what part of the country you're travelling from, but from London to Holyhead, you'll take the M6 up to junction 17, branching off at Sandbach on to the A534, then head towards Chester, picking up the A55 to cross the Menai Strait and on to Holyhead. The journey to Liverpool is quicker, following the M6 then the M62 into the city you can expect to take four hours at a comfortable speed, allowing an extra hour if you're branching off to Holyhead. If you're time-conscious and looking for the fastest route, remember that sailings from Holyhead to Dun Laoghaire take only three and a half hours.

If you're coming from Northern Ireland, most of the major border posts are open twenty-four hours a day. When you're going through any of these posts, be prepared to show your identification and driving licence. The border isn't a pleasant place to drive through, but as long as you obey instructions and don't stop in the 'no-man's-land' between the Republic and Northern Ireland, you should have no problems.

The standards of roads are variable. The main road between Belfast and Dublin is not dual-carriageway and there are no by-passes built around the small towns en route. Consequently, don't rely on making good time between the two capitals. Although the distance is only about one hundred miles, expect to take at least three hours to complete the journey. If you're driving into Dublin itself, a street-map is essential as signs for the city centre are few and far between.

A huge road-improvement scheme is currently being implemented throughout the country, with the help of EC money. However, this is going slowly so expect patchy road surfaces with plenty of 'loose chipping' signs. Do stick to speed limits on these stretches of road, as dozens of cars every day don't and end up with chipped or shattered windscreens. Main roads are wide, with a small buffer lane for slow-moving vehicles and cyclists. The volume of traffic is light – even in the busy summer months – and ideal for those on caravanning or cycling holidays. In remote areas, back-roads are often appalling with hundreds of pot-holes and few passing-places. The signposts in these areas are also pretty bad and frequently only in Irish, which is not much good if you've got an English map. A detailed map is essential, either Ordnance Survey or an AA/Michelin Touring guide. Watch out for donkeys, cows, sheep and horses wandering across roads in Galway and Donegal.

First-class roads are designated by the letter N (e.g. N1), L roads indicate link roads, whilst A and B roads share the same designation as in Britain. Signs indicating road distances are peculiar: the white signs indicate miles and the newer green ones are in kilometres. Both are common and can be confusing to unsuspecting drivers. The rule of the road is to drive and give way on the left.

To drive in Ireland, you will need the following documentation and equipment:

a current British or international driving licence
car registration documents
Green Card (international insurance certificate)

It is obligatory for front-seat passengers to wear seat-belts and children under twelve must travel in the back seat. Both petrol and diesel are widely available, although in rural areas petrol stations may close on Sunday so keep your tank filled up. Speed limits are 55 m.p.h. on main roads and 30 m.p.h. in built-up areas.

If you're a member of the AA, you are entitled to a full breakdown service in the Republic, from the Irish AA, but not a relay service. An extra insurance cover can be taken out for this before you go, and costs around £35 for 13–31 days. If you do break down, contact Cork on 021 276 922. Travellers are also strongly advised to have a suitable insurance policy to cover driving abroad. In the case of a serious car accident, phone 999 for the fire, ambulance and police services.

Everyone has their own preference when it comes to a driving holiday, but speaking as someone who has driven on the continent in everything from a Daimler limousine to a battered old Mini, I feel it's worth putting in a word here about what to look for when choosing a car to drive abroad in. Obviously, luggage capacity is an important consideration. Fuel economy, spare parts and comfort are the other major considerations. Don't try to squeeze too many people into a car, and remember, you'll return with more luggage than you set out with.

Hitch-Hiking

Hitch-hikers in Britain have variable success. The smaller roads on the way to the port are the best place to pick up a lift; the major motorway routes are a dead loss. Stopping is prohibited and the danger element, especially for girl hitchers, is unavoidable. In Ireland, lots of people try to hitch – both locals and foreigners, young people and old. Drivers in Ireland, however, don't appear to be any more willing to pick up hitchers than elsewhere. The best advice, if you're planning to hitch, is to take enough money for a bus ticket! The risk element in the Republic is generally considered to be lower than in Britain – although one should never, ever be complacent.

Generally Useful Information

TIME DIFFERENCES

Ireland keeps the same time as the UK, that is GMT during the winter months and GMT + 1 during the summer. New York is five hours behind Irish time.

ELECTRICITY

The standard voltage is 220 volt AC. Appliances should be fitted with three-pin plugs.

WATER

Water is safe to drink from the tap throughout the country. If you're travelling on car tours, consider packing a bottle of Irish spring water rather than fizzy drinks – much healthier and handy for long journeys.

Part Three
WHEN YOU'RE THERE

Tourist Information

As part of your holiday preparations it is a good idea to write to the Irish Tourist Board (Bord Fáilte) in London. This office issues general brochures and maps relating to the individual regions of Ireland. These will give you some idea of the main sights, the leisure and accommodation facilities available and some background information on the geography and history of the area. If you are keen on a particular sport, make a point of asking for the relevant leaflets to be sent to you. This way, by the time you get to Ireland, you'll not only have an idea of what to expect, but you'll also have a small dossier of useful information at hand even if you end up in the middle of nowhere.

When you're there, more specific information about each individual county can be picked up. Look out for the county touring guides, costing between IR50p and IR£1.50. These are definitely worth buying as they not only give you detailed historical and anecdotal information, but also point out local picnic spots and scenic walks. There are twenty tourist offices in the major towns and cities which stay open all year round, but many more which open during the summer months only. For a full list of locations, pick up a leaflet at any tourist information office or write off to London before you go. Tourist offices throughout the country are indicated by the green 'i' sign.

The literature available is generally very good, although you may have to pay for several of the more useful publications. Each individual tourist office specializes in its own particular area and may not have much detailed information about other counties. If you want more general advice, go to one of the larger tourist offices in Dublin, Cork or Limerick cities. The addresses of these are:

14 Upper O'Connell Street, Dublin 1 (Tel: 01 747 733)
Tourist House, Grand Parade, Cork City (Tel: 021 273 251)
Arthur's Quay, Limerick City (Tel: 061 317 522)

Inevitably the standards of service vary from individual to individual. At the peak of the summer, tourist office staff tend to be very busy and consequently rather snappy when they have thousands of tourists to deal with. Don't be put off – you are the customer after all and when they do get round to serving you, they are invariably helpful and informative. As far as accommodation goes, staff can suggest the main areas to look or, for a commission, find you a place for the night in a B&B or hotel. Commission ranges from IR50p for a local booking to IR£1 for a reservation in another county, and these costs are charged to cover phone calls. Information relating to local bus, train and boat tours can also be obtained from these offices, and it is often possible to book tours there and then, rather than having to search out the local bus or train stations.

Opening hours are usually 0900–1800 Monday to Friday, and 0900–1300 on Saturday, although times may vary from county to county. Offices at points of entry (Shannon Airport, Dublin Airport and Dun Laoghaire) are extended during the summer months.

Sightseeing

For a comparatively small country geographically, Ireland has a wealth of history to be discovered. Indeed, the sightseer will find that there is no corner of the land without its own individual character and history. There's always something to see or do in Ireland, and given the size of the country, it is entirely possible to take in the major sights (and more besides) in a week of leisurely touring.

The coastal regions are the areas of greatest interest, although one should never forget the numerous castles and monasteries in the country's tranquil interior, which can provide a basis for some most enjoyable tours far from the madding crowd. However, it is undoubtedly the busy metropolis of Dublin which is the premier tourist spot in Ireland, attracting both young and old with its internationalism and wealth of history. After the capital, the focus of tourism shifts to the South-west quarter, where attractions include Blarney Castle, just outside Cork city, the Ring of Kerry in Co. Kerry near Killarney, a local town with a tourist centre, and the historical streets of Limerick city. Moving further north, the main attractions become the natural landscapes, with the scenery of **Connemara** and **The Burren** eclipsing most of the man-made features in the region.

Obviously touring is the best way to see the countryside and its sights, and Ireland is the ideal country for car tours with its temperate climate and quiet back-roads. Don't underestimate the time each part of your tour will take – most journeys look short on the map, but end up taking longer because you'll be passing through numerous one-horse towns with very congested high streets. As a guide, the journey between Waterford and Cork will take about three hours minimum and between Belfast and Dublin two and a half hours – providing you don't get lost, of course! Another option for sightseers is coach or rail tours. Both local private firms and the national CIE buses put on tours to the major sightseeing attractions in their area, while rail/bus tours are also available. In terms of prices and services, Bus Eireann and Irish Railways are hard to beat, and as they have offices in most towns, it's easy to get up-to-date and reliable information about booking, costs, etc.

There's a small entrance fee for most museums and galleries. Opening times for museums, castles and stately homes vary from place to place, although most are open 1000–1700, and many of the larger sights stay open until 1800/1900 at night. Out-of-season, some places will close on Sunday and many of the minor castles and stately homes will shut down altogether for the winter.

Shopping

Shopping has the emphasis on quality rather than economy. Irish tweed, linen and crystalware are world-renowned – but don't expect to get them cheap in their country of origin. If you can afford to splash out a bit more than usual on souvenir shopping, however, you'll be buying items that will last a lifetime.

Handwoven Donegal tweed can be bought in department stores, either by the metre or made up in gentlemen's or ladies' garments, and countryside craftshops often sell the cloth by the metre too. Although Ireland is no longer a prolific producer of linen, the shops still stock plenty of it. Look out for good buys either in the classic linen suit or in skirts and jackets made up in bright primary colours. Woollens are another quality buy, and range from soft cashmere and angora garments to the chunky Aran sweaters, originating from the Aran islands in the west of the country. Remember that the hand-knitted article is more expensive but much longer-lasting than a machine-knitted one.

Waterford lead crystal is by no means the only quality crystal that Ireland produces. When in Galway, visit the **Galway Irish Crystal Visitors Centre** at Merlin Park (Tel: 091 57311). Open every day from 9 a.m. to 5 p.m., and selling seconds, ends of lines and so on from the fabulously intricate Galway crystal range, it's a bargain-hunter's paradise. Ceramics are available in the china sections of department stores, or in small out-of-the-way craftshops where the potter is in residence. Worked pewter and silverware are other possibilities. An unusual but utterly authentic and practical 'souvenir' from Ireland is a 'bodhrán' (pronounced bow-rawn): the Irish drum, played with a beater and made from goatskin and wood. The only full-time bodhrán maker in Ireland is Malachy Kearns. See his workshop – **IDA Craft Centre**, Roundstone, Co. Galway (Tel: 095 35808).

Shops are open 0900–1730 from Monday to Friday, although some places may open until 1800 during the summer months and large supermarkets are regularly open for evening shopping. In Dublin, shops have extended opening hours – sometimes until 2000/2100.

Food and Drink

At its best, food in Ireland makes generous use of the natural products of the country: lamb, seafood, salmon, trout and dairy products are unrivalled for their quality and freshness.

At the most mundane level, however, you could spend two weeks touring Ireland and not taste anything remotely different from your normal diet. Apart from a few distinctive dishes, Irish cuisine is plain, hearty and very good – but hardly exciting or diet-conscious.

At the bottom end of the scale, Ireland has an amazing array of fast-food shops: even the smallest hamlet has its hamburger joint or pizza takeaway. If you're planning on eating cheaply then these are the places where you'll get an inexpensive but filling meal. Don't go overboard though, as your palate will soon begin to tire of endless doses of starch and grease. Instead, look around for an inexpensive bar menu – the soup of the day is usually homemade and served with loads of delicious brown Irish soda-bread. Other cost-conscious measures include looking out for the special tourist menus. These cost either IR£5.60 or IR£7.50 for a three-course meal of simple but tasty food, and are especially good for family groups who are looking for an evening meal which won't make big inroads into the holiday budget. However, as only 370 restaurants around the country participate in this scheme (indicated by the 'smiling chef' sign), you can't rely on finding a tourist menu in every town.

The day begins with a traditional Irish breakfast, whether you are staying in a B&B, hotel or guesthouse. An Irish breakfast consists of the usual bacon, egg, sausage fry-up with cereal and/or fruit juice beforehand. Obviously this isn't ideal for vegetarians, so if you're in a hotel make alternative arrangements at the beginning of your stay, or ask your landlady if she can supply you with eggs, or a selection of cheeses, to make up for what you're missing. Bread, jam and toast are usually in plentiful supply at the breakfast table. Irish soda-bread is a brown bread with a deliciously nutty flavour, the kind of thing those with savoury tastes could easily get addicted to. Along with the food, tea and coffee are served, with as many refills as you're ever likely to want! Breakfasts are also widely available in restaurants and coffee-houses throughout the country. Costs for buying a breakfast range from IR£1.65 to IR£4.

With a hearty breakfast to set you up for the day, you may not feel like lunch, usually served 1200–1400/1430. Most bars and hotels do lunch menus, often featuring the same food as evening menus but at much cheaper prices – so this is the time to try out some of the more costly seafood or steak dishes. If you're just after a light lunch, remember that portions are usually more than generous, so some soup and a baked potato will easily suffice. A light lunch will cost around IR£4; for something more elaborate expect to pay between IR£5 and IR£7.

Mid-afternoon, when spirits begin to flag, a reviving cup of tea can easily be found in one of the numerous snack-bars. Not to be forgotten are the Irish bakeries with adjoining coffee-shops. Irish cream cakes and pastries are out of this world, whilst a request for tea and scones often results in a generous basketful of brown scones and lashings of tea. Definitely not a place for the figure-conscious or the weak-willed!

Dinner is usually available 1830–2100/2200. If you're staying in a hotel on half-board, check if your meal is flexible and may be taken at either lunchtime or dinnertime. Service charges may or may not be included in the cost of the meal, depending on the establishment, but tipping generally isn't treated as a big issue and it's left entirely up to the individual's discretion where he or she feels the service has been something special. The price of dinner depends on your standards: a fairly elaborate meal can set you back between IR£17 and IR£24. A more modest, but perfectly adequate dinner from the *à la carte* menu costs around the IR£8 and IR£10 mark. Prices at a good seafood restaurant range from IR£10 to IR£15.

Local specialities vary according to the county. On the west coast and the major inland water systems, fresh fish and seafood feature heavily on the menus. There are numerous seafood restaurants, especially on the west coast, and prices are not as high as might be expected. Moreover, it is often the most unlikely-looking restaurant built in someone's back-garden that serves up the most delicious seafood, so don't be put off by appearances. Don't pass up the chance of sampling some freshwater salmon and Dublin prawns – or indeed, the humble mussel and crab. Served *au naturel*, or in piquant sauces, they can't be beaten. Seafood chowder is a popular menu choice on the west coast, and the combination of freshly caught ingredients makes for a delicious, strongly flavoured soup. Galway oysters are a famous local delicacy – usually accompanied by a strong drink of beer or Guinness to wash them down. You could visit the Galway Oyster Festival, held in August/September in Clarinbridge, just south of Galway city. This annual event, sponsored by Guinness, is well worth a visit. Your reward is not only fine food and beverages, but a picturesque setting too. In Connemara, lamb is the special produce, either in a simple herb-flavoured roast or in the traditional Irish stew, a thick hearty casserole layered with onions and potatoes. Irish beef is also a quality product, and traditional preparations include Irish Spiced Beef, a rich blend of prime beef, cloves, herbs and garlic. More common, however, are the thick slabs of steak either grilled straight or cooked gently in any number of delicious sauces and indeed the traditional roast with all the trimmings is still first choice for Sunday lunch. Vegetables are not forgotten either. Potatoes are a staple part of any meal and Colcannon, made with cabbage and leftover boiled potatoes, sounds unappetizing but can be turned into something impressive by a good chef.

Puddings are nothing special and amount to the usual selection of gateaux, apple-pies and trifles – although a generous helping of rich Irish cream does help to add a touch of luxury to even the most humble pie. As for cheeses, there's the standard mousetrap variety, Irish Cheddar, which has a strong flavour and is suitable for simple lunches of apples and cheese. Otherwise cheeses vary according to county, and the Kerry soft cheeses or the slightly stronger Galway cheese would be welcome accompaniments to any picnic.

The usual range of German, Italian and French wines is readily available in the Republic. Wine is, however, much more expensive than in Britain. In an off-licence a standard bottle of Liebfraumilch can cost twice the price that you're likely to pay at home. Prices go up even further in restaurants, where the mark-up is greater. Expect to pay IR£8 at least for a bottle of cheapish wine and always go for the house-wine if there is one available. There are several varieties of Irish Whiskey, pot-stilled and matured in casks for seven years, but Old Bushmills brand has been produced for over three centuries, and many say that a

Bushmills malt can't be beaten. The other famous Irish spirit is that legendary beast poteen, a clear liquid of pure alcohol. The production of poteen is illegal, so you'll have to have a few good 'contacts' if you want to get hold of the stuff. It's not really a drink for the uninitiated anyway, as one small glass of the stuff has enough kick to put you well into next week!

After-dinner drinks include Irish Cream, a smooth mixture of whiskey and cream, Irish Mist, made of whiskey and honey, or the classic Irish coffee. A good Irish coffee should make use of indigenous Irish products – thick Irish cream and a measure of good malt whiskey. The coffee and whiskey are sweetened with several teaspoons of sugar, so that the liquid is dense enough to float the cream, making a delicious combination as the coffee is drunk through the warm layer of cream.

As for beers and lagers, Guinness is the national drink and is served everywhere. The distinctive brown pint, topped with a creamy head, has a strong, rich taste and those who are unaccustomed to it may find it heavy going and it does take a while to pull a pint of Guinness. The usual brands of lager, beer and soft drinks are available – although you may find the prices a bit off-putting. Canned drinks are IR£50p from supermarkets, and a pint of lager is IR£2. Prices in rural areas are slightly lower, but in Dublin or Cork, you could expect to pay around IR£2.10. If you're really keen on sampling Irish produce, try spring water (straight from one of the many peat bogs). A large bottle (handy for car tours) costs around IR£90p and is available from most shops and all bars.

Those in self-catering accommodation undoubtedly have the better deal money-wise when it comes to buying food. There are plenty of supermarkets and corner-shops where you can stock up on provisions, and butchers' and fishmongers' shops will supply you with the local fresh produce. Try some tasty pork sausages flavoured with local herbs or buy locally caught trout or Atlantic salmon. For picnics, a selection of delicious Irish soda-bread, fresh fruit and cheese is more than sufficient for a light lunch *al fresco*. For those who expect to spend much of their time dining in restaurants, the Irish Tourist Board issues a booklet, 'Dining in Ireland'. This gives the location of restaurants which offer tourist menus, as well as giving a quick résumé of special features and an average price for breakfast, lunch and dinner menus. This book is especially useful if you're staying in a fairly remote area, although if you're in one of the larger towns or cities, you'll need to be equipped with a good map in order to find the restaurants. If you're staying in B&B, ask your landlady if she can recommend somewhere – she'll generally be in a better position to give you an objective recommendation than staff in tourist offices.

Just recently established in Ireland is the 'Dinner for Two Club'. This could prove very useful for members from abroad. Participating restaurants, hotels, car rentals and other travel and leisure facilities are listed in the quarterly *For Two Guide* for Britain and Ireland.

Nightlife

Outside the major centres, the disco and nightclub scene is fairly tame, although you'll usually be able to find one or two in small towns which act as centres to a rural population. In the cities of Dublin and Cork, nightclubs range from the glossy establishments where the bright young things of Ireland party the night away, to the more modest pub/discos where the atmosphere is more relaxed and less competitive.

Pubs are the usual focus for nightlife throughout the country and many pubs have live music, ranging from jazz or folk bands to impromptu sessions on the fiddle and bodhrán, the traditional Irish drum. Folk music in particular is experiencing a revival in popularity – don't miss the chance to see some of the virtuoso performances from the Irish fiddle-players. Hotels frequently host Irish Nights and these may be a regular feature or a one-off, depending on the availability of bands. Otherwise, cabaret nights are often held in the larger city hotels, where you can have your evening meal with night-time entertainment inclusive.

The places with the best nightlife are **CORK** and **TRAMORE** on the south coast, **DUBLIN** and the seaside resort of **ROSSLARE** on the east coast, and **KILLARNEY**, **LIMERICK** and **TRALEE** in the west of the country. In the cities of Dublin, Limerick and Cork, a more cosmopolitan atmosphere prevails and here you'll find the best choice of discos, bars, theatres, cinemas and restaurants.

Horse-racing and theatre are other possibilities for an evening's entertainment. A number of race meetings take place in the evening, and as the social aspect of horse-racing is every bit as important as the racing itself, this can be a good way to meet people and enjoy a fine summer's evening outdoors (see 'The Socialite', page 19). The theatrical tradition is strong in Ireland, and the Abbey Theatre in Dublin puts on a season of works by famous Irish writers each summer: definitely worth a visit. Otherwise there's a National Folk Theatre based in Tralee, and Cork is the home-town of the Irish National Ballet Corps. If opera is more to your taste, then Wexford hosts a world-renowned festival in October, although, as with all the theatres detailed above, booking in advance is essential.

Communications

There are no problems keeping in touch with home from Ireland. International telephone calls can be made direct from most of the new-style telephone boxes, and it is equally possible to write, telegraph, telex or fax Britain. The mail service between Britain and Ireland is reasonably efficient – the delivery time is about four to five days – but this is obviously not much good if you run out of money halfway through your holiday and have to wait for extra funds to be mailed. It's a far better idea to avoid this situation altogether by taking an emergency fund with you in the first place.

POST OFFICES

Opening hours are from 0900–1730 Mon–Fri, and 0900–1300 Saturday. The General Post Office in Dublin's O'Connell Street opens seven days, Mon–Sat 0800–2000 and 1030–1830 on Sunday.

The mail service is reasonably priced and efficient. It costs 28p to send postcards and 32p to send a first-class surface letter. Post-boxes are the same as in Britain, except they are painted bright green. A lot of newsagents and corner shops will also sell stamps. Airmail costs depend on weight, although it is worth remembering that first-class post is cheaper and just as quick to the UK.

POSTE RESTANTE

Poste restante facilities are operative on weekdays only. Most post offices will hold mail for you, provided that it is clearly marked 'Poste restante', and proof of identity must be produced before mail is released.

TELEPHONES

There are three types of public telephone in the Republic: the first is the conventional payphone where you put your money in, then dial for a connection; the second is the older A/B model. In an A/B booth, you follow the standard procedure but press button A if your call is answered and button B if there's no reply and you want your money back. International phone calls can be made from any of the modern boxes, and as there are direct dialling links between North America and Ireland, there is no need to go through the operator, unless you are using the older A/B model. Calls to Britain are counted as STD, rather than international calls. The third type is a card payphone. Callcards are obtained at the post office, retail outlets located near the kiosk and Telecom Eireann Telecentres. For the location of nearest cardphone or callcard agents in your area ring Freephone 1800 250 250. The cards are available in three denominations: 20 units – £3.50; 50 units – £7.50; 100 units – £15.

You can arrange to phone home from your hotel room by going

through the hotel switchboard. Note that an extra charge will be levied for this service although most hotels do have direct dial now. The phone number for emergencies is 999 and calls are free. The operator can be reached by dialling 10.

Telephone charges are 20p (2 × 10p) for local calls. Charges are on a time basis for long distance and international calls.

Moving Around the Country

There are a number of ways for the independent traveller to move around the country. Trains, local bus services, express coaches, coach tours and car-hire are all possible modes of travel. For a less conventional method, try a week ambling along in a horse-drawn caravan.

Undoubtedly public transport is the cheapest way to travel. The local bus network covers practically every corner of the country, and is especially good if you are striking out for the remote parts in the North-west. The train service, too, is very good in terms of efficiency and speed, but the network is rather limited as it only connects the main centres of population and does not operate further north than Sligo town. Express Coaches, also run by Bus Eireann, offer the usual service and are an alternative to train travel on the routes between major centres. Coach tours are an obvious choice if you want to do a job-lot of sights in one day, but if you don't fancy the wide-eyed-tourists-on-a-bus bit, then you may consider car-hire. Unless you're sharing the costs with someone else, this is quite an expensive option, but as you'll discover, a car gives you the flexibility to go where you like at your own pace. Road standards are variable, and the big upgrading operation which is currently under way invariably means roadworks – lots of them!

CAR-HIRE

Car-hire in Ireland can be quite expensive: hiring a car for a week through one of the large firms in the months of June to September could set you back around £175 in total.

There are a number of local Irish car-hire firms, but if you are relying on car-hire as your main means of transport once you get to Ireland, the best idea is to book ahead through one of the major firms. That way you'll be able to choose the model and price range you want and not be subject to what's available: during the peak season, car-hire firms are busy and you may have to take what's left.

If you're hiring ahead in this country, there are two options open to you – to go through your tour operator or to book ahead with a large car-hire company, such as Hertz or Avis. Most of the major tour operators now offer car-hire facilities. Often the prices quoted are at specially negotiated rates with local firms, and are much cheaper than could be obtained if you were shopping around by yourself. Usually the cost of car-hire through tour companies includes local taxes, unlimited mileage, delivery and collection to and from your hotel, and some kind of insurance policy. The disadvantage of booking with tour operators is that this facility is inflexible: you often have to reserve your car either when you book your holiday or at least a month in advance of arriving in the country.

By contrast, major car-hire companies only require booking of up to seven days in advance before supplying you with a car in Ireland. Car-hire generally works out more expensive with a major car-hire firm, primarily because their quoted price excludes local tax charges. However, on the plus side, you do have the back-up and facilities of an international company. Obviously, the rates and services available differ from firm to firm, but usually if you hire through one of the international firms you get unlimited mileage, third-party insurance and an emergency breakdown service. It is also advisable to take out an additional insurance (a collision damage waiver) at an additional cost of £8 a day, as otherwise you may be liable for the first £800 of an accident claim. There is normally no charge for delivering cars to a different town, as long as the car-hire firm operates there; otherwise you'll be expected to pay for collection expenses (usually about 10p a mile from the nearest depot). As with the tour company car-hire, petrol and fines for driving offences are the driver's own responsibility.

If you are thinking of hiring through one of the major agencies, then Avis is the largest car-hire company in Europe and also, in our experience, the best. They operate in ninety-three countries, their prices are among the most competitive and their service is hard to beat. If you hire your car before you go, you get a guaranteed price which cannot be altered whatever happens to exchange rates, and you also have much more of a comeback if things go wrong. You can book either through your travel agent or through an Avis office.

For those of you who don't want to commit yourself to car-hire until you get to the country, Avis operates a scheme called 'Driveaway Cheques' – whereby you buy cheques in the UK on a no-commission basis – which allows you to choose car rental on the days you want and pay with these cheques. All the paperwork and hanging around is done in the UK, so no time is wasted when abroad, and you are entitled to all the same conditions of rental as if you had hired a car in advance; guaranteed price, unlimited mileage, etc. If you choose not to hire a car after all, the vouchers can simply be traded back in the UK at face value, so no money is lost. For flexibility and value this scheme makes a lot of sense, although if you are going to a busy resort in peak season you would still be better advised to make a definite booking in advance, as there can be no guarantee that the car you want will be there on the day you want it.

As regards documentation, British and International driving licences are valid. Application forms for International licences can be obtained from AA or RAC offices. Minimum age for driving a hired car is usually twenty-three, and you must have held a full licence for one year. Make sure you know what type of insurance is included in the car price and remember that most car-hire companies ask for a refundable deposit to be paid in advance.

Petrol comes in three grades: premium, super and regular, with premium being equivalent to British four-star grading. Diesel is also widely available, as is unleaded petrol. All fuel is sold by the litre (1 gallon = 4.5 litres). If you are involved in a serious accident, phone 999 for emergency services. If you're travelling in a hired car, remember you must first inform the car-hire firm before carrying out any repairs. For more details, see the 'By Car' section of 'Independent Means' (page 79).

TRAINS

Train services run by Irish Railways are surprisingly good. The trains are fast, efficient and most importantly, clean. There's no hanging around either, as most trains have ample seating space to cope with the busy summer months. The train network isn't overly extensive, but it does connect the major centres as far as Sligo in the north of the country. The commuter service DART runs a swift and frequent connection to east-coast towns close to Dublin, so if you're planning on sightseeing for a few days in Dublin you may consider commuting in from one of the quieter seaside towns. When you're there you can buy a rail-rover pass for a week's travel at around IR£55 per adult or IR£26 per child. This may seem expensive, but remember that petrol for one week's car touring costs around £60. Alternatively, Irish Railways also has a programme of day tours to major sights, at costs under IR£10. Check at the local rail office for details.

Eurail passes are valid for the Republic of Ireland, but unfortunately Interrail tickets bought in Britain are not: you'll have to pay half-fares on top of your Interrail card. Reservations are not necessary and there are buffet facilities on most services.

BUSES

Bus Eireann, the national bus service, has an extensive network which covers most corners of the country. The services are split into express services, connecting up the major centres, and local services. If you're planning to travel a lot by bus then an unlimited eight-day bus pass costs IR£55 per adult or around IR£25 per child (fifteen-day tickets available for about IR£80 and IR£40 respectively). For longer trips on express coaches, reserve your seat in advance or arrive in plenty of time to buy your ticket, as services can fill up quickly in summer months.

Bus Eireann also does a very good range of tours to the most scenic areas in Ireland: the Ring of Kerry or Connemara Park are popular favourites among holidaymakers. Prices are competitive at around IR£7 per adult, with discounts for children and for travellers holding Rambler bus/rail passes. One word of warning – book all tours well in advance as many can be fully booked up to a week beforehand.

To get the advantages of both rail and bus travel, buy the inclusive Rambler pass. At IR£75 per adult or IR£38 per child (IR£110 and IR£55 for a fifteen-day pass) these tickets are more suitable for individuals travelling alone than family groups. Eight-day Rambler tickets need not be used on consecutive days, but on the days that you nominate within a period of two weeks.

HORSE-DRAWN CARAVANS

This must surely rate as the slowest way to travel around Ireland, as you can expect to travel no more than ten miles a day. But as a method of getting away from all the hassles of modern living, this unique form of transport simply cannot be beaten. Caravans are the gaily painted traditional gipsy style and inside, facilities include bed-linen, cooking utensils and bottled gas. You'll receive a short course in how to look after your horse and after that you're on your own. Irish roads are ideal for horse-drawn caravans as they have a comparatively light volume of traffic.

Costs are reasonable – especially if you're sharing with someone – at around £300 for a four-berth caravan for one week in mid-summer, or £250 out of season. If you're interested contact **Slattery's Horse-Drawn Caravans**, 1 Russell Street, Tralee, Co. Kerry (Tel: 066 21722) or **Dieter Clissmann Horse-Drawn Caravans**, Carrigmore Farm, Wicklow (Tel: 0404 8188).

TAXIS

Taxis are available in all major cities, most usually at the normal pick-up points – hotels, rail and bus stations, or designated taxi ranks. Cruising taxis are not common outside Dublin and Cork, so don't expect to hail one in the street. The minimum fare is IR£1.80 and there is a standard charge of 75p per mile. Most taxis are metered, although you may find that taxi-drivers in smaller towns charge by agreement. A pick-up charge may be levied if a cab has been ordered. Fares are negotiable for larger distances. Tips are at the customer's discretion.

Problems/Emergencies

MEDICAL

If it's a minor problem, head for a chemist's shop, where the name and address of the nearest all-night chemist should be clearly displayed in the windows. If it's more serious, get to a hospital or phone an ambulance (dial 999), and remember British citizens are entitled to free emergency hospital treatment (see 'Health', page 41).

POLICE

The police, known as the 'Garda', must be contacted if any of your belongings have been stolen. Insist on a copy of your statement – insurance companies often require this as proof of theft before they will reimburse you. It is also a good idea to inform your travel rep if you're on a package holiday. Police cars are a distinctive light and dark blue with the sign 'Garda' on top. Telephone 999 in emergencies.

EMBASSIES AND CONSULATES

The British Embassy is at 33 Merrion Road, Dublin 4. The American Embassy and Consulate are at 42 Elgin Road, Dublin 4 and the Australian Embassy is at Fitzwilliam House, Wilton Terrace, Dublin 2.

WORK

Ireland has its own employment problems, so there are few opportunities for long-term work. Seasonal employment can be found in bars and pubs in the larger holiday towns or Cork and Dublin cities. If you're a qualified instructor in any particular sport, then you may get a place for the summer in one of the numerous watersports or recreational centres.

WOMEN

Socially, Irish men have a bit of a reputation for being chauvinistic. Because of the grip of the Catholic Church, divorce and abortion are not allowed in the Republic, although the more liberal elements in the cities are beginning to rebel against these strictures. As tourists, women should have no problems in Ireland. In fact Ireland (and especially rural Ireland) is very much safer for a young woman travelling alone than the vast majority of European countries (including Britain). Having said that, don't go courting trouble. The usual injunctions apply to cities; be sensible, don't walk alone at night, stick to lighted areas and don't get picked up by what your mother would call 'strange men'. There are no restrictions about what kind of clothes you wear, although skimpy T-shirts or shorts at places of worship are hardly considered respectable.

A Potted History of Ireland

It is sometimes hard to square the passion, the turbulence and the extremism which dogs any narrative of Irish history with the tranquil, easy-going face of Ireland today. From whichever angle you look at it – political, artistic or religious – Ireland's tale is an extraordinary one. Perhaps even more so, when we consider how many of the momentous events building up to Irish Independence occurred only seventy years ago – two generations. But, as they say, to begin at the beginning . . .

When the glaciers rolled back from the frozen land of Ireland, the scene was set for the first inhabitants, arriving about 8000 BC. The most important traces of these earliest dwellers can be seen in the huge tombs found in Knowth, Dowth and New Grange. These stone edifices form a tantalizing hint of a primitive society whose primary influences seem to have been the rotation of the seasons and planets. The origins of these tribes remain a mystery, but from the construction of the huge burial tombs and other prehistoric relics, it is apparent that this was primarily an agrarian society with a sophisticated grasp of mathematical and architectural principles. Little more is known about these primitive men, whose culture was inevitably swallowed up by the overwhelming dominance of the succeeding Indo-European tribe – the Celts. The Celts themselves appear to have travelled from Central Europe, and although the exact time of their migration is not known, by 300 BC their culture was securely established in Ireland.

Although the Romans conquered a substantial part of Britain, no attempt was made to take control of the island lying not far off the coast. As a consequence, Ireland was left to develop in its own way. Celtic society, despite the inevitable internal struggles for power, was notable for its sophisticated administrative, cultural and religious systems. Ireland was divided into the kingdoms of

Ulster, Leinster, Munster, Connaught and Meath, according to the *sept*, or clan, which was based on a concept of the extended family. In charge of each kingdom was the *ri*, or king. The high king, *Ard Ri*, who was theoretically the overlord of all the kings, is most commonly associated in myth and tradition with the O'Neill family in the Meath kingdom, whose headquarters were at the important centre of Tara. As far as art goes, the remarkable skill of the ancient Irish craftsmen remains one of the enduring legacies of pre-Christian Ireland. They fashioned native metals, including gold from the Irish hills, into exquisite works, and for entertainment, there were the myths, fairytales and folklore which would be sung by travelling poets and bards. Everything considered, Ireland before Christianization was by no means the country of barbarians which popular tradition paints it.

The first great cultural revolution Ireland experienced was the coming of Christianity. Although Celtic religion existed and was administered by the Druids in Ireland, the structures were comparatively loose, providing a fertile ground for the much more ascetic Christianity. St Patrick arrived in Ireland in AD 432, and proceeded almost singlehandedly to lay the foundations of the new religion. The Irish themselves accepted Christianity easily. The Christians were not interested in stamping out the old traditions entirely, and the methods which St Patrick adopted to convert the Irish were unconventional. The distance between Ireland and the European heartland of Christianity allowed him to be more pragmatic in his demands. What harm was an innocent belief in fairies, magic charms and harmless superstitions, when compared to the greater goal of Christian observation? So considerable was his success that in the space of seven years, church-building had begun, and by the end of his lifetime there were over fifty places of worship in the country. Ruins of the earliest buildings can still be seen in the important Christian centres of Armagh and Cashel, and for many years the Christian teachings emanating from these places existed side by side with the ancient lore. Gradually, traditional places of learning became assimilated into the Christian communities, and Irish scholars, with their knowledge of classical and indigenous traditions, became part of a movement which preserved a sense of Irish identity whilst also looking outwards and becoming part of the international Christian community.

The harmony which prevailed over early Christian Ireland was rudely disturbed by the arrival of the Vikings in the winter of AD 795. Initially the northern warriors launched only small-scale forays into areas north of Dublin, but gradually the temptations of the rich Irish monasteries in the centre of the country proved too great. Soon there was no part of the country untouched by threat of Viking invasions. One of the most immediate consequences of Viking occupation was the establishment of strongholds at strategic points on the main waterways: Wicklow, Wexford and Dublin, to name a few, were all founded in the Viking period. It was the southern part of the country where the Vikings scored their greatest successes, and over a period of two hundred years a fair degree of intermingling of Irish and Norse cultures took place. Although the Norsemen usually held the positions of power, the Irish tongue was still spoken and the Vikings themselves became converted to Christianity. At the beginning of the eleventh century however, the chaos and conflict of the preceding century came to a head at the Battle of Clontarf in 1014. The legendary hero, Brian Boru, was the prime instigator in attempts to throw off Nordic domination, although by now the two peoples had become so integrated that considerable numbers of Norsemen fought on the Irish side – and vice versa. King Brian's attempts to establish himself as *Ard Ri* of Ireland came to nothing, as he himself was killed in battle at Clontarf. The result was that Norse supremacy was replaced by warring factions of Irish clans, none of which had absolute control over Ireland.

Christian activity resumed in this period and the construction of monasteries and churches was prodigious. The tumultuous times dictated some architectural changes and the tall, slim towers, surviving at eighty sites throughout the country (including Glendalough), acted as safehouses where monks would store the precious objects of the monastery, pulling the ladder up behind them in the event of an attack. But the nature of the enemy changed. Soon it was not the Vikings or each other that the Irish had to fear, but the Normans.

The Anglo-Normans had had an eye on Ireland for some time, with a view to obtaining lordship. A splendid pretext for invasion came in the second half of the twelfth century, when Diarmuid MacMurrough, King of Leinster, asked Henry II of England for his help. MacMurrough, an unscrupulous character, had landed himself in hot water when he abducted the wife of a notable O'Rourke chieftain who was an ally of the O'Connor clan. The O'Connors took control of the high kingship and forcibly removed MacMurrough from his throne. MacMurrough fled to Wales, and at first attempted a few invasions with the help of Welsh Normans, but after he failed miserably, Henry II arrived in Ireland with his own force.

There was little resistance, with many of the Irish kings swearing fealty willingly, and Henry established the English domination of Ireland which was to persist until the twentieth century. One of Henry's first moves was to remould the religious and political structures of Ireland to suit himself. The feudal system – a lord supported by the law and the Church and submitted to by the tenants – was introduced, whilst the Church was modelled on the English example. Laws were passed prohibiting the Norman and Irish peoples to mix or marry and the Normans were expressly forbidden to speak the language or dress as the Irish natives did. The Irish people, unused to feudalism, rebelled and an internecine conflict ensued between the Normans and the Irish throughout the Middle Ages. A bid to wrest control from the Normans came from another quarter in 1315 when the Scot, Edward Bruce, brother of Robert the Bruce, invaded. In May 1316, Edward had himself crowned King of Ireland but his reign was shortlived and notorious for its brutality: he was killed in battle in 1318. Eventually, the area of real Norman control had contracted to the area around Dublin, which was fortified by a huge palisade to deter invaders and hence became known as the English Pale. Ireland's misfortunes were not over yet, for in 1348 the Black Death was carried to Dublin by rats. As the plague took its course, over half the population of Ireland died, with the capital Dublin left particularly devastated.

Over the next hundred years, English power was on the wane, as a result of ineffective directives from the English government, and

Ireland sank yet further into hopeless confusion and turbulence. Then in 1485, the War of the Roses came to an end in England and Henry VII acceded to the English throne. King Henry abolished the Irish Parliament, depriving the population of any say in their governance, and English officials were placed in positions of power. When Henry VIII succeeded his father, the same policy of anglicization was pursued – although now in a different direction. Henry's break with the Catholic Church, and his repudiation of Rome's authority, had effectively negated the English king's right to Irish lordship as William II had invoked the Pope's authority in his claims to rule Ireland. Henry's solution was to grind down the Norman-Celtic nobility to a point where no resistance was possible, and to institute the Reformation in Ireland.

Under Elizabeth I, the Reformation gained momentum in England, but largely failed in Ireland. The problem of the intractable, untameable Irish was once again up for review, and Elizabeth's solution was quite simple – beat them into submission. With the help of her Tudor troops, the Irish were beaten, massacred and murdered by a better equipped and organized army. The Irish nobility were detained in London or killed fighting, whilst English carpetbaggers took advantage of the prevailing atmosphere of confusion and claimed large tracts of Irish land as their own. The nobility in Ulster, almost to a man, fled leaving their estates to the Protestants, thus beginning the unequal weighting of Protestant and Catholic which forms the root of the Northern Ireland problem.

In 1641, the cauldron of bubbling hatred and tensions boiled over. The Catholic farmers rebelled against the Protestants who had been planted on their lands. Over 4000 Protestants were massacred by the Catholics and many more thrown off their recently acquired land. Cromwell's solution was decisive. Using the 1641 massacre as propaganda, he sailed to Dublin in 1664 with 20,000 men. Drogheda was one of the towns whose resistance to Cromwell is legendary, and like Wexford, it suffered the fate of complete extermination. Cromwell sailed back to England after a successful campaign, leaving a shattered Ireland behind him. In the next few years, many Irish people emigrated. Some were deported to the West Indies as indentured labour; others went to fight in armies on the continent; few came back. Laws at home made the conditions of the Catholic population insufferable. The country was divided into its thirty-two counties by English landowners and all Irish-speakers were prohibited from living in towns.

Things failed to improve when Charles II ascended the throne, although this proved to be a period of relative prosperity for Ireland, as it rebuilt its mercantile and trading links. When James II acceded to the throne however, the Irish were once again caught up in wars surrounding the English crown. James II was deposed by the Protestant William of Orange. James, a Catholic, attempted to rally the forces of France and Ireland behind him to regain the crown. The Irish perceived that of the two choices, James would be their best chance to gain some redress for what they had endured. Both William, supported by the Dutch and English, and James, heading the Irish (the French were too late!), met in the Battle of the Boyne in 1689 where King James made the infamous decision to desert his troops and flee to France. Fighting continued until the supporters of James eventually surrendered to the terms laid down in the famous Treaty of Limerick, which was endorsed by William of Orange.

The Treaty was supposed to alleviate the hardships which Protestant England had imposed upon the Irish Catholics. Religious freedom was to be granted and there was to be no property seizure. The English nobles, however, were not pleased with the terms of the Treaty, and did not see any reason to adhere to them. Once the Irish army had dispersed (one of the terms of the Treaty) and, in the main, left Ireland, the Treaty was flagrantly abused and the iniquitous Penal Laws were introduced.

Essentially, the Penal Laws were intended to stamp out once and for all the Irish nobility and prosperous middle-classes. Catholics were not allowed to attend university in Britain or sit in the Irish or British House of Commons. A Catholic was also not allowed to own a horse worth more than £5. The embargo remained on property – no Catholic had any rights to land ownership – so that by the end of the century, 75 per cent of the land belonged to 5 per cent of the people. In this state of oppression, with little prospect of hope, the Irish began the eighteenth century.

The climate was changing, both economically and politically, in the 1700s. The Industrial Revolution was beginning, with a prodigious growth in mercantile trade which was to turn Dublin, Cork, Limerick and Galway into important gateways for trade to America and Britain. At this time too, Waterford glass, silver and linen were beginning to be highly prized for their quality. Penal Laws were less rigorously applied, and talk of Irish Nationalism was allowed. Liberal attitudes prevailed, spearheaded by Swift and Bishop Berkeley, but it was not until the end of the century that calls for some measure of Irish independence were met.

In 1772, the Patriot Party was formed, under the leadership of Grattan. At a time when the English were preoccupied by the American and French wars, the growing demands from the Irish could not be refused. In 1778, the discriminatory Penal Laws were repealed and additional powers were given to the Irish Parliament. Catholics nevertheless still remained disadvantaged, and property and power would still remain in the hands of the Protestants. Ulster, with its predominantly Protestant community, had its own particular problems. Vigilante groups protecting the land rights among the lower classes sprang up on either side of the religious divide. In 1795, a fierce battle took place between Catholic and Protestant factions at Diamond, in Co. Armagh. The defeat of the Catholics caused thousands to flee from Ulster, and the Protestants of the area founded the Orange Order. The Order originally had lodges throughout the country, although now they remain a potent force only in Ulster.

A wind of change was beginning to blow through Europe with the events of the French Revolution. Irish Nationalists, organized as the United Irishmen, looked to France for help. In 1796, a large French force sailed into Bantry Bay, intending to march to Dublin and claim Ireland for the Irish. Half their ships however had been blown off course, and the French waited and waited, until they had no option but to turn back to France again. They did not set one foot on Irish soil. The failure of this attempt alerted the Irish landowners and government. They arrested the leaders of the United Irishmen, and conducted a reign of terror throughout the country in attempts to extract information from their followers. A mass uprising in the country took place in 1798, but was swiftly crushed by British troops, with the deaths of tens of thousands of Irish. The country being in a state of weakness and disarray, the British took the opportunity to rush through the Act of Union, effectively dissolving the Irish Parliament.

As the nineteenth century began, the desire for Irish nationalism had not abated and gave rise to such great leaders as Daniel O'Connell, who forwarded the cause of Catholic emancipation. Catholics were allowed religious freedom and were also able to take seats in the Houses of Parliament. Then a great tragedy struck, in the form of the Potato Famine. The causes of the Famine were complex. Potato was one of the staple ingredients of the Irish diet, but crops consistently failed in the period 1839 to 1841. During the same period, there was a large population explosion, especially among the lower classes, which gave rise to an even greater sub-class of poor, deprived people, scraping a living from the land. The combination of persistent crop failure and increasing numbers of mouths to feed resulted in the Famine. In less than a generation, the population of Ireland halved. Many people emigrated to Canada and the States, in the horrific 'coffin' ships. Others stayed at home to await their fate. The British Government hesitated: should they repeal the Corn Laws, which favoured the wealthy landowners, or should they do something more drastic? Thoughts of political expediency delayed any decisions and by the time the Corn Laws were repealed, it was too late. Public relief was organized on a massive scale. Poorhouses were set up and roads built for access. Yet throughout the whole Famine, some – but not all – landlords continued to take rent, in the form of wheat and livestock, and export it, whilst their tenants starved.

In the second half of the nineteenth century, the peasants of Ireland were more effectively organized by men such as Parnell and Davitt. Through their leadership, the Irish peasantry boycotted landlords, their agents, and withheld rent. This boycott proved to be more successful than any amount of petty violence. The Land War was ended with the introduction of the

'Kilmainham Treaty', allowing for the gradual dispersal of land amongst its tenants. This treaty was to prove the major triumph of Parnell's political career. But his success soon turned sour and only two years later, Parnell was embroiled in a disastrous divorce case. The affair of Mrs Katherine (Kitty) O'Shea and Parnell became headline news and the politician was eventually reviled by the Irish priesthood and his own political party. He married Kitty O'Shea as soon as the divorce allowed, but his career was in ruins. He died a year after his marriage, and after his death, many thought that Ireland had lost the leader who could have united Ireland in its quest for Home Rule.

Home Rule was passed through both Houses of Parliament and due to become law in June 1914. With the outbreak of war however, the legislation was postponed. Thus began the final stages of Ireland's struggle for independence. Disparate forces were united in their nationalist aims; Connolly and Pearse organized the rebellion in Ireland. Easter 1916 was to be the date for the revolution. Despite the fervour of these activists, it must be stressed that the vast majority of the Irish population was, at best, indifferent to the nationalist movement. As the rebels plotted, the British Government had already received detailed intelligence of their plans. At first, the rising took place only in Dublin and the rebels chose the Central Post Office as the spot to make their famous Declaration of Independence. The British reaction was swift. Gunboats sailed up the River Liffey into the heart of Dublin and shelled the city. All the rebel leaders were quickly arrested, tried and shot. Eamon de Valera was the only leader to escape death, citing his American citizenship as his defence.

A new kind of patriotism was crystallizing in Ireland. The death of the rebel leaders was a contributing factor, but the introduction of conscription also added to the disillusionment with the British Government. A loss of Irish youth on the battlefields of Europe gave a new impetus to the nationalist movement. In the 1918 elections, the Republican Sinn Fein party won a huge majority of Irish seats in Parliament. Following up their victory, they refused to swear an oath of allegiance to the Crown, thus effectively refusing to take their seats in

Parliament. A maelstrom developed with a growing tide of civil disobedience which threatened the rule of law and order. To deal with this, Lloyd George called the Black and Tans into being. This brigade of redundant soldiers was notorious for its brutality, but despite this, the skilful guerrilla leader Michael Collins of the IRA conducted a successful campaign against the British army. De Valera meanwhile, now working for the Irish cause from America, was recognized as the Irish Head of State. Eventually a meeting was set up between Lloyd George and the nationalists, led by Michael Collins. Lloyd George gave the rebels two alternatives: to accept Dominion status, and hence a greater degree of independence for Ireland, or to face the consequences of a greatly increased force of Black and Tans.

By this time, the coffers of the nationalist cause had begun to run low. Furthermore, Lloyd George had already rushed through a bill creating a British province in Ulster and setting up a parliament in Stormont. With these facts in mind, Collins accepted the compromise – only to be instantly disowned by de Valera. Although the proposal was finally passed by a narrow majority in the Dail, the Irish Parliament, there could be no peace and civil war finally broke out in 1922. In the course of the war, Collins was killed, along with many on both sides.

Even when order was restored, the controversy remained. De Valera and his colleagues refused to take the oath to the Crown until 1927, thus denying themselves their seats in Parliament. When de Valera did finally make it to Parliament, his party was called Fianna Fail, and was in government in the Republic for most of the succeeding period.

Only in the last twenty years or so has Ireland had full Republic status independent of Britain. From the time that de Valera took power until the present day, the changes in Ireland have been mainly of an economic nature. From the beginning, de Valera had very little time for the aims and methods of the IRA, and despite the problems which have dogged the North following Lloyd George's hasty segregation, the Republic of Ireland has maintained a polite distance from the trouble. Only recently, under the auspices of the Anglo-Irish agreement, have the two governments worked together on matters of security.

Economically, Ireland has moved from the backward rural country of de Valera's day to a country which courts the involvement of foreign industrial development. The Republic has benefited greatly from membership of the EC, which has spent millions upgrading Ireland's basic infrastructure. Today, tourism is a growing industry, with the Irish keen to expand into the British market. Americans, many with Irish heritage, come in droves to the Emerald Isle, but increasing numbers of Britons are also waking up to the possibilities of a holiday destination that is on their doorstep. The weather can't make any pretensions to Mediterranean temperatures, but the love of blarney, the unspoilt countryside and the friendly folk give Ireland a charm that many find hard to resist.

Be a Good Tourist

Tourism is the world's largest industry and while most of us think of travel as a good thing because it gives people enjoyment, encourages understanding between races and brings in needed foreign exchange, inevitably it has its negative side too – if uncontrolled it can change the face of the natural environment and break down traditional ways of life.

Many of the problems created by tourism have resulted from the desire to benefit from economies of scale: quite simply, we are now paying the environmental price of holidays that were sold too cheaply to too many people. Now tourists are recognizing the damage done by this industry and, as the Costas lose their appeal, a new breed of 'traveller' is emerging – one who does not leave his conscience at home but who travels with an enlightened approach and an open mind.

So how can you be a 'good tourist'? This brief checklist should provide a few pointers:
- With congestion such a major problem, consider travelling out of season. Even if you have to plan around school holidays, it is possible to travel in the Easter or autumn breaks.

- If you are travelling to a less-developed country, consider the leakage of foreign exchange from the economy. If you take a package in which the airline and hotel are foreign owned, only 22–25 per cent of the brochure price will stay in that country. If you then consume Western goods which are imported you further reduce the profits that country might make from tourism. If you can stay with locals, and try to consume only local goods.
- Take nothing in your case that you don't strictly need. In countries where waste disposal is poor, don't add to the problem. Remove toiletries, shirts and photographic goods from wrappings before you leave and take shampoos and sunscreens made from natural substances so that, if they get into the water, they won't destroy marine life.
- When arranging transport, look at what the locals do. To soak up the atmosphere without polluting it, use buses, bikes and your feet!
- If you're buying souvenirs, support the local arts and crafts market. But be careful not to buy goods made from endangered species.
- Be sensitive with your camera. Always ask someone before you take their picture, and don't click away in places of worship. Use your camera constructively – to photograph rather than pick wild flowers, for instance.

Being a good tourist is all about leaving as little negative impact as possible and where you can, making a positive contribution to the environment and people of the place you're visiting. If you would like more information, look at my book, *The Good Tourist*.

Part Four
GUIDE TO THE COUNTRY

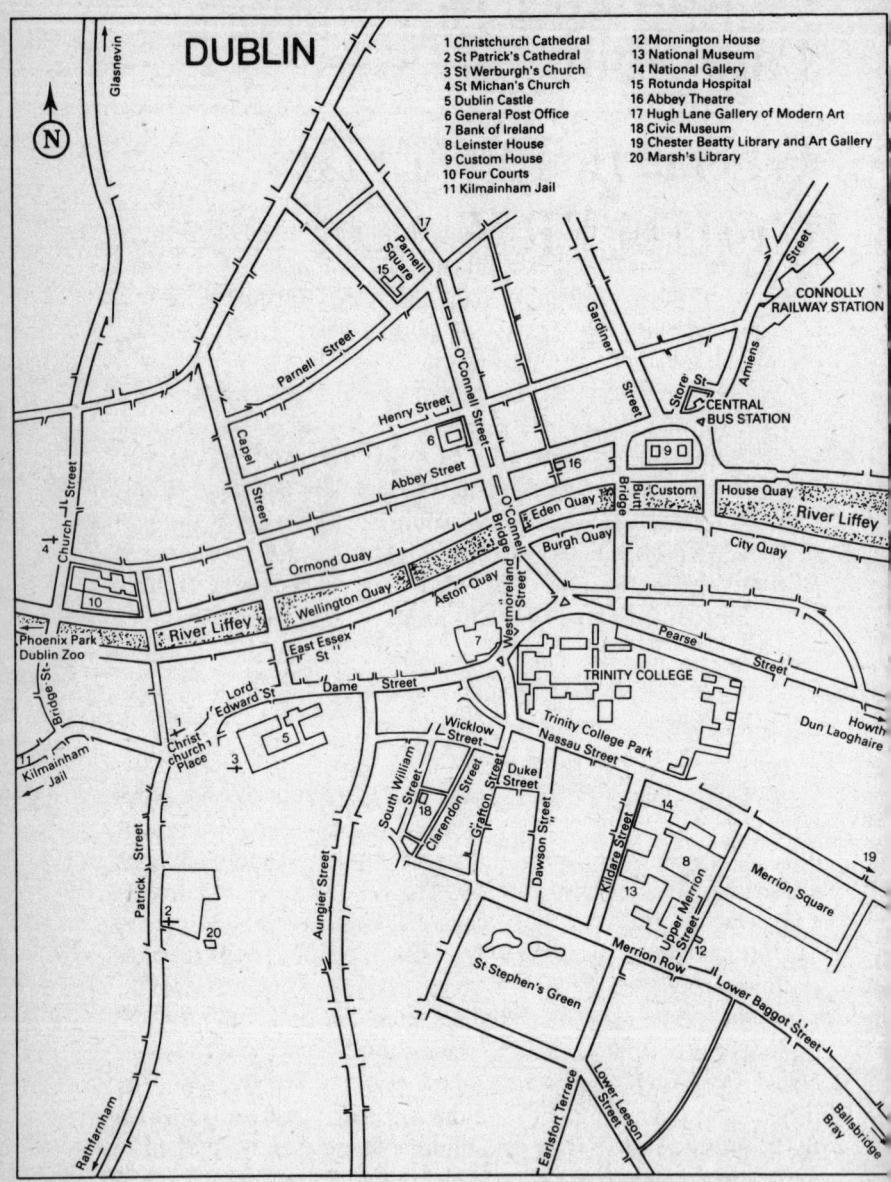

Dublin and Environs

INTRODUCTION

The Irish capital is often overlooked by British holidaymakers, but it is one of the most beautiful and relatively uncommercialized cities in Europe. Ireland's long and often turbulent history is epitomized in the history of both Dublin itself, and the surrounding County Dublin region.

County Dublin is a part of Ireland which offers something for just about every kind of holidaymaker, whether you are looking for picturesque coastline and fine, gently shelving beaches; facilities for the sporting enthusiast or sightseer; or quite simply some of Ireland's most beautiful countryside, found in the part of the region immediately south of Dublin.

In this chapter we introduce North and South County Dublin, but start with the City of Dublin itself.

HISTORY

Dublin (European City of Culture 1991) has undergone a social renaissance in recent years, which has transformed a previously dull, grey city into one of the most 'up-and-coming' holiday destinations in Northern Europe. The first recorded mention of a settlement in this part of Ireland, however, was by Ptolemy in AD 140; the village, as it then was, became known to the Romans as Eblana.

By the ninth century, Dublin's potential as a military and trading base became noticed by the invading Danes and the name *Dubh Linn*, literally meaning 'dark pool', first emerged. The Danes were defeated in 1014 by the legendary Irish patriot Brian Boru, but the formal date for Dublin's foundation is credited to the Viking invaders in 988; in celebration of this, the city held lavish millennium festivities in 1988.

Ireland's patron saint, Patrick, is thought to have visited Dublin several centuries before 988, and the present Cathedral stands close to the site of a well from which Patrick is understood to have baptized many Christian converts.

Brian Boru's victory for the Irish people was relatively short-lived, and Anglo-Norman invaders arrived in force during the twelfth century, led by the Earl of Pembroke (Strongbow). Under this new wave of invaders, semi-permanent Anglo-Norman fiefdoms gradually became established in and around what is now the City of Dublin.

Dublin became the centre of the Norman administration in Ireland and it was they who built the massive city walls, parts of which still stand. The expanding town became the focus of Irish resistance to Henry VII of England and the last, bloody, anti-English battle took place in 1601 when the clan chieftains rose up against their mainland occupiers. The few chieftains who survived were eventually forced to emigrate. It was to be another three and a half centuries before most of Ireland would finally be granted its independence from the mainland.

By the eighteenth century the long, gracious streets of the Dublin one sees today were being constructed, and the modern capital was born into a period of relative stability. The most traumatic years in Dublin's history, however, were yet to come, in the first quarter of the twentieth century, when a sharp increase in public support for the cause of Irish nationalism led to a decade of civil war that started during Easter Week, 1916. The ill-fated rebellion focused on Dublin's main post office, in O'Connell Street, and today you can still see some of the original bullet-holes on the supporting columns outside.

The Irish Republic was granted independence in 1922, and Dublin has prospered as the capital. Religion has played a central role in Irish history since the dawn of Christianity, and Dublin today remains a fiercely Catholic city. Despite the religious and political problems of the past, it is a safe, peaceful city to visit, with virtually all the 'troubles' concentrated in Northern Ireland. Although Dublin retains a special relationship with Britain, its history and development are unique among European cities. It deserves to be visited at least once in your lifetime.

HOW TO GET THERE

Dublin is one of the easiest cities to reach independently from mainland Britain, and the range of package holidays offered now is extensive. These are covered in detail in the Introduction.

For the independent traveller there are approximately a dozen flights daily from Heathrow alone, and several more flying from Stansted, Gatwick and Luton. The leading carriers are **Aer Lingus** (Ireland's national airline) and **British Midland**. **Ryanair** also offers a low-cost daily service from Luton or Stansted to Dublin.

A Saver return flight can cost as little as £79 if you book some time in advance, but the cheapest unrestricted fare is usually around £90–£100, flying with **Ryanair** from Luton to Dublin. In addition to the regular London services, there are a number of regional departures, including daily flights from Edinburgh, Glasgow, Birmingham and Manchester. The average flying time to Dublin is around sixty minutes.

By train, there are a number of routes by which you could reach Dublin, depending on your UK departure point. The most popular route, from London (Euston), is via Holyhead, on the Isle of Anglesey, by **Sealink Stena Line** to Dun Laoghaire several miles south of Dublin. Connecting coaches take arriving ferry passengers into the city centre, and the journey from London to Dublin takes approximately $10^1/_2$ hours, if you use directly connecting services. The fare is likely to be around £75 to £89 depending on when you travel. **B&I Ferries** travel into Dublin City Port.

From Scotland, your best route is via the West Coast railway line to Stranraer, the short ferry crossing to Larne in Northern Ireland, and finally the connecting train service south to Dublin. Although this route takes longer than the Dun Laoghaire crossing, it offers you the chance to see something of Northern Ireland on the train journey south.

By car, the best way to reach Dublin is via the same train/ferry route, via Holyhead and Dun Laoghaire. Liverpool is closest to London (200 miles), and the best roads to follow are the M1/M6 and M62; however, the crossing from Liverpool takes about seven hours, whereas, from Holyhead, the crossing is less than four. Ultimately, it's a personal decision whether you would rather spend more time on the road or at sea.

COMMUNICATIONS

Dublin's international airport lies six miles from the city centre, and there is a regular bus service, leaving from directly outside the door of the Arrivals terminal, to the Central Bus Station. The service operates throughout the day, takes about twenty minutes, and costs around IR£2.30.

Easily the best way of getting around Dublin itself is by bus, and full details are available from the CIE office, 59 Upper O'Connell Street. All parts of the city are served by regular bus services, most of which pass by, or through, O'Connell Street and O'Connell Bridge; the average fare is about 50p. The Central Bus Station, in Store Street, is the terminus for provincial services on Expressway buses.

If you are keen to visit the suburbs of Dublin, an electric commuter train service – DART – reaches HOWTH on the north side, and BRAY, County Wicklow, on the south. Fares are reasonable, and comparable to what you might pay for the equivalent bus journey.

Unusually for a capital city, taxis are not allowed to drive around picking up casual fares. Instead they must be hailed at official ranks, found near the better hotels, the Central Bus Station, the three railway stations, and at street ranks off O'Connell Street and on St Stephen's Green. Fares are higher than in the UK, and taxis are not a standard colour or make of car in Dublin.

Car-hire is a popular, though very expensive option, particularly if you are keen to explore the city environs. A number of major companies have offices in Dublin as follows: **Avis**, 1 Hanover Street East (Tel: 01 776 971); **Hertz**, Leeson Street Bridge (Tel: 01 602 255); and **Dan Dooley Kennings**, 42

Westland Row (Tel: 01 772 723). Two local firms are **Johnson & Perrott**, 12a South Leinster Street (Tel: 01 767 213); and **Murray's Europcar**, Baggot Street Bridge (Tel: 01 681 777).

TOURIST INFORMATION

Dublin's main tourist information office is right in the centre of the city, at 14 Upper O'Connell Street (Tel: 01 747 733). It is open daily 1000–1800, and has a wide range of literature relating to the surrounding region, and Ireland as a whole. Advance tourist information is available from the London office, 150 New Bond Street (Tel: 071 493 3201). There is a branch at Dublin Airport (Tel: 01 376 387) which is open all year round. The principal tourist office for the eastern region of Ireland, outside Dublin, is at St Michael's Wharf, Dun Laoghaire (Tel: 806 984/5/6). The office is open all year.

One or two useful addresses in Dublin are:
BRITISH EMBASSY, 33 Merrion Road (Tel: 01 695 211).
CITY AIR TERMINUS AND BUS STATION, Busarus, Store Street.
LATE OPENING POST OFFICE, O'Connell Street main office (open Mon–Sat 0800–2000, Sun 1030–1830).
CURRENCY EXCHANGE, at the tourist office (address above) until 1800, and at the GPO.

CLIMATE

The Dublin region is not generally known for fine weather, and the temperature rarely reaches the low 20s°C (low 70s°F) even in July and August. December to February are the coldest months, with the average afternoon temperature hovering around 5–10°C (41–50°F). The winter months tend to be very wet, although sudden showers are very much a feature of Dublin's climate, no matter what time of year you choose to visit.

WHEN TO GO

Summer is traditionally the most popular time to visit Dublin, although the later spring months are becoming increasingly favoured as people are now keen to avoid as many of their fellow holidaymakers as possible. Christmas and Easter are also popular times to visit Ireland as both events are celebrated enthusiastically by the Irish.

St Patrick's Week, in March, traditionally starts the main holiday season, and this can be a good time to catch something of the flavour of the 'real' Ireland as the country's patron saint is celebrated. The **St Patrick's Day** parade through the city centre usually attracts considerable attention from the world's media. Particular events worth seeing include the **Lord Mayor's Ball**, held at the end of the St Patrick's Week celebrations; the **Irish Football Cup Final**, in April; the **Dublin Horse Show**, and **Carroll's International Golf Championship**, in August; the **Dublin Theatre Festival**, **GAA Hurling** and **Football Finals** in September; and the **Dublin Film Festival**, in November.

CULINARY SPECIALITIES

The Irish are renowned for the warmth of their hospitality, and the quality and diversity of their traditional cuisine is evidence of this. The humble Irish potato features prominently in many dishes, notably the famous **Irish Stew**, although do not think for one moment that you will be expected to eat potatoes with every meal in Dublin!

The Irish capital has a good selection of international restaurants, but you should not miss the opportunity to sample some traditional Irish cuisine. Meals tend to be large affairs, beginning with a huge breakfast of fruit juice, porridge, fried eggs, bacon, sausages, toast, soda-bread, and tea or coffee; lunch and dinner are unlikely to be any less hearty, so prepare yourself to eat well – and often.

A popular pork favourite is **Limerick Ham**, smoked over chipped oak and served with juniper berries. **Dublin Bay Prawns** are a popular, if expensive, delicacy, and fresh mussels and lobster are worth trying if you get the opportunity. Fine quality local meat, however, is likely to be the centrepiece of any menu, and Dublin is renowned for its fine steaks. Lamb is likely to be offered either as tender chops, or as the principal ingredient in Irish stew.

An alternative to traditional Irish stew is **Dublin Coddle**, another form of stew made from sausages, bacon, potatoes, onions, parsley, and occasionally one or two other vegetables as well. A number of more unusual dishes, served in and around the Dublin area, are made from seaweed, reflecting harsh famine times in earlier years when that was literally all that could be found to eat; **Carrageen Moss Jelly** is the best-known survivor.

WHERE TO GO FOR WHAT

Dublin and environs offers something for just about every type of holidaymaker. The *Sightseer* should, of course, head straight for the City of Dublin itself, although there is plenty to see in DUN LAOGHAIRE, NAAS (in North Kildare), CELBRIDGE and KILDARE. The *Socialite* should also head for Dublin; although nightlife in Dublin tends to be more the 'traditional Irish' variety than swinging nightclubs and discos, there are now a number of good international-class nightspots in the city centre.

Both the *Nature Lover* and the *Recluse* will appreciate the beautiful countryside which surrounds Dublin; in particular, KILLINEY BAY beyond Dun Laoghaire, which is often compared to the Bay of Naples, and the confluence of the Liffey and Rye Water at LEIXLIP. The VICO ROAD, linking the villages of Dalkey and Killiney, offers outstanding views across the region's coastline.

This region is a veritable paradise for the *Sportsperson*, with even the smallest village never being more than a few miles from a golf course and stretch of river for freshwater fishing. To the north of Dublin, golf, game and sea fishing, and horse-riding can be enjoyed at **BALBRIGGAN**, **SKERRIES** and **MALAHIDE**. To the south, **DUN LAOGHAIRE** offers golf, bowling, squash, sailing, scuba-diving, fishing, horse-racing, cycling, tennis and indoor swimming. Golf and fishing are the two main sports which can also be enjoyed at **NAAS** and **KILDARE**.

The best beach resorts in this part of Dublin are in north County Dublin, and the gently shelving sandy coastline makes them ideal for *Family Holidays*. Among the more popular resorts are **BALBRIGGAN**, **SKERRIES**, **PORTMARNOCK** and **DOLLYMOUNT**, although both **RUSH** and **MALAHIDE** have good beaches as well.

Dublin

ACCOMMODATION

Finding somewhere to stay in Dublin could present you with a problem at some times of the year; it is always advisable to book ahead if possible during the summer months and at peak Christmas and Easter holiday periods. Hotel accommodation is not cheap, however, and summer room rates are comparable with those which you might expect to pay in London. Grade B hotel accommodation and guest houses are more reasonable. If you choose to travel as part of a package tour, particularly those offered by **Aer Lingus**, the saving on both travel and accommodation can be considerable. What follows is a selection of hotels and guesthouses in three broad price bands. Any tourist office will book accommodation for you at a small charge.

First Class

Berkeley Court, Lansdowne Road (Tel: 01 601 711) – A beautiful hotel, with 220 rooms, including twelve luxury jacuzzi suites. It has recently been refurbished and offers exemplary service; often used by visiting VIPs and politicians, including ex-US President Ronald Reagan in 1984.

Shelbourne, St Stephen's Green (Tel: 01 766 471) – Dublin's best-known luxury hotel, which has recently been refurbished to the finest international standards; 171 spacious bedrooms and one of the best restaurants in the city. A range of weekend breaks is available all year round.

Westbury, off Grafton Street (Tel: 01 791 122) – A first-class hotel, right in the heart of Dublin, with 150 bedrooms and six beautiful suites; facilities include the popular Winter Garden terrace and a large underground car park.

Jury's, Ballsbridge (Tel: 01 605 000) – Four hundred de luxe bedrooms in this large, modern hotel; popular with Aer Lingus as a luxury package hotel. Jury's is also a major conference venue and has great Irish cabaret entertainment.

Business Class

New Royal Dublin, O'Connell Street (Tel: 01 733 666) – One of Dublin's most central hotels, situated on the main street; more than 100 bedrooms, and a longstanding reputation for attentive service.

Lansdowne, Pembroke Road (Tel: 01 762 549/684 079) – A small, comfortable hotel, with less than thirty well-appointed bedrooms.

Marine, Sutton Cross (Tel: 01 322 613) – Another small hotel, located in the suburbs of the city; ideal if you are looking for peace and quiet; has a private swimming pool and is close to an excellent golf course.

North Star, Amiens Street (Tel: 01 363 136) – A good hotel if you are travelling by rail, due to its central location opposite Connolly railway station. The hotel was refurbished in 1987; all rooms have private facilities, although only a handful have baths.

Economy Class

Kelly's, 36 South Great George's Street (Tel: 01 779 277)
Clarence, Wellington Quay (Tel: 01 776 178)
The Beddington, 181–182 Rathgar Road (Tel: 01 978 047)
Hollybrook, Howth Road, Clontarf (Tel: 01 336 623)
Iona House, 5 Iona Park (Tel: 01 306 217)
Maples House, 81 Iona Road (Tel: 01 303 049)

SIGHTS

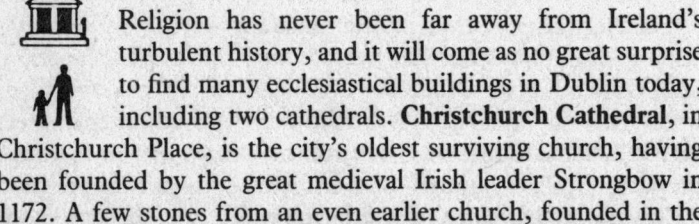

Religion has never been far away from Ireland's turbulent history, and it will come as no great surprise to find many ecclesiastical buildings in Dublin today, including two cathedrals. **Christchurch Cathedral**, in Christchurch Place, is the city's oldest surviving church, having been founded by the great medieval Irish leader Strongbow in 1172. A few stones from an even earlier church, founded in the early eleventh century, can still be seen; the building was heavily restored during the last century, but retains many medieval features, including the late twelfth-century crypt which extends under the entire length of the cathedral.

Christchurch Cathedral is not, however, Dublin's principal church building; that honour rests with **St Patrick's Cathedral**. St Patrick's stands nearby, in Patrick's Street, and carries the name of Ireland's patron saint. This larger cathedral was founded in 1190, although nothing of the present building predates the fourteenth century when it was rebuilt after a major fire. St Patrick's was also extensively restored during the nineteenth century, and has some intricate stonework spanning several centuries of architectural style.

Jonathan Swift, the eighteenth-century writer and satirist, served as Dean of St Patrick's for more than thirty years before his death in 1745. A collection of artefacts associated with his life and work are on display in the north transept, and a brass plaque near the main door marks his tomb. Three years before his death, Swift presided at the first public performance of Handel's 'Messiah', whilst the composer was visiting Dublin. The original holograph manuscript can be seen in **Marsh's Library** (Ireland's first public library), next door to the cathedral.

Two other ecclesiastical buildings of note are **St Werburgh's Church**, just off Christchurch Place, which has an outstanding Gothic pulpit, and **St Michan's Church**, in Church Street, with its creepy old vaults. This seventeenth-century building stands on the site of an eleventh-century church and its forty-three vaults house hundreds of bodies: due to an atmospheric phenomenon (the first church was built on the site of a prehistoric oak forest) the bodies decay very slowly. For the strong-willed, several remarkably well-preserved medieval bodies can be clearly seen.

The most historically significant modern building in Dublin is also the most unmemorable, and still serves its original function. The **General Post Office** in O'Connell Street was the place where the first Irish Free Republic was declared, after a street battle, in 1916. Bullet scars can still be clearly seen in the main supporting pillars outside. British forces eventually suppressed the 1916 uprising, after the command centre was isolated in the post office, and totally gutted the building by fire.

O'Connell Street itself dates mainly from the eighteenth century and, at its widest, is 150 feet across. A large statue of Nelson dominated the street until 1966 when a Breton hired by the IRA blew it up. No one was hurt and, amazingly, damage was almost entirely restricted to the offending statue. As a thoughtful gesture to Irish sensitivities, the statue was never replaced.

Within easy walking distance you can see **Parliament House**, a beautiful Georgian building, designed by James Grandon, and now the headquarters for the Bank of Ireland. Directly opposite is **Trinity College**, Ireland's most famous seat of learning celebrating its 400th anniversary in 1992; its equally famous library (see following section for opening hours) contains the *Book of Kells*, a priceless vellum tome dating from the early ninth century. The surrounding **Trinity College Park** is an ideal place to relax after a day's sightseeing, or perhaps enjoy a picnic.

Leinster House is another of Dublin's magnificent Georgian buildings, built in the eighteenth century by the Duke of Leinster. It is the largest Georgian house in Ireland and is now the seat of the Irish government. Leinster House is not normally open to the public, although guided tours are occasionally possible when Parliament is not sitting.

The River Liffey runs through the heart of the city, and you ought to see the old **Custom House** which stands close to Butt Bridge, on the north bank. With its distinctive copper dome, it is not difficult to see why many visitors feel this is the most beautiful building in Dublin. The House has been extensively restored over the last few years, although work first started more than sixty years ago, after the original eighteenth-century building was destroyed by fire during the civil war. A number of Ireland's leading trade unions still have their headquarters within sight of the Custom House.

The **Four Courts**, the seat of the Irish High Court of Justice, is along the North Quays, a short distance away, and is modelled very much on the English High Court in London. The formidable **Dublin Castle** has equally strong historical associations, as this was the seat of British rule for many generations. The building of Dublin Castle was started in the thirteenth century, probably on the site of a much earlier Viking settlement, although much of the present castle dates from the eighteenth century.

Over the last three hundred years the castle has served as a jail, courthouse, parliament building, and as the venue for more recent State banquets for visiting heads of state. Today you can visit the marvellous state apartments (open 1000–1700 Mon–Fri; 1400–1700 weekends) and Francis Johnston's **Church of the Most Holy Trinity** within the castle grounds.

Three other sights worth visiting are **Phoenix Park**, three square miles of parkland on the western edge of Dublin which houses **Dublin Zoo** on its north-eastern side; **Kilmainham Jail**, a formidable old building (guided tours only on a Sunday afternoon) which now houses a permanent exhibition dedicated to Irish nationalism; and **Mornington House**, at 24 Upper Merrion Street, where the Duke of Wellington was born in 1769.

Museums and Galleries

Dublin has a large number of museums and galleries – a tribute to Ireland's often turbulent historical development. The principal public collection is housed in the **National Museum** in Kildare Street, and here you can see a vast display of artefacts spanning the artistic, industrial and natural history of Ireland from prehistoric times to the present day. There is a particularly fine Antiquities collection, with many handsome relics from the centuries between AD 600 and 900, which was one of Ireland's most peaceful periods. The museum is open 1000–1700 Mon–Sat; 1400–1700 Sun; closed Monday.

Dublin's principal art gallery is the **National Gallery**, in Merrion Square, with its large statue of George Bernard Shaw near the entrance. The National Gallery has more than 10,000 works of art in its possession, but never more than a quarter of these can be on display at any one time. Two of the earliest works are twelfth-century frescoes taken from the Chapel of St Pierre-de-Campublic, in southern France. The main display features a large collection ranging from Old Masters to the works of modern Irish artists, and naturally Irish painters receive preferential treatment. Among those represented are Goya, Yeats (the portrait-painting father of the poet), Orpen and Gainsborough. The gallery is open 1000–1700 Mon–Fri; 1000–1300 Sat; 1400–1700 Sun.

As its name implies, the **National Portrait Collection**, in Malahide Castle a few miles north of the city, houses Ireland's main portrait collection. It is open 1000–1700 Mon–Fri (2100 Thu); 1000–1300 Sat; 1400–1700 Sun.

The **Hugh Lane Gallery of Modern Art**, in Parnell Square,

has been revamped and shows part of an enormous art collection bequeathed to the Irish nation by the late industrialist. It is open 1000–1800 Tue–Sat; 1100–1400 Sun. A more detailed collection of works by Irish artists can be enjoyed at the **Douglas Hyde Gallery**, Trinity College. This gallery is open 1100–1700 Mon–Sat.

For those keen to discover more about the city of Dublin itself, the **Civic Museum**, in South William Street, casts plenty of light on local history. It is open 1000–1800 Tue–Sat; 1100–1400 Sun. The **Guinness Museum and Visitors' Centre**, in James Street, gives an informal insight into the history and making of Ireland's most famous drink. The neighbouring **Museum of Brewing** has only been established a few years, and both are open to the public 1000–1500 Mon–Fri.

The **Chester Beatty Library and Art Gallery**, in a quiet residential part of the city in Shrewsbury Road, contains the oldest-known copy of the Old Testament as the centrepiece of a huge display of ancient and medieval manuscripts. It also includes a remarkable collection of picture scrolls and jades from the Far East, all of which were acquired by Sir Chester Beatty, a philanthropic American millionaire who retired to Ireland some years before his death in 1968. His enormous collection was bequeathed to the city. Guided tours are available at 1430 on Wed and Sat, and the Library is open normally 1000–1700 Tue–Fri, and 1400–1700 Sat.

Another smaller library/museum worth visiting is **Marsh's Library**, close to St Patrick's Cathedral, which has a wide range of old medical books and documents. Marsh's Library also houses a range of works devoted to Greek, Hebrew and Latin literature. It is open 1400–1600 Mon, Wed, Thu and Fri; 1030–1230 Sat.

Three other public collections of note are the **Trinity College Library**, reckoned to be the oldest surviving College Library building in the world and housing the beautiful *Book of Kells* and hundreds more early printed books (open 0930–1645 Mon–Fri, 0930–1245 Sat; closed Sunday and Bank Holidays); the **Museum of Childhood**, in Palmerston Park (open 1400–1800 all week) with its three and a half metre high doll's house; and the **Irish Jewish Museum**, in Walworth Road, which charts the long history of the Jewish people in Ireland. It is open during the summer: Sun, Mon and Wed 1130–1530; 1030–1430 on winter Sundays.

The **Dublin Experience**, an audio-visual show of inhabitants and lifestyles through the ages, (22 May–6 October 1000 daily).

City Tours

The range of city tours around Dublin is very limited, and the majority of visitors prefer to find their own way around the Irish capital since the city centre covers a relatively small area. **Aer Lingus** holidays occasionally include a simple introduction to the main sights of the city, usually a two- or three-hour bus tour, and one of the best is run by **CIE** who offer a 'Traditional Irish Music Night' as well as straightforward city tours.

Gray Line Sightseeing (Tel: 01 744 466) also offers one or two city tours, varying in length from two hours to a full day, and excursions to a number of the better-known towns and beauty spots within easy reach of the city. Full details of city tours are available from the Irish Tourist Board, Baggot Street Bridge, Dublin 2 (Tel: 01 765 871), or at 14 Upper O'Connell Street (Tel: 01 747 733).

For details of the 'Dublin Literary Pub Crawl' see pages 135–6.

Shopping

Dublin's reputation as a major shopping centre is growing steadily, and most of the major international boutiques and fashion chains are now represented in the Irish capital. Fashion goods are one of Dublin's best buys, and leading stores include **Michael Mortell**, at the Westbury Centre; **Ib Jorgensen**, 35 Dawson Street; **William Elliott** of Wicklow Street, and **Westbury Designs**, in the Westbury Centre.

Among the city's best department stores, you should find

time to visit either **Switzer's** on Grafton Street, or **Clery's** on O'Connell Street. The **Irish Cotton Industries** shop, at 18 Dawson Street, has a good range of traditional Irish clothing, and **Donegal Design**, near Roebuck Road, is a favourite for good mohair goods.

Kilkenny Design Workshops, in Nassau Street, have a first-class range of tableware and household goods; the nearby **Blarney Woollen Mills** has an equally wide range of Waterford glass and other gift items. Two other shopping areas worth looking out for are the **Tower Design Centre**, Pearse Street, for fine Irish craftwork; and the selection of antique shops in the Dawson Street area.

The key shopping areas are, Grafton Street, O'Connell Street and Henry Street. Dublin Tourism do a free guide to shopping in Dublin.

Parks and Gardens

Dublin is fortunate to have a good selection of parks and gardens where you can relax or enjoy a leisurely picnic during the summer months. The best known is probably **Phoenix Park**, some minutes' walk from the city centre, the largest park of its kind in Europe. It covers more than 1700 acres and has a popular zoo (admission about IR£2.60). You can also see the People's Park, a herd of tame deer and, in season, watch polo being played, free of charge.

Phoenix Park is vast, and through the woodland you can admire a distant view of the official residence of the Irish President (the *Arus an Uachtarain*), and that of the American Ambassador as well. The Park's Garden of Remembrance is dedicated to those who lost their lives during the long struggle for Ireland's independence.

Dublin's 'second' park is **St Stephen's Green**, at the top of Grafton Street. The Green is popular with visitors and locals alike, and features include a small lake complete with waterfall, and a striking sculpture by Henry Moore which is dedicated to one of Ireland's most famous literary sons, W. B. Yeats. During the summer concerts are regularly held in the bandstand, and there is a specially laid-out garden for blind visitors. The Park as a whole is usually open 0930–1800 Mon–Sat, 1200–1800 Sun, or until sunset during the winter months.

Covering an area of about fifty acres, the **National Botanical Gardens** are located at Glasnevin. The collection of plants, shrubs and flowers is very impressive, particularly during the summer months, and the Gardens are open 0930–1800 Mon–Sat, 1100–1700 Sun; admission is free, although visitors should note that the Gardens close at sunset during the winter months.

Herbert Park covers approximately thirty acres in the Ballsbridge district, quite close to the American Embassy. Although nothing remains of it now, this was the site of the enormous 1907 Dublin International Exhibition. Two other public parks of note are **Merrion Square Park**, in Merrion Square; and the 300-acre **Marley Grange Park** at Rathfarnham with its distinctive sculpture park.

WHERE TO EAT

Dublin has an excellent range of restaurants, and informal meals can be enjoyed at most of the city's pubs and wine bars. It is worth remembering that many of the city's restaurants close quite early, even during the summer months, so it is worth your while to make a quick telephone call to check opening hours and so avoid disappointment if you plan to eat late. What follows is a selection of good restaurants in three broad price categories.

First Class

Le Coq Hardi, Pembroke Road (Tel: 01 684 130) – Excellent international cuisine; specialities include breast of chicken stuffed with a mousse of Dublin Bay prawns, and loin of Irish lamb with a mousse of rabbit and morels.

Kish Seafood Restaurant, Jury's Hotel, Ballsbridge (Tel: 01 605 000) – Great seafood in a beautiful modern restaurant, within easy reach of the city centre.

Bon Appetit, 9 James Terrace, Malahide (Tel: 01 450 314) – An elegant restaurant in the heart of Malahide.

Business Class

Beaufield Mews, Stillorgan (Tel: 01 880 375) – A popular, traditional restaurant; the main dining area is decorated with a fine collection of antiques. Also has menus in Braille.

Kitty O'Shea's, Upper Grand Canal Street (Tel: 01 609 965) – A very traditional old restaurant offering wholesome Irish cuisine.

Rajdoot Tandoori, 26–28 Clarendon Street (Tel: 01 679 4274) – One of Dublin's best foreign restaurants, offering excellent Indian Tandoori specialities.

The Lord Edward, Christchurch (Tel: 01 542 400) – Offers an extensive menu of gourmet-style cooking, particularly seafood; good range of traditional Irish flavours.

Economy Class

Bewley's Café, 12 Westmoreland Street (also at 78 Grafton Street and 13 South St George's Street).

McDonald's hamburger restaurants at Grafton Street, O'Connell Street, Dun Laoghaire, Phibsboro Road, Rathmines, Rathfarnham, Stillorgan and Naas Road.

PUBS

Dublin is also blessed with some of Europe's liveliest public houses; it is no exaggeration that one of the warmest welcomes you can ever receive is likely to come from the locals at an Irish pub – particularly if you offer to stand them a drink! Opening hours are currently Mon–Sat 1030–2330 (2300 winter-time), Sun 1230–1400, 1600–2300.

You will not have to walk far to find a lively Dublin pub, but the following is a selection of the more traditional establishments in the city centre.

The Bailey, Duke Street – This is about as traditional as you will ever get; a pub has stood here since the late 1600s, and James Joyce immortalized it in his classic *Ulysses* when it was then known as Burton's.

The Brazen Head, Bridge Street – Probably the city's oldest pub, having been founded around the time of the Great Fire of London (1666), it has been serving weary travellers with Irish ale ever since.

Doheny and Nesbitt's, 5 Lower Baggot Street – The focal point for Dublin's professional people; lawyers, politicians and journalists regularly drink in this fine old watering hole.

The International Bar, 23 Wicklow Street – Named after the five nations rugby internationals, this bar keeps up the tradition of pouring Guinness with a patriotic shamrock scored into the head.

Kitty O'Shea's, Shelbourne Road – A sociable place where it is reckoned you should best be seen, rather than go out of your way to visit it as a 'sight' in its own right.

O'Donaghue's, 15 Merrion Row – The place where the Dubliners began their career, formerly known as Tom Kennedy's. The late Senator Robert Kennedy visited it hoping to find his family's roots but without success. He was forced to sing an old Irish ballad before leaving.

Paddy Cullen's, Ballsbridge – Real Dublin character, and excellent bar lunches.

Patrick Conway's, near the Rotunda Hospital – Plenty of charm and character; this is also the nearest public bar to the Gate Theatre.

Toner's, 139 Lower Baggot Street – Another traditional old pub which has changed little in the last few decades.

If you are interested in Dublin's literary heritage you might try the 'Dublin Literary Pub Crawl': an expert in Anglo-Irish literature will guide you around the various hostelries associated with famous writers such as Sheridan, Wilde, Shaw, Joyce and Beckett. The tour is available Tue–Thu, Jun–Aug, departing 1930 from The Bailey in Duke Street. It costs IR£5 per person with a reduction for students.

NIGHTLIFE

Dublin's nightlife is excellent, if a friendly pub with live music is your idea of a good time, though disco-goers will find fewer venues than in most European cities. There are plenty of lively pubs. A few of the most popular are **McDaid's**, in Harry Street; **Davy Byrne**, in Duke Street; and **Ryan's**, in Parkgate Street. In addition, all the good hotels have their own nightspots which open late during the summer months.

Traditional classical music entertainment can be enjoyed at the **National Concert Hall**, in Earlsfort Terrace, and further classical recitals are held regularly in the **Royal Dublin Society's Hall**, Ballsbridge; details about traditional Irish music can be obtained at the **Comhaltas Ceoltóirí Eireann Theatre**, 32–33 Belgrave Square, Monktown (Tel: 01 800 295).

Central among Dublin's many theatres is the **Abbey Theatre**, in Marlborough Street, which was founded in 1904. The original building was destroyed by fire in 1951, and the attractive modern building you can now see dates from 1966. The Abbey features the full spectrum of dramatic entertainment, and is worth visiting at least once during your stay in Dublin.

Other theatres of note include the varied **Olympia Theatre** in Dame Street; the city's oldest opera house, the **Gaiety Theatre**, in South King Street; the **Project Arts Centre**, at 39 East Essex Street; the **Gate** in Cavendish Row, and the **Lambert Puppet Theatre**, Clifton Lane.

Among the best social nightspots are a handful of 'dinner and dance' clubs in the city centre. These include **Jules**, in

Lower Baggot Street (Tel: 01 767 654); **Raffles**, Sach's Hotel, Morehampton Road (Tel: 01 680 955); and **Styx**, which you can find in Lower Leeson Street. The **Burlington Hotel** (Tel: 01 605 222), in Upper Leeson Street, generally has traditional cabaret in the summer evenings. Dublin Tourism's free guide to dining contains a cabaret and nightclub section.

EXCURSIONS

Excursion possibilities from Dublin are reasonable, and there are plenty of places you can visit within an hour or so's drive of the capital. Dublin is an excellent transportation hub, and there are buses to even the smallest villages. **CIE Expressway** operates to most of the region's towns and villages, once you need to travel beyond the limits of the city's suburban service. In addition, train services run south to Wicklow, Arklow and beyond; north to Drogheda and on to the border with Northern Ireland; and inland to Mullingar, or Kildare, and beyond. All the destinations suggested as possible excursions will be covered in greater detail in the rest of this chapter.

Heading to the south of Dublin, you can explore the beautiful east coast, with its rocky coastline and the town of Dun Laoghaire whose wide harbour was built for the mail ferries in the early nineteenth century. James Joyce lived, briefly, in the nearby town of Sandycove, and a museum dedicated to his life and work was opened in 1962. The museum is housed in one of Ireland's few Martello towers which are open to the public.

The village of Dalkey, further south, also has literary associations, as George Bernard Shaw lived here for eleven years until 1874. In the main street, you can still see the remains of a number of fifteenth- and sixteenth-century fortified mansions, and from Coliemore Harbour just outside the village, you can take a boat trip over to the bird sanctuary on Dalkey Island.

Immediately to the north of Dublin lies Howth Head, dominated by a harbour constructed between 1807 and 1809, and the medieval Howth Castle. From the point you can see Ireland's

Eye, a picturesque island where one of the earliest Christian monasteries (dating from the sixth or seventh century) is said to have been built. The remains of a much later stone church mark the site.

The Wicklow Mountains are one of the most historically significant areas of Dublin's environs, and also an extremely picturesque part of the Irish landscape to tour, even for a day. The road from Dublin to Wicklow town passes the large ruin of the Hell Fire Club on Mountpelier Hill. Founded in 1735, the club was eventually closed down due to the 'licentious and blasphemous conduct' of the 'devil-worshipping' members.

Other excursion possibilities within an hour or so of Dublin include the Great Sugar Loaf Mountain, in the north-east corner of Wicklow; the beautiful village of Enniskerry; Russborough House, near Blessington, which was once the home of copper magnate Sir Alfred Beit and now houses a vast private art collection; and the rolling countryside of County Kildare, to the west of the city.

North of Dublin

The region immediately to the north of the capital is well known for its beautiful coastline and a number of attractive, gently shelving beaches. Small resorts have developed around the best beaches, and these are particularly popular with families on holiday with young children.

Heading north, one of the first places you will come to is the village of **HOWTH**, known chiefly for the **Hill of Howth**, which is the most prominent natural landmark on this stretch of Ireland's east coast. The hill stands nearly 175 metres above sea level, and forms the northern arm of Dublin Bay. **Ireland's Eye** is a small island about a mile out from Howth Harbour, which you can see clearly from the hill – a peaceful spot for a picnic. Motor-boats can be hired from the harbour during the summer months.

Apart from the spectacular views from the summit of the hill – across the Bay and to **Baily's Lighthouse** – you should make the effort to see **Howth Castle** gardens. These are located on the side of the Hill of Howth and they contain one of Europe's finest collections of rhododendron bushes. The gardens are open every day of the year, except Christmas Day, between 0800 and sunset. There is a small admission charge during the flowering season, from April to June.

If you are keen to enjoy the natural beauty of Howth, a couple of suggestions for good accommodation are: the four-star **Deer Park Hotel** (Tel: 01 322 624), with three dozen bedrooms and outstanding views across the capital and out to sea, and the seventeen-room **Howth Lodge Hotel** (Tel: 01 390 288), which also overlooks the sea. The **King Sitric** restaurant (Tel: 01 325 235), at the East Pier, is one of Ireland's best, serving fine fish dishes in very pleasant, informal surroundings. Book early during the summer season.

Five miles to the north, **PORTMARNOCK** is another small resort, renowned for its fine eighteen-hole championship golf course. Green fees are high for non-members, and details are available from the local golf club on 01 323 082. The village also overlooks a magnificent three-mile stretch of sandy beach, known as the **Velvet Strand**, offering safe, clean bathing for all the family.

Two miles west of Portmarnock lies **St Doulagh's Church**, so named because it stands on the site of the stone cell of St Doulagh who lived there as a hermit in the early years of the seventh century. The oldest surviving part of the present church building is to the west of the fourteenth-century tower, dating back more than eight hundred years. A medieval tomb thought to be that of St Doulagh can be seen inside, as can an interesting sunken bath known as **St Catherine's Well**. The church is open only at weekends during the summer months, 1430–1730 (1800 Sun).

Quite nearby, on the southern side of a narrow estuary, lies the village of **MALAHIDE**. This is a popular centre for watersports of all kinds, and enthusiasts come from all over Europe to enjoy water-skiing and sailing in the estuary. The **Fingall Sailing**

School (Tel: 01 451 979), at the edge of the wide Broadmeadow estuary, offers basic courses in dinghy and sailboard handling, and water-skiing is available through the **Dublin/Balscadden Power Boat and Water Ski Club** (Tel: 01 450 970), at The Strand. Horse-riding is offered by the **Malahide Riding School** (Tel: 01 450 211) at Ivy Grange, Broomfield.

Visitors to Malahide should visit the **Castle**, a striking fortress of medieval origin which was home to the Talbot family from 1185 until 1976. The castle is now the property of Dublin County Council, and the National Gallery now house a substantial part of their portrait collection in the old building. Nothing of the original castle survives, but you can see parts of the tower, which dates from the fourteenth century. Malahide Castle is open 1000–1700 Mon–Fri; 1400–1700 weekends and Bank Holidays Nov–Mar (Sat 1100–1800 Apr–Oct). It is usually closed for lunch between 1245 and 1400, and there is a small admission charge. A combined castle/model railway family ticket is available. Tours are available in foreign languages.

A historical house and traditional farm can be found at **Newbridge House**, Donabare, just north of Malahide. Summer hours are 1000–1700 Tue–Fri (Sat 1100–1800), Sun and Bank Holidays 1400–1800. There is a small admission charge and tours are available in foreign languages.

The **Grand Hotel** (Tel: 01 450 633), in the centre of Malahide, is the village's best hotel. All fifty or so rooms have private facilities, and the Grand has an indoor riding school where residents are welcome to try a sample lesson.

Three miles inland, to the west of Malahide, is the village of **SWORDS**. This is one of the oldest villages in Ireland, with a monastic settlement which predates Dublin by several centuries. **Swords Castle** was built around 1200 as an episcopal manor house, although the five-sided structure was altered considerably in later centuries. The ruins can be visited at any time of the year, and archaeological work is taking place during the milder spring and summer months.

Another medieval site of note is Swords **round tower**, in the grounds of the village church (Church of Ireland). The seventy-five-foot tower stands on the site of the earliest known monastic settlement, founded in AD 563 by St Colmcille, although most of what you can see today dates from between 1400 and 1700. The cross on the roof is the 'youngest' structural addition, having been erected less than three centuries ago.

Lying fifteen miles from Dublin, RUSH is an attractive fishing village which is fast expanding as a popular summer resort. The village's round tower is the only surviving relic from a sixth-century monastery; a much later square tower, probably dating from the sixteenth century, adjoins it and there are three further towers which were constructed to resemble the original structure. Nearby, the Protestant parish church, dating from the mid-nineteenth century, houses a number of attractive medieval tombs.

The main resort in this part of the region north of Dublin is SKERRIES, a large village which is noted for its dry, bracing climate. Little of the old fishing village has disappeared, but Skerries has developed most of the modern amenities which you would expect in a sizeable resort. Attractions include **St Patrick's Island**, one of three small islands lying close to the shore. The ruins of an old church said to have been founded by St Patrick can still be seen. **Baldongan Castle**, three miles south of the village, is the ruined remains of a thirteenth-century fortress which served briefly as a residence of the crusading Knights Templar.

Skerries is a good destination for the sporting enthusiast, and most outdoor sports are available. Golf can be arranged through Skerries **Golf Club** (Tel: 01 491 567), and sailing through Skerries **Sailing School** at the harbour (Tel: 01 491 233). The resort has two first-class beaches, both offering safe family bathing. Accommodation in the village itself is limited to a couple of modest hotels.

Four miles north you'll find BALBRIGGAN, a quiet seaside resort at the edge of County Dublin. Deep-sea fishing is popular here, and there is both shore and boat fishing for conger, rock bream, cod, pollack, ray, dogfish and tope. Pre-booking with **Cardy Marina** (Tel: 01 411 047) is essential. Horse-riding can be enjoyed through the **Gormanston Indoor Riding Centre** (Tel: 01 412 508), in Knocknagin Road, and there is a good golf course at **Blackhall**.

There is an important prehistoric site at **Four-knocks**, about five miles to the west of Balbriggan. Three large earthen mounds were excavated here and it was discovered that one was covering what is known as a passage grave, in the cruciform pattern. The grave is thought to date back to approximately 1800 BC and the decorative uprights and lintels are particularly interesting.

Continuing northwards, the main coast road (N1) takes you past some of the region's most picturesque scenery before you reach the town of Drogheda. You have now entered the County of Louth; at just over 300 square miles, Louth is the smallest county in the Irish Republic.

The road to Drogheda goes past a number of small beach resorts, although most of them offer no more than a single hotel, or one or two self-catering apartments, and a relatively quiet stretch of coast. **BETTYSTOWN** has a particularly fine sandy beach, and the popular **Strand Races** are held here once a year during the summer months. You can also enjoy a first-class round of golf at the nearby course, and a fine meal at the **Coastguard Inn** (Tel: 041 27115). The tiny village of **Termonfeckin**, with its medieval stone cross in the square, is an interesting detour which few visitors seem to know about.

DROGHEDA is known in Irish as *Droichead Atha*, meaning 'the bridge of the ford'. The town has seen much bloodshed over the last three hundred years, and had several hundred of its inhabitants, and an entire garrison of soldiers, murdered or transported to the West Indies by Oliver Cromwell in 1649 when he attempted to subjugate the entire island. He failed in the end, but not before most of Drogheda had paid the ultimate sacrifice.

Little of the town survived the period of the English Revolution, although you can still see one of the original town walls in St Lawrence Street. The remains of a seventeenth-century abbey still stand in Abbey Lane, and part of a much older Dominican priory, including a two-floor tower, can be seen in Upper Magdalene Street.

One of the town's most attractive 'modern' churches is the **Church of St Peter**, although it is better known for its rather gruesome relic from the period of extreme religious suppression in the seventeenth century. The shrivelled head of Oliver Plunkett, one-time Archbishop of Armagh, has been kept here since his brutal execution in 1678 at Tyburn. The door of his cell is preserved in the church, and the Archbishop was finally canonized in the 1970s.

There is a small **Tourist Information office** in the centre of Drogheda (Tel: 041 37070) which can give you information about where to eat or stay. A couple of suggestions are the modest **Branagan's Restaurant** (Tel: 041 37407) in Magdalene Street, and the **New Rossnaree Hotel** (Tel: 041 37673/37811). For added luxury, the **Boyne Valley Hotel** (Tel: 041 37737) is a former mansion, now converted into a luxury hotel, a few miles outside Drogheda.

A few miles from Drogheda, on the main road west, lies the beautiful village of SLANE. The village has a number of quaint public houses which are perfect for a relaxing lunch, or a long drink far from the hustle and noise of the capital. A fine old castle overlooks the River Boyne, although it is best known today as one of Ireland's premier open-air rock venues; during the 1980s, Bruce Springsteen, Bob Dylan, the Rolling Stones, and Dublin's own U2 all played here. The castle has a good restaurant featuring seasonal Irish specialities.

In an earlier era, it was on the imposing hill near Slane that an unknown holy man, later revered throughout Ireland as St Patrick, lit his great bonfire and so proclaimed that Christianity was alive throughout the Emerald Isle. The view from the top of the hill is magnificent. Be sure not to leave Slane without having a look at the four distinctive Georgian houses, built in a neat square, which were once owned by four nosy spinster sisters. A suggestion for somewhere to stay in Slane is the **Conyngham Arms Hotel** (Tel: 041 24155), named after an ancestor of the spinster sisters, which offers bed and breakfast for about £20.

Much of this part of Ireland lies in the **Boyne Valley**, and about a mile outside Drogheda you can see a simple obelisk, on the north bank of the river, which marks the site of the **Battle of the Boyne** in 1690. This was one of the most important battles in both Irish and British history, and resulted in the Protestant forces of William of Orange (later King William III of Britain) soundly defeating those of the ousted Catholic king, James II.

Another site of historical interest is **Mellifont Abbey**, at the village of MONASTERBOICE. The original abbey was built during the fifth century, and was destined to be the site of Ireland's first Cistercian monastery. The most attractive feature of what little remains of the early medieval ruins is a magnificent High Cross, decorated with scenes from the Bible and reckoned to date back more than a thousand years. The abbey is still inhabited by Cistercian monks, who manage a model Friesian/Holstein farm which is known world-wide.

Another point of interest, close to Drogheda, is the untouched natural beauty of CARLINGFORD, looking across the River Lough towards the **Mourne** mountains. At Carlingford you can see the seventy-foot-high walls of **King John's Castle**, the largest Anglo-Norman fortress in Ireland, where Richard II was said to have imprisoned the future Henry V.

Another of Carlingford's historic sights is **Taafe's Castle**, which dates from the sixteenth century and is in a slightly better state of preservation. You can also see the remains of a fourteenth-century **Dominican abbey**, and a fortified house which served as the official Irish mint more than four centuries ago. A little way out of the town, **Faughart Hill**, where Edward Bruce was killed in the early fourteenth century, is one of a number of fine vantage points for the surrounding hills.

Further on, ARDEE is a thriving market town with a thirteenth-century church, and it served as an important base for English forces attacking Ulster in earlier centuries. It is here, legend records, the semi-mythical warrior Cuchulainn was born. It is also reputed that it was on the site of the present town that

Cuchulainn fought a bitter four-day battle with his best friend to prevent him stealing a sacred bull – he won.

Other places of interest in this part of the region include the small coastal resort of **BLACKROCK**, with a good stretch of beach popular for family holidays; the agreeable little village of **CASTLEBELLINGHAM**, and the small town of **KELLS**. Be sure not to miss the picturesque little village of **TRIM**.

Kells is best known, of course, for the world-famous *Book of Kells* (now in Dublin's Trinity College Library) and its five ancient **High Crosses**. Despite their religious significance, one was used as a gallows at the end of the eighteenth century. Kells also has a medieval round tower which was used variously as a place of storage for food and a refuge for persecuted rebels.

The largest town in County Louth is **DUNDALK**, a relatively dull, modern town with very little to recommend a specific visit. It makes, however, an excellent base for exploring the entire region and is particularly well placed for the beautiful **Cooley Peninsula**, which protrudes into the Irish Sea. There is a **Tourist Information office** in the centre of Dundalk (Tel: 042 35484) open all year.

Three suggestions for accommodation in Dundalk are: **Ballymascanlon House** (Tel: 042 71124), with three dozen well-appointed bedrooms, all with private facilities, and an exceptionally good leisure centre; the forty-room **Glendevlin Hotel** (Tel: 042 21500), with a popular all-day carvery; and the three-star **Derryhale Hotel** (Tel: 042 35471), which is a renovated old mansion on the outskirts of town.

The **Cooley Mountains** are one of the most striking natural features in this part of Ireland, and the perfect place for the *Nature Lover*, *Healthy Holiday* enthusiast and the *Recluse* to explore. The legendary giant, Finn MacCool, is said to have had his equally proportioned hound, Bran, buried in these mountains.

Be sure to visit the tiny village of **BALLYMASCANLON** from where you can walk to the **Proleek Dolmen**. These huge prehistoric stone structures have been found in various parts of Ireland and are reckoned to have been megalithic tombs with at least three huge supporting stones. The capstone alone at Proleek Dolmen is thought to weigh nearly sixty tons.

South of Dublin

The area to the south of the City of Dublin is regarded as one of the most beautiful in Ireland, and it is also one of the most accessible for British visitors arriving by sea (at Dun Laoghaire) or air at Dublin's international airport. The district of **Ballsbridge** lies immediately to the south of the city centre and this is where you can find some of Dublin's best residential areas, and a number of the city's better hotels – including both **Jury's** and the **Lansdowne**.

The first town of any size is DUN LAOGHAIRE (pronounced 'dunn leer-ey') which lies about eight miles south-east from Dublin, although there is virtually an unbroken conurbation between the two. Dun Laoghaire is the Irish Republic's principal seaport for both passengers and cargo from the United Kingdom. It has been a major gateway to Ireland for centuries, although the harbour you can see today dates back further than the start of the nineteenth century when it was built for the British mailboat service. The modernized international seaport is now said to be one of the most up-to-date in Europe.

Dun Laoghaire was known for a hundred years as Kingstown, in commemoration of an all-too-rare visit by George IV, in 1821, shortly after he became king. In response to growing nationalist sentiment, the town changed its name after the Irish Free State was established almost exactly a hundred years later.

Dun Laoghaire means, literally, 'Leary's fort' after a fortress which was built by a fifth-century king of Ireland. Nothing survives today, but you can still see **James Joyce's Tower** at Sandycove, one mile from the town centre, which was one of a number of such towers on Ireland's east coast. At one time they were the front line of Ireland's defence against the threat of invasion by Napoleon's forces.

One of Ireland's most famous literary sons, James Joyce, lived in the tower for a short time, and it appears in the opening chapter of his classic *Ulysses* along with one or two other local landmarks (including Burton's pub, now the Bailey, in the centre of Dublin). The tower is now a museum, dedicated to the life and work of James Joyce and containing some fascinating memorabilia. You can visit the tower 1000–1300 and 1400–1715 Mon–Sat, and 1430–1800 Sun between the months of May and September.

In Marine Road you can visit the town's newest church, **St Michael's**, which was rebuilt between 1965 and 1973 after the original early nineteenth-century building was destroyed by fire. Two other churches of interest are the **Presbyterian Church** in York Road, and the **Mariners' Church** in Adelaide Street. A second mariners' church, in Haigh Terrace, contains the **National Maritime Museum** which is open 1430–1730 Tue–Sun during the summer months.

The town's oldest church is **Monkstown Church**, about a mile from the town centre, a good example of an early nineteenth-century Gothic-style ecclesiastical building. The plaster vault is particularly interesting. About half a mile further south, **Monkstown Castle** is a fifteenth-century ruin where you can still make out the small keep, gate-house and part of the original curtain wall.

Dun Laoghaire is a veritable Mecca for sporting enthusiasts and is Ireland's main yachting centre. The headquarters of both the Royal St George and the Royal Irish yacht clubs, both of which were founded in the first half of the last century, are here.

There are three major golf courses within easy reach of the town, the best of which is supervised by **Dun Laoghaire Golf Club** (Tel: 01 803 916) at Eglinton Park. **Carrickmines** is a smaller (nine-hole) golf club (Tel: 01 895 972) and lies four miles from the centre of town. Sailing is possible through the **Dun Laoghaire Sailing School** (Tel: 01 806 654) in Lower Georges Street; scuba-diving and basic windsurfing tuition are offered at the **Fitzpatrick's Castle Hotel** (Tel: 01 851 533) at weekends.

Other sporting facilities include ten-pin bowling at the **Stillorgan Bowl**, Stillorgan; green bowling at **Moran Park**; squash and horse-racing at **Leopardstown Racecourse**; fishing from Dun Laoghaire harbour; and tennis at the **Clarinda Park** hard courts. During the summer months visitors can enjoy safe bathing at **Seapoint** and **Sandycove**, and there is an (unheated) swimming pool at **Blackrock**. There is a heated indoor pool at **Monkstown**.

Dun Laoghaire and its immediate environs offer an impressive range of evening entertainment, including one cinema (the **Forum**), and the **Lambert Mews Puppet Theatre** at Monkstown. There is a summer cabaret season at the **Victor Hotel**, in Rochestown Avenue, and ballad-singing sessions at the **Purty Kitchen**. More traditional Irish musical entertainment can be enjoyed at the **Irish Cultural Institute** (*Cultúrlann na Éireann*, Tel: 01 800 925). Their main programme runs between June and September, but off-season performances take place throughout the year.

For somewhere to stay in Dun Laoghaire, the best hotel is the **Royal Marine** (Tel: 01 801 911) with more than a hundred beautiful rooms overlooking the harbour. The **Victor** (Tel: 01 853 555), in Rochestown Avenue, is less expensive and offers residents the use of an in-house sauna and solarium. For budget accommodation try **Mrs Gavin** for bed and breakfast at 2 Mulgrave Terrace (Tel: 01 806 404).

Almost on the outskirts of Dun Laoghaire lie the picturesque villages of DALKEY and KILLINEY, in the heart of some of the most attractive scenery on Ireland's east coast. Dalkey is the better known of the two, with its quaint harbours of Coliemore and Bulloch, and **Archibold's Castle** in Castle Street. This is the only surviving reminder that the village was once part of a walled town and directly opposite, a sixteenth-century castellated house now serves as the Town Hall.

Lying a short way from the mainland, **Dalkey Island** has the remains of a small square church (St Begnet's), and a Martello tower; the church ruins are particularly noteworthy because they exemplify an early ecclesiastical style of architecture. Boats can be hired, or summer trips booked, at Coliemore Harbour.

On Torca Road, Dalkey Hill, you can see **Torca Cottage** where George Bernard Shaw lived between 1866 and 1874. The views from the summit of the hill across to Dublin and Bray are outstanding on a clear day. The Vico Road links the villages of Dalkey and Killiney, and one sight of note in Killiney is the hill of the same name, now a public park, from the top of which you can enjoy great views over the crescent-shaped Killiney Bay.

If you continue south on the main N11 you will quickly cross into County Wicklow and reach the town of **BRAY**. This is one of Ireland's longest-established seaside resorts and manages to combine a precious Edwardian charm with many of the popular modern attractions. Bray has a safe beach of sand and shingle which stretches south for more than a mile towards Bray Head, at the southern end of the windy promenade. One suggestion for accommodation is the respectable three-star **Royal Hotel** (Tel: 01 862 935) in the Main Street.

Bray Head stands nearly 500 metres above sea level and is the 'centrepiece' of a large public park. The ruins of a thirteenth-century church stand near the summit, and energetic visitors should attempt the three-mile walk around the Head's eastern side towards Greystones. The walk is perfectly safe, although it approaches the edge of the cliff in places and is not recommended for young children.

Dargle Glen Gardens, just outside Bray, was the home of the late patron of the arts Sir Basil Goulding. The gardens are open to the public on one Sunday each month. The house remains private, but you should check with a local tourist information office to find out if a forthcoming Sunday opening coincides with your own visit to this part of Ireland. It will be worth the effort.

Five miles west of Bray, the village of **ENNISKERRY** is an attractive estate village lying in the valley of the Glencullen River. Many of the original inhabitants were workers at the nearby Powerscourt Estate. The village's Catholic church was built in the 1840s, at the height of the great famine, and is one of the earliest Gothic revival churches in Ireland. The *Nature Lover* can enjoy some fine forest walks in the wooded countryside around the village.

The **Powerscourt Estate and Gardens**, formerly the property of Viscount Powerscourt and his family, are now owned by the Powerscourt Trust. The gardens are not unfairly described by the Irish Tourist Board as 'a magnificent example of an aristocratic garden laid out with taste and imagination'. Sadly the family house was completely destroyed by a fire in the 1970s, but the gardens remain as the legacy of one of Ireland's richest families. The Japanese and Italian gardens are particularly beautiful during the summer season, and there is a garden centre and plant shop open all year round.

Several picturesque villages lie within easy reach, either by bus or by car, from this part of the east coast. Immediately to the west lies a wide valley which stretches for about eight miles. The **Glencree River** flows through the heart of it and is surrounded by beautifully preserved woodland which has changed little since late medieval times when an English sovereign 'decreed' that this part of Ireland would be a royal forest. It no longer is, of course, but Glencree's natural beauty has not been altered. The Sally Gap lies two miles away and from here you can follow the old Military Road to Laragh, or head on to Roundwood eight miles further south.

ROUNDWOOD is another of County Wicklow's many undiscovered little villages, set amid a rugged landscape, and is said to be the highest in Ireland. From here it is only a short drive to the **Devil's Glen**, one of the best-known beauty spots in the county. A deep chasm, with craggy sides and dense shrubbery, is the perfect backing for a waterfall of more than thirty metres at the **Devil's Punch Bowl**. Two centuries ago the Glen gave temporary refuge to Joseph Holt's insurgents who had led an abortive rising against the English 'governors' in Ireland.

Continuing south, villages of note include GREYSTONES which has grown up on the southern slopes of Bray Head and is slowly developing as a seaside resort but has retained much of its authentic character as a traditional fishing village, and DELGANY, which lies close to the dry Glen of the Downs. The two beaches are covered with fine shingle and you can enjoy a cliff walk to Bray at the northern end of the village around Bray Head. **La Touche** (Tel: 01 874 401) is a small hotel worth considering if you plan to stay here, although not all the rooms have private facilities.

ASHFORD is another picturesque village, about eight miles south of Roundwood on the main road between Dublin and Wicklow. To one side of Ashford lie the famous **Mount Usher Gardens**, acres of rare (predominantly tropical) trees, flowers, plants and shrubs from most corners of the world. The River Varty forms the perfect setting for the gardens and there are a number of related shops within the estate. The gardens are open all year round and make a small admission charge.

Killruddery House and Gardens lie just outside Greystones and the park-like gardens are now thought to be the only surviving examples of seventeenth-century garden layout. The house was altered in 1820 but still contains a large collection of eighteenth- and nineteenth-century period furniture. The house is one of the venues for the annual **Festival of Music in Great Irish Houses** which is held each June.

RATHNEW, with its modern cottages built largely from clay, is another noteworthy village close by.

The *Nature Lover* or the *Recluse* might also consider a visit to the nearby villages of **NEWCASTLE** and **KILCOOLE** to experience some truly beautiful seaside walks. A combination of natural geography and reluctance on the part of the local authorities has ensured that development by the coast has been limited. One or two walks take you close to the main railway line, but the clatter of the occasional train is a small price to pay for the relative tranquillity the rest of the time.

A little way inland you can explore the natural beauty of **Glendalough**, or the 'valley of the two lakes'. There is only one road in and out of the valley, through the attractive crossroads village of **LARAGH**, and the region's history is encapsulated in the ruins of several churches which lie scattered around the banks of the valley's two lakes.

A pious monk, later canonized as St Kevin, founded a monastery at Glendalough during the sixth century and from these small beginnings grew one of the largest monastic settlements in Europe. Viking raids in the ninth and tenth centuries plundered much of the large monastic community, and invading English forces destroyed nearly all that remained at the end of the fourteenth century. One or two small monastic communes were re-established and remained until the final suppression of the monasteries, under Henry VIII in the sixteenth century.

St Kevin's Church, although not the largest, is the best preserved of the scattered ruins which survive. It once was a particularly fine barrel-vaulted building, with a high stone roof, but now stands as a tragic monument to the centuries of religious suppression which the reclusive holy men of Glendalough suffered at the hands of others. **St Kevin's Cell**, to the left of **Reefert's Church**, is a shattered beehive-shaped stone hut and was the monk's last known place of refuge.

The largest of the ruined churches is the **cathedral**, consisting of an eleventh-century nave and a chancel which still has a small sacristy attached to one side. Look out for the round tower which stands more than thirty metres high and is in a near-perfect state of preservation. The doorway is nearly four metres off the ground and the monks hid here (having entered by ladder and pulled it up behind them) in time of attack. On your way into the valley, be sure not to miss the fine entry arch which is the only surviving monastic gateway in Ireland.

A deep glacial glen, **Glenmacnass**, lies to the north of Laragh on the old Military Road. The River Glenmacnass crashes down into the glen from a height of more than eighty metres at its northern end. One of the highest peaks in this beautiful part of County Wicklow is Kippure which stands some 755 metres above sea level. The River Liffey has its source on the hill's southern slopes and the enormous transmitter on the summit is owned by Radio Telefís Eireann, Ireland's national broadcasting company.

Another popular beauty spot within relatively short driving distance of Glenmacnass is the great reservoir of the **Blessington Lakes**, which provides the southern half of Dublin with most of its water supply. The village of Blessington was built during the seventeenth century and has changed little from its original single tree-lined street in the days when it was a staging post for the Dublin to Carlow run on the mail coaches.

On the road to Poulaphouca village you can see **Russborough House**, a magnificent eighteenth-century stately home built by Richard Castle for the first Earl of Milltown between 1740 and

1750. The Alfred Beit Foundation now administers the house and the valuable art collection which includes works by Reubens, Goya and Velazquez. This is another venue for the Festival of Music in Great Irish Houses, held every June.

POULAPHOUCA lies on one side of the massive artificial lake of the same name. **Tulfarris** is a good place to have a quiet lunch before or after a visit to the nearby **Hollywood Glen**. St Kevin is believed to have constructed his first hermitage in the glen and today it offers superb views of the entire region.

Two other local beauty spots are the magnificent vantage point of **Wicklow Gap**, and the wide gorge known as **Glenmalure**. The two facing mountains which make up the gorge were carved out by glacial action. It was here that Elizabeth I's forces were routed by Fiach O'Byrne in 1580; an inscribed stone poignantly commemorates both Fiach O'Byrne and Michael Dwyer, an Irish rebel from two centuries later.

BALTINGLASS is about four miles north-west of **KILTEGAN**, a clean little village and former winner of the Irish Tourist Board's fiercely contested Tidy Towns competition. In Baltinglass you can see the remains of the Cistercian abbey of **Vallis Salutis** which was founded by the semi-legendary Diarmuid MacMurrough, King of Leinster. MacMurrough is thought to be buried somewhere near here, although the precise location of his grave has never been fully established.

AGHAVANNAGH is five miles from **DRUMGOFF** and this is the end of the old Military Road. Just before the end you can see another of the familiar blockhouses which appear at various intervals along the road. This particular one was used as a shooting range by Charles Parnell, and later as a residence by John Redmond MP, who urged Irishmen to join the British Army during the First World War in the hope of attracting government concessions for the cause of Irish Home Rule.

The county town of **WICKLOW** lies about thirty-two miles from Dublin. The town has a lovely setting on the slopes of a wide hill which overlooks the crescent-shaped bay and it takes its Gaelic name – *Cill Mhanntain* – from a fifth-century saint who established a church on the site of the present town around AD 430.

Danish invaders built a maritime station here around the ninth century, and in so doing established the town's reputation as a trading port. The modern name Wicklow is derived from *wyking alo* – 'Viking meadow' – which was bequeathed by the Danes, although nothing else from their period survives.

The town's oldest sight is the ruined twelfth-century **Black Castle** which dominates a narrow promontory overlooking the Irish Sea. This unremarkable medieval pile was extensively remodelled at the end of the fourteenth century and can be visited at any time of the year without restriction. Of more historical significance is the 1798 memorial, depicting a pikeman, in the centre of town. This commemorates a bloody insurrection which took place at the end of the eighteenth century.

The best hotel in Wicklow is the tiny country house hotel, the **Old Rectory** (Tel: 0404 67048) which has just five bedrooms and a beautiful setting. The house has been splendidly restored by owners Paul and Linda Saunders to bring everything, from the delicate plasterwork to the original marble fireplaces, back to its period splendour. The house is open only between April and October and advance bookings are essential given the size of the house. One small hotel in the town is the modest **Grand Hotel** (Tel: 0404 67337) with fourteen bedrooms, most with private facilities.

To the south of Wicklow, and north of Arklow, lie a number of reasonably good beaches which tend to be sheltered by large sand dunes. The best of these are **Brittas Bay**, **Silver Strand** and **Jack's Hole**. There are plenty of little villages inland from here which, individually or collectively, offer a pleasant way to spend an afternoon. GLENEALY is one such, lying about five miles south-west of Wicklow, close to both the Ballymanus Forest and Carrick Mountain.

A few more miles south-west will take you to **Avondale**, a sprawling estate which was once owned by Charles Parnell, the father of Irish land reform, but is now the property of Ireland's Forest and Wildlife Service. Parnell's house is now a museum and there are one or two forest nature trails open to visitors. For those with a scientific interest in forestry, this is where the Forest and Wildlife Service experiment with various types of trees and soil in order to establish which are best for particular locations within Ireland.

The area immediately to the south of Avondale is one of outstanding beauty, and the **Vale of Avoca** is the meeting point of the Avonmore and Avonbeg rivers. Thomas Moore's celebrated poem 'The Meeting of the Waters' was inspired by this place and he is reputed to have spent many long hours underneath a tall tree which stands almost at the point of confluence.

This part of the region once had vast quantities of copper deposits and the valley's distinctive red earth is a by-product of more than two centuries of mining the ore. Look out for the **Motte Stone**, an enormous boulder measuring, at its widest, four metres across; it stands 'guard' over the village of Avoca and lies exactly half-way between Wexford and Dublin.

The rivers Aughrim and Avoca come together at another attractive spot, **WOODENBRIDGE**, about a mile and a half south of Avoca. Towards the end of the eighteenth century an energetic prospector discovered a large gold nugget near here and so started a mini gold rush. Although it was hardly an early California, a total of 2600 ounces of pure gold was extracted over the next few years.

The village of CLARA is within easy reach, lying in the heart of Ireland, and this is the smallest village in Ireland with nothing more than a church, a schoolhouse, and a handful of houses. If you are on holiday with children you might like to visit the **Clara Lara Funpark**, which is a relatively new place for family recreation on the banks of the Avonmore River. It was originally a trout farm but now offers fishing, boating, an adventure playground and a picnic area. There is an admission charge, and a first-class restaurant serving great trout!

South-east

INTRODUCTION

The south-eastern corner of Ireland, stretching from Wicklow to Youghal, takes you from County Wicklow through County Wexford, County Waterford and into County Cork. It is a rugged, fertile region with a thriving agricultural community and a host of small seaside resorts which have grown up around picturesque little fishing communities.

Wicklow and Waterford, the two main counties which we introduce in this chapter, have evolved as a unique combination of three distinct cultures – the native Gaelic, and the Norse and Norman bequeathed by later invaders who eventually settled in this part of Ireland.

There is no shortage of sights or sporting activities if either is your preference, but most visitors reach this part of Ireland during the summer months when the region is basking in sunshine. It is hardly the Mediterranean, but the July and August temperatures in the South-east are consistently higher than in any other part of Ireland and the nature of the sheltered, sandy beaches makes most of them ideal for family holidays.

COMMUNICATIONS

The South-east has recently opened its own small international airport at Waterford, and there is a small airstrip just outside Wexford which is available to private aircraft. Daily services are operated by Ryanair from London's Stansted airport to Waterford. The region is easily accessible from Dublin airport by regular coach service, although to reach Waterford from there will take you approximately twice the time it took to fly from London in the first place. There is, however, a daily car-ferry link from

Fishguard and Pembroke Dock to Rosslare Harbour which takes about four hours. Also Irish Ferries travel between Rosslare and Le Havre/Cherbourg.

Road and rail connections are excellent; the main railway line runs south from Dublin through Wicklow, Arklow, Gorey, Enniscorthy, Wexford and Waterford before heading north towards Tipperary and Limerick. It does not reach Lismore, Dungarvan or Youghal. The main road south from Dublin is the N11, which by-passes Arklow and Enniscorthy and becomes the N25 at Wexford. The N25 continues west as far as Cork via New Ross, Waterford, Dungarvan and Youghal.

CLIMATE

This region has the reputation of being one of the mildest, if not *the* mildest, in Ireland. The July and August daily average regularly reaches the low 20s°C (low 70s°F) and it is not uncommon for the temperature to climb into the high 20s°C (low 80s°F) on particularly warm days. Even in late spring and autumn (May and October) the temperature is likely to be in the 15–20°C (60–68°F) range.

The winter months tend to be gloomy rather than cold and frequent bursts of light rain have to be regarded as a fact of life during the 'low' season. The east coast has some of the lowest levels of rainfall in Ireland, with the little resort of Courtown enjoying the enviable reputation of being the driest place in the country.

WHERE TO GO FOR WHAT

With the exception of the 'international' *Socialite*, most types of holidaymaker will find somewhere to suit them in south-east Ireland. The *Sightseer* will be impressed with the double cathedral city of Waterford, or the town of Wexford and village of Ardmore.

The *Sun Worshipper* and the *Family Holidaymaker* should consider any of the region's popular coast resorts such as Rosslare, Fethard-on-Sea, Courtown Harbour, Tramore, Curracloe (with one of the longest, safest beaches in the world) and Dungarvan. Although most of the beach resorts offer basic sports, none of the South-east's beaches are particularly recommended for the *Sportsperson*.

Both the *Nature Lover* and the *Recluse* should head inland to the beautiful but relatively unexplored Comeragh mountain range, Forth Mountain in Wexford and the volcanic Tara Hill. The Raven Point Peninsula, in County Wexford, is an officially protected Nature Reserve. The *Recluse* might also enjoy The Pike and Helvick Head, two of Waterford's many attractive and completely unspoiled little villages. There are equestrian activities at Horetown Equestrian Centre (Tel: 051 63706) and Laraheen Day Trekking (Tel: 055 28289). Borohill Equestrian Centre (Tel: 054 44117) specialize in tuition for children.

Although not quite into County Wexford, the town of **ARKLOW** in south Wicklow itself makes an interesting excursion from further north or south as this was another of the numerous settlements founded along the east coast by the Danes. It is expanding slowly as a resort in its own right and has a beautiful east-coast location at the mouth of the River Avoca. Arklow has a good sandy beach, known simply as Arklow beach, a little way to the north, which shelves gently and is well sheltered for safe family bathing.

The town also has a small **maritime museum** in St Mary's Road, with local exhibits dating back more than a hundred years; there is a small admission charge. The only hotel of note is the two-star **Arklow Bay** (Tel: 0402 32309) which has nearly forty rooms, most of which have private facilities. The hotel sits right on the coast, offering great views and opportunities for beach walks during the milder summer months.

The main road south from Arklow takes you to the small town of **GOREY** and into County Wexford proper. The first recorded mention of Gorey was in Norman records at the end of the thirteenth century and the origins of its wide main street can be positively traced to this troubled period of Ireland's development.

Edmund Spenser, the poet, lived here during the late sixteenth century. Interesting sights in Gorey include the town's **Market House**, and the **Roman Catholic Church** in St Michael's Road, much admired by its distinguished architect Augustus Welby Pugin who regarded it as one of his best works. Pugin was also responsible for the Loreto Convent which stands alongside the church. The town's **Church of Ireland parish church** was built by Wellan in 1861 and houses some of the finest stained-glass memorials in the country.

There is a **Tourist Information office** in Gorey (Tel: 055 21248) open during July and August. One of the town's best hotels is the four-star **Marlfield House** (Tel: 055 21124) which also has a very good restaurant. The hotel is a converted Regency period house and lies on the outskirts of the town, on the main road to Courtown.

The riverside village of INCH is worth a detour to see the famous *Innse Mocholmog* legend which is inscribed above the door of the **post office**. This is the last public place in Ireland where the name of the long-defeated royal house can still be seen, and the legend remembers one MacGiolla Mocholmog who was ruler of the old kingdom of Cuala in the twelfth century. The kingdom originally stretched from the city walls of Dublin down to the coastline of County Wicklow.

CASTLETOWN is a slightly larger village which, although it is in County Wicklow, falls within the archdiocese of Dublin by virtue of the fact that the colourful Cardinal Cullen originally consecrated the village church – and decreed that it would remain under his authority. Devotees of Irish history should search out the **grave of Liam Mellows** in the churchyard; he was one of a number of Irish rebels who were executed by the British during the Civil War period in the 1920s.

BALLYMONEY is a small but popular family resort offering a number of sandy coves and a long stretch of fine coastline which is popular with locals and visitors alike. You are now quite close to one of Wexford's most attractive natural features: **Tara Hill**. This volcanic mound stands over 250 metres high and was once part of the estate owned by Dubhtach, Ireland's chief poet. Apart from offering great views from the top it has a small oratory, known as Kildermot, on one side.

The village of COURTOWN is a little way further down the coast, and is one of the most appealing and picturesque seaside resorts in the county. Courtown lies at the mouth of the Ounavarra River and has more than two miles of blue-flag beach to offer. An added bonus is the resort's reputation for the lowest annual level of rainfall in Ireland! The resort has an eighteen-hole golf course and a pier which was built by the Earl of Courtown in the 1840s.

Riverchapel is generally regarded as a 'pleasant extension' of Courtown Harbour and this is where you will find the resort's places of worship. In antiquity, this was the very place where the first Bishop of Ferns (whose diocese covers all of County Wexford), and later the county's patron saint, first landed from Wales. The **Church of Ireland** building was completed in 1861 and is a good example of neo-Gothic architecture.

Nearby **BALLYGARRETT** represents the southernmost outpost of St Patrick's early Christian penetration. A church at Donaghmore, bearing his name, survived until 1859 when the present Church of Ireland was built. On the sea coast near Ballygarrett are the few ruined remains of the Order of Tiron, an Irish medieval religious order which lasted a few centuries.

The coastal village of BLACKWATER is also worth a visit, and you are sure to be struck by its cleanliness and tidy layout which have won it a number of prestigious national awards. Its early history is closely interlinked with legend as this is said to be the location of the 'Ardladhru' which is mentioned in the early Gaelic sagas. More positively, it is known that Ladhru, one of the leading Celtic nobles in the early Middle Ages, had a fortified position on the **hilltop earthworks** just outside the village. Although visitors can see this clearly, it is necessary to obtain special permission to examine the site closely because of its archaeological importance.

Within easy reach of Courtown is FERNS, a relatively quiet town but one of the most historically significant in Ireland. This was one of the earliest population centres in Ireland and is generally regarded as containing the 'root, bedrock and spirit of Gaelic mankind in this region'. In a more tangible sense, Ferns was the seat of both the most powerful noble and the most powerful cleric for a large catchment area. It suffered much more than most early settlements, having been burned, looted, sacked and generally pillaged, on average, at least once or twice every century from the Dark Ages to late medieval times.

The focal point of this unrivalled level of hostile interest was a grand **Cathedral of St Aidan**, a few ruined fragments of which can still be seen in the town's modern-day Church of Ireland cathedral. You can also see the **running stream**, said to ward off evil and be blessed with holy powers, various monastic ruins, a sacred well, and parts of a moated fortress which makes an excellent vantage point for the whole ruined site.

One of Ireland's lesser-known historical figures, one Father Ned Redmond, is buried in the churchyard adjoining the modern cathedral. Although he lived a relatively quiet, undistinguished life, Father Redmond is one of the few individuals who genuinely influenced the course of history. Whilst he was training for the priesthood in France he spotted a student drowning in an isolated stretch of water; he rescued the young man from certain death and, in later years, the student took the name Napoleon Bonaparte. The rest, one might say, is history . . .

Two other villages of interest in the immediate area are **CAMOLIN** and **CLOUGH**. Camolin grew up in the sixteenth century as more and more Englishmen came to settle in this part of Ireland. Lord Mountnorris, who served with the Camolin Yeomen Cavalry, had his country residence here.

The village of Clough was witness to one of the most decisive moments of the 1798 Rebellion when a well-armed Crown corps, led by Colonel Theodore Walpole, was attacked on its way to prevent rebel forces marching on Dublin. The Crown forces were overwhelmed by a surprise rebel attack and their captured artillery was turned against them. The end result was the total rout of the remaining Crown forces in County Wexford.

The main road south from Ferns to Wexford is the N11 which passes through the town of **ENNISCORTHY**, which means 'rock island'; it is often considered to be the most attractive little town in County Wexford. The town stands on the banks of the River Slaney, in the shadow of **Vinegar Hill**, and like so many towns in this part of Ireland has had a long and colourful history.

During the 1798 Rebellion the town was stormed twice in the space of four weeks, and on the second occasion, Vinegar Hill was the main rebel encampment until the Crown forces destroyed the stubborn pocket of resistance with heavy artillery fire. That skirmish was the last major confrontation of the Rebellion.

The town has an imposing old **castle** which was built by Raymond le Gros and subsequently owned by the Roche family. Although it saw little in the way of military action, it served as a makeshift jail during the 1798 Rebellion. The building was originally built in the fifteenth century by the MacMurrough Kavanaghs, and now houses the local **county museum** and a new seasonal **Tourist Information office** (Tel: 054 34699, open June–September). It has a good folk section and is open to the public throughout the year, although opening hours during the winter months are limited.

Another reminder of the "98" is the group of **bronze statues** by Oliver Sheppard which stands in the Market Square. The town has a small **Catholic cathedral** which was built between 1843 and 1848 under the supervision of Augustus Welby Pugin. Another attractive building is **St Senan's Hospital** which occupies a magnificent position close to the banks of the River Boro. Historians may be interested to know that the pioneer James Holland, who invented the submarine, and the mother of wireless inventor Marconi both lived here.

There is a seasonal **Tourist Information office** in the centre of Enniscorthy. One suggestion for accommodation is the three-star **Murphy Flood's Hotel** (Tel: 054 33413) in the centre of the town. The hotel has more than twenty bedrooms, most of which have private facilities.

The main road to the north-west of Enniscorthy will take you to **BUNCLODY**, a delightful little town built on the side of Mount Leinster, with one of those all-too-numerous Irish place-names which tend to make visitors smile when they first see them written! This was a busy market town, raised from lowly hamlet status by the Sheriff of Dublin in 1757, Alderman James Barry. Bunclody was also one of the last places in Ireland where Irish was spoken as the first language of the entire community, until the nineteenth century. The **parish church** belongs to the Church of Ireland and was commissioned by Lord Farnham in the eighteenth century. A Victorian writer described the adjoining churchyard as 'the most beautiful rural cemetery in the British Dominions'. The town also has a modern **Roman Catholic church**, built by E. N. Smith, which was completed in 1970.

The town has seen its fair share of military and ecclesiastical disputes over the last two or three hundred years, and the end result is one of the most unusual oddities of ecclesiastical jurisdiction anywhere in Ireland. The town has an old bridge, covering a 'V' shape of land which lies within the diocese of Kildare and Leighlin. However, the portions of land on either side of both the bridge and the 'V' strip are in the diocese of Ferns. The local vicars take the philosophical viewpoint that a diocese has to start and finish somewhere!

When you reach Enniscorthy be sure to drive a few miles north-west to see **KILTEALY**, a quiet little village which stands at the head of the **Sgollogh Gap**. This was one of the major passing points for travelling traders in the days before the railways came to Ireland and remains an outstanding beauty spot. Father Mogue Kerins, one of the heroes of the 1798 Rebellion, was born in the village.

Another village near here, **KILLANNE**, has a similar association with John Kelly, another of the central figures in the "98'. He was born in the house now occupied by Robert Rackard, himself one of the region's local sporting heroes. Kelly fought bravely during the Rebellion but was eventually captured after being wounded, and was subsequently hanged. Killanne has a much earlier association, however, with Ireland's religious beginnings, and the shapes of both its churchyard and graveyards are reckoned to indicate the site of an early Christian place of worship. Much of the traditional **circular stone bank** around the Church of Ireland still stands, and before the Dissolution of the Monasteries in the sixteenth century, the area was known to be served by the Cistercian monks of Graiguenamanagh. There is an **'ancient blessed well'** near the churchyard which is dedicated to St Anne, Mother of the Blessed Virgin.

Wexford

Wexford is the county town of this part of south-east Ireland and nestles in the heart of one of the country's most mysterious regions. The region is known simply as 'the Forth', which is short for *fór-tuatha mara* – literally 'the land of the foreign people by the sea'. A separate dialect, Yola, survived in this corner of Ireland as late as the nineteenth century, and a handful of words (including *stuke* which means a fierce woman) can still be heard.

The village of 'Weissfjord' was one of the first recorded Viking settlements in Ireland, although the town's origins predate that by several centuries. It was known to the early Gaels as Loch Garman, and to Ptolemy of Alexandria as Menapia at the end of the second century AD.

The town reached the zenith of its military power in the eleventh century when Diarmuid MacMaelnambo became the strongest of several senior county kings in Ireland. He achieved the distinction of being the last king of Ireland to lay siege to an English city, Bristol, when he launched a major amphibious operation in 1068, just two years after the Norman invasion of England. Successive Norman kings of England launched counter-attacks against Diarmuid MacMaelnambo's successors, and the Irishmen's bold defence was the origin of what is today regarded as 'the Irish question'.

Wexford continued to be fought over in the centuries which followed; Richard II personally led the English attack in 1394. However, in more modern times, an amicable Anglo-Irish peace has prevailed and during the First World War Wexford was 'host' to a British submarine detection base, an airship base, an American seaplane base, and a battery of large guns. During the Second World War, of course, the Irish Republic remained neutral.

The people of Wexford remain very proud of their town's long history and there is a flourishing Old Wexford Society which offers guided walking tours to interested visitors. They can usually be contacted at the Talbot and White's hotels (addresses and telephone numbers follow in the accommodation section). A good way to see the town other than on foot, is by bicycle and these can be hired through **Hayes** at 108 South Main Street (Tel: 053 22462). The town is home to the famous annual opera festival held in October. It has four blue-flag beaches at Courtown, Curracloe, Rosslare and Duncannon. The **Tourist Information office** is located at Crescent Quay (Tel: 053 23111) and is open all year round.

Wexford's most attractive historic building, **Johnstown Castle**, actually lies three miles south of the town. Evidence of settlement in and around this beautiful spot dates back many centuries, although the present castle is less than 200 years old. The castle itself is an agricultural research centre not open to the public, but the gardens and one of Ireland's finest agricultural museums, in the grounds, are open all year round. Opening hours are 0900–1730.

In the town the **Westgate Tower** is the only surviving fortified gateway from the five which the town once had. King Henry II spent Lent here in 1172, after the accidental murder of Thomas à Becket. It has been completely renovated by Wexford Corporation who received a 'Europa Nostra' Award in 1990. It is not open to the public at present but it can be viewed from the courtyard. The ruined **Selskar Abbey**, quite nearby, was the place where the first of several historic treaties between the Irish and the Normans was sealed in the mid-twelfth century. A more modern church building is **St Doologue's**, in the town's main street, which lies at the heart of the smallest parish in Ireland (covering barely three acres).

The **Franciscan Church** in John Street stands on the site of a thirteenth-century Franciscan friary and contains the bones of St Adjutor, a Roman child who was murdered by his father. The bones were gifted to the parish by Pope Pius IX in 1856 and are now buried beneath the altar.

Five miles to the south of the city is **Rathmacknee Castle**, a well-preserved tower house dating from the fifteenth century which is open to the public throughout the year. The **Irish National Heritage Park** (Tel: 053 41733/41911) at Ferrycarrig is on a thirty-acre site overlooking the River Slaney. It has full-size replicas of early Irish burial places, monastery buildings, living areas and includes examples of crannogs or motte and bailey. It is well worth a visit, although there is quite a lot of walking to be done to get round the exhibits. The Park is open from April to end October between 0900 and 1900. Family tickets are available.

Wexford has an excellent selection of hotels, guesthouses and restaurants, although there is little for the budget traveller other than a range of bed and breakfast establishments – the Tourist Information office has details. Good town hotels include **White's** (Tel: 053 22311) in George Street, with more than sixty pleasant rooms, and the **Talbot** (Tel: 053 22566) in Trinity Street, which has 103 bedrooms and a good leisure centre which includes a heated indoor swimming pool. The **Ferrycarrig** (Tel: 053 22999), at Ferrycarrig Bridge, also stands in its own grounds and has forty rooms, many with beautiful views over the River Slaney. Apart from eating in the hotels already mentioned, the **Farmer's Kitchen** (Tel: 053 23295), just outside the town on the main road to Rosslare, is a good restaurant if you are looking for hearty, traditional Irish cooking.

ROSSLARE HARBOUR lies about fourteen miles to the south of Wexford and is rapidly expanding as one of Ireland's main ferry ports, with daily sailings to and from Fishguard, Pembroke, Cherbourg and Le Havre. Although one or two hotels, shops, and even a church have sprung up in recent years, Rosslare Harbour cannot be considered a holiday destination in itself, rather a convenient arrival and departure point for visitors to Southern Ireland who are not travelling by air. The harbour now has a fine new terminal building, one of the best in Europe, with a bar, restaurant, shops, railway station, facilities for the disabled, tourist office and other travel services. Irish Ferries, the B&I Line and Sealink all dock at Rosslare.

Five miles north, however, lies the village of **ROSSLARE** which is expanding swiftly as a seaside resort. George Bernard Shaw spent many long summers here and captured the almost timeless atmosphere when he wrote: 'I was lost in dreams here.' Rosslare has about six miles of golden beach which cover both sides of a narrow promontory stretching out into Wexford Harbour.

There is a **Tourist Information office** at Rosslare Harbour (Tel: 053 33232) which can usually help with finding accommodation in Rosslare proper. There are a number of good hotels, the best of which are the four-star **Cedars Hotel** (Tel: 053 32124), with its smart leisure centre; and the Grade A **Great Southern Hotel** (Tel: 053 33233) which has nearly a hundred bedrooms, an indoor swimming pool, and a superb clifftop location overlooking the harbour. The **Hotel Rosslare**, also Grade A, is located a short distance from the ferry port. Popular with the Irish themselves is **Kellys Hotel** at Rosslare (Tel: 053 32114).

Rosslare is relatively close to one of the oldest and most venerated places of pilgrimage in Ireland: **Our Lady's Island**, which stands in Our Lady's Lake. This is thought to be part of a pre-Christian network of places of worship, although when Christianity swept through Ireland in the wake of St Patrick's mission, St Ibar 'absorbed' the island into the Christian church. Today it is dedicated to the Blessed Virgin and contains the ruins of an **Augustinian priory** and a **Norman castle**, which was built by Rudolf de Lamporte in the first half of the thirteenth century. There is a new boardsailing centre in Rosslare providing tuition and equipment, hire and storage. Information from any Tourist Information office in the area. There is a **Tourist Information office** at **KILRANE** (Tel: 053 33232) a mile from the ferry port on the N25. This is useful for car passengers coming from the ferry.

Continuing round the south-eastern tip of Ireland, try to make at least a brief visit to the picturesque fishing village of **KILMORE QUAY**. The village's **harbour** was reconstructed as a model harbour, after extensive research at Trinity College, in order to take weather and wave factors into consideration. Bird-watchers can take a boat from here to the nearby sanctuary islands of Saltee, and geologists regularly visit this part of Ireland to examine the surrounding rocks which are said to be among the oldest in Europe. It is here that the **Maritime Museum** is aboard the light ship *Guillemot*. It is open during the summer months and by prior arrangement (Tel: 053 23111).

A little way inland, BRIDGETOWN is as far south as you can get by train, but the village has little to recommend a stop. The village of DUNCORMICK is more picturesque, having grown up in the Dark Ages around the ancient **fortress** of Cormack. It stands on the river and it was here that Meiler Fitzhenry, from Henry I of England's illegitimate line, built a large castle. Inexplicably, the derelict building collapsed during the nineteenth century and practically nothing remains today.

CARRIG-ON-BANNOW offers fine views over **Saltee Islands** and further out to sea. **Bannow Island**, lying at the southern tip of the mainland, is now more of a peninsula than an island thanks to the silting-up in the seventeenth century of the deep-water channel which used to separate it from the coast. This ended maritime commerce in Bannow Bay, which in the Middle Ages had been both busy and prosperous. You can still visit the town's **parish church**, said to date back to 1260.

One of the best vantage points for Bannow's silted harbour is **Wellington Bridge**, on the River Corrach. The scale of the silting is most graphically revealed when you realize that the boggy fields on either side of the bridge have formed where once the Celtic Sea flowed. The river once formed the boundary between the Norman and Gaelic parts of County Wexford.

Inland a little way, TAGHMON is at the junction of a number of major roads. A large monastic complex was established here in early Christian times and St Fintan Munn lived and worshipped here. In more recent times the Reverend H. F. Lyte, composer of the favourite hymn 'Abide With Me', was rector of the Taghmon parish.

To the north-west of Taghmon, almost on the border between

County Wexford and County Waterford, is the peaceful town of **NEW ROSS**. Its modern-day tranquillity belies a tortuous past, steeped in religious controversy. It has endured at least one fierce papal interdict, the little-known medieval order known as the Curse of the Crutched Friars, and even a brief visit by the Devil himself. As if that were not bad enough, the town became a battleground for rival forces during the 1798 Rebellion and found itself battered by artillery fire on 4 June of that year. **St Mary's Church** and the surrounding ruins are the only sights of note in the town, but it is a good base for touring the surrounding region which is of outstanding beauty. One of the largest collections of sepulchral monuments is to be found in St Mary's Church. There is a seasonal **Tourist Information office** in New Ross (Tel: 051 21857) June to September. The town's best hotel is the three-star **Five Counties** (Tel: 051 21703) which stands in its own grounds overlooking the River Barrow. All thirty-five well-appointed bedrooms have colour television and private facilities.

One of the best-known public parks in Ireland is the **John F. Kennedy Memorial Park** which is quite close to New Ross. The ancestors of the assassinated US President came from nearby Dunganstown and a few Kennedys still live there today. The Park contains thousands of trees from all over the world, most of which were donated by foreign governments, and is beautifully laid out. It stands on the slopes of Slieve Caolite which was the main place of encampment for one of the largest groups of rebel troops during the "98".

Be sure to visit **Dunbrody Abbey**, which is undoubtedly one of the most beautiful ruined abbeys in Ireland. It was founded in 1210 and was known for several hundred years as the Abbey of St Mary of Refuge. The last abbot was Alexander Devereux who, when forced to surrender the abbey to the Crown, was created the first Bishop of Ferns by Henry VIII in 1539. Under the short but bloody reign of Mary I, Devereux became the common link in the apostolic succession for both Roman Catholic and Anglican churches.

The village of **BALLYHACK** is the main ferry point for south Munster, although between the thirteenth and sixteenth centuries it was better known as a place of hospitality for the Knights Templar and Knights Hospitaller. A car-ferry service operates between Ballyhack and Passage East in County Waterford. This saves a car journey of thirty miles. **DUNCANNON** is another of Wexford's ancient villages with origins dating back to the time of Finn MacCool and the Fianna during the third century AD. Duncannon had an obvious strategic attraction in its close location to Waterford Harbour, and a remarkable cross-section of kings and noblemen have paraded themselves along Duncannon's cobbled streets. In relatively recent centuries, Duncannon's 'visitors' have included Napoleon, James II (who was soon destined to lose his crown) and William of Orange (who had just won the crown from James II).

A little way down from Duncannon, at the very point where the southern tip of Ireland meets the Atlantic, is **Hook Head**. One of the oldest **lighthouses** in Europe still burns at the Head and a beacon has been recorded here since early Christian times when monks used to keep it alight. Ancient monks' cells have been discovered at the base of the lighthouse, but permission from the authorities is necessary if you wish to visit them independently. The modern lighthouse at Hook Head is built upon a Norman tower, the first stone lighthouse of which traces can still be seen. Hook Head is named after a Welsh missionary, Dubhan, whose name is the Irish word for 'hook'. Fishing from Hook Head is said to be first-class, although you are well advised to hire a local boatman as hidden rocks in and around the Head have surprised many an unwary mariner.

There is a scenic drive around the Hook Peninsula – the Ring of Hook – taking in the places mentioned above. One of many historical sites in the area is **Tintern Abbey**, a sister foundation to the Welsh establishment, founded by William Marshall in the early thirteenth century as a result of a vow he had made on a sea voyage from Wales, during which his ship nearly foundered. To gain God's blessing, he promised to establish a monastery wherever his ship landed safely in Ireland and colonized it with Cistercian monks from Tintern in Wales. It was dissolved as an abbey in 1540, and subsequently became the ancestral home of the Colclough (pronounced Coke-lee) family. They originated from

Staffordshire and the last descendant vacated the Abbey in 1959. It is now conserved as a national monument by the Office of Public Works.

Baginbin, formerly known as Dundonnell, is another fortress in the sprawling network of defences overlooking the sea around this point. Romantic Irish folklore recalls that 'at the creek of Baginbin, Ireland was lost and won' although history records a slightly less simplistic twelfth-century attack and counter-attack by the Norman Raymond 'le Gros' and Diarmuid MacMurrough. The latter eventually won, and proved it to a fleeing Raymond by breaking the legs of seventy captured Normans and throwing the screaming cripples over the cliffs into the sea.

Waterford

If you continue just a little way west you will cross into County Waterford, an area which combines some of Southern Ireland's finest scenery with many fascinating reminders of a long and often turbulent history. Stretching from the rugged cliffs around Waterford Harbour to the gentle inlet at Youghal Bay, it is not difficult to see why this diverse county attracts so many visitors each year.

As you tour Waterford it is helpful to know something of the county's geology in order to understand many of the natural features which you will see. The northern part of the county has a shale base, but from the Barrow river across to Stradbally on the Atlantic coast there are volcanic rocks. Three small mountain ranges, the Comeragh, Monavullagh and Knockmealdown, are formed from ancient red sandstone. The remaining, south-west corner of County Waterford has a soft, fertile limestone base which can be clearly seen in and around Dungarvan, Cappoquin and Lismore.

Waterford is one of several counties in Ireland where there is some outstanding forestry. All Ireland's roads were renumbered in 1980 so take note if you happen to be using an old guidebook to explore any of more than 400 designated forest areas in Ireland.

There are more than thirty of these in Waterford alone and what follows is a selection of about a dozen which are within easy reach of the larger towns and villages.

Ballylemon/Colligan Wood (Baile Uí Loimín): picnic site, and forest riverside walks; about five miles north-west of Dungarvan on the R672 to Clonmel.

Ballyscanlan (Baile Uí Scanláin): picnic site, forest and lakeshore walks, and several good viewing places; three miles west of Tramore on the R675 towards Dungarvan; turn right onto a third-class road for about a mile.

Carnglass (An Carn Glas): lay-by, picnic site and forest walks; eight miles south of Cappoquin, on third-class roads, heading towards Youghal; on west side of Blackwater less than two miles south of Ballyphillip.

Coolfin/Glenhouse Wood (An Chúil Fhionn): forest walks and rhododendron paths; less than a mile south of Portlaw on a third-class road leading towards the village of Kilmacthomas.

Dromana (Drom Eanaigh): lay-by, picnic site, forest and riverside walks, and a remarkable Hindu-Gothic arch; four miles south of Cappoquin on a third-class road leading towards Villierstown; on the east side of Blackwater.

Gairha (An Gaorthadh): lay-by, picnic site and forest walks; three miles west of Lismore on the R666 heading towards Fermoy (via Ballyduff); on right-hand side of the road.

Glendalligan North (Gleann Dealgan Thuaidh): forest walks and a popular vantage point; five miles north-east of Dungarvan on the N25 to Waterford; turn left for about a mile and a half.

Kilclooney (Cill Chluana): picnic site, forest and lakeshore walks, and access to Crotty's Rock; nine miles south-west of Carrick-on-Suir, on the R676 heading towards Dungarvan.

Killahaley (Coill Dá Sháil): lay-by, picnic site, forest walks and scenic views; three miles south-east of Lismore on a third-class road; lies on the west side of the River Blackwater.

Knockeen (An Cnoicín): lay-by, picnic site and access to Sugar Loaf Rock; about a mile south-west of Waterford on N25 heading towards Dungarvan; turn left for three miles on a third-class road.

Macollop Glen (Gleann Mhaigh Cholpa): picnic site, rhododendron paths and forest walks; six miles west of Lismore on the R666 towards Fermoy (via Ballyduff); turn right for about half a mile.

Rockets Castle/Curraghmore (Cúirt an Roicéalaigh): picnic site and forest walks; two miles north-east of Portlaw on the R680 towards Carrick-on-Suir; on the right-hand side of the road and adjacent to the River Suir.

Strancally Wood (Coill Shrón Chaillì): forest walks and good viewing points; seven miles east of Tallow on third-class roads, on the south side of the River Bride; on the west side of Blackwater.

The city of **WATERFORD** developed early and was a strong 'city state' of independent and mercenary alliances by the twelfth century. It received its formal charter from King John in 1205, a decade before the English barons forced him to put his seal to Magna Carta. The growing town witnessed many brutal battles between Waterford Norsemen, rival Irish clans, and invading English forces, but a new era of relative peace began in 1170 when the Norman commander, Strongbow, married the daughter of Diarmuid MacMurrough, King of Leinster.

During the sixteenth and early seventeenth centuries Waterford became the centre of intrigue and resistance to the anglicization of Irish religion, and the Catholic counter-revolution effectively started here. One of the leaders of the Catholic fightback was Luke Wadding, a Franciscan, who was destined to become the only Irishman to be proposed and voted upon during a papal conclave, in 1644. No Irishman has ever been elected to the papacy itself. Today Waterford is a flourishing town with a population of around 40,000, although technically it is a double cathedral 'city'. Both the Roman Catholic Bishop of Waterford and Lismore, and the Church of Ireland Bishop of Waterford have their cathedral bases in the town.

Of the two, the **Catholic Cathedral** in Barron Strand Street is slightly the less attractive to visit, having been built towards the end of the eighteenth century by a Waterford

Protestant, John Roberts. A number of holy treasures were uncovered during the building of the cathedral and these can now be seen in the National Museum in Dublin. The architect Roberts was the great-grandfather of Field Marshal Lord Roberts VC, the distinguished (if controversial) English military figure from the late nineteenth and early twentieth century.

The **Church of Ireland Cathedral**, generally known as Christ Church or Trinity Cathedral, stands in Cathedral Square and, unique amongst Europe's double cathedral cities, was built by the same John Roberts who created the Catholic counterpart. It predates the Catholic cathedral by approximately fifteen years and was built in the English Classic style. It stands on the site of the eleventh-century cathedral of the ancient independent diocese of Norse Waterford. Look out for the James Rice monument, an effigy of a decayed corpse which dates from the last decade of the fifteenth century.

Waterford's most famous sight is **Reginald's Tower**, originally built as a bastion of Viking authority by Reginald the Dane during the early years of the eleventh century. The circular guard tower was clearly built to last, and most of the ten-foot-thick walls are as sturdy today as they were nearly a thousand years ago when first built. Over the centuries the Tower has served as everything from a royal residence (more properly, a hideaway), an ammunition store, a mint, a jail and a barracks. For more than thirty years, however, it has served as one of County Waterford's most popular museums housing the town's archives and many relics from its long history. Reginald's Tower is open Mon–Sat throughout the year.

Among a number of interesting ecclesiastical buildings in Waterford is **St Olaf's Church** which was originally founded in the latter half of the ninth century and dedicated to arguably the Vikings' most revered saint. The Normans totally rebuilt the church although practically all you can see today dates from an eighteenth-century restoration carried out by Bishop Milles. In this area is Waterford's **Heritage Centre**. This is a well-presented interpretative centre for the Viking and early Norman settlement of Waterford. Open Monday to Friday 1000–1300, 1400–1700; admission £1.

A more striking building is **Grey Friars Church**, otherwise known as 'the French Church' after the volume of French holy men who came to take their pious orders in Waterford after the Normans had made their mark on the country. The Franciscans established a base here in 1240 and Henry III of England later enlarged and embellished the settlement. The church became a hospital in later centuries, once Henry VIII had suppressed its original monastic purpose, and by 1695 it had evolved into a place of worship for the French Huguenots. It fell into disuse after 1819 and the graceful ruins are now a national monument. Be sure to see the ruins of **Black Friars Church** in Arundel Square. These are all that remains of Ireland's oldest Dominican friary, established in 1226 and suppressed three centuries later by Henry VIII.

Visitors with an interest in Waterford's early history should see what remains of the original **city walls**; more survive at Waterford than at any other town in Ireland. The best-preserved chunk of the walls is an old tower which stands in St Patrick's Street, although the actual wall still runs as far as Newgate and on towards the French Tower at the end of Castle Street. Another part of the wall has survived in Manor Street, quite near the railway station, although the adjoining tower is younger than that in St Patrick's Street.

The remains of an old city fortification lie in the Palace Gardens near to the Theatre Royal. They stretch as far as the houses in Spring Garden Valley towards the town orphanage and represent only a fragment of the total fortifications which have been built up and demolished over the last nine hundred years.

Waterford's main street is known as **The Mall**, a wide eighteenth-century thoroughfare stretching from Reginald's Tower into the town. The City Hall and Theatre Royal are the most striking public buildings and both were built by the prolific John Roberts in 1788. The **City Hall** contains a collection of the world-famous Waterford glass, and includes one of Europe's finest glass chandeliers. The Meagher collection is housed in Reginald's Tower.

Catherine Street is Waterford's 'second' street and runs from the Mall to the Court House, which was designed by Sir Richard

Morrison and built in 1849. It stands on the site of another important monastic settlement, St Catherine's Priory for the Canons Regular of St Augustine, which was built in the early thirteenth century. Like so many of Ireland's ecclesiastical centres, it was suppressed on the sweeping orders of Henry VIII in the 1540s. The People's Park, close to the Court House, is a popular place to relax for an hour or so during the milder months.

Among the other places of interest in Waterford are the **Chambers of Commerce and Harbour Commissioners**, another of John Roberts' buildings which dates from 1795; the **infirmary** (John Roberts again, in 1770); **Mount Sion**, in Barrack Street, which was the site of Ignatius Rice's first religious order in a movement which was to cover the globe; and **St Patrick's Church**, one of the town's oldest places of Catholic worship.

No visit to Waterford would be complete without learning something about the beautiful crystal for which the town is so justly famous. The **Waterford Glass Factory** where the crystal is made lies a mile or so outside the town and free guided tours are available all year round between 0900 and 1630, Monday to Friday. It is best to make an appointment by calling the factory on 73311. Although the full production cycle can be seen, it is not normally possible to buy Waterford glass at the factory itself, apart from a few exclusive pieces which can be ordered. There is, however, no shortage of shops offering a good range in Waterford, Cork and Dublin.

Evening entertainment in Waterford is very good if you are keen to experience something of the traditional Irish nightlife. The town is host to the annual **International Festival of Light Opera** in September, although it is advisable to book accommodation well in advance if you plan to visit at that time. The town's Arts Centre hosts regular musical performances, poetry readings and other cultural events throughout the year. Two of the highlights are the Waterford Music Club and the Regional Youth Orchestra which both have their own 'seasons'. In addition, Waterford has the only remaining Victorian theatre in Ireland, offering a varied programme of dramatic entertainment.

As Waterford is the county town, eating out and accommodation are first-class although many smaller establishments are closed outside the summer months. Good eating places in Waterford include the **Reginald Restaurant** (Tel: 051 55087), in the Mall, which is probably the only restaurant and bar in Ireland to feature part of the old town walls; **Dooley's Hotel** (Tel: 051 73531); the **Granville Hotel**, Meagher's Quay (Tel: 051 5111); and two Chinese restaurants, the **Happy Garden**, 53 High Street (Tel: 051 55640) and the **Jade Palace**, 3 The Mall (Tel: 051 55612).

There is very little in the way of inexpensive accommodation for the 'economy' traveller in Waterford, but those with a slightly higher budget should have no problem finding somewhere to stay. Waterford's best hotel is the plush **Jury's Hotel** (Tel: 051 32111) which has a commanding location overlooking the whole town. The hotel has about 100 well-appointed bedrooms, all with private facilities, and an excellent restaurant which is open to non-residents; a leisure centre has recently been added.

One of the finest hotels in the county is **Waterford Castle** (Tel: 051 78203/80332), which stands on a small island at Ballinakill just outside the town. A castle was founded here in 1160 and the present hotel offers exclusive luxury country house accommodation in a refurbished medieval setting. There is a superb panelled restaurant, where you eat off Wedgwood plates and drink from Waterford crystal glasses, and 310 acres of private estate where a host of leisure facilities are available. Room-only accommodation starts at around £100 per night.

Other hotels in Waterford include the four-star **Granville** (Tel: 051 55111) which has sixty-six bedrooms and an interesting historical connection, having been the birthplace of Thomas Meagher; the **Tower Hotel** (Tel: 051 75801) which stands in the Mall; and **Dooley's** (Tel: 051 73531) which is the best of the few relatively inexpensive places to stay in Waterford.

The western side of Waterford Harbour contains a number of picturesque villages which make interesting excursions, either individually or collectively. **PASSAGE EAST** was the tiny port where Strongbow landed in 1170 and, just a year later, Henry II arrived with more than 4000 men in a total of 400 ships. You can still see a late eighteenth-century barracks which is being restored as a tourist attraction. Today the village of Passage East is a small seaside resort with a handful of shops and a reasonable stretch of sandy beach at Woodstown just south of the village.

From Passage East the drive-on/drive-off car ferry can be taken to Ballyhack. It operates in the summer from Monday to Saturday 0720–2200, Sunday 0930–2200; in the winter months 0720–2000 Monday to Saturday, 0930–2000 Sunday. Typical fare for car and passengers would be £5.50 return. For those going from Waterford to Wexford or vice versa this ferry is of great use.

A little further out of the town is Lough Gill, made famous in so many of Yeats' writings. A splendid view of the lake can be seen by taking the scenic route to the top of the Green Road.

A little way to the south lies **DUNMORE EAST**, an attractive village and bustling fishing harbour. The main catches are crayfish and lobster, much of which is exported at once but a reasonable amount of the day's haul finds its way into the hotels and restaurants of the region. The coastline around the village varies from sheer cliffs to secluded beaches and there is a **promontory fort** at Brownstown Head, just before you reach Tramore Bay. At the townland of Harristown you can see a remarkable V-shaped **Bronze Age grave site** set in a round cairn. At the time of its discovery this was one of the most important prehistoric sites in Southern Ireland. Places to stay include the **Candle Light Inn** on the sea front. Self-catering holiday villas are also available (Tel: 051 72800).

As its name implies, Tramore Bay is dominated by the village of **TRAMORE**, one of the liveliest resorts in this part of Ireland and not unfairly called 'one of the great seaside resorts of the Atlantic coast' by the Irish Tourist Board. The village itself is compact and unremarkable with a reasonable selection of shops and basic amenities (chemist, post office, bank and so on). There is a seasonal **Tourist Information office** (Tel: 051 81572) in the centre of the resort which is open during July and August.

 Its unrivalled attraction for thousands of visitors each summer, however, is its outstanding beach; more than

Above: Dublin's famous Georgian houses
Below: One of Dublin's traditional (and popular) pubs
Right: Phoenix Park, Dublin

St Kevin's Kitchen, Glendalough, Co. Wicklow   Blarney Castle, Co. Cork

Cashel Rock, Co. Tipperary   Clonmacnoise, Co. Offaly

Colourful John's Street, Waterford

The harbour at Passage East, Waterford

Left: Sailing off Howth Head
Below: Fishing in Killykeen Forest Park, Co. Cavan

Right: The beach and harbour at Derrynane in the Ring of Kerry
Right below: Pony-trekking in the Gap of Dunloe near Killarney

Left: The beautiful Irish Gardens on Garinish Island, off Co. Cork
Below: Bunratty Castle, Co. Clare

Above: Connemara Mountains, Co. Galway
Right: Cliffs of Moher, Co. Clare

Inisheer, Aran Islands

Twelve Bens, Connemara, Co. Galway

Dunluce Castle, Co. Antrim

Giant's Causeway, Co. Antrim

three miles of gently curving golden coastline which dips into the mild Gulf Stream Atlantic water. This is a bathers' paradise and the perfect spot for sun lovers and family holidays; this is one of the rare all-round resorts in Ireland where even the socialite and the watersports enthusiast are likely to find more than enough to enjoy a near-perfect holiday.

Apart from the beach, Tramore offers all the facilities of a large resort including a miniature railway, boating lake, numerous seaside bars and restaurants, and the inevitable amusement arcade. An eighteen-hole championship golf course and horse-racing track are also in the area. Other good beaches within easy reach are at the intimate little resorts of **ANNESTOWN** and **BUNMAHON**. From Bunmahon you can see yet another **promontory fort** on Dane's Island. Please note that the fort is virtually inaccessible and should only be attempted with the aid of an experienced local guide.

For the sightseer, there are plenty of possibilities for long walks around the surrounding countryside and the resort is adjacent to a host of chambered tombs, earthworks, portal dolmens and fragments of long-vanished fortresses which date back between two and four thousand years. The sites at **Knockeen Dolmen** and the **passage grave** at Matthewstown are particularly interesting and have been investigated in detail by Irish archaeologists.

Fenor is part of a Neolithic complex, and in medieval times became a stronghold of the mighty Power family, whose castle still stands at nearby Dunhill. A **Neolithic chamber tomb** can also be seen here, complete with a rare earth-fast capstone. The parish of **FENOR** has two attractive Roman Catholic churches which were both the work of the architect Terence Doolin during the last two decades of the nineteenth century.

There is a seasonal **Tourist Information office** in the centre of Tramore although it is unlikely to be able to offer much advice about where to stay if you arrive mid-summer without pre-booked accommodation. One of the few 'economy' hotels is the **Seaview** (Tel: 051 81244) although its twelve rooms fill up quickly. The **Grand Hotel** (Tel: 051 81414) has fifty bedrooms and fine views over the Bay, but costs considerably more for a night's bed and breakfast. A new hotel, the **Majestic**, is due to open in 1991.

Continuing along the coast, the next major inlet is Dungarvan Harbour which stretches out from the small town of DUNGARVAN. This busy market community, with a population of nearly 7000 which multiplies several times during the summer months, is another of County Waterford's popular seaside resorts. For generations this was one of the most fiercely independent corners of Ireland, its people bound together by the ancient Irish language. The language has survived, against all odds, in the adjoining An Rinn (Ring) peninsula and local people remain proud of the county's distinctive accent. An **Irish Language College** on the peninsula flourishes each summer as growing numbers of young people are keen to remember an integral part of their country's heritage.

Dungarvan lies in an area of outstanding natural beauty and whichever way you approach the town you cannot fail to be impressed. The Comeragh and Monavullagh mountains envelop the peninsula, and make Dungarvan an ideal base for a climbing or walking holiday. Three new hotels in Dungarvan are **Lawlers** (Tel: 058 41056), **Clohea Strand Hotel and leisure Centre** (Tel: 058 42416) and the **Park Hotel** (Tel: 058 42899). There is a seasonal **Tourist Information office** (Tel: 058 41741) in the centre of the town.

In earlier centuries the surrounding mountains offered excellent natural protection to the town, and it is not hard to understand why it quickly expanded as a fortress town; 'dun' in Irish means 'fortress'. Among the surviving reminders of its military past are the remains of British barracks which were destroyed during the War of Independence and a castle which was a confederate bastion during the Great Rebellion. One other site of note is **St Augustine's Church** at Abbeyside, which contains the remains of an Augustinian priory built during the latter years of the thirteenth century.

Helvick Head, just past the tiny village of Ballynagaul, is the beautiful western point of Dungarvan's natural harbour. It is a strangely isolated part of the county and totally untouched by the technology and development which has inevitably changed so much of rural Waterford further inland. Helvick Head is a superb vantage point to admire and respect the roaring Atlantic which crashes against the peninsula.

One of several other quaint villages in this part of the county is **KILMACTHOMAS**, which lies on the main road between Waterford and Dungarvan. This is a popular spot for climbing enthusiasts and nature lovers alike who may appreciate a reasonably quiet resort. It is well placed for the surrounding mountains and it was here that the Gaelic poets Tadhg Gaelach O'Suilleabháin (1715–95) and Donacha Rua MacConmara lived and worked. The actor and comedian Tyrone Power (1797–1841), great-grandfather of the Hollywood film-star of the same name, also lived here.

Heading inland from Dungarvan you reach a part of the county known as the **Nore Valley**, a relatively unpopulated area with a handful of quiet villages which collectively make an interesting excursion. The Comeragh Mountains shelter most of the valley until you reach the Knockmealdowns in the west. **BALLYMACARBERRY** village is the best place to admire the basin of the valley and pony trekking (available through the local public house) is one of the finest ways to explore the area.

The Nore Valley's best-known town is **CLONMEL**, a thriving community with a population of more than 11,000. Technically, only the part of the town south of the River Suir falls within the boundaries of County Waterford; the remainder is part of County Tipperary, making it that county's largest town. To confuse matters further, the entire town falls within the diocese of Lismore. A town is thought to have existed on the site since before the days of the Vikings, and it is known that a huge wall was built around the settlement in the fourteenth century. Parts of the original wall can still be seen although the turreted West Gate was rebuilt in the nineteenth century on the site of one of the town's earlier gates.

The town has a number of literary associations: it is the birthplace of Laurence Sterne (1713–68) who wrote *Tristram Shandy*; George Borrow (1803–81), whose father was an English soldier based in Tipperary, received part of his education here. A more colourful resident was Charles Bianconi, one-time Irish pedlar who created Ireland's first public transport system when he started running his 'Long Cars' between Clonmel and Cahir. Among the public buildings of note in Clonmel are the **parish church** of St Mary, which has a beautiful stained-glass east window, and the converted **Wesleyan chapel** which is now a small theatre. The chapel was originally designed by William Tinsley and has a varied (if irregular) programme of events during the summer months.

Clonmel's **Town Hall** stands in Mitchell Street and contains a fascinating collection of civic regalia which is normally on view to the public. The gold mayor's chain is extended by one link each time a new mayor is elected. More information about the town's history, including the horsebreeding industry which provided much of Clonmel's wealth for several generations, can be found in the museum and art gallery in Parnell Street. There is a seasonal **Tourist Information office** (Tel: 052 22960).

There are a number of good hotels in Clonmel, the best of which is the luxurious **Knocklofty House** (Tel: 052 38222) on the outskirts of town. This small country house hotel has fifteen rooms and a first-class reputation for style and comfort. It has a very good restaurant, specializing in French cuisine and also has tennis, fishing and a leisure centre. Another good country house hotel is the **Minella** (Tel: 052 22388) which overlooks the River Suir. In the centre of the town the **Clonmel Arms** (Tel: 052 21233) in Sarsfield Street has thirty-five comfortable bedrooms, and **Hearn's** (Tel: 052 21611) has twenty-five. Hearn's has a good little restaurant, offering traditional Irish cuisine, and it was here that Charles Bianconi launched his coaching service in 1815.

About two miles south-west of Clonmel lies **MARFIELD**, where you can see one of the foundations of Melaghlin O'Faolain, the medieval Gaelic ruler of the Decies. At Inishlounaght you can see the remains of a Cistercian abbey which was once one of the largest in this part of Ireland. A few tantalizing ruins of the **twelfth-century abbey** remain including the east window, some tomb fragments, and a transitional doorhead. One of the most significant pieces of twelfth-century Christian literature was St Bernard of Clairvaux's *Life of St Malachy* and this was produced at the instigation of St Bernard's 'dear friend, Abbot Comgan of Inishlounaght'.

The village of **RATHCORMACK** lies on the northern side of the Comeragh Mountains and is a place of remarkable solitude amid quite spectacular natural beauty. You can still see the remains of a **medieval church**, complete with a fortified tower, and the ruins of a castle a little way to the north of the village. The site of a small **Bronze Age chamber tomb** is at nearby Milvate, although this is not considered by archaeologists as one of Southern Ireland's most important prehistoric sites.

Back towards Waterford again, and one of the county's most attractive towns, is **PORTLAW**; curiously, this is also one of the least known and is overlooked by most guidebooks to Ireland. It lies on the River Clodiagh and began life as a handful of houses built (in the shape of a hand and fingers!) by a benevolent Quaker family for their mill workers. The first houses appeared in the 1820s and the original Quaker development 'plan' continued until the early years of this century. A small **parish church**, inevitably, was part of the early town although it was not until 1859 that the present stone church was started. The architect was the 'Irish Pugin', one J. J. McCarthy, and it is interesting to note that the modest stone tower was not completed for fully sixty years.

Ten miles outside the town is **Curraghmore House**, still the residence of the Marquis of Waterford, whose family name is Beresford. The house is considered a classic of eighteenth-century design, decoration and furnishing, and it incorporates a much earlier castle which belonged to the Power family. Among the many fine works of art inside the house are family portraits by Lawrence, Reynolds and Gainsborough. Public access to the house and its delightful gardens is possible between April and September on certain days; details are available through the local Tourist Information office, or by telephoning 051 87101.

One other village of interest in the immediate area is **KILMEADEN**, which is well known as the centre of a prospering local dairy industry. Gourmet-quality cheeses and cream are a speciality although the village retains an unrivalled reputation for traditional Waterford hospitality. It has one or two cafés and tearooms and you are likely to find it a peaceful haven.

Staying inland, County Waterford has a number of small towns and villages which offer a diverse range of options for the visitor. **CAPPOQUIN** lies on the Lismore to Dungarvan road, situated amid heavily wooded countryside between the River Blackwater and its Glenshelan tributary. This is one of Southern Ireland's most popular coarse-fishing areas and record catches of dace and roach have been recorded here.

Mount Melleray is a **modern Cistercian monastery** which welcomes visitors and still functions very much in the manner of medieval times. Although the monastery is practically an infant in monastic terms (having been founded in 1832 by Irish monks expelled from France ten years earlier) the close little community supports itself from the crops grown on the fertile stretch of mountainside which the members tend lovingly.

From here you may drive along one of the most beautiful inland roads in County Waterford, the 'V' road towards Clogheen and the Knockmealdown Mountains. The wide panoramic views are magnificent and the next village you are likely to reach is **BALLYPOREEN**. It seems an unremarkable little place, but it was in the village's small **parish church** that one Michael Reagan was baptized in September 1829. Michael Reagan became the great-grandfather of former US President Ronald Reagan, and the President returned to his village roots during a State Visit to Ireland in 1984. A number of his ancestors are buried in Templetenny Cemetery.

After Waterford itself, the county's best-known town is probably **LISMORE** which can boast historical connections as impressive as any town of its size (population 1000) in Ireland. The earliest recorded settlement was around AD 630 when St Carthage established a monastic centre for both nuns and monks. The centre expanded rapidly, both in terms of size and reputation, and very soon students, scholars and holy men were coming from all over Europe to study here.

In the eighth century the centre expanded further under

St Colman and before AD 900 it was effectively a university city with more than twenty sites of learning within its boundaries. It reached the peak of its power and influence during the twelfth century when the entire Christian Church was undergoing a period of reform led by St Bernard of Clairvaux and many Irish followers. Lismore played host to a visit and an extraordinary ecclesiastical conference with Henry II of England in 1171. Centuries of religious turmoil, however, were soon to undermine Lismore's position of strength and influence within the Christian world. Between 812 and 1207 a total of seven burnings and ten plunderings was recorded, including five sackings by Vikings; one of the most destructive took place in 1173, by Norman mercenaries led by Raymond le Gros.

The huge **medieval cathedral** was almost totally destroyed by Elizabeth I's forces, in the late sixteenth century, and within a hundred years the religious 'city' had all but vanished. By 1800 ruins of just eight churches survived and today only a handful of fragmentary remains bears witness to one of Europe's largest and most influential medieval religious settlements.

The town is understandably proud of its history, and there is evidence of the past more tangible than a few medieval ruins and some colourful manuscripts. A relatively modest Church of Ireland cathedral was founded in 1633 by Richard Boyle, the notorious Earl of Cork, on the site of the **pre-Reformation Cathedral**. It houses an attractive chapel dedicated to St Colmcille and a mid-sixteenth-century tomb (of the prelate Meyler McGrath) which is just about the only surviving relic of the medieval cathedral. The town also has a modern **Roman Catholic Cathedral** church built in Romanesque style with a distinctive campanile and altar. Lismore's most famous sight, however, is a secular rather than an ecclesiastical building. The town's enormous **stone fortress** overlooks the Blackwater and was built on the orders of Henry 11. It was completed under the personal supervision of his son Prince John (later King John) in 1185. Four centuries later Meyler McGrath presented the castle to Sir Walter Raleigh, who subsequently sold it to military adventurer Sir Richard Boyle in 1602.

The castle eventually passed into the hands of the family of the

Duke of Devonshire and still remains the official Irish home of the English Duke. The castle is not normally open to the public, although very wealthy visitors can rent it, complete with domestic staff, for a week at a time. The gardens are, however, usually open between early May and mid-September, and a number of old manuscripts from the castle are on display in the National Museum in Dublin.

On the Lismore to Fermoy road there are two small villages which may be of interest. **BALLYDUFF**, overlooking the Blackwater, is noteworthy because of its castle which resembles a fortified house. It was built in the 1620s by Sir Richard Boyle. The village of **TALLOW** was the birthplace of both the sculptor John Hogan (1800–58) and the folk bard of Dunclug, in 1780.

The south-west corner of Waterford has a lot to offer, and a good starting point is the small town of **ARDMORE**, seven miles east of Youghal, which is generally considered to be one of the best shrines of Irish nostalgia in this part of the country. Early legends recall how St Declan, a travelling missionary, arrived here and preached the Christian gospel even before St Patrick spread his more famous message further north.

Ardmore's early Christian credentials were recognized by the fact that a bishop and a diocese was firmly established by AD 1111 by the Synod of Rathbreasail, although the diocese was later merged with Lismore. The early bishops lived at **Ardmore Castle** although this was seized by Lord Warbeck, pretender to the English throne in 1497, and severely damaged in the subsequent siege. It was further ravaged in 1642 when confederate Catholic invaders were besieged by Lord Broghill's heavy artillery. A total of 117 Catholics were subsequently hanged.

The remains of the castle form only part of a collection of ruined early Christian buildings, the best known of which is the **Round Tower**. This tall, narrow stone structure dates from the eleventh century and marks the centre of a holy site where St Declan had his first settlement in the fifth century. The tower stands nearly 100 feet high and is the most complete of several similar towers in Ireland.

The fragmentary remains of **St Declan's 'cathedral'** and the cramped oratory which was probably his home can also still be seen. The oratory is also reckoned to contain St Declan's tomb, and there is a stone-lined grave in the floor. This is a place of veneration and pilgrimage amongst Irish Christians, and the saint's holy day is commemorated on 24 July. Most of the cathedral dates from the twelfth century, when it was restored in St Declan's memory. Look out for the west gable which shows Romanesque arcading and figure carvings which are unequalled anywhere else in Ireland. The nave and chancel display several gravestones and ogham alphabet memorials which are rather uncommon in this state of (relative) preservation.

At the end of Ardmore's beach lies what is probably the most famous relic associated with St Declan: his stone. This weighty object is said to have been used by the saint to carry his vestments and bell across the sea from his native Wales. One of the best-known local traditions is that rheumatism will be cured if you can crawl under the stone; the feat is impossible for those who have sinned! St Declan's well, at Dysert Church just outside Ardmore, is also said to have healing powers.

The village of GRANGE, two miles inland from Ardmore, has one of Southern Ireland's oldest-known graveyards, although most of the obvious tombstones are relatively modern in style. Just off the main Waterford to Cork road, KINSALEBEG occupies a commanding position overlooking Youghal Bay and the Blackwater estuary. The view is dramatic whatever time of day or year you happen to visit, but never more so than at sunrise or sunset.

Two more peaceful village communities worth at least passing through are CLASHMORE, on the Youghal to Clonmel road and overlooking Blackwater, and GORTEEN. The tallest of the surrounding Drum Hills, **Carronadavderg**, shelters Clashmore and this is a good access point for those keen to explore the natural beauty of the surrounding countryside. Gorteen lies alongside a tributary of the Blackwater and overlooks Dungarvan harbour, Helvick Head, and the rolling Atlantic.

The last town of any size in this part of Southern Ireland is YOUGHAL, pronounced 'yawl'. This takes you into County

Cork, one of the largest and certainly one of the most beautiful and varied counties in Ireland. Youghal is an ancient walled seaport town which stands at the mouth of the River Blackwater, although in modern times its walls have seen many more curious visitors than hostile invaders. The town is a lively coastal resort and was founded by Anglo-Normans in the thirteenth century. It was almost completely destroyed during the Desmond Rebellion of 1579 but the townspeople quickly rebuilt the town, the genesis of the thriving seaside community you can see today.

Easily the most colourful character from the town's past was the Elizabethan explorer Sir Walter Raleigh, who actually became Mayor of Youghal for a while. A potato festival is held in the town every year, and legend recalls that it was Raleigh himself who planted the very first potato in Irish soil more than 400 years ago. If the planting took place at all, it was in the garden of the beautiful Elizabethan mansion, **Myrtle Grove**. The house still stands and, indeed, is still a private residence so don't try to wander round the garden!

Another reminder of Youghal's medieval past is the remains of the town's **lighthouse** which was originally looked after by a convent of nuns. The scattered remains of their priory stand nearby. An ivory plaque from a neighbouring Dominican priory is now in the Dominican church in Cork. Much of the coastline around Youghal was used when the classic film *Moby Dick* was made. You are unlikely to see much sign of the mythical whale today, but there are one or two good beaches running west from the town towards **Knockadoon Head**; follow the signposts for Town Trail. **St Mary's collegiate church** is one of the county's most attractive parish churches and includes a monument to the colourful Sir Richard Boyle. Boyle had a total of two wives and seventeen sons; his mother was said to have lived until the age of 147 and eventually died in 1607 only because she fell out of a tree whilst picking cherries!

Youghal's narrow main street is dominated by a large **clock tower** which houses the local museum and art gallery. Also here is the town's seasonal **Tourist Information office** (Tel: 024 92390), which is open from mid-June until early September, Mon–Sat 1100–1900 (closed for lunch 1300–1400).

One suggestion for somewhere to eat in Youghal is **Aherne's Seafood Bar** (Tel: 024 92424) on North Main Street. A good place to stay is the **Hilltop Hotel** (Tel: 024 92911), with fifty bedrooms, all with private facilities.

South-west

INTRODUCTION

The south-west corner of Ireland comprises the counties of Cork, Ireland's largest, and most of the beautifully rural Kerry. It is no exaggeration to say that County Cork alone is a microcosm of the history, geology and anthropology which have helped make the country what it is today; from the bustle of the city of Cork, Ireland's second city, to the wide farmlands and still, quiet lakes, Cork is a truly remarkable place to visit at any time of the year.

County Kerry offers a gentle alternative with few towns of any size and plenty of rolling moorland which has changed little since medieval times. The pace of life is slow and even the weather seldom changes – it usually rains, due to its exposed Atlantic position. This is very much a county for the *Nature Lover*, the *Recluse*, or the *Healthy Holidaymaker*.

In this chapter we continue our tour of Ireland around its coastline, heading west from Youghal where the last chapter finished and concluding just before the westerly resort of Tralee.

HISTORY

Geologically speaking, this is one of the oldest parts of Ireland; Cork is built upon carboniferous and old red sandstone rocks which date back to the prehistoric Devonian age, whereas Kerry was formed as a direct result of vast geological upheavals up to 400 million years ago. For the last 200 million years Kerry has remained above the sea but the rugged appearance of its coastline is due to constant erosion; in another 200 million years it will have disappeared altogether.

The first human settlement in south-west Ireland was by

Palaeolithic man around 6000 years before the time of Christ. Small flints and large stone circles, dating from a slightly later period, chart prehistoric man's early existence in this part of Europe. Civilization as we might appreciate it today came much later – by 500 BC roads, field systems, promontory forts and thriving communities were established.

Christianity reached Cork before the time of St Patrick, through the preaching of St Ciaran of Cape Clear who was probably the first person to spread the Christian word to the Irish pagans. The message reached Kerry by the fifth century AD although, apart from a few early church sites in Cork, evidence of the 'popularity' of the new faith, particularly in Kerry, is sketchy.

The Anglo-Norman invaders brought a number of previously unheard-of religious orders to most of Ireland, and in medieval times, the remoteness of Kerry made it the ideal place of self-exile for Ireland's main ruling families as they tried to consolidate their opposition to the new settlers. Not until the seventeenth century was Kerry finally suppressed and the county's feudal independence shattered by land-greedy English adventurers who were 'expanding' with the full blessing of Elizabeth I.

Both Cork and Kerry suffered during the Elizabethan wars but the long process of recovery laid the foundations for most of the towns and villages which you can see today. A number of homes were built like forts, including Charles Fort and James Fort just outside Kinsale, and the constant threat of a French invasion prompted the construction of a great many circular Martello and coastal signal towers.

The people of Cork played a significant role during the Irish struggle for independence earlier this century and evidence of this can be seen in museums in Cork city. Neighbouring Kerry took a more active interest in preserving much of Ireland's traditional Gaelic culture and is now the focal point of a major revival. Whatever your motives for visiting south-west Ireland, you can be sure of finding a diverse, hospitable region, fiercely proud of its history and unique development.

PRACTICAL INFORMATION

The south-west of Ireland is well connected by road and rail to the rest of the country, and by sea and air to the United Kingdom. As Ireland's second city Cork has a major international airport, some three miles outside the city. Aer Lingus fly daily between Heathrow and Cork and Ryanair operates from Luton. Aer Lingus also fly to Cork from Birmingham, Manchester, Bristol and Jersey.

Road and rail connections are excellent and there are good coach links between most of Ireland's towns and cities. By road, it is 160 miles between Dublin and Cork travelling via the N7 and N8. The journey takes about four and a half hours, an hour less than the 192-mile journey from Dublin to Killarney (via the N7, N8 to Mitchelstown, N73 to Mallow, and N72 into Killarney).

The rail journey between Dublin and Cork takes about two hours forty minutes – but the single fare from Dublin (1991 price) is around IR£27.50. The railway line from Cork to Killarney and Tralee goes via Mallow, as does the line from Dublin if you are heading direct to Kerry. No other Kerry towns are linked by rail.

TOURIST INFORMATION

Cork City Tourist Information office is based at Tourist House, Grand Parade, Cork (Tel: 021 273 251) and is open all year round 0915–1730 Mon–Sat, with extended hours between June and September. Kerry's main tourist office is also open all year round and it is based at the Town Hall in Killarney (Tel: 064 31633). Further year-round offices are at Aras Siamsa, Godfrey Place, Tralee (Tel: 066 21288) and Skibbereen (Tel: 028 21766).

In addition, there are seasonal tourist offices open from mid-June until early September at: The Square, Bantry (Tel: 027 50229); Ashe Street, Clonakilty (Tel: 023 33226); Pier Road, Kinsale (Tel: 021 772 234); Youghal (Tel: 024 92390); Dingle (Tel: 066 51188); and Kenmare (Tel: 064 41233).

CLIMATE

The South-west has a generally temperate climate although Kerry's average temperature is likely to be slightly lower due to its exposed westerly location. July and August are County Cork's mildest months with the daily averages likely to be around 20°C (70°F) with six or seven hours of sunshine. May and June are also bright months, with less rainfall, but the temperatures are noticeably lower.

County Kerry has the distinction of some of Ireland's worst weather, with constant Atlantic winds all year, heavy rainfall (up to 200mm in December and January) and a summer daily average temperature of seldom more than 14–16°C (58–63°F). However, it is the combination of this climate with the rugged, undulating landscape which attracts most visitors to Kerry. Don't say you were not warned!

WHERE TO GO FOR WHAT

South-west Ireland offers practically nothing for the *Socialite*, apart from a few small clubs in Cork and plenty of traditional Irish nightlife all year round, but something for every other type of holidaymaker. The area is not usually rated highly for its summer sunshine but there are good family beach resorts at Kinsale, Clonakilty, Castlefreke and Glandore. There are further beaches at Slea Head and near Dingle but Kerry's weather seldom makes any activity other than beachcombing attractive.

For the *Sightseer* there is plenty to explore in Cork city itself, but other places of particular interest include Blarney Castle (with the famous stone), the prehistoric stones and burial sites near Ardgroom, Killarney, Inisfallen Island, the Castle of Dromore and Ardfert with its famous cathedral.

The outdoor *Sportsperson* will be at home in most parts of Kerry, where mountain climbing and hill walking are two of the county's main attractions. Inland Kerry and parts of north-west

Cork are perfect for the *Recluse* where you can walk for miles without coming across a fellow human being.

It is probably the *Nature Lover*, however, who will find most to see and do across the south-western region as a whole. There are literally dozens of outstanding beauty spots, including a host of forest trails and walks, and selections are outlined at the start of the geographical text for each of the two counties. Among the most picturesque places to visit in County Kerry are: Killarney Valley, Cromane, The Skelligs, Scotia's Glen, Mount Brandon, Caherconree, Glanmore Lake and Sheen Falls; and in County Cork: Fermoy, Kanturk, Lough Ine, Old Head of Kinsale, Barley Cove, Mizen Head, Ardgroom and Gougane Barra.

FOREST WALKS AND TRAILS IN CORK

Ardarou/Old Bride Bridge (Ard na Rabhaidh): picnic site and forest walks; adjacent to Glenville on the River Bride.

Ballintea/Glenanaar (Baile an Seibhe): picnic site, forest walks, scenic views in Canon Sheehan country; ten miles north-east of Mallow on the N73 towards Mitchelstown; turn north for three miles on third-class road to Shanagh crossroads.

Bealnamorrive (Béal Atha na Marbh): lay-by, forest and riverside walks and beautiful waterfall; five miles east of Macroom on the R618 towards Cork (via Coachford); turn left for about two miles.

Bottlehill (Cnocán an Bhuidéil): picnic site, forest walks and a scenic view, twelve miles north of Cork on third-class road leading towards Killavullen; turn right for a mile at Dalys crossroads.

Clashnacrona/Maulanimirish (Clais na Cróine): lay-by, picnic sites and forest walks; three miles south-west of Dunmanway on the R586, leading to Drimoleague.

Coolkellure (Cúil Cheiliúir): forest and lakeshore walks; two miles north-west of Dunmanway on a third-class road.

Corrin Hill (Cnoc an Chairn): picnic sites, forest walks and access to Carntiarna Iron Age fort; two miles south of Fermoy on the N8 to Cork; turn right for half a mile and the entrance is opposite a golf course.

Currabinny (Currach na Binne): car park, picnic sites, forest walks, scenic views, Bronze Age cairn, and a nature trail which can be followed from a leaflet available on site; four miles east of Carrigaline's Catholic church.

Farran (An Fearann): picnic site, scenic views, wildlife displays, and forest and lakeshore walks; eleven miles west of Cork on N22 towards Macroom.

Gortnatubbrid (Gort na Tiobraide): picnic site, forest walks, scenic views and access to St Gobnet's Shrine; adjacent to Ballyvourney.

Gougane Barra Forest Park (Páirc Fhoraoise Ghuagán Barra): car parks (not free), picnic sites, forest walks, nature trails (on foot) and car trail (guide available on site); three miles west of Ballingeary on R584 to Bantry; at the Pass of Keimaneigh.

Inchigeelagh/Coornahahilly (Inse Geimhleach): picnic site, extensive forest walks, scenic views and access to Memorial Cross; three miles south-east of Ballingeary on the south lake drive towards Inchigeelagh.

Travelling west into County Cork, **YOUGHAL** is the first coastal town which you will reach. This bustling resort is discussed in some detail at the end of the previous chapter. The area between Youghal and Cork Harbour contains some fine stretches of coastline and many old castles. **BALLYCOTTON** is one of the first villages you are likely to reach, best known for its harbour and distinctive black lighthouse. Ornithologists may be keen to visit the bird sanctuary which lies a little way inland from Ballycotton Bay.

GARRYVOE is the first of many good beaches in this county; the long sandy stretch of golden coastline reaches down from the small tower house known as **Garryvoe Castle**. A little way inland, **LADYSBRIDGE** is worth a detour to see **Ightermurragh Castle**. This is reckoned to be one of Ireland's finest fortified houses, built entirely from local limestone. The house was built in the mid-seventeenth century for the family of Edmund Supple although it later fell into its present state of disrepair.

Another nearby village of interest is **KILCREDAN** which has a beautiful ruined seventeenth-century church. Sadly the elements have taken their toll through the roofless ruins but you can still admire the carving on Sir Robert Tynte's tomb, and stroll through the enormous limestone headstones in the adjoining churchyard.

The village of **SHANGARRY** is known locally for its fine pottery, made from local clay, and you can still see plates, dishes and vases being hand-made. Neighbouring **CLOYNE** has one of County Cork's two surviving round towers – originally the bell towers of an early Irish church – and you can still climb to the top and admire the surrounding countryside. Cloyne also has a small cathedral church which dates from the thirteenth century and the alabaster tomb of George Berkeley, bishop of the diocese in the mid-eighteenth century.

MIDLETON is one of the larger towns lying close to Cork city. Today it is a busy market town but for nearly two centuries it has been Ireland's principal whiskey-producing centre. Midleton **distillery** is one of the most modern in Europe and now produces virtually all of the Republic's whiskeys, vodka and gin. It houses the world's largest copper pot-still with a capacity of some 36,000 gallons and you can also see what is said to be Ireland's largest water wheel and a beam steam engine which dates back to 1825.

Midleton was once a busy port of Cork Harbour from where troops embarked for many European conflicts, including the Battle of Waterloo. The town has a **craft centre** inside the local council offices where you can see some examples of the local pottery for which the area is well known. Many home-based potters have roadside signs inviting casual visitors to examine their wares and hopefully take home a unique souvenir of their visit to County Cork.

Leaving Midleton by road will take you past **BALLINACURRA**, a quiet old seaport which takes you towards **EAST FERRY**. The village's Church of Ireland parish church nestles amid secluded terraces, and **Rostellan Wood**, to the south of the village, is a peaceful spot to explore at leisure. You can see the few remaining fragments of an old folly tower and an ornamental pillar which belonged to a large country house that once stood on this spot.

Barryscourt Castle lies about half a mile south of the village of CARRIGTWOHILL; this beautiful late medieval building was completely rebuilt in 1585. Another village, WHITEGATE, was a base for American seaplanes during the First World War and even today retains some of the industry which brought prosperity to this corner of County Cork.

From here it is a short drive to **Roche's Point**, with its lighthouse at the edge of Cork Harbour, which offers an excellent vantage point for the entire area. This may be your first glimpse of COBH, formerly Queenstown and now the 'cove' (*cobh* in Irish but pronounced cove) of Cork. The town completely surrounds the harbour and is unusual in so far as it dates entirely from the nineteenth century.

Cobh lies about fifteen miles from the centre of Cork itself and it was from here that the great transatlantic liners and steamers used to sail. The wide harbour was often the last glimpse of Europe for countless thousands of emigrants – whether they were going to the 'New World' of their own choice or being transported because of a criminal offence, which was often no more serious than sheep-stealing or burglary.

Formerly known as Queenstown, after a visit Queen Victoria made in 1849, it was from here that the ill-fated *Titanic* set off on the last leg of her maiden voyage on 12 April 1912; just forty-eight hours later she lay on the bottom of the sea taking 1500 passengers with her. Three years later survivors from the *Lusitania*, sunk by a German torpedo, were landed here and a poignant memorial to those who died stands in the centre of the town. Many of the 1200 who perished are buried in or near the town, or in other nearby towns (notably Kinsale). The town has a small **cathedral**, St Colman's, which, like the rest of Cobh, was built during the last century. It is constructed in a late Gothic style and the foundation stone was laid in 1868. Other sights of interest include **Haulbowline Island**, the **Irish Naval Service base**, and **Great Island** which is linked to the mainland by an old bridge. A **tower house** and **Martello tower**, one of several erected near here during the Napoleonic wars, can also be seen.

Local tourist information is best obtained in Cork itself and most visitors to Cobh tend to stay in the city rather than its (albeit picturesque) satellite harbour town. If you are keen to stay here, one of the best hotels is the three-star **Commodore** (Tel: 021 811 277), which lies within half an hour's drive (less by train) from the city centre.

A short distance from Cobh, across Belvelly bridge, is **Fota Island**. The Fota estate is made up of more than 300 hectares of prime farmland, woodland and assorted parks and is owned by University College, Cork, but a reasonable proportion of it is open to the general public. When the park was first opened in 1983 it included the Republic of Ireland's first **wildlife park** (complete with breeding wallabies who took an instant liking to the Southern Irish climate!) and quickly became a major tourist attraction.

Fota House is also open to the public and has been completely renovated and restored to its original period splendour since it ceased to be a family home in the late 1970s. The house and furnishings date, predominantly, from between 1750 and 1880 and many of the paintings, including some fine Irish landscapes, are considered masterpieces of national importance.

Among the other attractions of the Fota estate are a public bee garden and an arboretum which includes representative collections of plants from China, Japan, South America, New Zealand, Australia and various corners of Europe.

Cork

The county town of Ireland's largest region is also the second largest city in the Republic; with a population of approximately 140,000 Cork is a popular tourist destination in its own right and a must for at least a day-trip if you are visiting Southern Ireland. Its name comes from *corcaigh*, the Irish word which literally means 'the marshy place'. The city stands on marshes originally created by the River Lee; the marsh was drained and the river diverted into two smaller streams which run through the

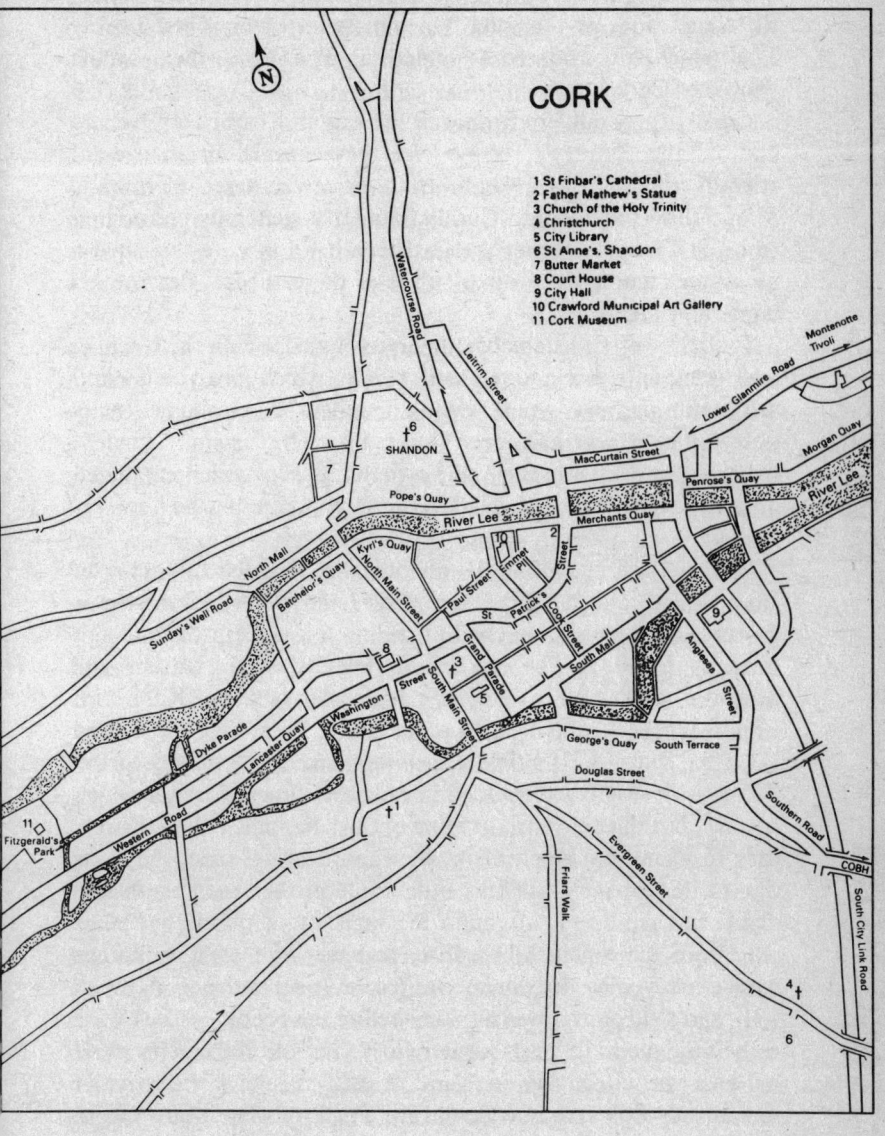

centre of Cork today. Once you know this, you will understand the significance of the song 'On the Banks of my Own Lovely Lee' which is considered as something of a folk anthem by the people of Cork.

Cork is generally regarded as the cultural capital of Ireland and, as the country's second city, has engaged in an age-old friendly rivalry with Dublin. Both cities can trace their roots to antiquity but modern Cork's founder is generally considered to be St Finbar. During the sixth century Finbar established a monastery where the Gothic spires of the cathedral bearing his name now stand.

Finbar's early settlement quickly included a church, a school and eventually became a small village which prospered until the ninth century when Viking invaders destroyed virtually everything which had been built up. They soon returned, however, and established their own settlement which expanded once the agricultural potential of the surrounding fertile land was known.

The modern city of Cork was officially founded by a charter from Prince John in 1185, three years before Dublin, which was a source of considerable civic pride when it celebrated its 800th birthday in 1985. The city briefly lost its charter in the late fifteenth century when local noblemen marched into Kent with Perkin Warbeck, the ill-fated pretender to the throne as Richard IV, after Richard III's timely demise at the Battle of Bosworth.

Large city walls were added in medieval times, parts of which survive, but the defensive location of Cork has never been entirely easy to maintain. Much of its later architectural prosperity was due to the expansion of its butter trade in the seventeenth and eighteenth centuries, although the majority of public buildings date from the nineteenth century or later. Many fine buildings were destroyed by fire during the War of Independence, between 1919 and 1921, but it was not long before the people of Cork were rebuilding their city to its former glory. The old walled city stood on what was effectively an island in the centre of a wide area of marshland. This area now lies on either side of what is now North and South Main Street, and you may be surprised to learn that all the city's main thoroughfares were once canals and waterways where barges used to ply. Even today you must cross at least one bridge to enter Cork and the city centre is a veritable labyrinth of one-way streets, making driving a nightmare unless you are familiar with the road system.

Cork's main street is Patrick Street and it is in and around here that you will find the best shops in the city. The street has a large statue of one of Cork's most colourful characters from the nineteenth century: Father Theobald Mathew. Father Mathew launched a major temperance campaign which quickly spread throughout Ireland, England, Scotland and even to the United States. At its peak, something like 160,000 people took 'the pledge' in a single year. The popularity of the movement declined after Mathew's death in 1861 but a depleted force still remains to spread the word of moderation to the people of Ireland. Father Mathew was also responsible for building the Church of the Holy Trinity (Capuchins) which was started in 1834.

Practically nothing survives of medieval Cork; the only building which remains is the tall **limestone tower** (known as the Red Abbey despite its grey colour) that was originally part of the fourteenth-century house of the Augustinian friars. The Duke of Marlborough is said to have watched his own troops laying siege to the city from the top of the tower, in 1690. Quite nearby, the **South Chapel** is an attractive eighteenth-century Catholic church which occupies a relatively inconspicuous location. The fact that a Catholic church is here at all was a direct result of the relaxation in penal legislation at the time and this was one of Ireland's first Catholic churches in the wake of Emancipation.

Cork's best-known public building is **St Finbar's Cathedral**, an imposing, if relatively modern cathedral, completed in 1870 by architect William Burgess. Burgess was a committed medievalist and his enthusiasm for the late Gothic style is reflected in the cheerfulness of the cathedral's exterior stone decorations. He was a strong anti-Catholic and the relative gaiety of his distinctive architectural style is said to have been his own defiant message to the austere world of Catholic Ireland. The cathedral is open daily 1000–1300 and 1400–1730 with no admission charge.

Christ Church, standing between the Grand Parade and South Main Street, is a beautiful building dating from the eighteenth century. Originally it served as a parish church within the original town walls but it is now the home of the city archives. The **Archive Centre** is open 1000–1300 and 1415–1700 Mon–Fri. The **City Library** is nearby and contains a curious wall which was built along the exact line of the old town wall.

St Anne's Church, in the city's Shandon district, has a famous 120-foot-high steeple. The church is built on the site of a much earlier building which was destroyed by the Duke of Marlborough during the siege of 1690. The steeple is shaped like a giant cruet pot and houses a fine collection of bells. You can climb the tower to read the inscriptions on the bells and, very occasionally, it is possible to have them rung on request. St Anne's is open 1030–1600 Mon–Sat and there is a small admission charge if you want to climb the tower to see the bells.

Other places of interest in Cork include the **Butter market**, close to Shandon, which for years was the focal point of the city's main industry; the limestone **Court House** and **City Hall**; **Crawford Municipal Art Gallery**, Emmet Place, which is open 1000–1700 Mon–Fri and 1000–1300 Sat (admission free); and the city's main **museum** in Fitzgerald's Park which is open 1100–1300 and 1415–1700 Mon–Fri and 1500–1700 Sun (small admission charge).

Cork is a good city to see on foot and much of the centre is marked out with green and white 'Tourist Trail' symbols for you to follow. These assume that you start your tour at the main tourist office, where you can buy a booklet outlining precisely where this mystery trail leads. Cork's main **Tourist Information office** is based at Tourist House, Grand Parade (Tel: 021 273 251) and can provide a wide range of literature about the city and surrounding county.

A good way of exploring Cork and the surrounding countryside is by bicycle – car-hire is not recommended unless you are heading straight out of the congested city centre. Two reliable cycle-hire outlets are **DMD Cycles Ltd**, 18 Grafton Street (Tel: 021 21529), and **Kilgrews Ltd**, 30 North Main Street (Tel: 021 23458). Bus tours of the surrounding area can be booked through **Bus Eireann**. This is the new national bus company of Ireland, which was developed from CIE. Tours leave from the Parnell Place terminus and information is available on 503 399 or through the Tourist Information office.

There are plenty of good pubs, cafés and restaurants in the city centre where you can enjoy just about every sort of meal from gourmet, traditional or international cuisine right down to a quick snack. The Irish Tourist Board lists all the approved options in a very helpful guide to eating out in Ireland but what follows is a sample of the better eating places in three broad categories:

First Class

Fastnet, Jury's Hotel, Western Road (Tel: 021 276 622) – *The* place for excellent local seafood; relaxing atmosphere and live entertainment nightly during the summer season.

Lovett's, Churchyard Lane (Tel: 021 294 409) – Popular among locals for a special night out (which is always the best recommendation); presentation and service impeccable; seafood a speciality.

Arbutus Lodge, Montenotte (Tel: 021 501 237) – The county's best-known restaurant; outstanding gourmet cuisine (traditional and international) and a first-class wine list; expensive but worth it – book early.

Business Class

Jacques, Phoenix Street (Tel: 021 502 387) – A busy, city centre location; varied menu with most tastes catered for.

Oyster Tavern, Market Lane (Tel: 021 272 716) – Seafood specialities (including oysters!) and an informal atmosphere; usually popular with local people so book early.

Economy Class

Canty's Bar, 6 Pembroke Street – A favourite haunt for young people; usually busy and known for its large meat-filled sandwiches.

Halpin's, Cook Street – Probably the best place for cheap food in the city centre; good selection (including vegetarian) but always crowded during the summer.

Bully's, Paul Street – A relatively new wine bar serving a good range of Italian dishes; large pizzas are good value for two and very filling.

Similarly you should have no problem finding somewhere to stay if you can plan your journey as far in advance as possible. The tourist office can help find accommodation but this can be difficult during the busy summer months. What follows is a small selection of the types of accommodation available in the city, which may help independent travellers book in advance.

First Class

Jury's, Western Road (Tel: 021 276 622) – Beautiful luxury hotel, part of the same exclusive group as Jury's Hotel in Dublin; 200 spacious rooms and excellent leisure facilities (including indoor and outdoor pools).

Imperial, South Mall (Tel: 021 274 040) – Fashionable hotel founded in the 1940s; good restaurant and relaxed atmosphere.

Arbutus Lodge, Montenotte (Tel: 021 501 237) – Outstanding luxury hotel with just twenty bedrooms; good location overlooking the city centre.

Business Class

Fitzpatrick Silver Springs, Tivoli (Tel: 021 507 533) – Modern hotel with more than a hundred bedrooms; a short distance from the city centre.

Ashbourne House, Glounthaune (Tel: 021 353 319) – Quiet hotel with twenty-six bedrooms, most with private facilities; leisure facilities include a sauna and heated swimming pool.

Metropole, MacCurtain Street (Tel: 021 508 122) – Recently renovated hotel with more than ninety rooms; city centre location and usually quite busy.

Economy Class

Ashford House, Donovan's Road (Tel: 021 276 324) – Good, clean accommodation in an old house near the City College.

Swansea House (Mrs O'Brien), Woburn Place (Tel: 021 501 441) – Basic bed and breakfast near the railway station.

Gabriel House, Summerhill, St Lukes (Tel: 021 500 333) – Twenty rooms available in a quiet part of the city.

Cork is well placed for visitors to make a number of excursions into the surrounding county. Easily the most popular is to **Blarney Castle**, just four miles to the north, with its famous kissing stone. This is the most visited castle in Ireland, and one of the country's main tourist attractions, although there is little to see other than the famous stone. Cormac MacCarthy had the castle built in the mid-fifteenth century, and certainly expected it to last. The main walls stand over twenty-six metres high and the walls are more than three and a half metres thick at the base – the length of two men placed end to end – in solid stone, every block of which had to be hauled manually from local quarries.

The **Blarney Stone** itself is set high up in the castle walls and is said to give the power of eloquence to all those who kiss it. The legend is thought to have originated in an exasperated comment by Elizabeth I, who was overwhelmed by the non-stop chatter of Dermot MacCarthy, the castle's sixteenth-century occupant, who refused to surrender it to the queen. To kiss the stone you need to lean back within the battlements, hold on to a rail, and touch the smooth object with your lips. It is both safe and hygienic as the stone is washed several times daily!

The castle and the stone can be seen at any time of the year, and you can buy a souvenir certificate to prove that you have kissed the Blarney Stone. Normal opening hours are 0900–1900 Mon–Sat and 0930–1730 Sun. The hours are shorter during the winter months – check with the Tourist Information office in Cork.

The castle stands amid some very picturesque parkland and the village of **BLARNEY** itself is worth a slight detour. The parish church has a traditional 'laird's loft' balcony, complete with cushioned seats and fireplace, which was reserved for the nobility of the castle. Blarney has a large craft centre, woollen mills and, to the north, Lisnaraha is one of the county's best-preserved **ring forts. The Blarney Park Hotel and Leisure Centre** is a Grade A family hotel offering swimming and tennis lessons for the active (Tel: 021 385 281).

To the south of the main road near Blarney are **Howards Mills**, Crookstown. They are owned by one of the county's oldest family firms and thought to be the only mills in Ireland where flour is still ground by stone. A nearby monument commemorates Michael Collins, the first Commander-in-Chief of the Irish Army, and a relic of an earlier era, a **ring fort**, can also be seen a few miles further south. St Finbar of Cork is reputed to have been born there.

The village of **FARRAN** lies close to the national park of the same name. Slightly nearer to Cork you can see the remains of two further medieval buildings erected by the same Cormac MacCarthy who created Blarney Castle. **Kilcrea Friary** is a well-preserved example of a Franciscan settlement but **Kilcrea Castle** is probably the more interesting of the two ruins. This fine old tower house was built towards the end of the fifteenth century and is one of the county's best surviving examples.

Among the other towns and villages in the immediate vicinity of Cork are **BALLINCOLLIG**, a major army base for centuries, where a keep which was built during the reign of Edward III can still be seen. Various ruined buildings beside the River Lee were originally used to make the town's main 'export' – gunpowder. The old powder mill area now forms Ballincollig Regional Park and Gunpowder Mills.

Heading south from Cork towards the coast, you will pass the city's international airport. This was opened in 1962 and, along with Shannon and Dublin, is one of three major airports in the Irish Republic. **RINGASKIDDY**, on the coast, is being developed as a ferry terminal and deep-water port and the modern Verlome dockyard can be clearly seen. In the heyday of sea travel, this used to be an important harbour for the construction of small ships. Ireland's first steam-ship was built here in 1812, and where the harbour narrows to Passage West, you can still admire the enormous drive shaft of the steamer *Sirius* in the car park of the Glenbrook Hotel.

The *Sirius* occupies a special place in maritime history: from here on 4 April 1838, she set out to become the first vessel to cross the Atlantic under steam power. It was a fraught journey as the amount of coal and wood needed to fuel the mighty boilers had been seriously underestimated. Most things which could be burnt were – including the wooden decks – but she made it to New York. Years later, the *Sirius* was wrecked at Ballycotton on a routine crossing to England, but after several years in a water mill the huge drive shaft came to rest in the ship's port of origin.

CROSSHAVEN is one of Ireland's leading centres for yacht enthusiasts. It has one of the Republic's best boatyards and the **Royal Cork Yacht Club** has its base here; the Royal Cork is the oldest club of its kind in the world, having been founded at Cobh in 1720. Among the more famous vessels built here was Tim Severin's skin-ship, the *St Brendan*. From here sea angling harbour trips and cycle hire can be arranged through the Crosshaven Sea Angling Club, Barry Twomey, Whispering Pines (Tel: 021 831 843). Canoeing and windsurfing take place at Oysterhaven (Tel: 021 770 738) or Cobh (Tel: 021 811 237).

Heading towards Kinsale, you are likely to pass through or by **CARRIGALINE**, depending on which route you have taken. The village is well placed for exploring the beautiful coastline of the area; the rugged cliffs are interspersed with countless tiny bays; two of the most attractive are **Robert's Cove** and **Rocky Bay**, within easy reach of any of Cork's satellite villages.

KINSALE is the first town of any size on the coast heading west from Cork. It lies about eighteen miles from the city and its Irish name – *cionn tSaile* – means 'tide head'. It has been popular as a seaside resort for decades, and along with Cork and Dublin, is one of only three town or city destinations which Aer Lingus Holidays promotes in their own right. The town has a beauty and character unequalled in Southern Ireland, and the fact that it is a mere thirty-minute car journey from Cork's international airport makes it a favourite with British visitors. Once Kinsale was a major naval base, although the only maritime activity which you are likely to see now is deep-sea fishing, for which the resort is justly popular.

The modern town of Kinsale was established during the eighteenth century and many of the original grey-roofed buildings remain. The bloodiest date in the old town's history, however, was more than a century before, in 1601, when Irish and Spanish forces joined to attack the Elizabethan invaders from England. More than 4000 Spaniards seized the harbour for ten weeks but they were eventually defeated, with the consequence that Kinsale became an English town (with the Irish refused permission to live there!) for more than 100 years.

In the early eighteenth century a young Scots mariner, Alexander Selkirk, set sail from Kinsale harbour in a ninety-ton ship bound for the spice-rich islands of the Pacific. His ship was wrecked and all aboard perished apart from himself. He was marooned on a lonely island for several years and his subsequent tale formed the basis of Daniel Defoe's classic *Robinson Crusoe*.

The town's main sight is its **museum**, which stands in the early eighteenth-century courthouse building, with a gruesome pair of wooden stocks in the vestibule. Among the artefacts of note are relics from the wrecked liner *Lusitania*, and uniforms, weapons, medals and documents relating to the town's military and naval past. The thirteenth-century **St Multose Church** is one of only a handful of medieval churches still in regular use in Ireland, and some of the *Lusitania* victims are buried in its churchyard.

Just outside the town lie two superb old fortresses, the more impressive of which is **Charles Fort** which was originally built in the late seventeenth century and extensively renovated after the Second World War. It was still in use as late as 1922 and its distinctive star-shape makes it all the more unusual. Guided tours are available and it is open 1000–1730 Tue–Sat from mid-June until mid-September. The second fort, **James Fort**, is another star-shaped construction but less impressive than its restored 'partner'.

Kinsale has a reputation for first-class cooking and Gourmet Weekends are possible with Aer Lingus Holidays. The town's Good Food Circle consists of ten restaurants who each contribute to a **Gourmet Festival** between 6 and 9 October each year, attracting visitors from all over Europe and North America.

Three of the ten, offering expensive, moderate and inexpensive alternatives respectively are: the **Blue Haven** (Tel: 021 772 209), in Pearse Street, offering award-winning seafood dishes in an intimate atmosphere; the **Cottage Loft** (Tel: 021 772 803), at Castlepark, which offers gourmet Irish specialities; and **Max's Wine Bar** (Tel: 021 772 443) in Main Street, offering a variety of Irish and continental dishes in a beautifully converted old townhouse.

There is not a wide range of accommodation in Kinsale, and you are advised to book early for what there is as the town fills up very quickly during the summer months. One of the best hotels is the three-star **Acton's** (Tel: 021 772 135) which has nearly sixty bedrooms and a commanding position overlooking the harbour. Two smaller hotels worth considering are the **Folk Guest House** (Tel: 021 772 382) which is basic but central; and the **Blue Haven** (Tel: 021 772 209) in Pearse Street. The proprietors of the latter also run the superb restaurant of the same name.

Excursion possibilities from Kinsale are very good, and you can see the remains of an early seventh-century settlement at Ballinspittle just outside the town. It was here that the large three-banked **ring fort** of Ballycatteen once stood and large finds of continental pottery have helped prove the region's importance as a trading centre in medieval times.

On your way down to the **Old Head of Kinsale** you will see an attractive beach at **GARRETTSTOWN**, and also the remains of an old manor house. The Old Head, as its name implies, is a long headland with a lighthouse at its tip. You might be surprised to learn that the name 'Old Head' actually comes from the Norse word *oddi* which meant a long, tongue-shaped bit of land which juts into the sea. In ancient times there was a promontory fort on the Old Head although the only traces of any buildings now are the remains of a later medieval wall and castle built by the de Courcys, and a nineteenth-century signal tower. Near the modern lighthouse you can also see what is left of two earlier beacons, including a conventional stone lighthouse which was built about 170 years ago.

The large village of Bandon, or, more correctly, **BANDON BRIDGE**, was one of several founded by adventurer Richard Boyle (the 'great' Earl of Cork) in 1608. Originally it was a walled market town and today it still has a flourishing cattle market. For the sightseer, **Kilbrogan** is the oldest surviving purpose-built Church of Ireland building in the Republic. On Cashel Hill to the rear of the village stands one of the best-preserved hillforts of its type in the country.

Travelling a little way to the north from Kinsale, the main road closely skirts the River Bandon until it reaches **INNISHANNON**. In the days before the railway came to Cork, the river was one of the county's main transport arteries. Ireland's first railway tunnel was cut at Kilpatrick, a little way north-west of Innishannon, although the line in this part of the county finally closed in 1961. The village is a peaceful stopover point for an hour or an afternoon if you are exploring inland Cork. There are one or two pleasing tearooms but no accommodation to speak of, apart from a couple of seasonal bed and breakfast options.

Returning to continue along the coast again from the Old Head of Kinsale, where you can see out to the lighthouse. Please note this is not a place to take small children as the cliff is very steep. You will pass through the quiet little villages of **COURTMACSHERRY** (overlooking Courtmacsherry Bay) and

TIMOLEAGUE before reaching **CLONAKILTY**, the next town of any size. Timoleague stands at the head of a wide inlet, and here St Molaga (who is buried at Labbamolaga, near Mitchelstown) founded an early Christian monastery. A Franciscan foundation succeeded this in the early fourteenth century and the extensive ruins are well worth a detour as they are among the best in Ireland. The village also has a relatively modern Roman Catholic church, with a distinctive round tower, and a road lined with cherry trees leading up to its front door. A castle once stood near the village, and although little remains now, the sprawling gardens can still be seen and enjoyed.

Courtmacsherry is one of the best sea-angling centres in Southern Ireland and the only hotel accommodation to speak of is the modest **Courtmacsherry Hotel** (Tel: 023 46198) in the centre of the village. The hotel has its own large gardens, although less than twenty bedrooms. These fill up quickly so book early.

Clonakilty is a compact but busy town a little further west. It has little to merit a special visit although it is a central base for touring the whole county, including a number of beaches to the west and on **Inchydoney**. This was originally an island but a causeway road now links it permanently to the mainland. Look out for Clonakilty's post office which is housed in a building that was once a Presbyterian church! At Templebryan, just north of the town, you can visit an outstanding example of an early **Celtic church** site. Field fences protect the original round enclosure and a medieval church was constructed in part of the area within this. A further stone circle stands nearby. The village of **BALLINASCARTHY**, on the road between Clonakilty and Bandon, was the ancestral home of the Ford family who founded the motor company. They left Ireland during the potato famine in 1847 and forty-nine years later, young Henry built his first motor car. The rest, of course, is history . . .

The road continues west towards Rosscarbery, although you could make a slight detour south to either one of two superb beaches – Owenahincha and the Long Strand – or to the Galley Head. The latter was once a fortified stronghold and the ruined remains of an old castle can still be seen. Quite nearby is Red

Strand, another good stretch of beach. A short distance inland from the Long Strand is **Castlefreke**, now a gently crumbling ruin but once the seat of Lord Carbery, the aviation pioneer, and inhabited until as recently as the mid-1950s.

ROSSCARBERY stands at the head of a sandy inlet and offers an attractive beach which is popular more for its convenient location than its beauty. In the village you can see the site of a medieval Benedictine monastery which was originally founded by the Order of St James of Wurzburg. Curiously, this short-lived German order was itself founded by Irish monks.

Coppinger's Court is a beautiful example of an early seventeenth-century **fortified house** which stands on the floor of a narrow, fertile valley. In more troubled times it was strongly defended and H. G. Leask described it as 'one of the most striking buildings of the house/castle type to be found in Ireland'. Another place worth visiting in the immediate area is **Drombeg**, a magnificent example of a west Cork **stone circle**.

Glandore is the next major inlet you will reach on the coast and this contains the villages of UNION HALL and GLANDORE. The latter is the more interesting, having been the first 'official' resort in western Cork. This is another favourite spot for sailing enthusiasts and a great **annual regatta** was initiated here in 1830.

CASTLETOWNSHEND is a quiet old village with a single street which slopes down towards the sea. Violet Martin, co-author of *The Irish R.M.* (dramatized on ITV in the 1980s), lived here and is buried in the churchyard. From here you can visit **Lough Ine**, a fascinating land-locked sea lake which is joined to the ocean by a single narrow water passage. It is now a centre for marine biological research, and the summit of the nearby hill (which towers nearly 200 metres above the lake) offers great views over the surrounding countryside and is well worth the climb.

Cape Clear (*Oileán Cléire* in Irish) is an island just off the south-western tip of Ireland. Trips are usually possible but depend very much on the tides. It was here that Ireland's first saint, St Ciaran, was born and subsequently built his first church. The ruins remain along with those of an inscribed pillar and holy well which were directly associated with him.

A ruined castle of much later date stands on the island's headland, as do the remains of a mid-nineteenth-century lighthouse. There is also a **youth hostel** and **bird observatory** on the island and ornithologists can make arrangements in advance to stay and study the birdlife (Cape Clear lies on a major bird migration route). The large rock just beyond Cape Clear is the **Fastnet Rock**, which the yachts in the famous race have to negotiate, with its huge lighthouse, completed in 1906. A passenger boat leaves from Baltimore each day. The times of sailings can be checked at Baltimore harbour. On the island, there are craftshops and a restaurant. It is hilly, but you'll be rewarded with fantastic views. Wear flat shoes and take rainwear!

Sherkin Island is a smaller offshore rock, closer to the mainland than Cape Clear or Fastnet. It can be seen from Baltimore harbour. It has one or two sandy beaches and an **outdoor pursuits and marine biology centre** together with the ruined remains of O'Driscoll Castle and a Franciscan friary. The friary is the younger of the two ruins, dating back to the mid-fifteenth century, and was founded by the O'Driscolls who owned much of western Cork in the High Medieval period. A passenger boat leaves frequently from Baltimore. On a fine day this is a good place to go with a picnic. The only bar on the island is said *never* to close.

Back on the mainland, the main coastal route west takes you through two more small towns – Baltimore and Skibbereen – before the coastline turns to the north. **BALTIMORE** was a prosperous port for centuries and the home of one of Ireland's best-known boatyards. During the early 1920s the boat *Saoirse* ('Freedom') was built for Conor O'Brien who later sailed around the world in her, the first Irishman to circumnavigate the globe. In earlier times, the town suffered a brutal raid by Algerian pirates in 1631 which saw more than 200 people, mostly English settlers, carried off to be murdered or forced into slavery. The town retains its appeal for overseas sailors and yachtsmen, although most tend to come with more peaceful motives in mind! A good little hotel is the **Baltimore House** (Tel: 028 20164) which has about ten simple but comfortable bedrooms. There are a few shops and restaurants in the town and Baltimore Yacht Club is situated on the harbour next to the boatyard. Two sailing schools are based here: Baltimore Sailing School and the Glenans Sailing School. Baltimore also offers a lovely cliff walk up to the nearby beacon.

Although **SKIBBEREEN** is effectively the hub of the day-to-day business of western Cork, it has little to recommend a special detour. It is the focal point of a thriving agricultural community and what industry there is in west Cork is largely concentrated in this town. Unusually, Skibbereen has a large French and German population. Having moved to this beautifully secluded area, they took to practising various fine arts, including painting, sculpting and pottery and the results can be seen today. The *Southern Star*, west Cork's own weekly newspaper, is based here and is noted for its prophetic warning at the turn of the century: 'The Skibbereen Eagle has its eye on the Czar of Russia'.

One suggestion for accommodation is the **West Cork Hotel** (Tel: 028 21277) which is a well-appointed middle-rate hotel with more than forty rooms available – all with private facilities. An added bonus is the in-house restaurant which serves traditional Irish dishes (and some standard 'international' fare) at moderate prices for a hotel of this grade.

The main coast road continues to **BALLYDEHOB**, with its brightly painted main street and enormous twelve-arch railway bridge which carried the Skibbereen to Schull light railway between 1886 and 1947. Mount Gabriel stands nearly 300 metres above the village, although visitors are not encouraged to explore the aircraft tracking station at the summit. Bronze Age miners dug away at the sides of the hill and you can still see the evidence of mine workings dating from as late as the nineteenth century. Take care not to let children explore too near the disused mineshafts. **SCHULL** is a pleasant seaside village just past Mount Gabriel, and a favourite spot for sea anglers. Two **megalithic tombs** lie about five miles west of the village although they are not immediately obvious to passing motorists.

CROOKHAVEN is another popular seaside resort a little way beyond Schull, and was a favourite stopover point for both

British and foreign ships during the last century. Here they took on provisions before the long Atlantic haul. In 1902 Marconi set up one of his earliest radio stations at nearby Brow Head; although it was moved to Valentia Island four years later, the new station retained the original CK (Crookhaven) call-sign until 1950.

There are some good sandy beaches at **BARLEY COVE**, and this is likely to develop into one of the South-west's major resorts in years to come. The best hotel at the moment is the middle-rate **Barley Cove Beach** (Tel: 028 35234) which has about a dozen bedrooms, all with private facilities.

This part of the coast ends at **Mizen Head**, with its striking vertical cliffs; these can be very dangerous so avoid taking children or pets if you possibly can. A lighthouse station is based on an islet which is linked to the mainland by a suspension bridge and this marks the most south-westerly point in Ireland. One sight of note near here is **Dunmanus Castle**, a beautiful old tower house which is set on a smooth ridge of rock. The castle was built by the O'Mahony family during the fifteenth century, and is occasionally used for clan gatherings. Further east you can see a stone circle, Dunbeacon, on the slopes of Mount Corrin. An old cairn stands on the 288-metre summit of Mount Corrin and the hill is a relatively easy climb.

The coast road skirts the long, narrow Durrus peninsula towards Bantry; alternatively, you could detour via the villages of Durrus and Kilcrohane to **Sheep's Head**, the tip of the peninsula, which offers commanding views of the surrounding cliffs and breaking waves. The peninsula is particularly attractive during the autumn months when the dwarf gorse is in full flower on the hillsides.

The small town of **BANTRY** is another of west Cork's many thriving market communities, and is believed by many people to offer one of the finest views in the world, over Bantry Bay. The view is certainly breathtaking, and one of the best places to admire it is from the Georgian splendour of **Bantry House**.

The house was built in the late eighteenth century and contains a collection of art treasures, including fine continental tapestries, amassed by several former Earls of Bantry during the last century.

The house is surrounded by some magnificent gardens, and both they and the house are open 0900–1800 all year daily; between May and September the estate remains open until 2200.

There is a seasonal **Tourist Information office** at The Square in Bantry (Tel: 027 50229) which opens 1100–1900 Mon–Sat between mid-June and early September. One good suggestion for accommodation is the **West Lodge Hotel** (Tel: 027 50360) which has ninety bedrooms, many with good views and all with private facilities.

GLENGARRIFF occupies a superb location a little way further up the coast. It is a small fishing port standing at the head of a wide bay amid beautiful woodland. Its principal attraction is **Garinish Island** whose large collection of subtropical plants and flowers is unrivalled anywhere else in Ireland. George Bernard Shaw was a regular visitor, and you can make the short crossing by boat from Glengarriff harbour between 1000 and 1730 Mon–Sat (1300–1800 Sun and church holidays). The island is only open to visitors between March and October except by special arrangement. A separate charge for admission is made on arrival.

Glengarriff stands against a backdrop of the **Beara Mountains** and you can admire the Glen of Coomarkane and the two corrie lakes at its head which were cut by melting glaciers tens of thousands of years ago. One of the highest peaks is the **Sugarloaf Mountain** which stands 596 metres high; the summit is a steep but invigorating climb and the views very rewarding. Do bear in mind, however, that the weather can change very quickly and climbers should *always* wear warm clothing, take a map (the large-scale Ordnance Survey is ideal), compass and food, and certainly tell someone exactly where they are going. Take care when you are descending as the rocks can often be quite loose.

Other interesting spots to visit near here include Adrigole, where you can climb the 686-metre Hungry Hill, and the fishing port of **CASTLETOWN BERE** which is considered one of west Cork's best centres for exploring the Beara hills. Hungry Hill was the inspiration and setting for Daphne du Maurier's novel of that title. There are a number of old ruins around here, including the castle and star-shaped fort of Dunboy. Here, in 1602, a joint Irish and Spanish force was besieged by advancing English troops led by Sir George Carew. **Dursey Island** is worth a visit, and is accessible via Ireland's only cable-car, weather permitting. It is a long, mountainous island and a haven for a variety of sea and coastal birds.

Continuing northwards along the coast, you will soon cross the invisible border between County Cork and County Kerry. One or two places of interest which you are likely to pass before doing so are **Allihies**, the site of extensive copper mining in the nineteenth century; the village of EYERIES with its five-metre, ancient inscribed stone pillar; and the fine **stone circle** at Ardgroom which effectively marks the end of County Cork.

Before you leave Cork, however, there are a number of other towns and villages away from the coast which you may like to consider, either together or individually, as excursion possibilities. The Kilmichael road, for example, leads to the **Lee Valley** and the **Gearagh**, an ancient marshland with small wooded islands which is now largely flooded by a reservoir which supplies a hydro-electric plant.

The villages of BALLYMAKEERA and BALLYVOURNEY are the focal points of another of Cork's areas of outstanding natural beauty. St Gobnet founded a monastery here in the sixth century AD and thousands of pilgrims still visit the spot each year (particularly on the saint's 'day' – 11 February). Archaeological excavations have revealed the remains of an early medieval round house and a nearby mound is widely believed to be St Gobnet's burial place. The local **museum** contains a number of relics which have been found in and around St Gobnet's site.

Gougane Barra is a dramatic corrie lake, set amid beautiful wooded crags. It is here that the River Lee has its source and wonderful woodland walks have been laid out. An island stands in the middle of the lake as a reminder of the medieval days when St Finbar had a hermitage here before moving east to Cork. The remains you can still see date back to no more than 200 years ago, when Father Denis Mahony built a retreat here.

The main characters from *The Tailor and Ansty* by Eric Cross are buried together in the small churchyard on the way up to Gougane Barra. The book was banned in Ireland in 1942 and caused quite a stir. On your way away from Gougane Barra, look out for the stone circle at Kealkil. The remaining inland places of note in County Cork all lie on a broadly easterly swathe from here, although obviously they are accessible heading north from Cork, or north-east from most of the other coastal destinations we have already covered in this chapter.

MACROOM is a pleasing market town which stands on the banks of the River Sullane. You can still see the entrance to a once-great castle, and the **museum** includes a number of relics from it. The nearby village of DRIPSEY was known for its woollen mills and you can still buy some fine locally-made garments from the one which remains. The original mill was powered from a large reservoir which is now an ornamental lake.

MALLOW is one of inland Cork's largest towns, although it is relatively small by mainland UK standards. This was where the first bridge across the River Blackwater was built and the town used to be a favourite spa resort during the eighteenth and nineteenth centuries, and was known as 'the Irish Bath'. **Mallow Castle** stands near the first river crossing, and was built by Sir Thomas Norreys in the sixteenth century. A herd of white fallow deer, descended from two animals given to Sir Thomas's daughter Elizabeth by Elizabeth I (the child's godmother), graze in the park. Mallow is also the birthplace of Thomal Davis, founder of the *Nation* newspaper at the end of the last century.

There is no Tourist Information office in Mallow but there is a Tourist Information point in the town. One suggestion for accommodation is the impressive **Longueville House** (Tel: 022 47156). This splendid Georgian country house was built in 1720 and has an outstanding restaurant specializing in the very finest home-produced Irish cuisine. Your meal is best accompanied by an estate wine produced by Ireland's only vineyard. The hotel has sixteen bedrooms, all with private facilities, and lies about forty-five minutes' drive from Cork airport.

The last remaining town of particular note is FERMOY, although one or two more northerly Cork villages are included in our Midlands chapter. The town stands astride the River Blackwater and began life as a major garrison for British troops. The old barracks were turned into a German-owned pencil factory after World War Two. Sights of note around Fermoy include **Corrin Hill**, just south of the town, which offers great views across the surrounding countryside (there are a few remains of a hillfort on the top); and the ruins of a **Carmelite priory** at Castlelyons. The town has a seasonal **Tourist Information office**, in Patrick Street, which is open 1100–1900 Mon–Sat from mid-June until early September.

COUNTY KERRY

County Kerry is the most rugged and independent of all Ireland's counties. It is predominantly rural and not dissimilar to the Scottish Highlands. The weather is usually as rugged as the landscape; a whole day of sunshine is rare and, as a result, there are no beach resorts to speak of.

This is the ideal part of Ireland for the *Nature Lover, Recluse*, or anyone looking for a healthy, outdoor holiday far from the smoke and noise of the city. There are approximately two dozen designated Forests and Trails in County Kerry and what follows is a selection of about half of these.

Ballaghisheen/Derreenageeha (Bealasch Oisín): picnic site and forest walks; twelve miles north-east of Waterville on a third-class road leading towards Glencar, near to Ballaghisheen Pass.

Caragh Lake (Loch Cárthai): picnic site, forest walks and viewing points; five miles south-west of Killorglin on a third-class road leading towards Caragh Lake; on the north-east shore of Caragh Lake adjacent to Lake Field.

Berrycunnihy/Ladies' Views (Doire Coinche): lay-by, picnic site and scenic views; eleven miles south of Killarney on the N71 heading towards Kenmare.

Dromore (An Drom Mór): lay-by, picnic sites, viewing point, and both forest and seashore walks; six miles west of Kenmare on the N70 heading to Sneem.

Gleensk (Glinsce): lay-by, picnic site, forest and seashore walks; seven miles west of Glenbeigh on the N70 to Cahirciveen.

Glenteenasig/Lough Slat (Gleann Tí an Easaigh): picnic sites, forest and mountain walks, scenic views; fourteen miles west of Tralee on the R559 towards Castlegregory; turn left for three miles at Augharcasla.

Kimego/Castlequin (Céim an Ghaba): lay-by, picnic site, forest walks, sea views and the picturesque ruin of an eighteenth-century turf-drying plant; four miles north of Cahirciveen on third-class roads, leading to Cooncrome Harbour via Castlequin village.

Lough Inchiquin (Loch Inse Choinn): picnic site, forest and lakeshore walks, and a waterfall; eight miles south-west of Kenmare on R751 to Lauragh; turn left for less than two miles at Coornagillagh.

Mangerton (An Mhangarta): lay-by, picnic site, scenic views, forest and mountain walks; three miles south of Killarney on the N71 towards Kenmare; turn left for about two miles at the Muckross Hotel.

Muckross Wood/Old Kenmare Road (Coíll Mhucrois): lay-by, picnic site, viewing points, forest walks and vantage points; five miles south of Killarney on the N71 towards Kenmare; turn right before the entrance to the Torc waterfall.

Parknasilla (Páirc na Saileach): picnic site, forest walks and viewing points; fifteen miles west of Kenmare on the N70 to Sneem; turn left for a mile at the entrance to the Great Southern Hotel.

Rossacrue (Ros an Chrú na Lua): lay-by, picnic site and forest walks; five miles north-east of Kilgarvan on the R569 towards Killarney; enter from the left-hand side of the road.

Entering Kerry from the south, the first town of any size which emerges from the rugged countryside is **KENMARE**. The town lies in a limestone niche in the surrounding red sandstone, and is very much a planned town, having been built on the orders of the first Marquis of Lansdowne in 1775. The two main streets form an 'X' shape with a park at the centre, and there are traces of an earlier settlement which grew up around mine works in the late seventeenth century.

Kenmare still has a number of its original houses. The market house, facing the park, is the best of these, and it stands close to an attractive **Catholic church** and the **Poor Clares convent** which was built in 1861. The convent's most famous nun was Mary Frances Cusack, the prolific Victorian authoress who wrote a *History of Kerry* and founded her own convent in 1861. Kenmare's oldest site, however, predates the modern town by several thousand years; fifteen huge stones, in a circle, are the best preserved of several stone circles in the Cork/Kerry region. They represent what was known as a **'boulder burial'** and this peaceful riverside location was probably the scene of a number of human sacrifices in prehistoric times.

The town is a popular destination for golfing and fishing enthusiasts, and it is a good base for exploring the natural beauty of the county as a whole. Locally caught fish is a speciality of the town's numerous restaurants and two worth visiting are **Hug's** (Tel: 064 41099) at Gortamullen, and **The Anchorage** (Tel: 064 41024) at Killaha East, which has a distinct nautical theme. There is a seasonal **Tourist Information office** (Tel: 064 41233) in the centre of town which can usually help visitors find accommodation. One of the county's best hotels is **The Park** (Tel: 064 41200) which stands in eleven acres of private gardens. The hotel has forty-eight bedrooms and offers luxury accommodation at luxury rates; the restaurant is one of the country's finest, boasting the only Michelin star in Ireland. The **Kenmare Bay Hotel** (Tel: 064 41300) has a hundred bedrooms and offers slightly more modest accommodation in the centre of town.

If you leave Kenmare by the Kilgarvan road you will reach the village of **KILLOWEN** after little more than a mile. The ruined church was where Sir William Petty's forces, led by his agent the Reverend Richard Orpen, took refuge during the religious struggles of 1689/90. The soldiers eventually escaped to Bristol by sea. Near here, you can visit Cnoc a Cappeen, a most peculiar mushroom-shaped rock which stands some ten feet high.

The **Beara Peninsula** can also be explored at leisure from Kenmare; at Killaha you can see the site of a major hoard of early swords and weapons dating back more than four thousand years. The Kenmare river offers some striking scenery before you head into the heart of County Kerry proper. **Inchiquin lake and waterfall** is one of the most striking beauty spots, and the surrounding forest is believed to date back to prehistoric times. The main road heads left over the lowest of the Cloonee loughs by Ardea bridge; close to here you can visit the remains of one of County Kerry's earliest castles, **Ardea Castle**, which was built on the site of a fort belonging to Aed Bennan, former king of West Munster who died in AD 621. Aed Bennan is one of the county's most colourful characters, not least because he had twelve sons including one whose visions of hell and purgatory inspired Dante's *Divine Comedy*. Aed Bennan also had a daughter, Mor, who married the king of Cashel; their descendants built the castle which is now the crumbling ruin you can see today.

Nearby Derreen was for decades the Irish family home of the Marquis of Lansdowne who was descended from the Cromwellian soldier Sir William Petty. Petty has his own place in Irish history as he managed to survey personally more than two thirds of the country in less than eighteen months. His 'reward' was vast areas of confiscated land, including a quarter of County Kerry, and he was one of very few of Cromwell's allies who actually flourished after the restoration of the monarchy under King Charles II, albeit quietly and far from his native England.

The village of GLANMORE stands amid Glanmore Lough, and the traces of a ruined megalithic tomb are still there. **Healy Pass** is a local beauty spot, right on the Cork/Kerry border, and it is named after Tim Healy who was the first governor-general of the Irish Free State when it became a dominion in 1922. The Pass offers outstanding views across two counties.

When you reach Kilmakillogue Pier you have the option of driving back into western Cork, towards Glengarriff or Castletown Bere, or north again into Kerry. Kilmakillogue itself is named after St Killian, who went to what is now Germany as an Irish missionary in the seventh century and was martyred at Wurzburg in 697. Heading back onto the main Cork to Killarney road again you will find yourself following what was roughly the old railway line – Morley's Bridge stands like a forgotten relic from the days when steam trains used to smoke their way through the quiet Kerry countryside. There are two extinct volcanoes close by, Stoompa and Crohane, and any detour from the main road will take you into some very rough, isolated countryside.

One suggested detour before you reach Killarney is **Temple Fiachna**, yet another **prehistoric burial ground**. The immediate area is noted for its distinctive glacier-rounded rocks and boulders. You can also see the ruined remains of an early Christian church and a *bullaun*, with seven large stones, where corn used to be ground. A terrible disaster is said to befall anyone who attempts to remove any of these stones.

Killarney

Killarney, the tourist centre of Kerry, is set in a valley which is one of the best known of all the Irish places of beauty. Killarney itself is a market town, fed by a wide catchment area, and although it generally gives the impression of being busy, this belies a much more peaceful town away from the two main streets. It was little more than an insignificant hamlet until the mid-eighteenth century when a forward-thinking local magnate, Lord Kenmare, began to develop an embryonic tourist industry. Arthur Young, the English traveller, wrote about the village towards the end of the century, and ever since there has been a steady stream of visitors from 'across the water'.

Today the town has a population of just over 9000, and the principal industry is tourism. The brightly painted pubs and souvenir shops along the main street are the most obvious manifestation of this, although most visitors sensibly spend very little time exploring the town itself as the main sights can be seen in an afternoon.

TRALEE, the county town of Kerry, is the site of the annual ten-day festival, 'The Rose of Tralee'. A town well worth a stop-off, though there is perhaps less for the tourist than in Killarney.

The main point of interest in Killarney is the **Catholic Cathedral**, a fine building by Augustus Pugin and certainly one of the best examples of neo-Gothic in Ireland. Work on it began in 1842, but took a leisurely seventy years to complete. Inside, the cathedral is more a complex of many different buildings, including the bishop's residence and St Brendan's seminary. It was extensively renovated in the early 1970s and the most obvious change was the removal of coarse late Victorian plasterwork to reveal the fine stonework underneath. The cathedral is open to visitors all year round.

Another church of interest in the town is **St Mary's**, in Main Street. It was rebuilt in the late Gothic style in 1870 on the site of at least one much older building (a church of one sort or another is reckoned to have stood there since the twelfth century). To the rear of the church stands Kenmare House, the last residence of the Earls of Kenmare and now the home for life of John McSwain, an Irish-American, who has donated the estate (and the house after he dies) to the Irish State.

Ross Castle, close to Lough Leane, was built by the O'Donoghue family during the fifteenth century although it, too, subsequently fell into the possession of the Earl of Kenmare. This was the very last stronghold in Ireland to hold out against Cromwell's invading forces but even it eventually fell, and little mercy was shown to the occupants. The castle has been altered considerably since it was first built, but most of it (particularly the Tower House) remains unmistakably late medieval.

Killarney has grown up around Lough Leane, and a small island in the centre of the lake, **Inishfallen**, held a monastery for more than a thousand years, from the seventh century. You can still see the remains of a twelfth-century Augustinian priory, and its long-gone predecessor is said to have been the secluded place where the legendary Brian Boru was educated in the late tenth century.

Beside Inishfallen stands **Ross Island** which is actually a peninsula. The ageing woodland makes this a very beautiful place for a walk, and it can be most romantic if there is a low mist floating over the lake. The ruins of Castlelough, built by the MacCarthy Mor family, lie a short distance from the end of the peninsula. Another local spot worth seeing is Killegy churchyard which is the last resting place of Henry Herbert, a local worthy who built the large house at Muckross and played host to Queen Victoria in 1861, and of the author Rudolf Erich Raspe.

Muckross Friary stands opposite the churchyard, and is undoubtedly one of the best-preserved medieval friaries in Ireland. MacCarthy Mor founded it in 1448 for an order of Observantine Franciscans, although the striking towers were not added for another two hundred years. Much of the intricate stonework above windows and doorways can still be seen and there are innumerable plaques dedicated to the life and work of great men and women who have been associated with the friary. These include the first (and last) Earl of Clancarre and Aodhgan, reckoned to be the Republic's greatest poet from the seventeenth or eighteenth centuries.

If you turn back onto the main road, you will soon reach **Muckross House** and its famous gardens, which are one of Kerry's most popular tourist attractions. The house was built by Henry Herbert in 1843 and is now a **folk museum** complete with authentic folk artists practising their art for visitors to see first-hand. The Herbert family gave the house and gardens to the State in the 1880s, and it is open 1000–1900 daily mid-March to June; 0900–2100 daily in July and August; 1000–1900 daily September and October; and 1100–1700 Tues–Sun for the rest of the year.

Killarney has a range of good restaurants and hotels in the city centre. Three of the best restaurants are **Gaby's** (Tel: 064 32519) in the High Street which specializes in local seafood; **Foley's** (Tel: 064 31217), also in the High Street, which offers a wide range of Irish and 'international' dishes; and the upmarket

Malton Rooms (Tel: 064 31262), in the Great Southern Hotel, for a first-class meal in beautiful surroundings.

Accommodation in Killarney is best booked in advance, but a few suggestions are the **Great Southern** (Tel: 064 31262) which is a large luxury hotel with 180 bedrooms; the **Cahernane** (Tel: 064 31895) in Muckross Road which offers fifty comfortable bedrooms, all with private facilities; and the **Three Lakes** (Tel: 064 31479) with seventy bedrooms, all well furnished and with individual bathrooms.

Several beautiful lakes are within easy reach of the town centre; the **Torc waterfall** stands close to Lough Leane and the nearby Friars' Glen was a refuge for Franciscan friars during periods of religious persecution. The Lower, Middle and Upper lakes lie close to the waterfall. Derrycunnihy Woods are worth exploring, if you have the time, and are one of the most varied botanical sites in the county. Among the other places of natural beauty near here are Moll's Gap, the Black Valley, and the Gap of Dunloe. Moll's Gap was shaped by glacial rocks coming from Kenmare over a prolonged period of time, and the Black Valley contains Ireland's highest mountain, Carrantuohill (1038 metres). The Gap of Dunloe is another striking relic of glacial action, and it is best visited in late afternoon or early morning when there are few fellow tourists around.

An alternative route out of Killarney takes you west around the **Ring of Kerry**, a famous scenic journey through the Iveragh Peninsula. What follows is generally regarded as the 'standard' tour, as recommended by the Irish Tourist Board, which can be completed by car or bus in an afternoon. Two possible extensions are given at the end of the tour if you plan to spend a bit longer in this part of the county.

Following the Killorglin road out of Killarney, you will reach **Ballymalis Castle** after about nine miles. The castle stands on the banks of the River Laune, flowing from the Lower Lake, and was originally built as one of the first Anglo-Norman structures after this part of Ireland was conquered in the thirteenth century. It was largely rebuilt in the sixteenth century and was restored during the 1980s. **KILLORGLIN** is one of only a handful of towns and villages in this part of Kerry, and it grew up around another Anglo-Norman castle which has not entirely disappeared. It has no sights of note unless you happen to be here during the annual **Puck Fair**, usually held in the second week of August, when a wild goat is captured and ceremoniously crowned in the town square. This Celtic celebration signals the start of several days of entertainment and drinking – but the goat is eventually released unharmed. The **Bianconi Inn** (Tel: 066 61146), with thirteen rooms, is the best of a handful of modest guesthouses.

Caragh Lake lies close to Killorglin; a short hike to the summit of one of the surrounding hills will reward you with what is surely one of the finest views anywhere in Ireland. The quaint little fishing village of CROMANE is an alternative detour from Killorglin, although it is usually feasible to visit both Cromane and Caragh Lake if you allow yourself enough time before darkness (and if the infamous Kerry mist does not spoil your excursion!).

The village of GLENBEIGH is a good base if you plan to explore the Ring over a period of days rather than hours. Be sure to visit the ruined **Victorian Towers**, on the outskirts of the town, built by the architect Godwin for 'Mad' Lord Headley. Godwin's mistress was the actress Ellen Terry, and he was subsequently sued by Lord Headley for excessive fees. The old house was burnt to the ground in 1922, during the Civil War, and never rebuilt; today it is a sad reminder of an all-too-brief period of late Victorian upper-class opulence, and the views from here are magnificent. Seven lakes, noted for their good fishing, stand near the Towers and legend recalls that these appeared after the seven-year elopement of Grainne, daughter of an early medieval king of Ireland, and Diarmuid. Grainne was betrothed to another, but fled with Diarmuid to live in a cave at Glenbeigh for fully seven years before they were discovered.

A little way further on is ROSSBEIGH, with its distinctive long spit of sand which has helped sink many unwary ships which have sailed too close to the coast. Many legends have grown up around this part of Kerry, but few are recalled as often as the tale of Oisin, son of Fionn (who was originally betrothed to Grainne), who fell from a magical horse and immediately became an old man. A steep road from Rossbeigh takes you to **Kells Bay**, a beautiful vantage point and the reputed burial place of St Fionan, one of Ireland's earliest religious leaders. A small power station is one of the few reminders that you are in the late twentieth century rather than the twelfth, and the next village you will reach is tiny CAHIRCIVEEN. The main point of interest here is the **O'Connell Memorial Church**, built in 1875 to honour the centenary of the birth of the Catholic patriot Daniel O'Connell. The plans for the church were approved personally by Pope Leo XIII. One other sight of interest is the remains of a fifteenth-century castle built by the MacCarthy family.

Leacanabuile is the site of a ninth- or tenth-century **stone fort**, and it has been extensively excavated in recent years. From this part of County Kerry you can see **Valentia Island** and the small village of KNIGHTSTOWN which flourishes there. There is a bridge at Portmagee if you want to explore the island in any detail; the views from the island can be breathtaking and it was here that the first transatlantic telegraph cable was anchored. Valentia was noted for its slate industry in the past, and with typical Irish ingenuity, the abandoned quarry has now been converted into a religious grotto! A one-eyed magician, Mug Roith, lived here during the first century AD and it was widely believed that it was he who beheaded John the Baptist. The 'popularity' of this claim ebbed and flowed throughout medieval times, but it reached a peak in the eleventh century when local people began a period of long fasting and almsgiving to try and dispel the story. Even today Mug Roith's name is uttered with more than a little contempt on the island.

Back on the mainland you can visit **Killabuonia**, originally a pagan place of worship and now known as a pre-Christian grave site. The nearby **St Finan's Bay** is beautiful to admire and photograph but considered very dangerous for bathing. Another medieval religious site is the ruins of an Augustinian priory at Ballinskelligs, shortly before you reach the main road again.

The village of WATERVILLE overlooks Ballinskelligs Bay, and it is here that Cessair, disgraced grandson of Noah (who built the biblical ark), is said to have landed on 15 September 2958 BC. The precise time of day is not clear, but Cessair and a motley band of renegades are credited with laying the foundations of the village. Two more historically credible figures, Scéne, wife of one of the eight leaders of the Milesians who invaded Ireland in antiquity, and Erronan, another leader, are said to be buried at nearby Eightercua. Continuing the trend for precise dates, Erronan is believed to have landed in Ireland on the morning of Thursday 1 May 1700 BC. The **Waterville Lake Hotel** is the first Club Med holiday location in the British Isles. There are three tennis courts, a swimming pool and golf can be arranged (at extra cost) at the eighteen-hole Waterville golf links (Tel: 066 74133).

If you drive on past the crest of the road to Coomakista you will be rewarded with another of the county's outstanding views across to two small islands. Scariff, the larger and nearer of the two, has **Bronze Age remains** and the ruins of a seventeenth-century Franciscan settlement. Returning to the mainland, you find the village of DERRYNANE which has long trading associations with France and Spain. The eighteenth-century customs men had a continuing battle with the ruling O'Connell family, who dominated the usually illicit trade, but the unorthodox export trade in practically every moveable good imaginable survived.

A number of old copper mines can be seen shortly before you reach the village of CAHERDANIEL. These were first worked around 2000 BC, when the ore used to be exported to Spain for smelting. Caherdaniel is one of the Ring's larger villages, with a busy main street and a couple of hotels. The best available accommodation is the **Derrynane** (Tel: 066 75136), with fifty-one bedrooms, all with private facilities, and a good restaurant which specializes in traditional Irish cuisine. It also boasts a heated indoor swimming pool. The legendary military invaders of Ireland landed at Caherdaniel in 2680 BC, or more precisely, on Tuesday 14 May 2680 BC! One thousand sword-wielding Greeks, led by Parthalon (who had recently killed both his parents), plundered the shore and promptly left. There are no traces of this early invasion, but later local sights include the ruins of a coastguard station taken over by Republican extremists during the Civil War, and an early copper mine said to have been used as a refuge by St Crohane.

One other local sight which you must not miss is **Staigue Fort**, one of the best-preserved ancient forts in Europe. It dates from around 1000 BC and originally housed both humans and cattle within its strong stone walls. You can still admire the cleverly placed stone lintels, sloping walls, and neatly inset steps. **White Strand** is a nearby beauty spot and a safe place for bathing.

The last village in the standard Ring tour is SNEEM, nestling in Sneem Valley which mighty glaciers carved more than 20,000 years ago. This is an appealing little place, and the perfect spot to stop for lunch or afternoon tea on a mild summer's day. Sneem River is particularly popular with salmon fishermen, and you should consider the modest **Stone House Hotel** (Tel: 064 45188) if you are keen to stay here. It has just five bedrooms so try to book in advance. A large, anonymous private house stands near the village, amid acres of woodland, and this is one of Kerry's few internationally famous places of interest. The secluded country house is not normally open to the public, as it is regularly used as a hideaway for international statesmen; two former residents were President Charles de Gaulle of France, shortly after he resigned in 1969, and Queen Beatrix of the Netherlands, who stayed here in 1978 whilst contemplating abdication. She handed over the throne to her daughter, the present Queen Juliana, eighteen months later.

The Castle of Dromore is within easy reach of Sneem, although there is little to see of the former seat of the O'Mahony family. Another ruined castle, that of O'Sullivan Mor, stands in the grounds of the more modern Dunkerron Castle. The older of the two fell into disrepair after being vacated by its last regular occupant, a military adviser to both James VII of Scotland (the Old Pretender) in 1715 and his son, Bonnie Prince Charlie, in 1745.

If you have time to spare after the standard 115-mile tour of the Ring of Kerry, try to visit **The Skelligs**. This huge rock is a must for nature lovers as it is home to more than 20,000 pairs of nesting gannets, kittiwakes, guillemots, petrels and other seabirds. A ruined monastery still stands on Great Skellig, although the approach can only be made by long flights of often slippery stone steps. The monastery was founded by St Fionan in the early seventh century and lasted about seven hundred years.

A final suggestion if you have any time to spare is **BALLAGHISHEEN**, which is worth visiting if only to admire the fine views from the Pass of the same name. Many legends are associated with this part of Kerry, but the strongest association is with Oisin who sat at the Pass on his white horse (see Rossbeigh earlier in this chapter), looking in vain for his long-dead fellow soldiers.

The final part of Kerry we plan to cover in south-west Ireland is the **Dingle Peninsula**, a geological jumble of rocks, cliffs, mountains, lakes and beautiful stretches of coastline. You can tour the peninsula in a full day, including one or two breaks, and the following guide is broadly that suggested by the Irish Tourist Board, covering about a hundred miles assuming you start from, or presumably skirt, Tralee.

The R559 road along the southern side of Tralee Bay is a good starting point, and runs beside a disused eighteenth-century canal. Among the first sights you will see is a medieval parish church at **ANNAGH** which is thought to date back as far as the twelfth or thirteenth century, and may even have been built on the site of the birthplace of the sixth-century St Brendan the Navigator who was reputed to have discovered America. At 953 metres high, Mount Brandon looms large at this point. County Kerry also boasts Ireland's highest peak. Standing at 1040 metres, Carrantuohill forms part of the well-known Macgillicuddy's Reeks. The coast road continues past a **Bronze Age tomb** at Maumnahaltora, and Mount Caherconree. A rare inland **promontory fort** still stands on the summit, dating probably from the late fifth or early sixth century AD. **Inch Strand**, a little distance away, offers a good sandy beach although, sadly, the weather is seldom mild enough for bathing.

The main Dingle road continues via the magnificent **Anascaul Lake** and the **ancient burial place** at Ballintaggart, the latter offering a good vantage point to admire the harbour. **DINGLE** itself is a small community, virtually self-sufficient from fishing and tourism, although it had greater importance in medieval times when it was the county's principal harbour. It returned two Members of Parliament until as late as 1800. Among the points of interest in the town are an attractive eighteenth-century **Catholic church**, built from local red sandstone, and an unassuming old house at the end of John Street which was once owned by James Louis Rice. Rice was a distinguished soldier, friend of Emperor Joseph II of Austria, and a conspirator in the 1791 plot to rescue Joseph's sister, Marie Antoinette, during the French Revolution. The flamboyant French queen was to have been spirited across to Dingle but she refused to leave Paris, believing wrongly that the revolutionaries would not dare execute an anointed queen.

There is a seasonal **Tourist Information office** in the centre of Dingle (Tel: 066 51188) which can give accommodation advice. One suggestion is the smart **Skellig Hotel** (Tel: 066 51144) which commands a magnificent location overlooking the wide harbour. The hotel has fifty bedrooms, all with private facilities, and a good restaurant.

The road out of Dingle runs towards Slea Head via Milltown, although the latter has little to merit a stop unless you are keen to see a few traces of the county's early Spanish metal workers. Much more interesting is **Ventry harbour**, just beyond the village of the same name. The harbour occupies an interesting place in Irish folklore as it was from here, in the third century AD, that Fionn MacCumhail eloped with both the daughter and wife of the King of France. With Spanish help, the French king arrived with a large army although he failed to capture Fionn or secure the return of either of his two ladies. A good restaurant at Ventry is **The Cormorant** (Tel: 066 59858).

The small town of FAHAN, a little way further on, has many relics of Kerry's earliest prehistoric settlers – some 500 in all – although it has yet to be developed as one of the county's major tourist attractions. **Slea Head,** on the other hand, is well known as one of Kerry's most popular beauty spots; several vessels, including two ships from the Spanish Armada in 1588, have sunk here.

Dunquin harbour is another beauty spot within easy reach of Slea Head, and you should note the distinctively coloured Silurian rocks which form the surrounding cliffs. These date back more than 400 million years and archaeologists have found a remarkable range of fossils in and around this part of the coast. Across from Dunquin are the Blasket Islands, no longer inhabited, but a trip to Great Blasket Island, home of not only Thomas O'Calomhthain who wrote *An tOileánnach (The Island Man)* but also Peg Sayers, whose autobiography in the native Irish, depicted life on these islands, is a must for anyone interested in island life. One of the islands is now owned by Irish prime minister, Charles Haughey. Sightseers should not miss the ruined **Castle Sybil** of the Anglo-Norman Ferriters, at Dún An 'Oir. It is built within the perimeter of an Iron Age fort and is said to be named in honour of one Sybil Lynch of County Galway, who ran off with a member of the marvellously named English Order of the Ferriters. Her father chased her to the castle, and in a frantic effort to escape, Sybil hid in a cave underneath. She had not reckoned on the rising tide and eventually drowned. Another Ferriter, Piaras the Poet, was hanged by the Cromwellians in 1653 within the castle grounds.

Visitors with an interest in Ireland's early history should see the **oratory** at Gallarus. This is the best-preserved early building in Ireland, and the triangular religious building still has all its roof and walls intact; it is thought to date from the eighth century AD.

Kilmalkedar church is a fine Romanesque building, dating in part from the twelfth century, although there are traces of an even earlier building within the present structure. It stands to the left of a crossroads above Gallarus, and contains a seventh-century cross which is the oldest-known Irish relic showing Roman script. A fifteenth-century priest's house stands within the church grounds.

The nearby Brandon Creek is named after St Brendan, who reputedly started his missionary journeys by following this stream. Conor Pass and Brandon Point are two more local vantage points which you will reach if you also follow the riverside road. When you reach **CASTLEGREGORY** you can relax at one of several small sandy beaches. Lough Gill, a short distance away, is a favourite spot for bird-watchers to admire Bewick's Swan, a migratory bird from Siberia.

West

INTRODUCTION

After the Midlands, West Ireland is the largest area of land covered in this guide. A total of seven counties make up West Ireland – Limerick, Clare, Galway, Mayo, Roscommon, Sligo and Leitrim – although for the purpose of tourism it is only the first four which deserve detailed attention.

A region as large as West Ireland offers a diverse range of holidays, from the healthy outdoor walking holiday to the lazy beach-based vacation, or a detailed tour which would keep even the most energetic sightseer content. The region has the added advantage of a major international and domestic airport at Shannon, which is Ireland's gateway to the United States and Canada, though overland connections with the rest of the country are very good if you are travelling from Dublin or Cork.

In this chapter, our tour begins in the south of the region in County Limerick and continues north through the three other main counties – Clare, Galway and Mayo – before concluding with a brief introduction to Counties Roscommon, Sligo and Leitrim. In view of the size of West Ireland, our look at each of the four main counties begins in the county town and continues approximately anti-clockwise around the main resorts and places of interest in that part of the region.

HISTORY

Many of the oldest rocks in Ireland have been found in the West. In County Limerick, for example, Silurian rocks have been found which date back more than 400 million years, and the sediment which led to the formation of quartzites in County Galway may be as much as 200 million years older than that.

The earliest settlers in West Ireland established their primitive homes in the Lough Gur area of Limerick around 3000 BC, and this is now one of the region's main tourist attractions. Christianity came to West Ireland in the fifth century AD, beginning in the south and first taking root in the Limerick area. Celtic paganism gradually died out as Christianity spread north.

In the ninth century the Viking invasions began, initially on the Shannon Estuary, but they too soon spread north. The Vikings established a few semi-permanent bases, the most significant of which was destined to become the modern town of Limerick. By the time the Normans came in the eleventh and twelfth centuries, previously unpopulated parts of West Ireland – notably County Clare and much of Galway – were now inhabited.

The Normans laid the foundations for much of modern Galway and built large castles in various parts of the region, notably Limerick, Galway and Clare. Elizabethan invaders during the sixteenth and early seventeenth centuries forced many of the leading families out of the West. Many of those who remained later fled to the New World during the Great Famine of the 1840s, but a hard core survived against all the odds and helped lay the foundations for the diverse, independent region to which tens of thousands of visitors flock each year.

COMMUNICATIONS

This region contains one of the Republic of Ireland's three main international airports, Shannon, which lies sixteen miles west of Limerick. This is Ireland's main transatlantic gateway and there are daily flights to Boston, New York and Washington. Internal air links with Cork and Dublin are excellent and there are daily summer services to Shannon from Birmingham, Bristol, Edinburgh, Glasgow, Leeds/Bradford, Manchester and London Heathrow. There are also airports at Knock, an international airport, and at Sligo and Galway.

There are excellent road links between all parts of the region, but rail services are patchy. There are regular connections between Dublin and Galway, via Athlone, and less frequent services between Athlone (and stations further east or south) and Claremorris, Westport and Ballina. A separate line runs north-west from Dublin to Sligo via Mullingar.

TOURIST INFORMATION

There are Tourist Information offices in all the main population centres in West Ireland. Major offices, which are open all year round, are located as follows: Arthur's Quay, Limerick (Tel: 061 317 522); Aras Fáilte, Eyre Square, Galway City (Tel: 061 63081); Aras Reddan, Temple Street, Sligo (Tel: 061 61201); and at Shannon International Airport (Tel: 071 61664).

CLIMATE

During the summer months warm air tends to brush the coast from the Atlantic Gulf Stream, although the opposite often occurs between October and April when a cooler Gulf Stream wind usually blows.

July and August are the warmest months to visit West Ireland with the daily average likely to be 17–20°C (63–68°F). Rain falls throughout the year but is heaviest between October and March. Visitors should bring some form of waterproof clothing whatever time of year they visit West Ireland.

WHERE TO GO FOR WHAT

Ireland's long west coast offers a number of good beaches; one of the most developed resorts which is suitable for *Family Holidays* is **KILKEE** in County Clare, although there are a number of beautiful, lonely beaches on the Mullet Peninsula in County Mayo which may suit families with older children.

For the *Nature Lover*, there is plenty to see including the **Cliffs of Moher**, which offer rugged natural beauty with a wide range of birdlife; the **Ashleigh Falls** near LEENANE, site of the recent film *The Field* starring Richard Harris; the attractive surroundings of FOXFORD in County Mayo; and the **Clare Glens** which lie between the counties of Limerick and Tipperary. Spa enthusiasts will be interested to learn that the only **active spa** in Ireland is at LISDOONVARNA, a popular holiday resort in County Clare, and the site of an annual 'Bachelor Festival' which attracts large numbers of people, not least middle-aged American women!

For the *Sightseer* and outdoor *Sportsperson* there is an abundance of places to visit, not least LIMERICK and GALWAY cities themselves, the famous religious site at **Knock**, and **Lough Gur**, probably Ireland's most significant archaeological site. One or two suggestions for fishing enthusiasts are: the villages of CROSS and KINVARA, in County Galway, and BALLYVAUGHAN (mainly sea fishing) in County Clare.

There are many fine forest walks and trails in West Ireland, and what follows is a selection of four in each of the four main counties.

Limerick

Combaun/Temple Hill (An Carn Bán): lay-by, picnic site and forest walks; six miles north-west of Kilbeheny on a third-class road leading to Anglesborough.

Curraghchase (An Currach): picnic site, gardens, arboretum, and the ruin of Curraghchase House which was once owned by the poet Aubrey de Vere; thirteen miles west of Limerick on the N69 leading to Askeaton – turn south for two miles on a third-class road.

Fanningstown/Greenwood (Baile an Fhainínigh): picnic site, forest walks – real Canon Sheehan country; six miles south-east of Kilmallock on the R512 heading towards Kildorrey.

Galty Castle (Caisleán na nGaibhlte): picnic site, and riverside, forest and mountain walks; five miles north-east of Mitchelstown on the N8 towards Caher – turn left for two miles on a third-class road.

Clare

Ballycuggaran (Baile Uí Chogaráin): lay-by, picnic site, forest walks and a hill climb to Slieve Bernagh; two miles north of Killaloe on the R463 to Tuamgraney.
Cullane (Coilleán): beautiful lakeshore picnic site, forest walks and ruins of Cullane House; one mile west of Tulla on a third-class road to Fair Green.
Dromore (Drom Mór): lakeshore picnic site, forest walks and access to Dromore Castle; two miles west of Crusheen on a third-class road.
Lough Atorick (Loch an Tóraic): lay-by overlooking Lough Atorick forest, mountain walks and fine scenic views; six miles south-west of Woodford on a third-class road heading towards Feakle (on the border between County Clare and Galway).

Galway

Coole Demesne (An Chúil): car park, picnic site, forest walks, nature trail, and the former estate of Lady Gregory; one mile north of Gort on the N18 heading towards Galway City.
Portumna Forest Park (Páirc Fhoraoise Phort Omna): car park (small charge), picnic sites, toilets and an information office, forest walks, stands for viewing wildlife (including deer herds and wildfowl ponds), marina and a nature trail; adjacent to Portumna, on the north shore of Lough Derg.

Mayo

Ardnageeha (Ard na Gaoithe): picnic site, forest walks and scenic views; two miles south-west of Cong on a third-class road which takes you past Ashford Castle.

Beleek (Beal Lice): picnic site and forest walks; a mile north of Ballina on the R314 to Killala – on the west bank of the Moy estuary.

Clydagh Bridge (Droichead Chlaoideach): picnic site, forest walks, good fishing and a beautiful waterfall; three miles north of Castlebar on the R310 heading towards Pontoon.

Moore Hall (Mac-Chluain): picnic site, access to Lough Carra, forest walks, scenic views, fishing and the ruin of Moore Hall; eight miles north of Ballinrobe on a third-class road leading to Carrownacow. Turn left for a mile before Carrownacow when you reach Lough Carra.

Pigeon Hole Wood (Coill Pholl na gColm): picnic site, forest walks, cave and an underground river; one mile west of Cong village on the R345 to Clonbur – turn left for half a mile.

Tourmakeady Demesne (Tuar Mhic Eadaigh): car park, picnic site, forest walks, waterfall and a nature trail (information leaflets are available on the site); five miles south-west of Partry on a third-class road leading towards Tourmakeady – on the west shore of Lough Mask.

The county town of Limerick is **LIMERICK CITY**, a beautiful old town which was founded as a Viking settlement about AD 922. After Dublin and Cork, this is the third largest city in the Republic of Ireland, with a population of 61,000, and the fourth largest in Ireland as a whole. The city centre is small enough for visitors to be able to walk between the main sights with relative ease. There's a map of the city available from the Tourist office with points of interest and historical sites marked out. Also there is a guided walking tour during the summer months.

Rather like Derry further north, Limerick was at the centre of some of the most bloody conflicts during the religious struggles of the late seventeenth century. A period of bitter persecution continued into the eighteenth century, although a resurgence of the old Gaelic culture took place at the same time and ultimately outlived the persecution.

Limerick has produced a number of notable individuals who have been influential in various movements dedicated to Ireland's independence. William Smith, for example, was instrumental in the ill-fated 1848 rising for Irish freedom. Three young men who lived for a time in Limerick helped lead the 1916 uprising in Dublin. Although two were subsequently executed, the third – Eamon de Valera – led his people through the War of Independence (1919–23) and was President of Ireland between 1959 and 1973.

There is plenty to see in Limerick, although very few buildings survive from before the late seventeenth century. The most significant exception is **St Mary's Cathedral** which was built in 1172 by Dónal Mór O Brien, King of Munster. The original Transitional church has been 'reformed' and restored several times in the eight centuries since it was built, but much of the original medieval architecture can still be seen. St Mary's is open to the public throughout the year when not in use, and one of the most attractive features is the black oak choir stalls which date from the fifteenth century – the oldest surviving church stalls in Ireland. Other features of the Cathedral include some beautiful late medieval carving in the Arthur Chapel, and an evening Son et Lumière presentation from May to September telling the story of the Cathedral. There is a fine view over the city from the top of the tower.

Standing near the Cathedral, in Michael Street, is the **Granary**, which is a superb example of an eighteenth-century Georgian building which has been converted to modern use. It contains the city library, archives, a pub, a restaurant, the School of Art and Design and various offices.

The Exchange, in Nicholas Street, was rebuilt in 1777 as the meeting place of the Limerick Businessmen's Corporation. The exterior columns are the most distinctive feature of the original architecture. From here it is a short walk to **King John's Castle**, built around 1200 and one of the best surviving examples of Norman architecture in Ireland. Twin towers flank the entrance on the north side, and guided tours are available during the summer months. The small **Old Church**, near Barringtons Pier, is the only building in Limerick which predates the Castle, having been built in the twelfth century.

Thomond Bridge stands opposite the Castle. According to historical tradition, the **Treaty Stone** which stands on a pedestal near the bridge was the stone on which the 1691 Treaty of Limerick was signed, thus ending the two-year Jacobite-Williamite War which culminated in a siege of John's Castle.

Another of Limerick's attractive bridges is **Sarsfield Bridge**, modelled on the Pont Neuilly over the Seine in Paris and built between 1824 and 1835. The **Sarsfield Memorial** stands in the grounds of St John's Cathedral, and both this statue and the bridge are named in honour of Patrick Sarsfield who helped defend Limerick during the sieges of 1690 and 1691.

St John's Roman Catholic Cathedral is an early nineteenth-century building of the Gothic revival style with a distinctive eighty-six-metre spire, the highest in Ireland. Visitors can enjoy a pleasant walk around the nearby **St John's Square** where most of the stone houses date from the mid-eighteenth century. Many of the buildings were restored as part of Ireland's contribution to European Architectural Heritage Year in 1975.

The city's main **museum** currently stands on the west side of St John's Square though there are plans to move it to the New City Hall at Merchant's Quay. It houses a vast collection of artefacts dating back to 4000 years BC. The **Hunt Museum** at Plassy, three miles from the city centre, houses an equally broad range of items which the art historian John Hunt donated to the Irish State. Visitors with an interest in art should find time to see **Limerick Art Gallery** in Pery Square, which is open 1000–1300 and 1400–1800 Mon–Fri and 1000–1300 Sat.

Among the other points of interest in Limerick are a few fragments of the **medieval town walls**, behind Lelia Street, the **People's Park** near Pery Square, and the **Good Shepherd Convent** in Clare Street where the famous Limerick lace is made. Admission to the lace room is free and it is open 0945–1645 Mon–Fri.

There is a reasonable selection of places to eat and stay in

Limerick City, and the **Tourist Information office** at Arthur's Quay (Tel: 061 317 522) can provide a comprehensive selection. The city's best restaurant is probably the **Copper Room** (Tel: 061 55266), at Jury's Hotel, Ennis Road. This beautiful restaurant specializes in French cuisine and has won a number of awards in recent years. A more modest restaurant, in the city centre, is **Olde Tom's** (Tel: 061 45961) in Thomas Street. Olde Tom's offers more traditional Irish cuisine and a variety of evening entertainment throughout the year.

What follows are a few suggestions for accommodation in Limerick.

First Class

Jury's Hotel, Ennis Road (Tel: 061 327 777) – Part of the prestigious Jury's Hotel Group, with luxury hotels in Dublin, Cork and Limerick; one hundred plush bedrooms, all with private facilities; good city-centre location. Recently refurbished and a leisure centre added.

Limerick Inn, Ennis Road (Tel: 061 51544) – A slightly larger hotel, located close to Jury's; most rooms have good views over the city or the River Shannon. It is about three miles from the city centre and also has a leisure centre.

Business Class

Limerick Ryan, Ennis Road (Tel: 061 53922) – Limerick's largest quality hotel with more than 180 bedrooms, all with bathrooms. The Limerick Ryan is located on the Ennis Road one mile from the city centre heading towards Shannon Airport.

Economy Class

Royal George, O'Connell Street (Tel: 061 44566) – A popular budget hotel right in the city centre; all sixty bedrooms have a bath or shower.

Woodfield House, Ennis Road (Tel: 061 53023) – This rather old-fashioned hotel offers a quiet location and a homely atmosphere; most of the two dozen bedrooms have private facilities.

Assuming Limerick City is your base, the surrounding county offers a good range of excursion possibilities.

ANNACOTTY lies about four miles east of the city, on the main road heading towards Dublin, and the nearby River Mulcair is a popular excursion for salmon-fishing enthusiasts. CASTLECONNELL, a few miles further on, also offers good salmon fishing and a wide range of walks and nature trails. Outdoor enthusiasts can enjoy more walks around the twin villages of MONTPELIER and O'BRIEN'S BRIDGE which link County Limerick with County Clare.

KILLALOE overlooks the River Shannon and has more for the sightseer. The village became the centre of a diocese in the twelfth century and remains so to the present day. The ruins of **St Flannan's Cathedral** reveal that it was a plain building, dating from the thirteenth century, although the attractive stone cross shaft by the main entrance is thought to date from around AD 1000. Two other points of interest are **St Flannan's Oratory**, in the grounds of the Cathedral, and **St Molua's Oratory** in the grounds of the modern Roman Catholic church. St Flannan's was erected in the twelfth century, around the same time as the original cathedral, but St Molua's was rebuilt only in 1930 when its original location was due to be flooded during the construction of the Shannon hydro-electric scheme.

The remains of **Brian Boru's fort** are near Killaloe but the village's main attraction to family holidaymakers is its broad range of recreational facilities. These include facilities for swimming, boating and sailing as well as a picturesque picnic area and one or two hills which can be climbed at a leisurely pace on a summer afternoon. The old **Lock House** on the bridge spanning the Shannon at Killaloe House is an interpretative centre for the area, plus a new Tourist office.

Two miles south of NEWPORT are the **Clare Glens** which form the boundary between Limerick and Tipperary. Despite their name, the Glens are actually one enormous gorge through which the River Clare flows. They are wooded, with dark conifers, oak and ash trees, and visitors can follow a carefully marked Nature Trail.

Just north of the village of MURROE is **Glenstal Abbey**, built initially as a private home in the 1830s and given to the Benedictine Order in the 1920s. It has many features in common with a Norman abbey – a Norman-style gate and round tower – and visitors can enjoy the magnificent gardens and the ornately decorated church.

The **Slievefelim Mountains** form a beautiful backdrop to much of north-east Limerick, and one of the best ways to enjoy the countryside is to follow the seventy-mile Sarsfield's Ride. This signposted route follows that taken by the patriot Patrick Sarsfield who led 600 troops to intercept and destroy a Williamite siege en route to Limerick.

One of the most important religious sites in this part of Ireland is **Holy Cross**, about ten miles north of CASHEL on the R660. The abbey has recently been renovated and is now a fine example of the architecture of that era. The village is named after a **monastery** which was founded here in 1169, although the surviving ruins date from no earlier than the fifteenth century. The original monastery was said to possess a fragment of the True Cross although, if that were the case, the tiny relic has been lost for many centuries.

Travelling into south-east Limerick, you will find one of the most attractive features of this part of the county, **Lough Gur**, which is arguably the most significant archaeological site in Ireland. Remains of human settlement dating back to 3000 BC have been found here, including stone circles, wedge-shaped gallery graves and a vast collection of artefacts, including weapons and prehistoric pottery. The most impressive site is the stone circle, which has a diameter of nearly fifty metres and dates positively from 2000 BC. Three other sites of particular interest are the enormous 'Giant's Grave', a well-preserved ruin of a fifteenth-century castle, and a prehistoric artificial island. A Stone Age Interpretative Centre is open daily throughout the summer (May to September) and offers a colourful audio-visual explanation of the main attractions of the Lough Gur area.

Eight miles south-east of Lough Gur the main road takes you through the village of HOSPITAL, so named after a base of the Crusading Knights Hospitaller Order which existed briefly here. South-east again, for a few more miles, and the outdoor enthusiast can enjoy the isolated splendour of **The Galtees** hills. ANGLESBOROUGH is a quiet little village hidden away in the heart of the hills.

Further west, the **Glen of Aherlow** is one of the county's widest and most fertile valleys. From here it is only a short drive to KILFINANE where it is possible to enjoy some of the finest vistas in this part of Ireland. Self-catering visitors may be interested to know that many of the beautiful thatched cottages around this area are available for rent, and full details are available through the Irish Tourist Board, or any Tourist Information office throughout the country.

At BALLYHOURAS there is a very rounded little green hill. Although there is practically nothing left to see apart from the stump of a **round tower**, St Patrick is said to have founded a monastery on the hill in the sixth century. The views from here are very good, and it is a short drive to the **Greenwood**, a large State-owned forest offering dozens of possibilities for long forest walks along clearly signposted paths and trails.

Ten miles north from the Greenwood is KILMALLOCK, a lovely little town standing amidst some very fertile arable farmland. The town's principal attractions are **King's Castle** and the **medieval collegiate church** of Saints Peter and Paul. The church has some magnificent seventeenth- and eighteenth-century carvings, including those on the grave of the Gaelic poet Aindrias MacCraith, better known as An Mangaire Sugach or the Jolly Pedlar, who died in 1795.

CROOM lies almost at the centre of County Limerick and this was the home of the Kildare branch of the Geraldine family who carried the famous war-cry 'Crom-Abú' (Croom Forever) into battle in more troubled times. The remains of the old **Geraldine castle** can be seen just outside the village, mostly hidden from the main road by a high modern wall. **Manister Abbey**, three miles east of Croom, is a ruined Cistercian abbey which was founded by Donncha O Brian, King of Thomond, in 1148. It was burnt down and all the monks murdered by English troops in 1579, after the English had defeated the Geraldines. The Abbey was never inhabited again.

Continuing into west Limerick you reach ADARE, a good base or starting point for a tour of this part of the county. The attractive hamlet lies ten miles south-west of Limerick City and has the enviable reputation of being the most beautiful village in Ireland. It stands in a magnificent woodland setting and really should be a must on any visit to Limerick. The oldest buildings are the **Church of St Nicholas** and the adjoining **Chantry Chapel**. The church is thought to date back to the twelfth century and the round-headed windows are typical of the style used in High Medieval times. Chantry Chapel was used for minor services and such chapels are relatively uncommon in Ireland due to the proliferation of 'full-scale' churches.

The **Trinitarian Abbey** was founded around 1230 for the Trinitarian Canons of the Order of the Redemption of Captives, an obscure medieval order which never had more than this single abbey in the whole of Ireland. The order was suppressed in the mid-sixteenth century and although the building was allowed to fall into disrepair, it was eventually restored to its present use as both a Roman Catholic church and a convent. The village's Church of Ireland building has also been 'reclaimed' from disuse; it was once an **Augustinian priory**, founded in 1315 by John Fitzgerald. A Franciscan friary which was established a century later still lies in a state of graceful ruin and is now the centrepiece of a modern building owned by Adare Manor Golf Club. Private visits are possible but it is necessary to check with the golf club first.

Desmond Castle, on the banks of the River Maigue, is a fine example of feudal castle architecture. Despite its name, it was built and occupied mainly by the Kildare Geraldines rather than the Desmond branch. Although much of the castle now lies in ruin, it is still possible to make out the square keep, bakery, kitchens, stables and the two great halls which are thought to date from the thirteenth century.

There is a **Tourist Information office** (Tel: 061 396 255) in Adare which is open between May and October. A good place for accommodation is the **Dunraven Arms** (Tel: 061 396 209) which has forty-four bedrooms, all with private facilities, and the relaxed atmosphere of a country hunting lodge. The hotel also has a good restaurant where large roasts and traditional Irish cuisine are among the most popular items on the menu. **Adare Manor** (Tel: 061 86566) was built in the eighteenth century as the private residence of the Earl of Dunraven. It is now a prestigious hotel, set in 840 acres of woods and parkland with salmon and trout fishing. **The Mustard Seed** (Tel: 061 86451) is a restaurant in a small old-style terrace on the old estate of Adare. It is comfortable and intimate. The standard of cuisine is very high but it is open only during the evening.

The town of RATHKEALE, eight miles west of Adare, is the second largest in the county. A **Palatine Museum** has recently opened there. **Castle Matrix** is a beautiful Geraldine castle about a mile south-west of the town. Built around 1410, the castle was extensively renovated in the seventeenth century and its unique combination of architectural styles makes it one of the more unusual castles in West Ireland. It is still in habitable condition and both the castle and the extensive grounds are open to the public during the summer months.

Another eight miles south-west on the N21 takes you to NEWCASTLE WEST. The town is named after the large **castle** which was built here in the early thirteenth century. The castle stands a little way from the main town square and is worth a visit to see the two fifteenth-century banqueting halls. Newcastle West is a relatively modern town and accordingly offers little else for the holidaymaker apart from the usual amenities of any reasonably large town.

Killalianthan Church is an attractive little medieval building about four miles south-west of **DROMCOLLOGHER**. Measuring just fifteen metres by nine, this is one of the smallest churches in Ireland. Parts of an even earlier Christian building, a seventh-century monastery founded by St Beircheart, are retained in the walls of a ruined fifteenth-century church at nearby Tullylease.

The **Mullaghareirk Mountains** occupy much of southwest Limerick and two of the most popular beauty spots are at **Sugar Hill** and **Barna Gap**, from where you can see for miles. The town of ABBEYFEALE lies nine miles west of the Barna Gap and takes its name from a **Cistercian abbey** founded on the banks of the River Feale in 1188.

Another former **Geraldine castle** can be seen at PORTRINARD, although the two-metre-thick medieval walls now only stand to a height of five or six metres. The nearby village of ATHEA is a nationally recognized centre for traditional Irish music and any of the public houses will be able to give you more information about where and when musical events are taking place.

Nine miles further north is GLIN, an attractive village which is laid out in the shape of a square. This is the seat of the Knight of Glin whose family, the Fitzgeralds, have owned much of the surrounding land for more than seven centuries. Among the places of historic interest are the ruined **Old Castle of the Knights**, on the banks of the Glencorby stream, and the late eighteenth-century **Glin Castle** where the Fitzgerald family still live.

One of the most restful parts of County Limerick is KNOCKPATRICK, about a mile south of the county's only seaport at FOYNES. Here there is an **Aviation and Maritime Museum** (Tel: 069 65416). During the 1930s and early 1940s the port of Foynes was the fulcrum point for air traffic between the USA and Europe. It was here that the famous flying boats could be seen. The new museum recalls this era with a range of exhibits, graphic illustrations and an audio-visual show. The **round hill** commands a fine view over the Shannon Estuary and it is from here that St Patrick is said to have blessed County Kerry. The ruins of a **medieval church** stand on the summit and the poetess Charlotte Grace O'Brien is buried in the adjoining churchyard.

Six miles east of Foynes is the small industrial town of ASKEATON. The Munster Geraldines founded and expanded the town and three ruined medieval buildings survive as a reminder of Askeaton's former importance. **Desmond Castle** dates from the fifteenth century and is the most significant of the three. A fifteenth-century banqueting hall, with several ornately carved stone window arches, lies to the west of the tower.

Two other places of interest in west County Limerick are the **Curraghchase Forest Park**, owned and maintained by the Irish State, and **Dromore Castle** five miles east of the entrance to Curraghchase. The roofless castle stands on high ground overlooking **Dromore Lake** and was built in the second half of the last century. It was inhabited for only a few years, then abandoned because of dampness, and visitors should note that the grounds are not normally open to the public.

County Clare lies to the north of Limerick, and the fact that there are traces of nearly two and a half thousand stone forts and castles testifies to the particularly turbulent history of this part of Ireland. Our tour begins in the county town of **ENNIS** and takes a broadly clockwise direction before reaching the border with County Galway.

The name Ennis means an 'islet' or 'river meadow'. The town overlooks the River Fergus and grew up around a large castle built by the O'Brien family in the thirteenth century. Ennis' religious and commercial importance grew quickly; it became a borough in 1612 and was also designated as the cathedral town of the Roman Catholic diocese of Killaloe. In more recent times Ennis came to national importance earlier this century as the campaigning base for Eamon de Valera (1882–1973). Although he was born in New York, de Valera's family settled in Ireland. After narrowly escaping execution during the Civil War (because he was born an American citizen) he went on to lead his country to independence, and after the Second World War he served two terms as President.

The best way to explore Ennis is on foot and the **Tourist Information office** (Tel: 065 28366) on the Limerick Road can supply a booklet giving details of a walking tour. A good place to start is the **county museum** in Harmony Row. The museum includes a Presbyterian church and a library, but the most interesting feature is a section devoted to the life and work of Eamon de Valera who represented this part of County Clare in Parliament from 1917 until he first became President in 1959. A **monument** to him occupies a commanding position close to the attractive **Court House**, a wide-fronted building which dates from 1850. Visitors to the county museum can also see a spade used by Charles Stewart Parnell to dig the first sod for the laying of the Ennis–Clare Coast railway line in 1883. The line was discontinued in 1961 and one of the original locomotives is on display at the railway station.

The oldest building in Ennis is the **Abbey** which was founded by the O'Brien family in 1250. Parts of the Abbey have been restored, and two of its more interesting features are the enormous east window, one of the tallest in any Irish abbey, and the large fifteenth-century MacMahon tomb with its distinctive carvings of the Feast of the Passion.

Ennis' **Pro-Catholic Cathedral** was built in 1831, just two years after Catholic Emancipation began. It is a relatively unassuming building in neo-Gothic style. Two other sights of interest in Ennis are **monuments** devoted to three men executed by the British in 1867 for their part in an unsuccessful Fenian rescue, and to the Irish patriot Daniel O'Connell who was MP for County Clare for three years in the nineteenth century.

Ennis has a few good restaurants and two of the most popular in the medium price range are **Brogan's** (Tel: 065 29859), O'Connell Street, and the **Auburn Lodge** (Tel: 065 21247) in Galway Road which offers a first-class range of traditional Irish cuisine. The **Cloister** (Tel: 065 29521) in Abbey Street opens its patio garden to customers during the summer months.

The best hotel in Ennis is the plush **Old Ground Hotel** (Tel: 065 28127) which has sixty bedrooms, all with private bathrooms. The hotel has been extended and restored to its pre-war splendour over the last ten years. A less expensive alternative is **Queen's Hotel** (Tel: 065 28963) which has about thirty bedrooms, all with private facilities, or the **West County Hotel** on the Limerick Road (opposite the Tourist office) which has 110 bedrooms all with private facilities (Tel: 065 28421).

There are a number of ruined churches and hermitages within easy reach of Ennis. A **round tower** and **late twelfth-century church** once stood at Drumcliff, and the remains of a **fifteenth-century castle** stand near the Dromore Lake. One of County Clare's earliest sites is **O'Dea's Hermitage** near Corofin. St Tola, who died AD 737, is credited with founding the first church here although most of the remains, including St Tola's Cross, are believed to date from no earlier than the twelfth century.

The **Clare Heritage Centre** at COROFIN offers a detailed introduction to the difficult years of the nineteenth century and also offers a genealogical research service to help people with Clare roots to trace their ancestry. The village is well placed for visitors to explore a number of older sights nearby. **Fiddaun Castle**, nine miles from Corofin, is a well-preserved sixteenth-century castle built by the O'Shaughnessy family, who also founded the quiet market town of GORT and were known to be regular visitors to the **Church of the Son of Duach**, the romantic ruins of a major tenth-century religious site. Part of the small cathedral, one of several ruined buildings here, was built during the tenth century.

A restored sixteenth-century **tower house** can be seen at Thoor Ballylee, and it was here that W. B. Yeats lived during the 1920s. It is now a museum dedicated to his life and work. The remains of a **medieval parish church** are in the centre of the village of TULLA but most visitors carry on to see a number of **prehistoric passage graves** which have been discovered in the vicinity. A particularly striking wedge-shaped **passage grave** has been found near the village of QUIN.

At CRAGGAUNOWEN there is a beautiful **castle** which was built by the MacNamaras around 1550. In recent years a number of prehistoric buildings have been reconstructed on the site, including a *crannog* (man-made island) and a Bronze Age fort. There is a lake nearby which is popular with boating and fishing enthusiasts. SIXMILEBRIDGE is one of many small villages in this area founded in the eighteenth and nineteenth centuries as various new industries, notably iron-working, came to County Clare. The forest behind CRATLOE is one of the oldest in Ireland, and it is said that the original beams in the roof of Westminster Hall came from trees felled here.

BUNRATTY is home to Ireland's most popular tourist attraction: a **folk park** and **medieval castle**. The world-famous **Bunratty banquet** is held in the Banqueting Hall of the castle, sometimes twice nightly if demand allows. The banquet costs approximately IR£26 per person for food, wine and medieval entertainments. **Bunratty folk park** contains a reconstruction of a nineteenth-century Irish village where you can enjoy a real Irish céilí (traditional Irish food, music and dance). The céilí takes place from May to September and costs IR£21 per person. Traditional Irish crafts, which had been flourishing since long before the nineteenth century, are still practised at the **Ballycasey Workshops** three miles west of Bunratty, and visitors are welcome.

Among the places to visit in the easternmost corner of County Clare are the pleasant market town of **SCARIFF**, which sits high above Lough Derg, and the picturesque little eighteenth-century village of **MOUNTSHANNON**. A small boat can be hired from Mountshannon to take you over to **Holy Island**, with its early **monastic ruins**. The first religious settlement here was founded by St Caimin in the seventh century.

Two other places of interest in east Clare are **Mooghaun Fort**, a famous Iron Age ring fort near the village of **NEWMARKET-ON-FERGUS**, and the sixteenth-century **Ralahine Castle**, which is still largely intact, although it has not been occupied for some time.

Continuing into west Clare, the visitor will find the islands of the Shannon Estuary, which are picturesque and historically significant. One of the largest is **Canon Island** on which the ruins of a **thirteenth-century priory** still stand. From **KILLIMER** there is a car ferry service, during daylight hours, over to Tarbert in County Kerry. This twenty-minute journey will save eighty-five miles by road. The ferry leaves every hour on the hour.

KILRUSH is a bustling market town and from here it is possible to take a boat across to **Scattery Island**. St Senan founded a monastery here in the sixth century although subsequent Viking invasions all but destroyed it. Brian Boru recaptured the island around 970. In the centre of Kilrush there is a **memorial** to the Manchester martyrs of 1867 (mentioned earlier in this chapter) which was designed by the father of former British wartime Cabinet Minister Brendan Bracken.

Visitors to west Clare by car can follow a beautiful coast road round the **Loop Head** and back to Kilkee. Among the many vantage points on this popular route are **Poulnasherry Bay**, the little villages of QUERRIN and DOONAHA, and the **Loop Head lighthouse**. The village of CARRIGAHOLT faces the wide Bay of the same name and at the pier it is possible to visit the remains of **MacMahon Castle** which was built in the fifteenth century.

Further north, the **Bridges of Ross** are a remarkable product of natural erosion by the sea and thousands of years of stormy weather. Two natural 'bridges' were formed but only the smaller of the two, and the central arch of the larger one, still remain. Between the villages of CROSS and KILKEE lies some of West Ireland's most dramatic cliff scenery, including an enormous column of rock known as **Bishop's Island** which has a ruined medieval oratory on its summit. Kilkee is a busy little summer resort with a magnificent beach in Moore Bay. A wide reef protects the beach from the full force of the Atlantic Ocean. The resort was one of the first of its kind to expand during the Victorian era. In addition to a **folk museum** on nearby Corbally Hill, and the **Sweeney Memorial Library**, visitors can enjoy a full range of sporting and leisure facilities, including golf, swimming and sailing. There is a seasonal **Tourist Information office** (Tel: 068 56112) which can provide details of accommodation availability. Two places to stay in the town centre are the medium range **Thomond Hotel** (Tel: 068 56025), which has twenty-three bedrooms, eight with private facilities, and the more modest **Halpin's Hotel** (Tel: 068 56032) which has eleven rooms, seven with showers or private bathrooms.

Two further local beauty spots within easy reach of Kilkee are **Donegall Point**, where the remains of a **promontory fort** still stand, and **Spanish Point** which offers excellent swimming at the Silver Strand. Nearby MILTOWN MALBAY is a smaller seaside resort than Kilkee but the range of sporting and leisure facilities is no less extensive. Deep-sea diving is an additional feature of Miltown.

Moving into north-west Clare, visitors can expect some of the most beautiful scenery in West Ireland. The Irish Tourist Board offers a particularly good guidebook, *Burren Journey West*, which features this part of the region in considerable detail. ENNISTYMON is a small market town and likely to be one of the first places you reach. A late medieval **O'Brien castle** and a modern **Catholic church**, built in 1953, are two places of interest in the town.

A little further north is the small coastal town of LAHINCH. It has a beautiful beach and a first-class range of leisure facilities for all the family, including an eighteen-hole championship golf course. Lahinch's best hotel is probably the **Aberdeen Arms** (Tel: 065 81100) which has fifty-five well-appointed bedrooms. Less expensive accommodation is offered by the **Atlantic Hotel** (Tel: 065 81049) which also has a good restaurant, specializing in traditional Irish cuisine. Another good choice for quality Irish food is **Kenny's Pub**, which serves both lunches and dinner.

A ruined **castle**, built by the O'Connor family, is worth a detour at the village of LISCANNOR, and the nearby **Cliffs of Moher** are a must for any visitor to this part of County Clare. These steep, beautiful cliffs reach a height of more than 200 metres above sea level. The most striking vantage points are **Hag's Head** and **O'Brien's Tower**, and a **visitor centre** near the approach road from Liscannor offers an introduction to the geological and past military significance of the cliffs.

The beaches near the small fishing village of DOOLIN are unsafe and should not be used. From here the new approved passenger ferry crossing to the three **Aran Islands** can be made on Doolin Ferry (Tel: 065 74189). Most of the Aran limestone is bare, its surface eroded away by Ice Age glaciers. The islands have been populated for over four thousand years and their inhabitants speak mostly Gaelic. Apart from being the home of the world famous Aran jumper, the islands have fired the imaginations of many artists, writers and poets. The largest island is INISHMORE. Made up of fourteen small villages, the island has a number of small beaches as well as forts and many early

Christian churches. Accommodation is available at **Ard Einne Country Home**, Cill Einne, Inishmore (Tel: 099 61126).

INISHMAAN is the middle island, linked by an airstrip with the other islands and with Galway. The cottage where the poet and dramatist John Millington Synge lived can be visited here.

INISHEER is the most southern of the islands. The ruin of **Teampall Chaomhain** (Church of Kevin) is dedicated to the island's patron saint. It is worth noting that accommodation is limited on these islands and inquiries should be made before leaving the mainland via a Tourist office in the region.

Nearby points of interest on the mainland include the recently restored **Doonagore Castle**, now a private residence, and **Slieve Elva**, the highest peak in County Clare. There are a number of **underground caves** open to the public at **Poll na Gollum**. Also of interest are the Allwiee Caves, which offer many fine examples of stalagmites, stalactites, pillars and underground lakes. Guided tours are available. And sun lovers may be interested to know that the best beach in this part of the county is a little way further on at FANORE. The only active spa in the Republic of Ireland is at LISDOONVARNA. This has been a popular holiday spot since Victorian times and the **Spa Wells Health Centre** still houses the main sulphur spring and pump-house. The surrounding countryside is quite beautiful for touring by car, and much of it is State-owned forest.

The final stretch of County Clare is known as **High Burren** and is the least-populated part of the county. KILFENORA is one of only two villages of any size, and the **Burren Display Centre** is worth visiting to learn more about this varied part of West Ireland. The plant-life of the Burren is particularly diverse and information about this is displayed in the Centre, which is open throughout the year.

There are several significant prehistoric sites in the Burren. Full details are available from any Tourist Information office in County Clare, but three of the most important sites are: the remains of an **Iron Age fort** at Caherballykinvar, a **portal dolmen** dating back to 2500 BC at Pulnabrone, and a collection of **wedge tombs** at Gleninsheen.

North of County Clare is County Galway, one of Ireland's most romantic and best-known regions which makes up more than a third of the land-mass of West Ireland. Much of the county is rich farming land although tourism plays an important part in the economy of Galway.

GALWAY CITY is the county town and the capital of West Ireland. It is a former Norman settlement and has a history which goes back more than 1000 years. Its independent commercial status was recognized by a Charter granted in 1484 by Richard III, and it grew in importance even more during the eighteenth and nineteenth centuries when it became the administrative centre for the British government in the western counties of Ireland.

There is a lot to see and do in Galway City, but everything can be explored easily on foot. Details of accommodation and walking tours are available from the region's main **Tourist Information office** (Tel: 091 63081) which is located near Eyre Square. The beautiful eighteenth-century **Eyre Square** is the centre of town and two **monuments** stand at opposite corners. One is dedicated to Padraic O'Conaire, a Galway-born writer who died in 1923, and the other is a metal fountain depicting an old Galway sailing vessel.

Galway's oldest building is the **Collegiate Church of St Nicholas** in the city centre, erected by the Anglo-Normans in 1320 and expanded a century later. Christopher Columbus is said to have prayed in this majestic building before setting sail for the Americas. Many of the church's authentic medieval carvings are among the finest in Ireland, and they can be viewed any day of the year when there are no services taking place.

The **Franciscan Abbey** in Francis Street was built in the last century but stands on the site of a friary founded in 1296. The **Spanish Arch and Spanish Parade** are the next oldest points of interest in the city, and date from 1594. The Arch was built to protect the quays where Spanish ships unloaded their cargoes, and the Parade is said to be where the Spanish merchants would stroll and relax in the evening after a busy day's trade.

The **Old Merchant Houses** in Shop Street date from the

seventeenth and eighteenth centuries although many are now disused. **Lynch's Castle**, at one end of Shop Street, now houses a bank but is believed to have been a private residence as long ago as the sixteenth century. **Galway City Museum** is near here, and offers a more detailed introduction to the city's thousand-year history.

Other places of interest in Galway are the **Salmon Weir**, near the modern **Cathedral** in Gaol Road, and **University College, Galway**. The college was founded in 1845 and specializes in the study of Celtic languages, notably Irish. The **college library** houses a vast collection of books and archive material including the city's municipal records from 1485 to 1818. The **Galway Irish Crystal Visitor Centre** at Merlin Park (Tel: 091 57311) is well worth visiting (open every day from 0900 to 1700). Intricate Galway crystal items can be purchased at a bargain price as the Centre sells seconds and end of lines.

Galway City has a good selection of both restaurants and hotels. One of the best places to eat out is the **Oyster Room** (Tel: 091 64041) at the Great Southern Hotel, in Eyre Square. This plush, refurbished restaurant offers a fine range of international and more traditional Irish specialities. Two less expensive restaurants in the city centre are: the **Lydon House** (Tel: 091 64051), in Shop Street, which is very informal, and the **Malt House** (Tel: 091 67866) in the Olde Malte Arcade, which offers a wide selection of dishes in an 'olde worlde' setting. **Eyre House**, in Eyre Square, is another establishment offering fine food and unique dishes.

A few suggestions for accommodation in Galway City.

First Class

Great Southern Hotel, Eyre Square (Tel: 091 64041) – A beautiful luxury hotel offering exemplary service and a superb range of leisure facilities – including a sauna and heated indoor swimming pool. 120 spacious bedrooms and good nightlife.

Corrib Great Southern, Dublin Road (Tel: 091 55281) – A slightly smaller hotel with a similar range of leisure facilities; many of the bedrooms have lovely views over Galway Bay.

Business Class

Galway Ryan, Dublin Road (Tel: 091 53181) – Popular with business visitors and close to the city centre; ninety-six bedrooms, all with private facilities.

Economy Class

Adare Guesthouse, Father Griffin Place (Tel: 091 62638) – Simple but comfortable accommodation.
Glendawn House, Upper Salthill (Tel: 091 22872) – Good budget accommodation in the seaside suburb of Galway City.

Mid and south Galway is known as Oyster Country because of its long association with the harvesting of that most exotic of seafoods. An International Oyster Festival is still held in CLARINBRIDGE every September. **Paddy Burke's Oyster Bar** in the village is as good a place as any to sample the tasty product in as traditional an environment as you will find anywhere in County Galway.

Dún Ghuaire Castle is near the market village of KINVARA and overlooks Galway Bay. This dramatic sixteenth-century castle holds traditional medieval banquets throughout the summer. The main market town in southern Galway, GORT, is a little way to the south. The nineteenth-century **Lough Cutra Castle** and the **Punchbowl**, a wide natural crater, can be seen near here. It is worth a small detour from Gort to see **Kilmacduagh Church and round tower**, as these both have a close association with St Colmán, who flourished here in the early sixth century.

Thoor Ballylee is a sixteenth-century tower house near **Coole Park**, which was owned and lived in by W. B. Yeats shortly after the First World War. Now an interpretative centre, it offers restaurant and bookshop facilities, audio-visual presentations and multilingual guide commentary as well as woodland walks with picnic areas over the stream. It is open to the public 1000–1800 daily between May and October, and many rare examples of Yeats' published work are on display here. A little way further on, near CRAUGHWELL, is the grave of the poet Raftery in the grounds of **Lilleeneen Church**.

The ruins of the medieval **Athenry Castle** stand just outside the Norman-founded town of ATHENRY. The fifteenth-century **market cross** and the thirteenth-century **Dominican Priory of Saints Peter and Paul** are further reminders of the town's long history. The best-preserved **medieval town walls** anywhere in Ireland can also be seen here.

LOUGHREA is one of only a handful of towns of any size in east Galway, and as well as being the professional and service centre for a wide area, it is also the cathedral town for the diocese of Clonfert. **St Brendan's Cathedral** was built between 1897 and 1903 and has a beautifully artistic interior, including several fine stained-glass windows. A good range of sporting and leisure facilities is available to visitors in Loughrea, and the town's **museum** traces more than a century of history of the Gaelic Athletic Association.

Portumna Forest Park, near the village of WOODFORD, is a pleasant excursion and the nearby **Portumna Castle** is a national monument dating back more than 300 years. Two even earlier ruined buildings of note are **Clonfert Cathedral**, built on the site of a monastery founded by St Brendan the Navigator in AD 563, and **Clontuskert Abbey**, near the village of CLONFERT, which dates from late medieval times.

BALLINASLOE is the largest town in east Galway, and this ancient settlement came to prominence when Turlough O'Conor, King of Connaught, built a castle here in 1124. Among the places of interest today are the ruins of **Ballinasloe Castle**, the nineteenth-century **Garbally College**, and **St Michael's Church** which was built in the 1850s by a pupil of Pugin.

Returning west, the ruined **Franciscan Friary** in the village of KILCONNELL is reputed to be the burial place of St Ruth. A more attractive ruin is the **Augustinian Priory** at DUNMORE. The doorway and central tower are remarkably well preserved, and Walter de Bermingham is credited with founding the Priory in 1425.

 For the nature lover, one place of particular interest is **Mountbellow Lake and Bird Sanctuary**, a man-made

expanse covering about sixteen hectares. This is the breeding ground of the rare Irish Crane, and visitors are welcome to explore the site (quietly) at their leisure throughout the year.

Past the village of MILLTOWN, one final suggestion for somewhere to visit is TUAM, a town which was originally a religious settlement founded by St Jarlath in the early sixth century. It was upgraded to a monastic settlement in the eleventh century, and among the surviving ruins are the late twelfth-century chancel, and the medieval High Cross, in the Victorian **St Mary's Cathedral**.

Back west again, past Galway City, the village of MOYCULLEN is well placed for exploring the natural beauty of this part of the countryside around **Lough Corrib**. Quite apart from the natural beauty of this part of the county, two of the many ruined castles worth seeing near here are **Ross Abbey**, a large old seventeenth-century building, and the austere **Aughnanure Castle** which was built by the O'Flahertys in the fifteenth century and later besieged by Cromwellian troops.

OUGHTERARD is a popular place for fishing enthusiasts, and is often described as a gateway to Lough Corrib. From here, boats can be hired to take you to **Inchagoill**, the most beautiful island in Lough Corrib and best known for its early **monastic ruins** including **Teampall Phádraig** which is tenuously associated with St Patrick. The village of CLONBUR, on the northern side of the lough, is also well placed to see the lough at its best. Nearby, the village of CONG takes you (just) over the border into County Mayo and was the location of the 1951 film *The Quiet Man* which starred John Wayne and Maureen O'Hara.

The southern tip of Galway is one of the best-known Irish-speaking regions in West Ireland. This is part of beautiful CONNEMARA, a thinly populated region with a host of fine vantage points, secluded little beaches and tiny hamlets. BEARNA is one such hamlet, about five miles west of Galway City, with a long, sheltered beach.

The coastal road west goes through the village of SPIDDAL, with its Romanesque-style **parish church**, and past the **ruined castle** at INERVIN which has legendary associations with St Colmcille. CASLA is roughly the centre of southern Connemara, where several roads converge. This is a popular spot for fishing enthusiasts – the surrounding lakes are teeming with salmon. The artist Charles Lamb lived and worked at nearby **CARRAROE**. The **Hotel Carraroe** (Tel: 091 95116) has twenty bedrooms available, and a further ten self-catering cottages.

Try to make a brief visit to **Ros Muc**, a small peninsula jutting out into Kilkieran Bay. This is close to **Lough Aroolagh** and on one side of the lough stands the **cottage of Padraig Pearse**, who was executed for his part in the 1916 uprising. The village of **KILKIERAN** is so named because it was here that St Kieran came ashore on his way to Aran from Clonmacnois. A more recent visitor to this part of Ireland was President de Gaulle who spent some time at **CASHEL** and the neighbouring resort of **ROUNDSTONE** in 1969.

 Heading into north-west Galway, you'll find that the only town of any size is **CLIFDEN** which is generally regarded as the capital of Connemara. The town is a flourishing seaside resort, and stands above an inlet of **Ardbear Bay** against a backdrop of the beautiful Twelve Bens Mountains. Clifden was carefully planned by John D'Arcy in the early years of the nineteenth century, and the tall spires of both the small **Catholic Cathedral** and the **Protestant Church** dominate the town's skyline.

Two suggestions for somewhere to stay in Clifden, in the middle to upper price range, are: **Abbeyglen Castle** (Tel: 095 21201) which has forty bedrooms and a range of leisure facilities including a heated indoor swimming pool and tennis court, and is situated in ten acres of garden. It has a highly recommended restaurant. The other is the **Rock Glen Manor House** (Tel: 095 21035) with twenty-nine bedrooms. The Rock Glen is a converted nineteenth-century hunting lodge just outside the town.

Coral Strand, about four miles south-west of the town, is the best beach near Clifden. A local beauty spot is **Owenglin Cascade** where the River Owenglin tumbles over huge boulders just south of the town. More of Connemara's stunning scenery can be enjoyed on the **Sky Road**, a popular tourist route leading past Clifden Bay towards **KINGSTOWN**. Beside the Atlantic sea is

Connemara Golf Club, Bally Conneely, Clifden (Tel: 095 23502). This eighteen-hole par 72 course is challenging and testing.

The village of **BALLYNAHINCH** lies close to some good fishing lakes and several of the surrounding Ben peaks. From here it is a short drive to the **Inagh Valley** and the **Connemara National Park** with its Visitor Centre which is open 1000–1830 between April and October. The coastal village of **CLEGGAN**, near here, is the main fishing port for this part of West Ireland.

At Roundstone (south-west of Cashel Bay on the coast) is the **IDA Craft Centre** where Malachy Kearns makes all the traditional Irish instruments: bodhráns, tin whistles and Irish harps. Other suggestions for excursions in west Galway are: **Inishbofin**, a large island accessible by mailboat from Cleggan, with some medieval ruins and good beaches; the bleak **Renvyle Peninsula** made famous by the writings of Oliver St John Gogarty; and the rugged beauty of **KILLARY HARBOUR**. **Killary Lodge**, Derrynasliggaun, Leenane, County Galway (Tel: 095 43411) is set in twenty acres of its own land. The range of outdoor pursuits on offer include canoeing, coastal and hill walks, sailing, orienteering, archery, clay-pigeon shooting, cycling, swimming and tennis. Two special interest breaks offered are photography and painting. There are fifteen bedrooms, all ensuite, and the cooking is cordon bleu.

County Mayo lies to the north of Galway and is another of Ireland's largest counties. The county town, **CASTLEBAR**, is a busy, friendly market town offering plenty of souvenir shops, cafés and bars as well as an indoor swimming pool. **Breaffy House Hotel** is a stately home (Tel: 094 22033).

WESTPORT, the largest town in County Mayo, dates mainly from the late eighteenth century. Apart from the **Romanesque Catholic Church** and the octagon-shaped town centre layout, its main attraction is **Westport House**. This magnificent Georgian mansion has a superb collection of art nouveau glass and carving, and a good collection of artefacts from the 1798 Rebellion. There is also a **children's zoo** and once the admission is paid most of the attractions are free. This makes for a great day out for the family. There is also a camping site here. The house is open to the public throughout the summer. There is a good **Tourist Information office** (Tel: 098 25711) in the town centre. From here it is possible to get written information in French, German and English on walking, horse-riding and cycling holidays in the area. Westport is a base for the famous Glenans sailing centres providing resident sailing courses and sailboard training. Details from the Tourist office or Glenans, Collanmore Island, Westport. Two suggestions for accommodation are: the **Westport Ryan** (Tel: 098 25811), in Louisburgh Road, which has nearly sixty bedrooms and stands in its own grounds overlooking a lake; and the more modest **Castlecourt Hotel** (Tel: 098 25920) with forty bedrooms, all with private facilities. **Westport Golf Club**, Carrowholly (Tel: 098 25113), is on the shores of Clew Bay. A beautiful eighteen-hole course has been a venue for the Irish amateur championships.

Croagh Patrick is one of the tallest peaks near Westport (2,510 ft) and a place of pilgrimage for many Roman Catholics. It is from here that St Patrick is said to have rung his bell and so attracted all the snakes in Ireland to come to the summit and throw themselves over the edge. St Patrick prayed here for the forty days of Lent in AD 441. Over 60,000 faithful climb to its summit on the last Sunday in July every year. A more modern site of religious importance is the **Emancipation Cross**, near the fine beach just west of MURRISK. This is one of several such crosses in Ireland which commemorate the granting of Emancipation for Catholics in 1829. From **Ronagh Point** it is possible to visit **Clare Island** and **Inishturk Island**. Both are strikingly beautiful, and the former has a number of religious ruins. Back on the mainland, TOURMAKEADY is the centre of another pocket of native Irish-speakers. There are a great many forest and lakeside walks available in this part of County Mayo, and two places of particular interest are **Lough Carra** and the ruined **Abbey of Ballintubber** which stands on the site of a sixth-century abbey founded by followers of St Patrick.

Achill Island is well worth a visit. It can be reached from the mainland via a bridge. The island is fifteen miles wide and twelve miles long. It has a fantastic landscape with mountains, moors, lakes, beaches and bays. It's a haven for the photographer as the light is very special. Mountain walks and rock climbing are there for the active; all the beaches are accessible by road, Keembay and Minaon heights should not be missed. There is a fantastic array of sport and activities on the island: surfing for beginners and experts; canoeing and boating on lakes and sea; sea angling from boat and shore; tennis; six-hole golf links; orienteering; mountaineering; hang gliding; subaqua diving. All you need is the weather!

The eastern side of County Mayo is best known for the village of KNOCK – and the famous vision of the Virgin Mary which local people claim to have seen in the **Church of John the Baptist** in August 1879. Knock was subsequently granted the status of a genuine shrine by the Vatican, and Pope John Paul II visited the site in September 1979. Although the original church where the reputed vision was seen still stands, an enormous **new church**, with a capacity of 20,000, was opened in 1976. More than 750,000 people visit Knock each year, and accordingly the village has a large number of souvenir shops and cafés to meet the demand. One good local hotel is the **Belmont** (Tel: 094 88122) with nearly thirty bedrooms, all with private facilities.

Many of the small villages of east County Mayo have ecclesiastical ruins of some description. A **round tower** and **medieval tomb** survive at BALLA, and a restored **Augustinian friary** can be seen at BALLYHAUNIS. Only a few fragments of buildings remain at MAYO, the small hamlet which gave the county its name. It is difficult to believe that this sleepy village was once one of Ireland's largest religious communities. A final sight in this part of Mayo is the ruined **seventeenth-century church** at TURLOUGH, which has a twenty-three-metre-high tower.

Further north, the **Mullet Peninsula** dominates the north-west corner of County Mayo. BELMULLET is the main town in this part of the county, a good base for fishing or outdoor enthusiasts keen to explore the area at leisure. It also has a nine-hole golf course. Among the many isolated ruins in or around the peninsula are the medieval remains of **St Dervia's Church** at FALLMORE, and a collection of scattered buildings which may have been associated

with St Brendan at **Inishglora**. Spectacular views can be seen at
BALLYCASTLE just along the north coastline. For the fisherman
small boats can be launched for inshore fishing at Belderrig and
Ballycastle. Fish waiting to be caught are cod, whiting, gurnard
and ling. The beaches are safe and ideal for children. Information
on walks can be obtained from Tourist offices in the region.

The final part of County Mayo is the north-eastern corner
which borders County Sligo. This district is dominated by Loughs
Conn and Cuillin. In the middle of the larger of the two, **Lough
Conn**, lies the small island of **Pontoon**, which was the home of
the nineteenth-century robber and highwayman by the name of
Gallagher. Gallagher went down in history as the only known
Irish criminal for whom the rope broke whilst he was being
executed. Unfortunately for him, he didn't have time to escape
and, after a glass of wine and a chat to the crowd, a new rope
was found which this time did the job.

CROSSMOLINA is a good fishing centre and sightseers can visit
the sixteenth-century **Deel Castle** just outside the village. There
is a large beach at nearby Ballycastle and **Downpatrick Head** is a
favourite spot for walking enthusiasts. The wide open countryside
and striking cliff scenery form a perfect place in which to enjoy the
fresh, outdoor air. Much of the surrounding countryside provides
peat, one of the principal sources of fuel in West Ireland.

Further associations with St Patrick have been claimed by the
town of KILLALA, although historians believe it more likely that
St Muireadach founded the first Christian church in this part
of County Mayo. Killala was the base for an ill-fated French
military force who, in 1798, had come to spread the gospel
of Revolution. They attracted a number of Irish allies, but
despite one or two early successes against the British army, the
1100-strong army was ultimately defeated. The earliest surviving
church is the seventeenth-century **Church of Ireland Cathedral**,
although to the west of the town there are a few remains of
a thirteenth-century **Dominican priory**. Another of Killala's
interesting features is its **round tower**, a former lighthouse
which was converted to a belfry and safe refuge during a
period of religious persecution. One recommendation for bed

and breakfast accommodation in the town is with Mrs Caplice at **Avondale**, Pier Road (Tel: 096 32229).

BALLINA, the largest town in County Mayo, is on the River Moy, Ireland's prize salmon fishing river; with the famous 'ridge pool' in the town centre, frequently visited by honorary Irishman, Jack Charlton. Contact North Western Fisheries Board, Ardnaree House, Abbey Street, Ballina (Tel: 096 22788) about rod licences. The town was the first to fall during the short-lived French incursion of 1798. Locals lit the road still known as the 'Road of the Straw' with straw bales to guide the French troops towards the British army. Ballina is the cathedral town of the diocese of Killala, and the nineteenth-century **Cathedral of St Muireadach** is just about the only sight of note in the town.

Ballina's **Tourist Information office** (Tel: 096 22422) is open between mid-June and September. A fine country house hotel near Ballina is the **Belleek Castle** (Tel: 096 22061), which has sixteen rooms and a beautiful forest setting. The **Downhill Hotel** (Tel: 096 21033) is the best place to stay in town and it offers an excellent range of leisure facilities and heated indoor swimming pool. During July and August the hotel runs a Children's Club from three years and over, and lots of activities are on offer. The **Imperial Hotel** (Tel: 096 22200) is a less expensive alternative. Bord Fáilte in connection with Mayo Leisure holidays (Tel: 098 41647) arrange holidays to suit the individual. They have a host of experts in horse-riding, rock climbing, hill walking, bird-watching, photography, watersports, farm life, historical tours, and fishing. Accommodation is arranged in a local hotel and there are facilities for children to join in or be looked after.

The long, thin county of Roscommon borders Galway, Mayo, Sligo and Leitrim. This is rich agricultural land, and the principal town, **ROSCOMMON**, lies at the heart of this farming community. The town grew up around a large **Norman castle** which can still be seen a little way to the north of the town. The Irish destroyed the original castle in 1329 and built an almost identical fortress in its place twelve years later.

Roscommon's best-known sight, however, is probably the old **county jail**. The most intriguing fact about the jail is that its last official hangman was a formidable *woman* known as 'Lady Betty', the only female 'hangman' known to have worked in the British Isles. The **Tourist Information office** (Tel: 0903 26356) is based here, although it is only open between mid-June and the end of September.

Two other points of interest in Roscommon are the **Georgian Courthouse**, now owned by the Bank of Ireland, and a ruined **Dominican friary** which was founded by a former King of Connaught, Felim O'Connor, in 1254. His tomb lies within the friary and has several beautifully sculpted stone figures. Just over the county border in County Sligo is ENNISCRONE, a small seaside resort. There is a fine eighteen-hole championship golf course. The beach is over three miles long and the latest craze 'sand skiing' can be tried there.

For visitors to neighbouring County Sligo or Leitrim, KEADUE in the north-east of the county is a popular excursion. From here it is possible to visit **Slieve Anierin**, further east, and an ancient **church site** near **Lough Meelagh**. Further south, the town of BOYLE lies between **Lough Key** and **Lough Gara**. Among the places of interest in Boyle are a **Cistercian abbey**, founded in 1161, and the burnt-out shell of **Rockingham House** whose grounds form part of the **Lough Key Forest Park**. Further south-east, the village of FRENCHPARK was the birthplace of Douglas Hyde, the first President of modern Ireland. Much earlier rulers of Ireland were crowned at the **Hill of Connaught**, six miles south of Frenchpark. A **redstone pillar** marks what is believed to be the grave of Ireland's last pagan monarch, Dathi, who died in the early Dark Ages.

Two other places in Roscommon worth making an excursion to are STROKESTOWN, an attractive Georgian town lying at the foot of the 263-metre-high **Slieve Bawn**, and BALLINTOBER OF BRIDGET, where visitors can see a ruined **castle** built by the O'Connor family. The castle was besieged several times during its active history, including at least once by Cromwellian forces.

Sandwiched between Counties Mayo, Roscommon and Leitrim is County Sligo, one of the most rugged and remote parts of West Ireland. Physically County Sligo has a lot in common with neighbouring County Mayo – steep cliffs, wide loughs and only a handful of small towns and villages to interrupt the beautiful countryside. On the road between Roscommon and Sligo is **Markree Castle** at COLLOONEY, which has fifteen bedrooms with private bathrooms and direct dial telephone. This would make an interesting overnight stop or you could sample a lovely afternoon tea. Children are very welcome. The dining room of Markree is the **Knockmoldowney** restaurant (Tel: 071 67800). Very close to Markree on the Coolaney road is **Glebe House**, a guesthouse and restaurant, five bedrooms all ensuite, children welcome (Tel: 071 67787).

The county town of Sligo is **SLIGO TOWN** located in the north-east of the county. It is now possible to fly twice daily from Dublin to Sligo Town with Aer Lingus. Sligo Town is the largest in the north-west of Ireland, with a history dating back to before medieval times when it was plundered by the Vikings, and a colourful association with the family of the county's most famous poet, William Butler Yeats.

Sligo Town has two cathedrals both of which date from relatively modern times. The striking **Church of Ireland cathedral, St John's**, was the first to be built; it was designed by the distinguished architect Richard Cassels. It is here that concerts are held during the Sligo Arts Festival in September each year. The acoustics are superb and commented on by many visiting musicians. The **Roman Catholic Cathedral** is much larger and built out of locally quarried limestone. Of special interest are the stained glass windows.

Sligo Abbey is the oldest building in the town, having been founded as a Dominican priory in 1252 and rebuilt in the fifteenth century. Like so many of Ireland's medieval ecclesiastical buildings it was almost burnt to the ground by Cromwell's forces in the seventeenth century. A number of attractive cloisters have, however, survived and can still be seen.

The **Sligo County museum and art gallery** is an impressive local museum with a broad collection of artefacts ranging from prehistoric times right up to the Irish civil war earlier this century. A special room in the museum is devoted to the life and works of

W. B. Yeats. The museum and gallery are open 1000-1700 Tue, Wed, Fri and Sat, 1200-1700 on Thu, closed on Sun and Mon.

Travelling out of town you will find **Lough Gill**, made famous in so many of Yeats' poems. A splendid view of the lake can be had by taking the scenic route to the top of the Green Road.

Heading north out of town on the Bundoran road turn off for ROSSES POINT, a picturesque seaside village. There are two blue flag beaches excellent for swimming and a life guard is on duty during the summer months. Here you will find Sligo Yacht Club and the challenging Rosses Point Golf Course, well known for its beauty and spectacular views (Tel: 071 77186). Sea angling trips can be arranged from the village. Here there are two restaurants, **Reveries** (Tel: 071 77371) and the **Morrings** which serves wholesome food at a moderate price.

The main **Tourist Information** office (Tel: 071 61201) for County Sligo and the North-west is in Temple Street beside the Hawks Well Theatre. Here you will get plenty of information for bed and breakfast accommodation in the area. Two ideas for hotels would be the **Sligo Park Hotel** (Tel: 071 61201), Pearse Road (the Dublin road out of town). It has ninety bedrooms, all with private facilities, and a leisure complex. The more modest **Southern Hotel** (Tel: 071 62101), convenient for the railway station, has around fifty bedrooms, all with private bathrooms.

STRANDHILL is a coastal resort and lies about five miles from the centre of Sligo Town. It has a lovely long stretch of beach marked by a great black and yellow cannon. It must be made clear that this is a very dangerous beach for swimming as it has strong tidal undercurrents and has claimed lives. Although not one of Sligo's most attractive villages it none the less does possess an air of a traditional seaside resort. Strandhill also has an attractive eighteen-hole golf links on the sea front. From here it is possible to follow by road the signs to the start of the climb of the imposing **Knocknarea Mountain**; the ascent is easy except for one bit when a scramble on hands and knees may be needed but on a good day the views are rewarding from the top of the stone cairn which is said to be the grave of Queen Maeve of Connaught. A possible place to stay would be the **Glen Lodge**, two miles from Strandhill on the Ballisodare road. This is a Georgian house open from March to November. It has a good if not expensive restaurant open for dinner from 1930 (Tel: 071 68387).

Europe's largest and oldest collections of megalithic remains are at **CARROWMORE**. There is a visitor centre where information on the collections can be obtained and quite a lot of walking is involved. Sligo Riding Centre is beside the visitor centre where lessons can be given for adults or children. Also horses can be hired for treks (Tel: 071 61353).

Taking the Manorhamilton road out of Sligo Town past the hospital you will come across the **Glencar Lake** after a few miles. Follow the signs down to the **Glencar Waterfall**. Yeats enthused about this waterfall in his poem 'The Stolen Child'. This would make an ideal spot for a picnic.

Going back into town take the Drumcliff to Rathcormac road past Sligo Tennis Club. At **DRUMCLIFF** you will find the grave of W. B. Yeats. Although he died in Paris during the Second World War, when it was over he was brought back to be buried in the Church of Ireland churchyard where his great-grandfather had been rector. It is also here that you will find the carved High Cross which is all that remains of a sixth-century monastery which St Columba founded before sailing to Iona.

Lissadell House, west of Drumcliff, is a magnificent old mansion which is still owned by the Gore-Booth family. Yeats was a regular visitor to his friend Constance. She subsequently married a Polish artist, Count Markievicz, and became very active in the struggle for Irish independence. Standing for Sinn Fein in late 1918, she became the first woman elected to the British parliament although she deliberately never took her seat. Nancy Astor, who succeeded her husband as MP for Plymouth a few months later, did take her seat and is often wrongly called Britain's first woman MP.

Two other places of interest in north County Sligo are an early Christian site at **Inishmurray** (Tel: 071 67126), and the small coastal resort of **MULLAGHMORE**. This is a popular self-catering area and the views of the Atlantic are breathtaking. Sailing, windsurfing and waterskiing take place here. The **Beach Hotel** has a swimming pool (Tel: 071 66103) and **Zithna's** restaurant is open throughout the summer. **Classiebawn** – a Victorian castle, the family home of the late Earl Mountbatten of Burma – stands on the headland overlooking Mullaghmore. (It was shortly after leaving the village's small pier, in August 1979, that his small boat was blown up by the IRA, killing him and several members of his crew and family.)

Turning inland, County Leitrim, the most northerly of the seven counties which make up West Ireland, is also the least known. It has only a handful of quiet towns and villages and offers a very secluded destination for a holiday. Relatively few holidaymakers spend much time in Leitrim, preferring instead to make it the destination of a day-trip from one of the neighbouring counties, or else simply passing through it on their way to another part of Ireland.

The county town is CARRICK-ON-SHANNON, which is the centre of a small river-cruising industry. It is possible to hire boats from here to cruise the Shannon for a few days, or even a few weeks, and the town is well placed for visitors to explore the nearby **Lough Key Forest Park** and the **Arigna Mountains**, which still have a number of working coalmines. Overlooking Lough Arrow at CASTLEBALDWIN just off the Boyle–Sligo road (N4) is **Cromleach Lodge**, a modern country house, all bedrooms ensuite. The restaurant is excellent, and worth a visit (Tel: 071 65155).

The principal town in north Leitrim is MANORHAMILTON, which was founded by Sir Frederick Hamilton in the seventeenth century. His **manor**, after which the small town was named, is now a stately old ruin covered in ivy. The **Bonet Valley** stretches out to the north of Manorhamilton, and it is only a short drive to ROSSINVER where a **Holy Well** associated with St Mogue can be seen. A **megalithic tomb** has been located near KILTYCLOGHER, and this magnificent court cairn is known locally as Prince Connell's Grave. One other place of interest in County Leitrim is the attractive village of DROMAHAIR. **Creevelea Abbey** in the village was founded by the wife of Owen O'Rourke, chieftain of this part of Ireland in the sixteenth century.

North-west

INTRODUCTION

The chapter covers County Donegal, Ireland's largest northern county, often regarded as a microcosm of the country as a whole. Donegal is a county of considerable contrasts, with beautiful inland scenery and a long, rugged coastline broken only by the occasional stretch of golden sand and small seaside resort. It has no large towns, but countless little villages and hamlets which remain largely undiscovered by tourists.

County Donegal guarded its strong individuality during several centuries of conflict involving both religious and political upheaval; even today it has the largest concentration of native Irish-speakers in Ireland. This is a county primarily for the *Nature Lover* or the *Recluse*, or anyone who is keen to enjoy a holiday far from the hustle and bustle of a large town or city.

Our tour of County Donegal starts at Ballyshannon, just over the border from County Leitrim, and continues roughly clockwise around the coastline until we reach the north of the county.

HISTORY

County Donegal is exposed to the full force of the Atlantic Ocean on three sides – and has been for many thousands of years. Although its geological base is one of the oldest in Ireland – much of the county is the southernmost tip of the Caledonian mountain system which stretches from Scandinavia down through the Scottish Highlands to Ireland – a lot of the original rock has been eroded. What remains is essentially a rugged plateau, with an average height of 366 metres above sea level, and a number of jagged mountain peaks near the north-west corner of the county.

The earliest human settlers are believed to have flourished in the Irish Mesolithic period, around 7000 BC. More than a tenth of the 1400 different varieties of prehistoric tomb found in Ireland have been located in Donegal. Ui Neill was the first Dark Age local king to make his mark, and his family line eventually became the O'Neills whose military significance in Irish history was to manifest itself in later centuries.

St Patrick, who was born in Donegal, brought a level of Christianity to the county, but St Columba of Iona did much more to spread the Christian word. The Vikings and the Normans made a number of brief forays into Donegal but made little impression. In later centuries, however, Donegal was one of the few lasting strongholds of Irish independence, and the survival of Gaelic Irish is largely due to the efforts of the people of Donegal.

The county suffered greatly during the Great Famine in the 1840s, and had barely recovered before Ulster's main port at Derry was decreed to remain part of Britain when Irish independence was granted in 1922. Nevertheless, the county's tourist industry began to grow after 1945 and today it is one of the principal sources of revenue for Ireland's most northerly county.

COMMUNICATIONS

The nearest international airport to County Donegal is at Derry, just over the border in Northern Ireland. There are regular scheduled flights from Glasgow and Manchester. Loganair has flights to and from Glasgow from Carrickfin, thirty miles north of Donegal Town. Road connections with Donegal are good. There is a small airstrip just outside Letterkenny, in the county itself, but this is only suitable for visitors arriving in private aircraft. There is an airport at Sligo with daily flights to Dublin and Luton.

There are no rail links into Donegal and the nearest you can get by train is Derry, to the east, and Sligo in the south. Road connections are good and it is possible to make a circular tour of most of central and southern Donegal on the N56 alone. The N15 links Sligo with the town of Donegal, and the N56 and N13 will take you to or from Derry.

TOURIST INFORMATION

The main Tourist Information office for the county is based at Derry Road, Letterkenny (Tel: 074 21160). This office is open all year round and can provide you with information about most of the villages and places to stay in the county, together with suggestions for places to stay in all price categories. In addition, there are seasonal Tourist Information offices in Donegal Town and Dungloe.

CLIMATE

The North-west has a reasonably mild climate between May and September, and this is reflected in the number of popular seaside resorts which have developed along the Donegal coastline. Winter temperatures fall considerably, and strong Atlantic breezes combine with heavy rainfall to make the North-west a most inclement part of Ireland to visit outside the summer months.

Average temperatures between May and September vary from about 14°C (57°F) up to a maximum of 21–24°C (70–74°F). Coastal breezes can be anticipated throughout the year and the weather can change quickly so always bring a change of clothing no matter what time of year you visit Donegal.

WHERE TO GO FOR WHAT

The scenery and countryside of north-west Ireland is varied, and it is not difficult to see why W. B. Yeats was at his most inspired when he regularly travelled north to Donegal from his home in Sligo. Among the best beach resorts are Greencastle, on Lough Foyle, Culdaff, Malin Head, Ballyliffen and Rathmullan. Two particularly good family resorts are Moville, on the Inishowen Peninsula, and Buncrana, which has a wide range of recreational facilities.

Much of inland Donegal is ideal for those looking for a touring holiday, or for visitors who are keen to explore the natural beauty of this part of Ireland. A number of Donegal's resorts are suited to the outdoor sporting enthusiast, particularly those who enjoy fishing, and some resorts worth considering are: Ballyshannon, Bunbeg, Bundoran, Donegal Town, Fahan, Glencolumbkille, Rossnowlagh and Dunfanaghy.

County Donegal also offers a wide range of forests and trails and what follows is a selection of ten of the most popular.

Ards Forest Park (Páirc Fhoraoise na hArdadh): car park, picnic site, toilet facilities, forest walks, nature trails and scenic views; three miles north of Creeslough off the N56 to Dunfanaghy – on the south-west shore of Sheephaven Bay.

Crownasillagh (Croaghacullin – Cró na Saileach): forest walks; six miles west of Killybegs on the R263 to Kilcar – turn right for two miles on a third-class road.

Crocknacunny (Cnoc na Coinne): lay-by, picnic site, forest and riverside walks, access to Lough Derg; two miles north of Pettigo on the R233 to Lough Derg.

Derryloughan (Doire Luacháin): forest and seashore walks; three miles north-east of Glenties on the R250 to Letterkenny. Turn left on a third-class road for two miles.

Derryveagh (Doire Bheitheach): picnic site, forest walks and fine views of Claggan Lough; a mile north of Church Hill village on the R251 to Gweedore. Turn left on a third-class road for two miles.

Glengesh Pass (Malaidh Gleanna Geise): picnic site, forest walks and scenic views; a mile south of Ardara on the N56 heading towards Killybegs. Turn left on a third-class road for two miles, towards Glencolumbkille.

Lough Derg (Loch Derg): car park a mile from the pier for Station Island, picnic sites, lakeshore drive, forest walks, and access to St Brigid's Well; six miles north of Pettigo on the R233 leading to Lough Derg.

Meenirroy (Mín an Fhir Ruaidh): forest walks; twelve miles west of Letterkenny on the R250 to Glenties.

Murvagh/Mullanasole Strand (Murbhach): picnic site, forest walks and access to the beach; four miles south of Donegal on the

N15 to Ballyshannon – turn south-west at Laghy for just under three miles.

Woodquarter (Ceathrú na Coilleadh): picnic site, forest walks and scenic views; two miles north of Milford on the R245 heading towards Cranford. The turn-off is on the right-hand side of the road.

From the south you will enter County Donegal just before **BUNDORAN**, one of the best-known seaside resorts in the Irish Republic. Centuries before the first holidaymakers arrived, the brisk Atlantic winds shaped many of the coastal rocks into some bizarre shapes, the largest and most striking of which are known as 'The Wishing Chair' and 'The Fairy Bridge'.

Bundoran is a typical seaside town – bustling with life and activity between May and September, but practically dead for the rest of the year. There is a long stretch of clean sand and a range of sporting attractions, including several golf courses. The town has all the main amenities, including a seasonal **Tourist Information office** (Tel: 072 41350) which can give you information about the extensive range of activities and excursions available during the summer months.

The resort is not ideal for independent visitors during the summer season unless accommodation has been pre-booked. Two suggestions for somewhere to stay are: the **Great Northern** (Tel: 072 41204), which has nearly a hundred bedrooms, all with private facilities, and stands in the middle of a golf course; and the more modest **Maghery House Hotel** (Tel: 072 41234) which has fourteen bedrooms, all with bathrooms.

BALLYSHANNON, a mile or two further up the coast, is a much older and altogether more relaxing town for those who prefer not to be part of the package market. The town is thought to have been founded in the sixteenth century BC by a small group of Scythians who were fleeing from persecution further south in Europe. The mighty O'Donnell family held the town for many centuries in medieval times, and several bloody battles with English forces took place near here.

Among the places of interest are the old **parish church** of St Anne's, where Donegal's bard William Allingham (1824–89) is buried, and the barracks which were built in 1700 by Colonel Thomas Burgh. A small island, **Abbey Island**, stands in the estuary just off Ballyshannon and here visitors can see the ivy-covered ruins of a twelfth-century **Cistercian abbey**.

Three ideas for somewhere to stay in Ballyshannon are **Dorrian's Imperial Hotel** (Tel: 072 51147), a grand old middle-range hotel with nearly thirty bedrooms, all with private bathrooms; the less expensive **Creevy Pier** (Tel: 072 51236) which has ten rooms, also with private facilities; and the five-bedroomed **Danby House** (Tel: 072 51138), a registered Grade A guesthouse with a good restaurant.

ROSSNOWLAGH is a smaller resort a little way north on the west coast. It has another fine strand stretching nearly three miles round Donegal Bay and the little village here is an increasingly popular holiday destination – particularly if you are a surfing enthusiast. The O'Sgingin family come from this part of Donegal originally, and a member of that family held the post of hereditary historian to the O'Donnells for generations.

BALLINTRA and **LAGHEY** are two small villages you will pass through before reaching the town of Donegal. A beautiful detour from the town itself, or a possible excursion, is along a narrow road heading south-east from Ballintra. After a few miles, the countryside spreads before you with not a house to be seen, and the mysterious charm of **Lough Derg** and **The Black Gap** stretches out in front. Lough Derg has been a place of Christian pilgrimage for centuries, despite no obvious early religious significance and the efforts of various medieval popes and monarchs, as late as Queen Anne, to prevent it. Every summer thousands of pilgrims still flock to the island to enjoy a few days of silent prayer.

The town of **DONEGAL** takes its name from a Viking fort established here in the ninth century, Dún na nGall, which means 'the fort of the foreigners'. Donegal stands on the estuary of the River Eske and it grew in both size and importance as the main seat of the O'Donnell family who ruled over this part of

Ireland until their chiefs were forced out during the Flight of the Earls in 1607.

Sir Basil Brooke was the English landlord who settled here after 1607, and he is largely credited with the layout of the modern town. Among the places of interest are a large **square tower** with two turrets, which was built by the O'Donnells in 1505, and a **small castle** which was the main O'Donnell home and subsequently was refurbished by Brooke as his own residence.

The remains of a **medieval abbey** stand on the banks of the river and its associations with the O'Donnell family go back many centuries. Several leading members of the family are buried in and around the abbey, including the warrior Red Hugh O'Donnell, who offered the friary many endowments in the late fifteenth century.

There is a **Tourist Information office** (Tel: 073 21148) at The Quay, which is open between May and September. There is much in the way of accommodation in Donegal itself, and two suggestions are: **The Hyland Central** (Tel: 073 21027), with seventy-two bedrooms, all with private facilities, and the more modest **Abbey Hotel** (Tel: 073 21014) which has forty-nine bedrooms, also with private facilities.

North from the town of Donegal the countryside really opens out. A circular tour of Donegal Bay and the southern part of the county covers barely fifty miles yet takes you through some of the most beautiful scenery in Ireland. The village of MOUNTCHARLES is a good starting point for the tour, and visitors can admire (from the outside only) the eighteenth-century **family house of the Conyngham family** whose titles include that of the Earl of Mountcharles.

A little way along the coast is DUNKINEELY, a picturesque village with a good reputation for sea fishing. An ecclesiastical building of some description has stood on the site of the village's **Transitional church** since the seventh century, although the only relic from this period is an **early stone cross slab**. The ivy-clad walls of the church date mainly from the twelfth century.

KILLYBEGS is the next village around the Bay, and one of the largest on the tour. The village's early history is uncertain, but St Catherine is said to have saved the harbour from destruction in 1513. This is a major fishing port for both commercial fishermen and sporting enthusiasts. Even those who are not interested in fishing will find a certain fascination as the catches are unloaded, washed, and made ready for the next stage of the journey to the fishmongers and restaurants of Europe.

One of the village's most impressive buildings is **St Catherine's Church**, designed by J. B. Papworth and built during the 1840s. The interior is beautifully proportioned and the spacious nave measures thirty metres by twelve metres. Standing close to the church tower is the decorated tomb slab of Niall Mor Mac Sweeney, a leading member of one of the most powerful families in north-west Ireland in late medieval times.

Killybegs was well known for its hand-tufted carpets. Examples of the 'Donegal Carpet' are on display in Dublin Castle, the White House in Washington, and the Vatican. Small carpets can be bought as souvenirs, but remember that the carpets are not cheap as you are paying for genuine craftsmanship.

The walls of a **medieval castle** still stand on St John's Point, a narrow promontory which protrudes out into Donegal Bay. During the summer months visitors can also enjoy one of the finest – and busiest – beaches in north-west Ireland. The views of Donegal Bay are simply breathtaking, whatever time of year you visit the Point.

There are one or two good restaurants and modest places to stay in Killybegs and a full list is available from the Tourist Information office in Donegal.

The tiny village of KILCAR is worth a stop to admire the **Roman Catholic Church**. Although built as late as 1904, it is a very attractive building and a good example of the church architecture of its period. Visitors can also see local handloom weavers at work, producing Donegal tweed. The nearby village of CARRICK stands above **Teelin Bay** and is a good base for outdoor enthusiasts keen to explore the **Slieve League cliffs**. These rise to more than 600 metres above sea level and offer endless possibilities for walks for the energetic visitor.

GLENCOLUMBKILLE occupies just about the most westerly position in County Donegal. As locals will tell you, beyond here there is nothing but sea until you reach America! The village has a large **folk museum** which is open daily 1000–1200 between Easter and the end of September.

The **Glencolumbkille Valley** was named after St Columba of Iona and he is credited with establishing an early monastery near here. It is possible to make a three-mile 'pilgrimage' around fifteen cross slabs, pillars, and ruined chapels known as 'the Stations of the Cross'. The fifth is particularly worth seeing as this is reckoned to have been St Columba's chapel; the eleventh stop is said to have sheltered sailors who were washed ashore from a storm-wrecked Armada vessel in 1588.

The main road continues inland to **ARDARA**, a popular little village for a short stop to admire **Loughros More** and **Loughros Beg Bays**. Steep cliffs lead down towards **Tormore Head** and **Ballagh Pass**, two of southern Donegal's best-known beauty spots. Ardara also has a flourishing handwoven tweed industry, and it is usually possible during the summer months to see the looms in use.

There are one or two good beaches against a mountain backdrop near **PORTNOO**. An interesting walk is over to **Inishkeel Island**, when the tide is low, where some early Christian monastic ruins can be seen. Another local attraction is **Doon Fort**, on an island in Doon Lough, which can only be reached by boat. The early medieval fort still has much of its four-metre-high walls intact and is an impressive sight, even from a distance. When it was originally built, the fort was designed to house both animals and people, and small islands such as this were a popular base because they were easier to defend.

North-east of Ardara, where two glens meet, is the village of **GLENTIES**. Small-scale industries are developing here and include home woollen spinning and Ireland's only State-funded fish hatchery. Among the public buildings worth seeing in Glenties are the **Court House**, built during the 1840s, and the **Market House** which was constructed around the same time.

The parish church is one of the newest in Ireland, having been completed in 1975. One suggestion for accommodation is the **Highland's Hotel**, twenty-one bedrooms (Tel: 075 51111). There is little to see or do if you head inland from Glenties; only one minor road cuts through the **Blue Stack Mountains** to a handful of scattered villages near the border with Northern Ireland.

BALLYBOFEY and **STRANORLAR** are two such villages, standing on the River Finn and connected by a bridge. Fishing and game shooting, in season, are excellent in this part of County Donegal, and the possibilities of exploration in the bleak Blue Stack Mountains are endless.

The north-west coast is dotted with attractive little villages, most standing on or close to a good stretch of beach with a rugged cliff-face backdrop. Past **Crohy Head**, a local beauty spot, **DUNGLOE** is a small fishing port which lies in the heart of one of the few remaining Irish-speaking parts of Ireland. This is a rural, agricultural community which has learned to adapt to very poor soil conditions over the last few hundred years. The village of Dungloe is known locally as the 'Capital of the Rosses', after a beautiful lake and rocky area of land which links the village with Inishfree Bay.

One of the best beaches here is at **MAGHERY**, a little way south-west from Dungloe. Sightseers can visit a **megalithic portal tomb** a little way west of the village, and there is a **late medieval church** less than two miles away. The church measures just thirteen metres by six metres, making it one of the smallest in Ireland, and was in regular use until 1829. The **Ostan na Rosann** (Tel: 075 21088) is a delightful hotel overlooking Dungloe Bay and offering forty-eight bedrooms, all with private facilities. The hotel also has a small heated indoor swimming pool.

Aranmore Island is within easy reach of the small port village of **BURTONPORT**, from where regular ferries operate. The island is the largest of several off the Rosses coast and a small community has lived there for many centuries. Visitors can enjoy both trout fishing and sea angling, and there are many fine cliff walks.

The fragmentary remains of a promontory fort still stand on the southern end of the island.

Back on the mainland again, visitors should try not to miss another fine beauty spot at **CROLLY**, where there is a magnificent waterfall on the River Gweedore. Nearby **GWEEDORE** itself is a popular village which stands in a part of County Donegal which is often described as 'spectacularly wild'.

Gweedore is rapidly becoming one of north-west Ireland's major holiday destinations for game-fishing and outdoor enthusiasts, although there are still very few places to stay. Holidaymakers might be interested to know that much of Gweedore's electricity is generated by a local turf-burning power station.

If you have your own transport, a scenic road out of Gweedore takes you past the beauty of **Loughs Nacung** and **Dunlewy** into the **Derryveagh Mountains**. The highest peak in north-west Ireland is Errigal, 750 metres above sea level, and this can be seen at close quarters if you take this route. The mountain can be climbed in good weather but the loose scree and steepness of the summit make it unsafe for inexperienced climbers.

The village of **DUNLEWY** is the nearest town or village to Errigal, and it, too, is a popular base for fishing enthusiasts keen to explore the numerous rivers and lakes round about. Sightseers may prefer to look inside the village's **Church of the Sacred Heart**, with its thirty-metre-high tower, which was built by William Augustine Ross of London in 1877. Ross owned the surrounding Dunlewy estate at that time.

The main road east – the R250 – reaches **LETTERKENNY**, the largest town in north-west Ireland and the only place with a **Tourist Information office** (Tel: 074 21160) which is open all year round. The town stands on the River Swilly, close to Lough Swilly, and grew up as a market town in the last quarter of the nineteenth century. Today Letterkenny is the cathedral town of the diocese of Raphoe, and the town centre is dominated by **St Eunan's Cathedral** which was built, in late Gothic style, between 1890 and 1900. A **statue of Patrick O'Donnell**, the distinguished Cardinal Archbishop of Armagh between 1925 and 1927, stands outside the Cathedral.

Although much less impressive to look at, the town's **Church of Ireland church** is considerably older. It dates from the late seventeenth century and the stonework is in extremely good condition. Count Redmond and his seven sons are among the many local personalities buried in the adjoining churchyard. Redmond was a discontented nobleman who had been disowned by his family in the second half of the seventeenth century. In search of excitement and money, he and his seven sons formed an unusual band of outlaws and made their living from highway robbery. Redmond died in 1681 although the law allowed few of his sons to die in their beds as their father had.

Other places of interest near Letterkenny include the **remains of a medieval church** at Conwal cemetery, two miles from the town, and **Scarrifhollis**, three miles south-west, where Oliver Cromwell's army routed the opposing Catholics led by Bishop Heber MacMahon. The Bishop and the surviving Catholic soldiers were executed shortly after the defeat, despite Cromwell's personal promise of clemency.

There are few restaurants and hotels in Letterkenny, which is perhaps surprising considering that it is the largest town in the county. The best suggestion for somewhere to stay is the A-grade **Mount Errigal Hotel** (Tel: 074 22700), in the town centre, which has nearly sixty bedrooms, all with private facilities. The hotel has a good restaurant offering a varied range of Irish and international specialities. Another popular restaurant is **Rumpoles** (Tel: 074 24227), in Port Road, which offers mainly traditional Irish cuisine in an informal setting.

A final village worth visiting before you return to the west coast again is DOOCHARRY. The main road to and from Letterkenny winds up (or down) from this peaceful little hamlet through some of the most strikingly beautiful countryside in the entire county. The River Gweebarra cuts through the hills on its way to the sea and visitors can enjoy fine views over the surrounding **Glendowan** and **Derryveagh mountains**.

Back on the coast again the main road north continues past BUNBEG, a small resort with an enormous golden beach and a quaint early nineteenth-century Gothic-style church. This part of Donegal is known as 'Bloody Foreland' because the sun, particularly during the summer months, turns the rocks to a reddish shade which can be both beautiful and eerie.

Ballyness Bay is one of several such bays along the Donegal coastline, and the principal resort overlooking it is **GORTAHORK**. This is the heart of the Irish-speaking community of County Donegal and a good base for climbing enthusiasts or those keen to learn more about the traditional crafts and culture of this part of Ireland. **Ballyconnell House**, a restored seventeenth-century estate house, is now a college which teaches Irish during the summer months. During July every year the town hosts a major exhibition of local paintings and crafts in the **exhibition and crafts centre**, opposite McFadden's Hotel in the town centre. This is usually a good place to pick up an original work of art, albeit by an unknown local artist, at a relatively low price.

The **Muckish Mountain**, 670 metres above sea level, is the highest peak in the immediate area and has a number of cliff and rock faces offering varying degrees of difficulty to climbers. A small church, the Church of Christ the King, was built on the mountain in the early 1950s. A good hotel in Gortahork is **McFadden's** (Tel: 074 35267), in the Main Street; it has eighteen bedrooms, sixteen with private facilities.

A short distance up the coast, the village of **FALCARRAGH** is one of the few Irish-speaking villages left in Ireland. English is spoken, of course, but Irish is likely to be the first language you hear. This is the best village from which to climb Muckish Mountain, through the **Muckish Gap**. Fishing in the local streams is another attraction of Falcarragh, although many visitors come to see the ruins of an interesting **rectangular church** at Ray, which dates from the late sixteenth century. A High Cross has been erected in the centre of the ruins.

Three miles north from Gortahork is **Magheraroarty Pier** where visitors can catch one of several ferries across to **Tory Island**. Although the island lies just nine miles off the mainland, the sea crossing tends to be quite rough. Before a regular helicopter service was introduced in the 1970s, the island was often cut off for days, occasionally weeks, on end.

Tory Island offers plenty of possibilities for both the *Sightseer* and the *Recluse* although there is practically nothing in the way of tourist accommodation so visitors are best advised to return to the mainland by evening. It has been inhabited since prehistoric times and there is considerable evidence of the island's long history. The most impressive man-made sight is the **medieval round tower**, built from pink Donegal granite cemented with a lime made from sea-shells; it still retains part of its original conical top. The tower stands near the shore at the village of WEST TOWN and the circumference measures nearly sixteen metres. Although the tower is partially ruined, it has stood for more than 1000 years despite constant buffeting from the fierce Atlantic gales.

Tory Island is thought to have had five churches at one time, although the only remains of an early church are the foundations of one which was known as the **Church of the Morsheisear**. There is no sign of the church (probably legendary) said to have been inhabited by St Columba. However, the large 'hole' in the centre of the island is said to have been created by St Columba's staff when he threw it from the summit of the Muckish Mountain. Other points of interest on Tory Island include a **T-shaped cross**, carved from a single two-metre-high block of stone, which stands at the West Town harbour, and the remains of a **four-walled fort** at the east end of the island. The promontory fort is known in Donegal as Balor's Fort after the Celtic God of Darkness, a baleful figure from Irish legend who is believed to have used the island as a safe haven during many of his pirate missions in the mortal world.

Back on the mainland again to the next coastal village, DUNFANAGHY, which overlooks an attractive isthmus on **Sheep Haven**. The village has a fine long beach and the surrounding coastline offers many possibilities for long walks. There are local beauty spots at Rosguill, Horn Head and a **natural blowhole** – known as MacSwiney's Gun – at Trawmore.

CREESLOUGH stands at the head of Sheep Haven Bay, and it was here that the powerful MacSweeney family settled in medieval times. The family 'inherited' the magnificent **Doe Castle** in 1440, and this can still be seen in all its fifteenth-century glory about two miles outside the village. The MacSweeneys lived here for a couple of centuries, but the castle remained occupied until 1890. Few can deny that the castle's dramatic position, overlooking the Bay, is one of the finest of any castle in Ireland. Above the doorway visitors can admire the carved initials of General George Vaughan Harte, British hero of the Battle of Seringapatam during the Indian Wars and owner of the castle in 1798. Among the other notable features of the castle are a seventeen-metre-high keep and a tomb slab dedicated to the original MacSweeney.

ROSAPENNA is the next small resort and its main attraction is a superb eighteen-hole championship golf course. The nearest good beach is a little way further on at **Downings** which has a good reputation for watersports. Local attractions include a collection of unusual rock patterns at **Muslac**. A good middle-range hotel in Rosapenna is the **Rosapenna Golf** (Tel: 074 55301) with forty bedrooms and a location close to the golf course.

Visitors to this part of the North-west should not miss the opportunity to see something of the **Rosguill Peninsula**. To see the Rosguill at its best, it is necessary to walk some distance although it is possible to do a 'basic' tour by car along the Atlantic Drive from Sheep Haven to Mulroy Bay. Among the many beauty spots worth looking out for are **Tranarossan Bay, Melmore Head** and **Horn Head**. The towering height of the Muckish Mountain is seldom far from view and is a good landmark to guide your tour if you are not following a prearranged route.

Two villages of particular interest along this section of coast are **CARRIGART** and **MILFORD**. Carrigart stands on an inlet of Mulroy Bay and is often used as a base by caravan and camping holidaymakers touring northern Donegal. Milford stands on the southern end of the same Bay and is well placed for visitors keen to enjoy the excellent fishing generally available on the Leannan River and Lough Fern. **St Columba's Tullyferne Church**, in the village, was built in 1870 and is a good example of the style of Gothic revival often seen in County Donegal. Both villages are conveniently located for visitors to explore the **Fanad Peninsula**. By car, it is possible to follow the Fanad Peninsula Scenic Tour which was built and officially opened in 1980. The tour is well signposted and covers forty-five miles past lakes, beaches and countless beauty spots where you can stop for a while, take a few photographs, and perhaps enjoy a picnic if the weather is fair.

The village of KERRYKEEL has a fine location overlooking Mulroy Bay, and visitors will also be rewarded by good views over the Knockalla Mountain, rising to the north-east, and the **Knockalla Fort** on a nearby ridge which was built in the early nineteenth century as a precaution against possible invasion by the French. A much older site, the **Kildooney More portal tomb** which dates from the Neolithic period, is close at hand.

Three more scattered little villages are within easy reach. TAMNEY stands by a lough on an inlet of Mulroy Bay and the **ruins of a sixteenth-century castle** built by the MacSweeney family are here. KINDRUM, on the other hand, is a relatively modern village, having grown up with the expansion of the local linen industry in the early years of this century. PORTSALON offers a contrast again, with a long stretch of sand which is safe for family bathing.

RATHMULLAN, on the south-east corner of the Fanad Peninsula, is another relatively quiet village, but it has a more colourful past than most of the picturesque hamlets in this part of the county. In 1587, Hugh O'Donnell, the fifteen-year-old son and heir of the O'Donnell family, was kidnapped from Rathmullan by the English Lord Deputy, Sir John Perrott. Young Hugh was kept prisoner in Dublin Castle until he managed to escape on Christmas Eve 1591. His understandable bitterness against the English manifested itself in various military conflicts, but he was eventually driven out of Ireland and died in exile in Spain in 1602. Among the points of interest in the village are the **wide harbour**, a major anchorage for British ships during the First World War, and the remains of **Rathmullan Priory**. The Priory was founded by Owen MacSweeney in 1516 for the Carmelite Order, and was severely damaged by the English in 1595. It was subsequently restored, and the most striking feature remains its tall tower.

Among several good restaurants in Rathmullan is the **Water's Edge** (Tel: 074 58138), near the harbour, which specializes in delicious seafood. Two suggestions for accommodation are the middle-range **Fort Royal Hotel** (Tel: 074 58100), with fifteen bedrooms, private beach and a wide range of sporting facilities including tennis and sailing; and the higher grade **Rathmullan House** (Tel: 074 58188) which stands in its own grounds overlooking Lough Swilly.

At the base of the Fanad Peninsula is RAMELTON, one of the largest villages in the northern part of County Donegal. It was founded by William Stewart in the first half of the seventeenth century and quickly expanded. A number of early buildings can still be seen, including a small row of houses in Castle Street and the ruins of **Tullyaughnish Church**, with a decorated Romanesque carving in its east wall which was taken from an even older church. Most of the later town, including what is now the main street, grew up on just one side of the river – the other side is lined with trees. Among the more interesting later town buildings are a number of three-storey **Georgian houses** facing the river at Shore Road, and the **Ramelton Public Hall** which was completed in 1878. Three miles to the south of the village, visitors can see the ruins of **Killydonnell Friary**, which was founded in 1471 for the Franciscan Third Order Regulars.

A good restaurant in Ramelton is the **Mirabeau Steak House** (Tel: 074 51138) which, as its name implies, specializes in enormous steaks served with any one of a number of tasty home-made sauces. One suggestion for bed and breakfast accommodation is with Mrs Scott, at **The Manse** (Tel: 074 51047), near the village centre.

Before heading on to the rugged north-east corner of the region, do not overlook the excursion possibilities inland in central and northern Donegal. KILMACRENNAN, for example, is a beautiful little hamlet which stands at the junction of roads leading from Letterkenny, Milford, Ramelton and Creeslough. In early Christian times, it was from here that St Columba was sent to foster-parents from his birthplace at Gartan.

St Columba returned to the village and founded a church, later converted to an abbey which was in regular use until the mid-sixteenth century. The remains of the **abbey** can still be seen half a mile to the north of the village. It is a graceful old ruin, even if very little now remains. Traces of one or two later churches can be seen near the revered abbey.

GARTAN itself is worth a visit since it was here that Columba – whose name means 'dove' – was born in AD 521. A **flagstone** marks the actual spot, at Lacknacoo in the Glenveagh Estate, where he is said to have been born of Royal parents more than 1400 years ago.

Much of this inland region forms the magnificent **Glenveagh National Park** whose scenery and castle are simply breathtaking. **Lough Beagh** is a long, narrow lake which is a centrepiece for the whole Park, and this really is a magnificent part of Ireland for the *Nature Lover, Recluse*, or the romantic visitor to explore at leisure. Be sure not to miss catching a glimpse of one of only two herds of red deer in Ireland, which live in a fenced-off area of the Park.

The north-east corner of County Donegal is known as the **Inishowen Peninsula** and stretches from Lough Foyle and Lough Swilly to the most northerly point in Ireland, **Malin Head**. The centre of the peninsula is very hilly, although the highest peak (Slieve Snaght) reaches no more than 615 metres above sea level. Our route through the peninsula broadly follows that recommended by the Irish Tourist Board as 'a good day's touring' by car.

MANORCUNNINGHAM is a small village at the foot of the peninsula and among several ruined buildings near here are the remains of a **fifteenth-century friary** which still has a magnificent east window – one of the best in Donegal. Evidence of much earlier settlement is the Grianán of Aileach, a partly restored **prehistoric stone fort** on the summit of the 250-metre **Grianán mountain**. Most of the restoration was completed by a Dublin archaeologist in the 1870s, although it ceased to be used as a fort in AD 674.

The village of FAHAN stands on Lough Swilly and its 'formal' name is Fahan Mura after an early Christian settler, St Mura. A few fragments from his original **seventh-century abbey** remain, including a flat twin-faced stone cross. There is a very good **Yacht Club** at Fahan which welcomes visitors during the summer months. A little way further north is BUNCRANA, a small seaside resort overlooking the eastern shore of Lough Swilly. There is a first-class family beach and sightseers can visit a **tower house** erected by the O'Dohertys in the early fifteenth century and a **six-arched bridge** over the River Crana which was built on the orders of Sir John Vaughan around 1718.

The road passes through the **Mamore Gap**, offering magnificent views out to sea. The climb reaches its peak at the village of CLONMANY whose main attraction is the large **waterfall** at Glenview. The nearest beach is at Binnion, just over a mile from the village; there is also a raised beach at nearby Rockstown.

BALLYLIFFIN is another of Inishowen's little seaside resorts, with a popular stretch of sandy beach at Pollan. The village is well placed for visitors to enjoy climbing **Crockaughrim**, or viewing the ruined **Carrickbrackey Castle** with its large circular tower. From here it is only a short drive to **Carndonagh**, an early Christian site with the oldest standing cross in Ireland. **St Patrick's Cross**, as it has been known since antiquity, dates from the seventh century and is one of the finest examples of an early cross outside mainland Europe. Nearby MALIN is the most northerly village in Ireland, and its main attraction to visitors is Malin Head which is as far north as you can go before reaching the Atlantic Ocean. Another village close to Malin is CULDAFF where visitors can see the **stone 'boat'** in which St Boden is said to have crossed to Ireland from Scotland. A four-metre-high **stone cross** stands just outside the village and there are a number of small sandy beaches within easy reach.

This whole northern area is fine territory for hill walking, although visitors with children should be wary of sudden cliff-faces (up to 300 metres high) in and around Malin Head. One of the peninsula's best beaches can be enjoyed at **Greencastle**, although it is better known for the remains of the magnificent **castle** built by Richard de Burgo – the Red Earl of Ulster – in 1305. The castle remained occupied until the last century, and then quickly fell into disrepair.

Among the remaining villages of interest on the eastern side of the peninsula are MOVILLE; tiny MUFF, right on the border with Northern Ireland; RAPHOE, with a number of ruined ecclesiastical buildings including a monastery which dates back to the tenth century; and **LIFFORD**, with an attractive eighteenth-century **Court House**. One suggestion for somewhere to stay in Lifford is the farm guesthouse run by Mr and Mrs McKean. The **Hall Greene** (Tel: 41318) offers an ideal base for touring, fishing and golf within a relaxed and peaceful atmosphere.

Midlands

INTRODUCTION

This chapter, dealing with the sprawling Midlands region of Ireland, covers a wider area and more counties than any other in this guide. The vast majority of Ireland's best-known resorts and larger towns are located along the coast, so it is an easy misconception to assume that the Midlands have little to offer the visitor. We aim to show that this is far from being the case.

This region is commonly known as the Lakelands, due to a conscious effort on the part of the Irish Tourist Board to attract more visitors to this beautiful, often ignored area of Ireland. Parts of the Midlands actually contain more water than land so the cruising and fishing enthusiast will have literally hundreds of possible places to visit. Apart from the lakes, there are few wide, flat parts to this region, and this is undoubtedly part of its charm. Much of the countryside is bleak, undulating and sparsely populated – the perfect setting for the ultimate 'away-from-it-all' holiday. In this chapter, we will introduce you to the remaining counties of Ireland which make up its 'secret' heartland.

HISTORY

The Midlands have had a less colourful historical development than other parts of Ireland, largely because strategic and trading considerations favoured the development of coastal towns and cities rather than the boggy inland areas. Large chunks of the Midlands have never been populated, while others, particularly in the north, saw only token human settlement during prehistoric times before much of the present bogland had completely formed.

A number of significant early Christian settlements grew up in this isolated part of Ireland, and the surviving ruins at

Clonmacnois were once part of one of Ireland's foremost religious sites. The Celts and the Vikings built and plundered parts of the Midlands, and there are a number of surviving castles which date from the late medieval period. From early times, this has been a popular part of Ireland to escape to, whether to build a country castle or enjoy a quiet holiday.

By the nineteenth century, the Grand Canal which runs through the southern part of the region was reaching the peak of its commercial importance, transporting goods, notably peat, from one part of Ireland to another. It is still navigable, and like so many of the smaller canals in the Midlands it is very popular with canal-boat enthusiasts. In recent years, the economy of the region has received a modest boost from the expansion of the tourist industry, a trend which looks set to continue.

COMMUNICATIONS

Although not a major holiday destination, the Midlands are still well connected to the rest of Ireland. The region has no public airport – although no part of the area is more than three hours' drive from Dublin – and obviously there are no seaports either. Road links are good, with the N3 running north between Dublin and Cavan, the N4 connecting Dublin to Sligo, the N6 linking Dublin and Galway, and various other 'N' roads heading further south.

The main railway lines which cross through the Midlands link Dublin and Sligo, via Mullingar and Longford; Dublin and Galway, via Mullingar and Athlone; and Dublin and Limerick via Naas, Port Laoise and Nenagh. Additional lines link Port Laoise with Athlone, Dublin with Carlow and further south, and Port Laoise to Cork via Thurles and Tipperary.

TOURIST INFORMATION

The main Tourist Information office for the Midlands is in Dublin Road, Mullingar, in County Westmeath (Tel: 044 48650). It is open all year round, as is another principal office in Athlone (Tel: 0902 94630). There are seasonal offices in Birr (Tel: 0509 20110), Cavan (Tel: 049 31942), Port Laoise (Tel: 0502 21178), Monaghan (Tel: 047 81122), Longford (Tel: 043 46566) and Clonmacnois (Tel: 047 74134).

CLIMATE

It has been said that the Midlands of Ireland have a relatively 'undistinguished' climate, and that is probably the best description. Away from the coast, there are few extremes of heat or cold, although winter frosts across the bogland are a regular occurrence. Rainfall, particularly in the north of the region, is heavy during the period from October to March. The mid-afternoon summer temperature is unlikely to reach more than the low 20s°C (low 70s°F). Visitors at any time of year should bring some waterproof clothing and be prepared for sudden changes of weather.

WHERE TO GO FOR WHAT

Very few parts of the Midlands feature on the conventional tourist map of Ireland. There are no major resorts and this is not a part of the world for the *Socialite or Sun Worshipper* to consider. Neither is this an area for families with young children, although older children with an interest in fishing or the great outdoors may well love the region.

The Midlands are ideal territory for the touring independent visitor, particularly the outdoor enthusiast or those who participate in outdoor pursuits such as fishing and hill-walking. In and around **BANAGHER** is one of the best of several particularly good parts of the Midlands for pike, perch, trout and bream fishing.

For the *Sightseer*, places to visit include **CLONMACNOIS**, one of Ireland's most famous holy places, the attractive shopping town of **BIRR**, the market town of **ATHLONE** with its large medieval castle, the thirteenth-century **Norman settlement** of Athy, and a **Franciscan abbey** at Castledermot.

Monaghan

The outstanding feature of County Monaghan is its tranquillity. The landscape comprises rounded hills and scenic lakes and is dotted with farmhouses and market towns. It has much to offer in the way of outdoor pursuits; in stretches of water abundant in fish; quiet country lanes, ideal for the cyclist; and gently undulating terrain, perfect for hill walking. The history of the county predates the Bronze Age, and the remains of the tombs, forts and cairns of the period are to be found among the hills today. The present county was shaped in the sixteenth century by the English, in their uniting of the territories of the two ruling families of MacMahon and McKenna. It is a small and rural area, and its main towns can be toured in a circuit of around ninety miles.

In the south is **CARRICKMACROSS**, a town of 350 years standing, whose name means 'rock of the wooded plain'. It grew up around the castle built by the third Earl of Sussex in the 1630s, on the site now occupied by the convent of St Louis. In town, the most outstanding building is the **Catholic Church**, while **Glor na nGael**, which means 'the voice of the Irish', is an attractive folk museum. Three miles to the north is **Mannan Castle**, whose origins date back to the twelfth century, and at a similar distance to the west is the splendid scenery of **Dún a Rí Forest Park**.

Ten miles north-east is **INISHKEEN**, birthplace in 1904 of the poet and novelist Patrick Kavanagh, whose formative years in the area are evoked in his first book of poetry, *The Ploughman and Other Poems*. Directly north from Carrickmacross is **CASTLEBLAYNEY**. The town lies beside Lake Muckno and had its origins in the church founded here by St Maoldoid, although it was not until the early seventeenth century that the town was developed, when Sir Edward Blayney built a castle near the present site of **Hope Castle** (and thus gave the place its name). The latter structure was built under the auspices of Henry Thomas Hope of Surrey. He bought the estate from the last Lord Blayney who died in 1874. The castle, along with the **Courthouse**, is the outstanding architectural feature of the town. Its attractive woodland grounds extend along the banks of Lake Muckno, the largest in the county and a good spot for fishing.

Due west is BALLYBAY, which prospered in the eighteenth century from manufacturing linen. Nowadays it serves as a convenient base for the angler. The nearby Dromore river teems with coarse fish, while northwards are a series of little lakes notable for their bream and other species.

MONAGHAN has been a town of strategic importance since the days when it was a stronghold of the MacMahons, who ruled over much of the area now covered by Monaghan county. Among the most attractive buildings are **St Macartan's Catholic Cathedral** from the nineteenth century, and the **Market House**, completed in 1792. The **Courthouse** of the same date contains the town's museum, which, only six years after opening, won the 1980 Council of Europe Museum Prize. Three miles to the south are the lakes and hills of **Rossmore Forest Park**. Six miles to the north-east is the village of GLASLOUGH, which has won awards for tidiness and has an equestrian centre with horses available for hire.

On the western border of the county is CLONES, whose remaining elegant Georgian houses are a reminder of its eighteenth-century prosperity. It was the site of a monastery founded in the sixth century by St Tighearnach and later of a twelfth-century **Augustinian abbey**, the remains of which can be seen in Abbey Street. In the market place is a **sculpted cross** depicting famous biblical scenes. The attractive **county library**, of Italianate design, was built in 1847 as a market house. **Hilton House** is worth a visit, not only because of its Georgian architecture but because of its scenic wooded grounds, **Hilton Park**. There is also a nine-hole golf course nearby. Anglers will enjoy the River Finn, Lough Ooney and the surrounding lakes.

Accommodation can be found at **Ashleigh House Guesthouse**, 37 Dublin Street (Tel: 047 81227) at an economy price; more expensive is the **Hillgrove Hotel** (Tel: 047 81288), and the **Westenra Arms**, The Diamond (Tel: 047 82298).

Tourist Information is available from the Market House, Monaghan (Tel: 047 81122).

South of Clones are a number of quiet villages which were once thriving centres of the linen industry. Five miles south-east, amid gentle hills and lakes, is NEWBLISS. Further on in the same direction is ROCKCORRY and the nearby **Dartry Estate** whose sylvan grounds are now a forest park. The lakes around SHANTONAGH make it another rewarding halt on the angler's itinerary.

Cavan

County Cavan is a sparsely populated upland region. Its many stretches of water offer rewarding fishing, and it is well served by a quiet, but extensive, road network. **Cuilcagh Mountain** in the north-west is the source of the River Shannon which, at almost 250 miles, is the longest river in Britain and Ireland.

CAVAN, the county town, has a chequered history. It was the seat of the O'Reillys in the ancient kingdom of East Breifne. Their thirteenth-century castle, **Cloughoughter**, lies three miles to the north-west in Killykeen Forest Park. A few miles to the north-east, on the Cootehill Road, are **'Finn MacCool's Fingers'**. These standing stones were the coronation site of the Princes of Breifne.

Accommodation is available at the **Farnham Arms**, Main Street (Tel: 049 32577/32523). Slightly more expensive is the **Hotel Kilmore**, Dublin Road (Tel: 049 32288).

Tourist Information is at Farnham Street, Cavan (Tel: 049 31942).

To the south-west is the village of KILMORE. The **Church of Ireland Cathedral** here has in its churchyard the grave of the seventeenth-century Protestant Bishop, William Bedell. His work to promote the Irish language included the translation of the New Testament and the compilation of an Irish grammar. Further on is the village of CROSSDONEY ('Church of the Cross'). At nearby CORNAFEAN there is a folk museum at **Corr House**. From here the road to ARVAGH passes **Bruce Hill**, an archaeological site, and **Coronea Mass Rock**, where Mass was celebrated in secret during the time of the prohibition on Catholicism.

The road north from Cavan to Belturbet passes through DRUMLANE, site of a sixth-century monastery and reckoned also to have once had a church founded by St Columba of Iona. BELTURBET is a popular tourist resort whose position on the banks of the River Erne and surrounding lakes has made it a centre for boating and angling. On **Turbet Island** is a thirteenth-century castle erected by Walter de Lacy. Overlooking **Lough Oughter** are Killykeen Forest chalets: twenty two- to three-bedroom chalets, each set in its own clearing. A recreation centre, games room, children's play area, tennis court and laundry facilities are on site (Tel: 049 32541).

To the west is BALLYCONNELL, an attractive village which has won awards in the national 'Tidy Town' competition. An interesting feature of the **seventeenth-century church** is the Tomregon stone, carved in the form of a human head. Less than a mile from Ballyconnell is the new **Slieve Russell Hotel** (Tel: 049 26444). Set in the country it has a fully-equipped leisure centre, tennis and squash courts and beauty salon. During the summer, they have crêche facilities. A golf course is under construction at present and there is plenty of fishing in the area. Five miles to the west is BAWNBOY which acts as a gateway to the county's hill-walking region in the remote and rugged north-west corner.

Due west from Cavan, by the border with County Monaghan, is SHERCOCK, once the home of the playwright Richard Brinsley Sheridan. Nearby is **Lough Sillan**, which is noted for its coarse fishing.

Nine miles away in the south-east corner of the county is KINGSCOURT, whose **Catholic church** has some outstanding work by the renowned stained-glass artist, Evie Hone. From here the road west passes through Bailieborough and heads south through Killinkere to **VIRGINIA**. This is an attractive town whose history is dominated by its literary figures. Four miles north is the site of **Cuilcagh House**, where Jonathan Swift used to visit his friend, the Reverend Thomas Sheridan. On the site today is the mound called **Stella's Bower**, where Swift is said to have conceived the idea for *Gulliver's Travels*. Sheridan's grandson was none other than the playwright, Richard Brinsley Sheridan.

Longford

Longford is mainly a low and flat county. The River Shannon flows along its western border and is fed by a number of small streams which traverse the county's pastoral land. This is the landscape that inspired the literary imagination of local authors Oliver Goldsmith, Padraic Colum, Maria Edgeworth and Leo Casey.

At the centre of the county is **LONGFORD TOWN**, on the south bank of the River Camlin. It grew up around the castle of the O'Farrells, Princes of Annaly, of which no trace remains, although visitors can still see the ruins of a later structure, the **castle** built in 1627 by the first Earl of Longford. The town is dominated by **St Mel's Cathedral**, fashioned in nineteenth-century Renaissance style from grey limestone, to the rear of which is an **ecclesiastical museum**.

Accommodation is available at the **Longford Arms**, Main Street (Tel: 043 46296), while just along the road is the **Annaly** (Tel: 043 46253); there is a good selection of boarding houses.

Tourist Information is at Main Street (Tel: 043 46566), from late May to mid-September.

Three miles north-west is the village of **NEWTONFORBES** and nearby **Castle Forbes**. This fine seventeenth-century mansion, seat of the Earls of Granard, stands in beautiful grounds which may be viewed if permission is obtained in advance. Two miles west of the village is **Lough Forbes** which is continuous with the River Shannon, and contains trout, pike and perch.

Travelling north from Longford, you will pass through **DRUMLISH**, the starting point for climbing **Cairn Hill**, the highest in the county, before reaching **BALLINAMUCK**. This town is famous for the battle fought here in 1798 between a combined force of French and Irish and the English. The latter were victorious. The battle was commemorated, first of all, by a monument erected in 1928. It then featured in Thomas Flanagan's historical novel, *The Year of the French*, which formed the basis for a film whose success prompted another monument, erected on the battlefield on **Shanmullagh Hill** in October 1983.

In the east of the county, near the Cavan border, is the busy market town of **GRANARD**, whose proximity to the River Inny and Loughs Gowna and Sheelin make it a good angling centre. The castle at the south-west end of the town, which was once an Anglo-Norman fortification, now bears a **statue of St Patrick**, erected on the occasion of the fifteenth centenary of his arrival in Ireland. In 1981 the Granard **Harp Festival** was revived and is now held annually at the beginning of August. The **Greville Arms** (Tel: 043 86521) has ten bedrooms.

Two miles south-west is the village of **ABBEYLARA** with the remains of its thirteenth-century **Cistercian abbey**. Nearby, close to the shore of Lough Kinale, is the start of the defensive earthwork known as **'Black Pig's Dyke'** which runs north-west for six miles to the shore of Lough Gowna. Visitors interested in the writer Maria Edgeworth may be prepared to make the journey to **EDGEWORTHSTOWN** to see the **Maria Edgeworth Museum** in St John's Church of Ireland.

The south-east corner of Longford constitutes another literary trail, this time in the wake of poet and playwright Oliver Goldsmith. He was born in **PALLAS**, a few miles east of **BALLYMAHON**, and throughout the area are places which served him as a setting or inspiration for his work. The main attraction of the west of the county is the River Shannon which is suitable for cruising, while the towns on its banks, such as **TERMONBARRY**, **LANESBOROUGH** and **NEWTOWNCASHEL**, are ideal spots for the angler.

Westmeath

Except in the north, where the terrain is gently undulating and there are numerous low grassy hills, County Westmeath is flat. The many lakes make the county ideal for an angling holiday and have excellent supplies of trout, as well as coarse fish such as bream, tench, rudd and pike; the River Shannon in the west is also recommended for coarse fishing.

MULLINGAR is a thriving commercial centre which lies at the heart of the county. It contains some notable early nineteenth-century architecture, although the most imposing building is the 1930s **cathedral**, with mosaics of St Patrick and St Anne by the Russian artist Boris Anrep. Other buildings worth viewing are **All Saints Church**; the **market house**, which contains the **local museum**; and the **town library**. Hotel accommodation is available at **Bloomfield House** (Tel: 044 40894) and at the **Greville Arms** (Tel: 044 48563). **Tourist Information** is at Dublin Road (Tel: 044 48650). **Crookedwood House Restaurant** was a recent award winner and is an excellent restaurant located approximately nine miles north of Mullingar – one mile off the Mullingar–Castlepollard road. Dinner from £17 Sunday lunch £11 (Tel: 044 72165).

Not far north of Mullingar is **Lough Owel**, which combines splendid scenery with the opportunity for fishing and swimming. The same attractions are to be found further north at **Lough Derravaragh** which features in the legend of the Children of Lir, who were changed into swans by a jealous step-mother. North-east of the lough is the town of **CASTLEPOLLARD**, a mile from the early nineteenth-century Gothic **Tullynally Castle**, seat of the Earls of Longford. It features a fine woodland demesne and gardens and is open to the public.

A few miles east of Castlepollard is **FORE**, site of a seventh-century monastery founded by St Fechin, although nothing remains of it today. The oldest structure in the town is **St Fechin's Church** from the tenth century, while the **Benedictine Priory** survives from the thirteenth century.

The road south-east from Castlepollard passes through Collinstown on its way to **DELVIN**, a picturesque village surrounded by pleasant countryside. On the south-west side of town is the thirteenth-century **Delvin Castle**, and nearby is the medieval **Clonyn Castle** and the eighteenth-century **Killua Castle**. Near the latter is an **obelisk** which commemorates the introduction of the potato to Ireland by Sir Walter Raleigh.

In the south-west corner of the county is its largest town, **ATHLONE**, a site of strategic importance for much of the last thousand years. On the west bank of the River Shannon is the thirteenth-century **Athlone Castle**, whose original design remains clear despite frequent repair and alteration. Within the central keep is a **museum** with displays on local history. The **Old Walls of Athlone** can be seen from Railway View on the east side of town, while the ruined **Franciscan Abbey** of the thirteenth century is on Abbey Road.

There is a good choice of hotel accommodation at **Newpark House**, Kiltoom (Tel: 0902 89130/89124); **The Paddock** (Tel: 0902 72070/78481); and **Shamrock Lodge** (Tel: 0902 92601).

A few miles north of Athlone is **Lough Ree**, one of the Shannon's three major lakes. It is an excellent site for a day of outdoor pursuits, offering trout, coarse and pike fishing, boating, sailing, swimming and water-skiing. At lunch-time, consider the picnic sites at Hodson Bay, Coosan Point, and Muckanagh.

The area just north of Athlone, between the villages of Glasson and Tang, is known as 'Goldsmith Country' because of its strong associations with the poet and playwright Oliver Goldsmith. GLASSON is believed to have been the model for 'Sweet Auburn' in his poem 'The Deserted Village', while a few miles north, the village of LISSOY was his home from the age of two.

Offaly

Offaly is a mostly flat county with extensive stretches of bogland. Along the south-eastern boundary with Laois are the misleadingly named Slieve Bloom Mountains, which are really no more than gently rolling hills. The earliest evidence of settlement in the county dates back 9000 years, and the countryside is dotted with monuments testifying to Offaly's ancient past.

In the centre of Offaly is the county town of **TULLAMORE** on the banks of the river of the same name. It contains a number of fine buildings and is the home of the liqueur whiskey 'Irish Mist' whose production centre is open to visitors by arrangement. On the north side of the Grand Canal is the sixteenth-century **Sragh Castle**, while four miles to the west are the remains of the seventeenth-century fortified house, **Ballycowan Castle**. **Charleville Castle** (Tel: 0506 21279) was designed in 1798 by Francis Johnston, a legendary architect of Ireland. This is an occupied castle and the owners plan to restore it to its former glory. Personally conducted tours are by appointment, group rates are available. The approach is by private avenue using the gates facing Tullamore town, beside Offaly Historical Society on Birr Road.

Accommodation is available at the **Phoenix Arms**, Bridge Street (Tel: 0506 21066/21980), which has seventeen rooms, and at the ten-bedroom **Oakfield House**, Rahan Road (Tel: 0506 21385/51072).

Not far north of the Kilbeggan road are the remains of **Durrow Abbey**, founded by St Columba in the sixth century, and a place of pilgrimage on his feast day, 9 June. The famous *Book of Durrow*, a copy of the Gospels, was produced here in the seventh century, and now resides in Trinity College, Dublin.

In the north-west of the county, on the banks of the Shannon, is the extensive monastic settlement of **CLONMACNOIS**. It was founded in AD 548 by St Ciaran, and soon developed into a monastic city, then a medieval university. The buildings on the site, the oldest of which dates back to the ninth century, include two round towers, a cathedral, eight churches, and a thirteenth-century ringwork castle. There is a **Tourist Information** centre here (Tel: 047 74134), open March to October.

South from Clonmacnois is the town of **SHANNONBRIDGE**, originally a fortified river-crossing and now a spot popular with coarse anglers. Not far to the west is the ruined **Clonony Castle** of the sixteenth century. Further south, beside the Shannon, is the picturesque town of BANAGHER where Anthony Trollope wrote his first novel in 1841. Across the river, and into Connacht, **Clonfert Cathedral** is worth a visit to view its twelfth-century Romanesque doorway.

Ten miles south is the Georgian town of BIRR at the confluence of the Little Brosna and Camcor rivers. Along with two others, it claims to be the geographic centre of Ireland. **Birr Castle**, home of the Earl of Rosse, is not open to the public, but its magnificent grounds are. They contain an extensive variety of trees and shrubs with particularly interesting species from China and the Himalayas. Also in the grounds is a **museum** devoted to the first Earl of Rosse, an astronomer, and the display includes the telescope he built in 1845 which was the largest of its day.

Accommodation is available at the **County Arms** (Tel: 0509 20791/20193), and at **Dooly's** (Tel: 0509 20032), both hotels with eighteen bedrooms.

Tourist Information is available from May to October (Tel: 0509 2011).

Kildare

County Kildare has a flat terrain composed almost entirely of bog and plain. The Grand Canal bisects the north of the county and once brought the area prosperity with the transport of passengers and freight. There has been no freight traffic since 1959, but this stretch of water has recently been revitalized by its use for pleasure cruises and canal-boat holidays. It is also a rewarding fishing ground.

In the north-east corner is MAYNOOTH and the thirteenth-century **Maynooth Castle**. Not far from this is **St Patrick's College** whose **ecclesiastical museum** is open to visitors by appointment. An outstanding example of mid-Georgian architecture can be seen in the east of the town at **Carton House**, although visitors can only admire its exterior as it is closed to the public. It was designed by the German, Richard Cassels. A few miles further south is the village of CELBRIDGE and the eighteenth-century country house **Castletown** (Tel: 062 88252). The largest private house in Ireland, it belongs to the Irish Georgian Society and is open to the public April–September Mon–Fri 1000–1800, 1100–1800 Saturdays and in winter 1000–1700. 1400–1700 Sundays and Bank Holidays. It contains much of its fine original furniture. There is a coffee shop and the West Wing restaurant situated in the original old kitchens. Open all year it serves good food at candlelit tables. Booking essential.

Further south is the principal town of Kildare, **NAAS** (pronounced 'nace'), the gateway to the heart of the Irish racing world. There is a racecourse here, while a few miles south-east is the famous steeplechase centre of **Punchestown**. Naas has a good selection of accommodation in the county, including the **Harbour View Guesthouse**, The Harbour (Tel: 045 79145) and the **Town House Hotel**, Limerick Road (Tel: 045 79226).

South-west along the N7, just after **NEWBRIDGE**, is the **Curragh**, which at twelve square miles is the largest area of public land in the country. It is a popular exercise ground for the many racehorses in the area, while Curragh Racecourse is the home of the Irish Derby. Further along in the same direction is the town of **KILDARE**. St Brigid founded a nunnery here in the sixth century and a **round tower** on the site has survived from the tenth century. The nineteenth-century cathedral incorporates some of the earlier thirteenth-century structure. Nearby at **TULLY** is the famous **National Stud** where top stallions are brought in for breeding. A tour of the stables is available and in the grounds is the **Irish Horse Museum** and the ornate **Japanese Gardens**.

Down in the south-west of the county is **ATHY**. The River Barrow flows through the town, and on its banks stands the sixteenth-century **White's Castle**. The **Dominican church** is an interesting modern design in the shape of a pentagon. On the northern outskirts are the remains of **Woodstock Castle** and the Norman **Ardswell Motte** lies five miles to the north-east.

Laois

Apart from the Slieve Bloom Mountains in the north-east, Laois (pronounced 'leesh') is a low undulating land of unremarkable scenery. Strictly speaking the Slieve Bloom range, with the highest point at only 610 metres, consists of hills rather than mountains. Nonetheless, the countryside in this part of the county is very attractive. On the other side of the county, in the north-east, is the town of **PORTARLINGTON**. In the late seventeenth century it became a major centre for Huguenot refugees from France. Although no one any longer comes here to learn French, the pronounced Gallic connection is still evident in **St Michael's Church**, known as the French church because that is the language in which many of the tombstones are inscribed, and, until the late nineteenth century, the language in which services were conducted. There are also signs of Huguenot architecture in **Patrick Street**. Nearby, off the road to Monasterevin, are the remains of **Lea Castle**.

Going south to Port Laoise, a small detour off the N7 from Monasterevin will be rewarded by a visit to **Emo Court**. The eighteenth-century Emo house, designed by the renowned architect James Gandon, is not open to the public, but the gardens are. Another interesting Gandon design is the **Church of St John the Evangelist** at nearby **COOLBANAGHER**.

In the centre of Laois is the county town of **PORT LAOISE** whose only real distinction is the nearby top security prison. Its position does, however, make it a convenient base from which to explore the county. Hotel accommodation can be had at the **Montague Hotel**, Emo (Tel: 0502 26154), and **The Killeshin**, Dublin Road (Tel: 0502 21663). For lower prices try **The Regency**, Main Street (Tel: 0502 21305).

The road to Stradbally in the west passes the **Rock of Dunamase**, the summit of which has the remains of a castle and a superb view. **STRADBALLY**, for the visitor, is dominated by locomotion in one form or another. In the first weekend of August it is the venue for an annual steam engine rally, while a more regular attraction is the **Stradbally Traction Engine Museum**. At **Stradbally Hall**, built in 1699 and remodelled in Italianate style in the mid-nineteenth century, there is a narrow-gauge railway on which a steam train, formerly used at the Guinness brewery in Dublin, runs each weekend.

South of Port Laoise on the N8 is **ABBEYLEIX**. The town is on the site of a twelfth-century Cistercian abbey, and was extensively redesigned in the eighteenth century by Viscount de Vesci. **Heywood Gardens**, near Ballinakill, was designed by Edwin Lutyens in the early part of this century. The oval garden and terraces have recently been restored. The estate is now a College under the Salesian Order. Admission by appointment (Tel: 0502 55245).

Kilkenny

The countryside of Kilkenny is verdant and well cultivated, and a large proportion of the land is made up of limestone rock, which turns black when well polished. It is used extensively in the buildings of Kilkenny city and from this derives its nickname, the 'Marble City'.

On the banks of the River Nore, **KILKENNY** is a fascinating and ancient city. It has been a centre of population since St Canice founded a monastery in the sixth century on the site of the present cathedral. It is from the saint that the city takes its name; in Irish it is 'Cill Chainnigh', meaning 'Canice's Church'. **Kilkenny Castle** is an imposing building in the town centre overlooking the river and along with its fine gardens it is open to the public. The castle stables now accommodate the **Kilkenny Design Workshops** producing high quality ceramics, textiles, and silver and metal work. There are numerous examples throughout the town of Kilkenny's architectural splendour. **Rothe House** in Parliament Street is a fine Tudor merchant's house from 1549, and home of the museum collection of the Royal Society of Antiquities in Ireland. It is open each day from April to October. Across the road is the sixteenth-century **Courthouse**, and the corner of Parliament Street and St Kieran's Street is the location of **Kyteler's Inn**, the oldest house in the city. The ruins of the nearby **St Francis Abbey** date from the thirteenth century, as do those of the Dominican **Black Abbey**. The latter site in the north-west of the city is near **Trinity Gate**, the only remaining gate of the wall which formerly ran around the city. Across **St John's Bridge**, which gives a good view of Kilkenny Castle, is the eighteenth-century **Kilkenny College**. Its Georgian architecture is interesting, as indeed is its alumni list, which includes Jonathan Swift and the philosopher bishop George Berkeley.

As one would expect from such an illustrious city, Kilkenny offers a good choice of accommodation. **Newpark Hotel** (Tel: 056 22122) is a medium-sized, medium-grade hotel; among the most reasonable is **Central Guest House**, John Street (Tel: 056 21926). Slightly more expensive is **Brannigans Glendine Inn**, Castlecomer Road (Tel: 056 21069).

Tourist Information is at Rose Inn Street (Tel: 056 321755) from March to November.

Several miles due north of Kilkenny is **Dunmore Cave** in the limestone rock, one of the few which are safe for visitors to explore. To the south-west on the N76 is the town of CALLAN and the remains of **Skerry's Castle, Callan Castle**, and **Butler Castle**. The town is also notable as the birthplace in 1762 of James Hoban, an architect who emigrated to Philadelphia and achieved lasting fame as the man who designed the White House in Washington.

Fourteen miles south-east of Kilkenny is THOMASTOWN and the remains of its outstanding **thirteenth-century church**. Nearby is **Dysart Castle**, former home of Bishop George Berkeley. Visitors to the town should not fail to make the short journey across the River Nore to see the ruins of the twelfth-century **Jerpoint Abbey**.

Tipperary

It is not really a long way to Tipperary. The name was immortalized in song in 1912 by two Englishmen for no reason other than its euphony. It is the largest inland county in Ireland, yet its waterways are a salient feature and an outstanding recreational asset, while the Galtee Mountains in the south-west are the highest in the county.

The N7 from Dublin runs through **ROSCREA** in the north-east corner of Tipperary, and coming from this direction the first thing the visitor will see are the remains of the thirteenth-century **St Cronan's Abbey** with its exemplary Hiberno-Romanesque architecture at the west door. The town's chief attraction is its thirteenth-century **Norman castle** in Castle Street, whose tower provides a superb view of the surrounding countryside. Within the grounds is the Georgian **Damer House**, open from Easter to September for the public to see its majestic carved wooden staircase, paintings, period furniture, and local museum. The nineteenth-century Roman Catholic church, **St Cronan's**, incorporates some of the Franciscan Friary built on the same site in 1490. Two miles south-east of the town are the monastic ruins of **Monaincha**, while the same distance to the west are the remains of **Mount St Joseph's** Cistercian monastery. Still inhabited, the area houses a 3000-acre farm with a bakery. It is unique in that it is the only monastery in the world with a boys' boarding school as the centrepiece to its existence.

Accommodation is available at the **Pathe Hotel**, Castle Street (Tel: 0505 21301), and at **The Tower Guesthouse**, Church Street (Tel: 0508 21774/21616).

The N7 continues south-west to **TOOMEVARA** – which has a ruined **Augustinian priory**, and opposite that a **folk museum** where traditional music is performed in the summer evenings – before reaching **NENAGH**. In **Nenagh Castle** is the thirty-metre-high circular keep, one of the best examples of its kind in the country and formerly part of a much bigger thirteenth-century castle.

Five miles further north-west is **DROMINEER**, a harbour on the shore of Lough Derg at the foot of the Arra Mountains. The scenery here is magnificent, there are frequent cruises on the lough, and the town is an excellent resort for angling, swimming and dinghy sailing.

Thirty miles south-east of Nenagh is **THURLES**, on a route which passes between the Silvermines and Devil's Bit mountains. The gap in the hills, visible from the main road, is explained by the legend which claims that it was bitten out by the devil in a rage. He then spat it out further south near Cashel, thus forming the Rock of Cashel. Thurles was once a town of great military importance, and this is borne out by the two **fifteenth-century castle keeps**, one guarding the bridge over the River Suir and another near the town centre. The road south-west to Cashel passes **Holy Cross Abbey**. Founded in the twelfth century, most of the present structure, scenically located by the River Suir, dates from the fifteenth century.

The chief reason for visiting **CASHEL** is to see the aforesaid **Rock of Cashel** on the northern outskirts. The Rock is a limestone outcrop rising to a height of sixty metres with buildings grouped at its base and on top. For seven centuries it was the seat of the kings of Munster. It was also here that the shamrock emerged as the national emblem, one being picked by St Patrick to illustrate his explanation of the doctrine of the Trinity. To fully appreciate the history and the attractions of the Rock it is advisable to take advantage of guided tours available. Accommodation is offered by the **Golden Vale House Hotel**, Dundrum (Tel: 71218), **Grants Castle Hotel**, Main Street (Tel: 61044), **Dundrum House** (Tel: 71116) or **Rectory House** (Tel: 71266).

South-west on the N74 is **TIPPERARY**, a pleasant Georgian town without any single outstanding feature. From here there is a very scenic route south-east through the Glen of Aherlow to **CAHIR** (pronounced 'care'). There is good salmon and trout fishing in the River Suir which flows through the town and also in the River Aherlow to the north. **Cahir Castle** is an impressive structure dating from the fifteenth century and will be recognized by some as the location for the film *Excalibur*. The village of **BALLYPOREEN** in the south-west has been added to the tourist trail following Ronald Reagan's visit there in 1984 and the discovery that his paternal great-grandfather was born in nearby

Templetenny. Souvenirs of the Presidential visit are available in the **Ronald Reagan Lounge** and a **Ronald Reagan Museum** was opened in the centre of the village in 1985.

Bordering on County Limerick lie the **Mitchelstown caves**, more than 500 metres of underground passages which are open to the public. The enormous stalagmites and stalactites have fascinated visitors for centuries, and tours of the carefully lit caves are always accompanied by experienced guides.

Northern Ireland

INTRODUCTION

Six counties – Antrim, Armagh, Down, Fermanagh, Derry and Tyrone – make up Northern Ireland – the part of Ireland which remains an integral part of the United Kingdom. The province is often called Ulster, although strictly speaking, Ulster includes three counties of the Irish Republic as well.

Northern Ireland shares a border some 250 miles long with the Irish Republic, and the province covers an area of some 5500 square miles – one sixth of the total landmass of Ireland. The distinctive Lough Neagh, the largest lake in the British Isles, lies in the middle of Northern Ireland.

At one point, Northern Ireland is only thirteen miles from the British mainland, the distance between Torr Head and the southern tip of the Mull of Kintyre in Scotland, yet the province is different from the rest of the United Kingdom in so many respects, not least in its troubled religious and political development. The real character of this beautiful province has been clouded by the latest spate of 'troubles' which began in earnest in 1968. Mercifully, these are confined to a relatively small part of the province, and what you see on the television news should not colour your views of all Northern Ireland.

In this chapter, we start our tour in and around the capital, Belfast, travelling as far north as the ferry port of Larne, then heading south to make a circular tour of the Six Counties ending up just north of Belfast again.

HISTORY

The history of Northern Ireland reflects more the history of Ireland than that of mainland Britain. Geologically, it is one of the oldest parts of Northern Europe, and one of the most striking reminders of its early development is the magnificent Giant's Causeway, in County Antrim, which dates back more than sixty million years.

Northern Ireland has always retained close links with Scotland. A famous Irish visitor to Scotland was St Columba, who set sail from the province before establishing his Christian community on the isolated Scottish island of Iona.

A two-way migration between Scotland and Ireland endured for several centuries (both countries feeling threatened by neighbouring England), but the most dramatic period occurred in 1607 when the Irish earls were forced to flee their native land by James VI and I – who wanted complete control over Ireland – and lowland Scots were encouraged to take over the abandoned estates. The Scots brought a different culture and character to Ireland, and to the present day, family and business links between Northern Ireland and Scotland remain very close.

The most enduring legacy of the early seventeenth-century Scots migration was the birth of Protestantism in Northern Ireland. This still flourishes, with regular 'Orange' parades being staged by the most devout followers in commemoration of the Battle of the Boyne in 1690 when the Protestant William of Orange defeated the Catholic James II, and so claimed the British throne.

The origins of the present troubles stem from the late seventeenth century – though some say even earlier – but they reached a turning point in 1922 when, after a period of virtual civil war, the British government granted Ireland her independence. The overwhelmingly Protestant North, however, wanted to remain as part of the United Kingdom under British sovereignty and so the present partition of Ireland came about.

The North was given its own parliament, Stormont, which lasted until 1972, followed by a short-lived Northern Ireland Assembly in the mid-1980s, but Republican opposition to British rule remained as strong as ever. The Catholic minority in the North still retain a fierce loyalty to their fellow-countrymen in the Republic, and the tiniest handful of extremists, mainly in the provisional Irish Republican Army, have waged a terrorist campaign against British targets ever since the partition.

British troops entered the province in 1968 to quell serious disturbances between the two divided religious communities, and have remained there ever since. Visitors may have their cars searched, particularly in Belfast and when crossing the border from the Republic. The military presence is reasonably unobtrusive, although occasional bag searches can be expected when entering some Belfast hotels and department stores. Sadly this is the price that has to be paid for security, until some distant day when the two communities can put their differences behind them and reach a peaceful settlement.

PRACTICAL INFORMATION

Northern Ireland is easily accessible from mainland Britain and Eire, and the most direct way to reach the province is by air. **British Airways** and **British Midland** fly fifteen times daily from London Heathrow to Belfast. The other airline on this route is **Britannia Airways** who fly from Luton. There are also daily connections from Birmingham, Blackpool, Bristol, Cardiff, East Midlands, Exeter, Guernsey, Isle of Man, Newcastle, Jersey, Liverpool and Leeds. **Loganair** fly three or four times daily (less at weekends) from Edinburgh, Glasgow and Manchester. Belfast has an international airport twenty miles outside the city, and a 'city' airport close to the centre. Of the airlines mentioned, only **Loganair** fly to the city airport, although **Jersey European** operate a year-round service from Birmingham, Blackpool and Exeter to this central airport.

Three British ferry companies offer regular sailings to Northern Ireland. You can sail direct to Belfast from Liverpool with **Belfast Ferries**, and to Larne from Stranraer with **Sealink**. From Cairnryan there is a regular service to Larne with **P&O**. The Stranraer/Larne and Liverpool/Belfast services connect with trains at either end, and there is a connecting boat-train service from London Euston to Belfast. All three ferry services are available to visitors wishing to take their own car. Driving regulations in Northern Ireland are the same as in mainland

Britain, although unattended car parking is prohibited in most of central Belfast. **Supabus** is one of a number of companies offering London/Belfast bus connections; the journey takes about fourteen hours, including the ferry crossing.

Ulsterbus operates a wide range of day tours every year including such places as Dublin, the Lakes of Fermanagh, the Antrim Coast and Giant's Causeway, the Mountains of Mourne, Sligo, the Donegal Highlands, the Ards Peninsula. Information on these tours can be obtained from Ulsterbus offices at Oxford Street and Glengall Street, from Easter.

Ulsterbus also offers one-day and seven-day tickets for unlimited travel on all scheduled bus services within Northern Ireland. These operate all year round. 'The Irish Overlander' ticket, also available from Ulsterbus offices, offers fifteen days' unlimited travel *anywhere* in Ireland on all scheduled bus/rail services. This also operates all year. For further information, telephone 0232 320 011/235 282.

Further rail excursions include 'The Irish Rover', offering unlimited eight days' rail travel within a sixteen-day period, or fifteen days within a thirty-day period – on all scheduled services *anywhere* in Ireland. This operates all year. Tickets are available from the Intercity Travel Centre, 17 Wellington Place, Belfast (Tel: 0232 230 671), Central Station, Belfast (Tel: 0232 235 282) or Larne Harbour Travel Centre (Tel: 0574 70517).

'The Rail Runabout' offers seven days' unlimited travel on all scheduled rail services within Northern Ireland and to Dundalk. This service operates from April to October. Tickets are available from main railway stations.

Belfast Citybus operates one-day tours taking in sights such as the shipyard, Stormont and Belfast Castle and the University. Buses leave Castle Place, Belfast. This service is available from June to September (Tel: 0232 246 485).

There are also a number of rail excursions on a steam train available. 'The Portrush Flyer' makes round trips to Portrush from Belfast via Antrim and Ballymena. 'The Steam Enterprise' makes round trips to Dublin from Belfast Central Station, via Lisburn, Portadown and Newry. For further details contact Central Station (Tel: 0232 235 282).

TOURIST INFORMATION

Initial enquiries should be directed to the Northern Ireland Tourist Board whose head office is at River House, High Street, Belfast. Further information on the range of publicity available, and details of the excellent accommodation booking service, can be obtained by calling 246 609 or writing to the above address. The office is open 0900–1715 Mon–Fri and 0900–1200 Sat between June and September; 0900–1715 Mon–Fri for the rest of the year. There are tourist offices in many other towns including Derry, Enniskillen, Larne, Newry, Strabane and Portrush (the nearest to the Giant's Causeway).

Visitors touring the North should invest in a copy of *The Visitor's Guide to Northern Ireland* (Moorland Publishing, 1987, £7.95), available from UK bookshops. It covers the province comprehensively and is *the* authoritative guide to the North.

CLIMATE

Northern Ireland's climate is very similar to that of much of northern England and southern Scotland. You are unlikely to see much sunshine whatever time of year you visit, it is often windy and some rain is virtually guaranteed. The province receives an above-average rainfall (806mm compared with 649mm in London), although the autumn and winter months tend to be much wetter than spring or summer.

One peculiarity about the Irish weather is how rapidly it can change; a crisp, bright summer afternoon can quickly become wet and miserable so bear this in mind if you plan to spend much time out of doors. Because of the Gulf Stream off its northern coast, Northern Ireland enjoys a climate free from extreme cold. Average summer temperatures seldom reach more than the low 20s°C (low 70s°F); the winter average is unlikely to be more than 10°C (50°F).

WHERE TO GO FOR WHAT

The *Sun Worshipper* has some scope in the province's lively beach resorts, and there is no shortage of nightlife all over Northern Ireland. Belfast offers some possibilities for the *Sightseer*, although it does not lend itself to random strolling. The *Sightseer* should make a point of visiting the **Giant's Causeway** and the dramatic ruin of **Dunluce Castle** in County Antrim; DERRY, the province's second city; and OMAGH, the county town of Tyrone. Georgian ARMAGH is another attraction.

The *Nature Lover* and the *Recluse* will appreciate the peace and solitude of much of inland Northern Ireland. There are **forest parks** at **Tullymore** and **Castlewellan**; the beautiful **Mountains of Mourne**, and the **Sperrin Mountains** south of Derry; the picturesque **Clogher Valley**, and the varied charms of the shoreline of **Lough Erne**.

Belfast

A third of Northern Ireland's 1.5 million population live in, or within ten miles of, the province's capital. A village has existed here, at the head of Belfast Lough, since medieval times, but it was the Industrial Revolution which transformed a prosperous but tiny agricultural community into the city you see today.

In terms of population it is roughly the size of Edinburgh – but there the similarities end. First-time visitors seldom know what to expect of Belfast; some expect a virtual war zone, others a relatively poor city with little to see or do away from the countless pubs for which all of Ireland is famous. In reality, Belfast fits neither picture, and if you look beneath the surface you will find a vibrant, modern city with plenty to offer the short-stay visitor.

Your first sight of Belfast is likely to be from the air, and if you fly with Loganair from Manchester, Glasgow or Edinburgh, you will sweep low over the outskirts of the city and Belfast Lough, before landing at the small airport. The airstrip has been built close to the site where the Short Brothers tested many of their early aircraft, including the Sunderland flying boat and the very Short 360 aircraft which you are flying on, if you have chosen Loganair.

Belfast was little more than an undistinguished coastal town until the early nineteenth century, and as late as 1810 it had less than 20,000 inhabitants. The Industrial Revolution soon took hold in Northern Ireland in the early 1800s and a host of new industries, including rope-making, shipbuilding and tobacco processing, grew up. Belfast's shipbuilding industry, now in its twilight years (despite having the world's largest dry dock), produced many famous vessels, including the ill-fated *Titanic* which sank with the loss of more than 1500 lives in April 1912. The city's most successful industry was, however, linen, and Belfast became a linen 'boom town' during the nineteenth century. People flooded into Belfast from all over Ireland. By 1911 the population was 390,000, and by the start of the Second World War, 440,000 – more than any other city in Ireland, including Dublin. The traditional industries declined quickly after the war and, although a handful of lighter, predominantly electronic, companies established themselves in the city, Belfast today is essentially a shadow of its former self, with high unemployment and few obvious prospects for the future.

The only good by-product of the 'troubles' is that Belfast is just about the only city left in Western Europe which does not have a significant drugs problem.

Navigating your way through the city presents few problems. All major car-hire firms are represented. Security arrangements prohibit car parking anywhere in the city centre other than designated car parks, and these tend to fill up quickly, and much of the city centre is now 'pedestrians-only'.

The main city-centre bus stop is outside the City Hall, in Donegall Square, and the Tourist Information office can give details on routes and fares. Empty taxis do not normally drive around the city looking for fares so check the local Yellow Pages and book one by telephone. There are some taxi ranks – a large one located at the City Hall.

The oldest buildings in modern Belfast are almost entirely of Victorian origin; only three public buildings predate the mid-nineteenth-century industrial boom. The oldest building in the city is **Knockbreda parish church**, built in 1737, although technically speaking it lies just a little way outside the city, on the A24 ring road heading south. The architect, Richard Cassels, also designed Leinster House in Dublin, and one of the most regular worshippers at Knockbreda was the Duke of Wellington's mother, Lady Anne Hill.

In Belfast proper, the best starting point for a walking tour is **Donegall Square**, which is dominated by the magnificent **City Hall**. Built from white Portland stone, it stands on the site of the much less impressive White Linen Hall that was demolished to make way for a building 'fitting to Belfast's status' when it was declared a city in 1888. The most impressive room is the oak-panelled banqueting hall, destroyed by a German bomb in 1941 and rebuilt in time for the Coronation twelve years later. King George V opened the first devolved Northern Ireland parliament here, although perhaps there was a premonition about its eventual failure when the building's architect, Sir Brunell Thomas, only got his fee after taking the city fathers to court in 1906!

Among the **statues** near the City Hall is one to Sir Edward Harland, founder of the city's great **dockyard**, and another dedicated to the memory of those who lost their lives on the *Titanic* in 1912. In happier times, the Belfast docks built the luxury cruise liner *Canberra* and the oil tanker *Myrina*, the largest ship afloat when it was launched in the late 1960s. The remainder of the square is dominated by an enormous Victorian office building, now occupied by Scottish Provident. It has an ornamented façade featuring countless animal heads, ropes and nautical sculptures. A warehouse to the rear of the City Hall is decorated with images of famous men, from Shakespeare to George Washington.

Walking round to Great Victoria Street, visitors can admire the city's **Opera House** which was originally designed by Frank Matcham and restored in 1980. **Kelly's Cellars**, in nearby Bank Street, is one of the city's oldest public houses, and it was in here that many supporters of the 1798 Rebellion quenched their thirst before going off to fight further south. At 46 Great Victoria Street is the famous **Crown Bar**, so good an example of an archetypal Victorian boozer that it is now in the care of the National Trust.

The **Albert Memorial clock**, on a tower which now leans about four feet from the vertical, is one of the city centre's tallest landmarks. It is a good direction finder if you ever get lost, and stands close to the city's oldest public building, a converted **market house** on the corner of Waring Street. It was originally built in 1769 and now serves as a bank.

One of Belfast's two main places of learning is the **Royal Belfast Academical Institution**, whose most distinguished former tutor, towards the end of the nineteenth century, was Lord Kelvin's father. Kelvin himself was born in a small house (now demolished) near the Institution in 1824 and it was he who later pioneered the absolute scale of temperature. Most of the Institution's buildings date from the last century and it first opened its doors in 1814 as an interdenominational school.

Northern Ireland's main seat of learning is **Queen's University**. The oldest buildings date from 1849 and today more than 8000 full-time and 10,000 part-time students take courses here. The **botanical gardens** lie next door to the university and the central palm house, built in the 1840s, is believed to be one of the earliest examples of cast-iron and curvilinear glasswork anywhere in Europe. The gardens are open daily until sunset throughout the year.

The **Ulster Museum** stands within the botanical gardens, and here you can see a fine collection of exhibits relating to the history of the province. One of the non-Irish exhibits is the body of a *coelacanth*, an enormous prehistoric fish, thought to have been extinct until this one was caught off the coast of Madagascar in 1973. Treasures from the Armada shipwreck *Girona*, of world importance, can also be seen here. The museum is open 1000–1700 Mon–Fri, 1300–1700 Sat and 1400–1700 Sun.

The **Transport Museum**, in east Belfast, houses a relatively small collection of exhibits depicting the development of Irish transport over the last two centuries. It is open 1000–1700

Mon–Sat. One other building of note in the suburbs is the **Public Records Office**, with a good public search room. Among the archives deposited here are the private papers of Lord Castlereagh from the period 1790–1822; the public room is open 0930–1645 Mon–Fri.

As you might expect, Belfast has a large number of churches which holidaymakers are welcome to visit. The two oldest city-centre churches are the **May Street Presbyterian**, built for the outspoken Victorian theologian Henry Cooke in 1829, and the **First Presbyterian Church** in Rosemary Street, where John Wesley preached, which was completed in 1783. It regularly holds lunchtime concerts.

St Malachy's Roman Catholic Church, which was opened in 1844, is particularly striking because of its vaulted ceiling and attractive turrets. One of the city's cathedrals, **St Anne's**, is a relatively unattractive modern building in Donegall Street. It was started in 1899 and is not yet officially complete! The cathedral contains the tomb of the great Unionist patriot Sir Edward Carson, and stands close to the offices of Northern Ireland's two morning newspapers, the *News Letter* and the *Irish News*.

One final church which has as much in common with a maritime museum as it has with a place of worship is the **Sinclair Seamen's Church**, in Corporation Square. Opened in 1857, this fine, solid old building has a distinctly nautical feel to it, having been constructed of ships' parts. It even boasts port and starboard lights on its huge organ. The exterior was the work of Charles Lanyon who also built the city's custom house around the same time, as well as being the designer of Queen's University.

Other sights of note in Belfast include **Cave Hill**, on the north side, with **Belfast Castle** standing on the slope facing the city. Cave Hill is a popular place for long summer walks and is named after five man-made dwellings near the top which are reckoned to have been built in Neolithic times. **McArt's Fort**, on the very top, was the scene of a major plot in the name of Irish independence in the last years of the eighteenth century. The **city zoo** is also located on the slopes of Cave Hill. The **Royal Courts of Justice** are in Chichester Street and it is possible to see round the main buildings, although opening times vary due to frequent high-level meetings by various Northern Ireland Ministers, which are often convened at short notice. Ask at Tourist Information in Belfast if you are keen to visit this historically significant building. One other place of interest is **Stormont Castle**, four miles outside the city. First opened in 1932, this was the purpose-built parliament building for Northern Ireland until direct rule was reintroduced in 1972.

ACCOMMODATION AND EATING OUT

Belfast has a reasonable selection of hotels and guesthouses with rates to suit most pockets. Hotel rooms are significantly cheaper than in Dublin or London, particularly at the higher end of the scale. What follows is a selection of popular hotels in three broad price categories.

First Class

Conway Hotel, 300 Kingsway, Dunmurry (Tel: 612 101) – A popular hotel on the outskirts of the city in its own grounds; seventy-eight bedrooms, all doubles except for two family rooms, and all with private facilities; good golfing nearby.

Culloden Hotel, 142 Bangor Road, Holywood (Tel: 02317 5223) – A de luxe hotel to the north-east of the city; seventy-six spacious bedrooms and an excellent *à la carte* menu in their main restaurant.

Europa Hotel, Great Victoria Street (Tel: 327 000) – A twelve-storey tower block in the city centre and Belfast's best hotel; 199 bedrooms, all with private facilities; ninety-nine single rooms and popular with business visitors; good restaurant and nightclub.

Business Class

Stormont Hotel, 587 Upper Newtownards Road (Tel: 658 621) – A spacious 'A' class hotel (the second-highest official grade); sixty-seven bedrooms, mostly doubles except for eight family rooms.
Wellington Park Hotel, 21 Malone Road (Tel: 381 111) – Comfortable hotel with fifty double bedrooms; offers a good programme of evening entertainment and an impressive range of outdoor leisure pursuits including fishing, shooting, golf and sailing.
Hotel Drumkeen, Upper Galwally (Tel: 491 321) – A small hotel, with just twenty-eight rooms, but an excellent base for family holidays as all but three bedrooms can accommodate children; the hotel has a large garden and a relatively inexpensive restaurant for an 'A' class hotel.

Economy Class

Regency Hotel, 13 Lower Crescent (Tel: 323 349) – A clean and comfortable hotel near the city centre; thirteen bedrooms, seven of which have private bathrooms.
York Hotel, 59 Botanic Avenue (Tel: 329 304) – Eighteen bedrooms, all but three with bathrooms; telephones in most rooms and facilities for children.
Duke's Hotel, 65/67 University Street (Tel: 236 666) – Twenty-one bedrooms all inclusive of private facilities.
Camera Guesthouse, 44 Wellington Park (Tel: 660 206) – Eleven bedrooms available in one of the city's best guesthouses; children and dogs are welcome and there are reduced rates for senior citizens.

Belfast is not renowned as one of Europe's great culinary centres, but it does have a reasonable spread of restaurants for a city of its size. There has been a spate of fast-food places opening over the last few years in the city centre, but pubs are as good a place as any to get an inexpensive meal at lunchtime. The Northern Ireland Tourist Board publish an excellent little pocket guide each year which features every eating place in the province, from the Woolworth café to the best hotels. It costs about £1 and is available from bookshops. A selection of restaurants in Belfast follows.

First Class

Oscars, 34 Bedford Street (Tel: 247 757) – Excellent restaurant offering the finest cuts of local meat and seafood; specialities include chicken with prawn sauce and salmon with two fish sauces; good wine list.

Restaurant 44, 44 Bedford Street (Tel: 244 844) – Practically a Belfast institution and one of Northern Ireland's few Egon Ronay listed restaurants; fish dishes are the house speciality, although game, in season, has to be tasted to be believed.

La Belle Epoque, 103 Great Victoria Street (Tel: 223 244) – Good city-centre location for this fine French restaurant; specialities include lobster and pheasant.

Business Class

Truffles, 3a Donegall Square West (Tel: 247 153) – Popular and relaxed businessman's favourite in the city centre; house specialities include lemon and mushroom pork and peppered steak with brandy sauce; closed Sundays.

House of Moghul, Andras House, 60 Great Victoria Street (Tel: 243 727) – Award-winning Indian restaurant; open daily; superb *à la carte* and set menus.

Scruples Steak House, 32 Bradbury Place (Tel: 234 573) – Open every evening until midnight; good steaks and a variety of French dishes available in informal setting.

Economy Class

Jenny's, 18 Donegall Road (Tel: 249 282) – As typically Irish as you will find; superb Irish stew and a first-class range of light snacks and fresh sandwiches.

Manor House, 47 Donegall Pass (Tel: 238 755) – One of the city's best Chinese restaurants; exotic Cantonese dishes are a speciality; open daily until midnight.

Barnett Restaurant, Barnett Park (Tel: 681 246) – Informal atmosphere and a varied traditional menu in this restored Victorian house, unlicensed so bring your own wine.

Excursion possibilities from Belfast are numerous, and there are several parks along the **Lagan Valley** on the south side of the city just outside the main urban area. **Barnett's Park** is the most picturesque, offering fine views over the River Lagan. You can relax and enjoy a coffee or light meal in the restored Georgian mansion, which was the headquarters of the National Trust in the province until a devastating fire in 1976.

Past the old mill village of **EDENDERRY**, you come to the **Giant's Ring** if you travel via the Ballynahatty Road. Little is known about this man-made phenomenon, but you can admire a late **prehistoric stone dolmen** (a structured mound of large stones) in the middle of an enclosure which measures about 200 metres across. Four thousand years ago it was a place of ritual and worship to the early pagans; in more recent centuries, it has simply been another place of interest on the tourist trail, and a surprisingly peaceful spot within easy reach of the bustling city centre.

You are quite close to what is reckoned to be the busiest part of the **Ulster Way**, a well-trodden footpath which stretches for more than 500 miles all the way around Northern Ireland. Many visitors like to say they have walked at least a little of the Ulster Way, and the stretch at nearby Lisburn tends to be the most popular for brief visits.

Continuing north of Belfast, the A2 coastal road takes you on to the busy port town of **LARNE**, where many people first set foot in the province if they arrive on one of the regular ferry services from Stranraer or Cairnryan. Before reaching Larne the road passes **CARRICKFERGUS**, a similar-sized town to Larne, with a population of about 17,000.

The town developed around an **Anglo-Norman castle** which was the creation of John de Courcy in the late twelfth century. For five centuries thereafter it remained the seat of English power in the North. The castle served as a prison in the eighteenth century and subsequently as an armoury and magazine until 1928. Today it is a fascinating museum. In 1690 William of Orange passed through the town before going on to victory at the Battle of the Boyne. Among the points of interest in Carrickfergus are **St Nicholas' parish church**, also built by de Courcy, in the twelfth century, but heavily restored around 1615 after a devastating fire; and the **Andrew Jackson Centre**, which is a reconstructed cottage and museum dedicated to the former American President who was born here. The Jackson Centre is open 1000–1700 and 1800–2000 daily between June and August. Jonathan Swift also lived in this area. In his youth he was Church of England incumbent at Kilroot, just past Boneybefore. He wrote 'A Tale of a Tub' here in 1695. The ruins of Swift's church stand in an ancient graveyard by the shore.

There is a **Tourist Information office** (Tel: 63604) at Castle Green which is also open between June and August. Carrickfergus is an alternative to Belfast for accommodation in this part of the province, and one or two Tourist Board recommended suggestions are: the **Coast Road Hotel**, 28 Scotch Quarter (Tel: 51021) with fifteen comfortable bedrooms, all with private facilities; the **Dobbins Inn Hotel**, 6 High Street (Tel: 51905), with thirteen bedrooms; and the **Marathon Guesthouse**, 3 Upper Station Road (Tel: 862 475) with four double bedrooms.

The town of Larne is a busy place, but it has nothing to recommend a special visit, or even a short delay if you arrive here by ferry. If you arrive late, or plan to leave early, two accommodation suggestions are: **Magheramorne House Hotel**, 59 Shore Road (Tel: 79444) which has twenty-three bedrooms, all with private bathrooms; and **Mrs Eileen Mills' guesthouse**, 2 Prince's Gardens (Tel: 73269).

Just outside Larne you can visit one of the province's many beauty spots – the **Glencoe Waterfalls**. The village of GLYNN was the setting for the film *Luck of the Irish* although it has undergone some modern development since the film-makers left. Try to visit the seven-mile-long **Islandmagee peninsula** where the last witch to be tried in Ireland – in 1711 – originally lived. The steep basalt cliffs were witness to a horrific atrocity in 1641 when soldiers from the English garrison at Carrickfergus threw dozens of the local inhabitants to their death on what later proved to be an exaggerated charge of treason.

Heading inland a little, towards Lough Neagh, you come to **Ballylumford Dolmen**, another of Ireland's prehistoric sites. The great stone structure almost obscures the entrance to a private home! The nearby village of WHITEHEAD is a small coastal resort with a reasonable beach made up of tiny stones and pebbles. The Irish Railway Preservation Society is based here and occasionally short steam-train journeys can be enjoyed along a stretch of privately owned railway line.

The county town of **ANTRIM** overlooks Lough Neagh. The modern council estates and shopping centres belie the origins of one of Northern Ireland's most ancient towns; the oldest building you can still see is a **round tower** dating from the tenth century which stands in **Steeple Park**, just over a mile from the town centre. A monastery stood here from the sixth until the twelfth century, and the tower is one of the two best-preserved examples in Ireland.

Later places of interest in Antrim include the **Courthouse, Market Square**, which dates from the early eighteenth century, and an eighteenth-century cottage in Pogue's Entry, just off Church Street. Antrim's oldest church is **All Saints parish church** which was built in the last few years of the sixteenth century. The church contains some fine Renaissance stained glass, but the large steeple is relatively modern, having been added in 1816.

Heading south again, past Belfast, the next large town is **LISBURN**, with a population of more than 40,000. The town's origins go back to medieval times, but few public buildings predate a fire which virtually destroyed the town in 1707. The only significant exception are the **Assembly Rooms**, now a museum and exhibition centre devoted to the town and the local linen industry. John Wesley preached here in 1756 and Henry Munro, the Irish rebel, was hanged in the street in front of the building; his severed head later stood on a pole for weeks afterwards as a warning to other nationalist leaders, still at large.

The town has a small **Cathedral** which was built in 1623. It contains the tomb of Louis Crommelin, who did much to encourage the prosperous linen industry in the town. Within easy reach of Lisburn is the village of HILLSBOROUGH, best known for the **castle** bearing the same name, which is regularly used for high-level government and diplomatic meetings. In recent years, the Northern Ireland Secretary and the Irish Republic's Foreign Minister have met here on a regular basis.

You are now well into County Down, the first region of Ireland visited by the country's patron saint, St Patrick, more than 1500 years ago. The county's landscape is dominated by the twenty-three-mile-long **Ards peninsula**, where a concentration of Scottish immigrants settled in the early years of the seventeenth century.

The town of BANGOR stands at the head of the peninsula, and it was here that an early Christian abbey was founded in the mid-sixth century. The Vikings plundered the early community, and all that has survived from that period is a small section of wall close to the **Bangor Abbey parish church**. The church does, however, still have a fifteenth-century tower and an unusual octagonal spire, which dates from 1693. The separate **clock tower** was added by a rich local benefactor during the First World War.

A few miles back along the road is the town of HOLYWOOD – note there is only one 'l' and it has nothing whatsoever in common with its glamorous Californian soundalike! Yet another early Christian **abbey** was founded here in the seventh century, by St Laiseran, only to be replaced by a Norman church four centuries later.

The other large settlement on the Ards peninsula is NEWTOWNARDS, a manufacturing town with a population of more than 20,000. The town's origins date back to the thirteenth century when a Dominican priory was founded by Walter de Burgh. Nothing now remains of the priory other than the **nave** which was built into a now ruined seventeenth-century tower in Court Square. Ruined **Movilla Abbey**, where St Columba studied, can be found on the outskirts of Newtownards, in the direction of Donaghadee.

One of the oldest buildings is the **Market House**, now the Town Hall, which dates from 1765. An autumn fair is held outside the Market House every September, and has been going strong since 1613. One suggestion for accommodation in Newtownards is the **Strangford Arms Hotel** (Tel: 814 141) which has thirty-five bedrooms, all with private facilities.

There are a number of smaller towns and villages on the Ards peninsula which make an interesting visit, either collectively or individually. At GROOMSPORT, for example, you can see the place where Marshal Schomberg landed with more than 10,000 soldiers faithful to William of Orange in 1689; the town of COMBER has a large **monument** dedicated to Sir Robert Gillespie, a distinguished local soldier who died in action in Nepal.

DONAGHADEE is a popular little seaside town with a population of just over 4000. The town is the closest Irish point to Great Britain, and is dominated by a lighthouse and an enormous **harbour**. The harbour was enlarged in 1820, and throughout the first half of the nineteenth century a busy ferry service over to Portpatrick in south-west Scotland operated. The ferry service changed to the Stranraer–Larne route in 1849, but local fishermen used to offer to row people over to Scotland for the princely sum of £5.

Among the many visitors to this part of Ireland from Portpatrick were James Boswell, in 1769; John Keats in 1818; Daniel Defoe; composer Franz Liszt; William Wordsworth – and it is even said that the Russian Tsar, Peter the Great, stayed at **Grace Neill's Inn**, still standing in the High Street, at the end of the seventeenth century.

At GREYABBEY, on the main route from Newtownards to Portaferry, is situated a ruined **Cistercian monastery**, founded in 1193 by Affreca, daughter of the King of Man and wife of John de Courcy.

Two other places of interest are at **BALLYHALBERT**, where **Burr Point** and **Burial Island** represent the most easterly points in Ireland. Ballyhalbert also houses a mysterious Celtic **tumulus**. At **PORTAFERRY** on the southern tip of the peninsula, you can take a five-minute journey over to Strangford on the mainland. Portaferry is a popular spot for fishing and sailing enthusiasts, and a marine aquarium opened here in 1987 as part of the **marine biology research centre** connected with Queen's University, Belfast. Numerous species of fish live in the lough, which is a wildlife reserve and sanctuary for thousands of migratory birds. About 130 species are on record and almost half the world's population of Brent geese winter on the lough. A subaqua diving centre is also based at Portaferry.

The rest of County Down stretches to the border with the Irish Republic. The **Mountains of Mourne** are the most distinctive natural feature; forty-eight peaks standing within a twenty-five-mile circle, and all but two (**Bearnagh** and **Bignian**) with smooth, rounded tops. **Lough Shannagh** and **Silent Valley** are two of the most beautiful parts of County Down for the rambling enthusiast. From **Slieve Donard**, on a clear day, you can make out the coast of England.

The only coastal resort of any size before you reach the border is **NEWCASTLE**, one of Ulster's three main seaside holiday destinations, the other two being Portrush and Bangor. Newcastle has a population of 6000, although countless thousands more arrive whenever the weather is fine to take advantage of the long, sandy beach. One of Europe's early aviation pioneers was Harry Ferguson. A large stone monument on the promenade commemorates his first flight, in a shaky home-made monoplane, along the beach in 1910.

There is a wide range of accommodation in Newcastle, reflecting the town's popularity with package and independent visitors alike. The largest hotel is the A-grade **Slieve Donard** (Tel: 23681) in Downs Road which has 107 bedrooms, all with private facilities. An excellent country club hotel is the **Burrendale** (Tel: 22599), 51 Castlewellan Road, while medium-grade suggestions are the **Enniskeen** (Tel: 22392), 98 Bryansford Road and the

Brook Cottage Hotel, 58 Bryansford Road (Tel: 22204); a couple of good guesthouses are the **Arundel** (Tel: 22232), 23 Bryansford Road, and the **Savoy** (Tel: 22513), at 20 Downs Road.

A large nature reserve, **Murlough**, is about two miles north of Newcastle, and this is a favourite haven for many varieties of seabird. **Castlewellan Forest Park** also lies nearby, and here you can find an **arboretum** dating back two and a half centuries. A designated area for the *Nature Lover* is **Tollymore**, Northern Ireland's first forest park, which opened in 1955. Quite apart from the natural attractions, there is an Information Centre with café for visitors to enjoy.

Before you leave the heart of County Down, try to make a visit to **DOWNPATRICK**. The **Cathedral** here was originally built in the mid-thirteenth century but was destroyed and rebuilt at least three times between then and the early nineteenth century. What one sees today is virtually all nineteenth-century. The massive organ was donated by King George III in 1802.

The town's most famous sight is the **reputed grave of Ireland's patron saint**, St Patrick, which stands close to what remains of an old round tower in the churchyard adjoining the Cathedral. A huge granite monolith was placed over the grave in 1901 and the site is revered as a place of pilgrimage on the saint's day, 17 March. Interestingly, a medieval crusader is said to have buried the bones of St Columba and St Brigid in the same grave.

A little way to the north of the town is **Inch Abbey**, a graceful old ruin which was founded as a Cistercian abbey in 1180. It was built on the site of a much older monastery, but this was virtually destroyed by Viking invaders in the early years of the eleventh century. Traces of a hospital and a bakery have also been uncovered nearby.

There is a limited selection of accommodation in Downpatrick, and the only recognized hotel is the **Abbey Lodge** (Tel: 4511) in Belfast Road. It has twenty-two bedrooms, all with private facilities. There are very few guesthouses in the town; one option for bed and breakfast is **Mrs Vera McCormick** (Tel:

2695), at 69 Saul Road, who has two double rooms available throughout the year.

Within a few miles of Downpatrick lies **CASTLEWARD**, a showplace in care of the National Trust. It includes a magnificent **Georgian mansion** filled with works of art and period pieces – Castleward also houses an ornamental lake, a temple and a demesne.

Back on the coast, the village of **ANNALONG** is set against a beautiful mountain backdrop, and is one of the finest stopping points for seeing the rural life of the county. It still has a busy little harbour, but the coast's main fishing fleet is based a little way further down at **KILKEEL**. A ruined **fourteenth-century church** stands in the town centre, and a mile or so to the northeast a prehistoric **stone dolmen** with an enormous capstone can be seen. The road north towards **HILLTOWN**, via the **Spelga Pass**, has a number of fine vantage points.

NEWRY is the last town of any size before you reach County Armagh. It is a busy town with a population of nearly 20,000 and occupies a strategic position at the head of the Gap of the North. Modern Newry is on the Newry river and canal. Newry takes its name from the legend that St Patrick himself planted a tree – a yew – by the banks of the river. No surviving buildings are directly associated with Ireland's patron saint, but an **abbey** on the east bank of the river was built only a couple of centuries later. It was expanded in the twelfth century by the Cistercians although nothing now remains apart from a granite slab inside a local bakery. To the east of the **Town Hall** stands Ireland's first post-Reformation (Protestant) **church**, dating from 1578. This unobtrusive church was built by Sir Nicholas Bagenal, Elizabethan Marshal of Ireland and founder of the modern town. His impressive coat of arms is displayed on a tablet inside the church's porch.

Newry has a **Roman Catholic Cathedral**, built in Tudor-Gothic style in 1825 by Thomas Duff. The transepts and tower were not added until much later. In and around the town centre there is plenty of evidence of Newry's prosperous commercial past: large town houses are common and the oldest, at 1 Trevor Hill, is an imposing granite building dating from the late eighteenth century.

There is a **Tourist Information office** at the Arts Centre, Bank Parade (Tel: 66232), which is open all year round. The choice of accommodation in the town is limited; the only actual hotel is the **Mourne Country Hotel** (Tel: 67922), in Belfast Road, which has forty-four bedrooms, all with private facilities. Two suggestions for bed and breakfast accommodation are: **Millvale House**, 8 Millvale Road (Tel: 3789), and **Oisín House**, 4a Canal Street (Tel: 5715).

One suggested excursion from Newry is the resort port of WARRENPOINT. The volume of shipping handled by the town's small **harbour** has expanded considerably since the closing of Newry's port in the 1970s. The main goods received here are paper, grain, timber and coal, and the lively **promenade** is one of the best places in County Down for people-watching. Another excursion might be to BANBRIDGE, close to Newry and the birth place of Patrick Brontë – father of Charlotte, Emily and Anne. The **Brontë Homeland Centre** is located at Drumballyroney Church and Schoolhouse.

County Armagh is Northern Ireland's smallest county but it occupies a special place in early history as it was here that St Patrick based his first Christian mission.

If you enter the county from the north, via the A3 heading from Belfast, the first town you will reach is LURGAN, which prospered as a result of the expanding nineteenth-century textile industry. The famous *Book of Armagh*, one of the oldest and most precious illuminated Irish manuscripts, was found in the private collection of an eccentric seventeenth-century Lurgan bibliophile. It is now preserved in the library of Trinity College, Dublin.

The A3 continues through PORTADOWN, another town whose prosperity once relied on the production of textiles. Today the town's economy is based on the manufacture of a diverse range of goods, ranging from carpets to industrial ceramics. A big cattle market is held in the town every Friday.

Portadown's most famous former resident is Sir Robert Hart,

the Victorian founder of both the Chinese postal service and the Chinese lighthouse service. His former home is in Woodhouse Street. Among the surviving points of interest in the town are the unusual **triangular 'squares'** at either end of the main street, and a number of churches representing all the main religious denominations. Twenty minutes' drive from Newry lies **ROSTREVOR**, one of the most attractive villages in Ireland. The **Cloughmore** or 'big stone' sits on a fine viewpoint on Slieve Martin and is approached by a forest drive. Rostrevor also incorporates a 'fairy glen' and a 'fiddlers green'.

The main road continues to **ARMAGH**, the ancient capital of Ulster and still regarded as Northern Ireland's spiritual capital. Armagh is referred to as 'the garden of Ireland' as it is the centre of such a fertile district. It is an attractive town, with a population of 13,000 and a good selection of things to see and do. St Patrick founded Armagh and built his first stone church on a hill near the town in the fifth century from which Christianity spread throughout the island. The seat of both the Roman Catholic and the Anglican Archbishops of Northern Ireland, Armagh's religious links stem from its connection with St Patrick. The late eighteenth-century Archbishop, Richard Robinson, commissioned many respected architects and thus was responsible for many of the fine Georgian buildings in the town centre.

If you travel to Armagh by car, a sensible place to park is on the **Mall**, a beautiful tree-lined promenade which once served as the town's racecourse. The Mall is also a good starting point for admiring the Georgian architecture as it is lined with beautiful town houses and is within easy reach of the **Anglican Cathedral**, the older and more historic of Armagh's two cathedrals. It stands on the site of a much smaller medieval church, and building started in the 1760s under the close supervision of Archbishop Robinson. An early visitor was the poet Thackeray who admired the eleventh-century stone cross and pagan stone figures which are now preserved in the chapterhouse. The legendary Irish warrior Brian Boru was killed near Armagh and his remains allegedly lie close to the large stone plaque which is built into the west wall of the north transept. The Cathedral is open to the public 1000–1700 daily throughout the year.

The adjoining **Cathedral Library** is *the* famous library of Armagh. It is fascinating, and among its many exhibits are an early copy of *Gulliver's Travels* with many handwritten notes by the author, Dean Swift, and a fine collection of church records dating back to medieval times. The library is only open 1400–1600 Mon–Fri (and not at all during July and August) unless you have special permission from the Keeper.

In Abbey Street there is a **Presbyterian church** which was completed in 1722, four years before Dean Swift published *Gulliver's Travels*. It was built from stones taken from a medieval Augustinian priory which stood next to the church, where the Anglican Cathedral now stands.

Work began on the **Catholic Cathedral** in 1840 and took thirty-five years to complete. Building was suspended during the period of the Great Famine, in the 1840s, and the Cathedral stood for several years with its outside walls reaching no higher than five metres. The building style is a combination of Perpendicular Gothic and ornate Decorated Gothic. Indeed the Cathedral is almost Byzantine in its lavish colouring, mosaics and carving. The ceiling and walls feature every Irish saint, and it is interesting to reflect that nearly all the funds to build the Cathedral came from public subscription; the Pope provided the rest.

The **Archbishop's Palace** was built in 1770 and contains a number of treasures including contemporary portraits of King George III and Queen Charlotte. The Palace now serves as council administration offices, and is not normally open to the public. The officials are unlikely to object, however, if visitors have a brief look at the magnificent entrance hall with its enormous chandelier and the Royal portraits.

Another attractive Georgian public building is the **Court House** at the northern end of the Mall. From here prisoners had to walk the length of the Mall to reach the jail, now disused. The jail had a public gallows outside until 1866. To the north of the Court House is the **Armagh County Museum** with a varied collection of local artefacts neatly laid out in a late Georgian schoolhouse. It is open 1000-1300 and 1400-1700 Mon-Sat. The stone left over from the construction of the Court House went towards building the nearby **Sovereign's House**. This grand building now houses the regimental museum of the Royal Irish Fusiliers. Its opening hours are restricted mainly to weekday afternoons but are liable to change; for up-to-date information telephone Armagh 522 911.

One other relatively modern place of interest in Armagh is the **planetarium** which stands in the grounds of an eighteenth-century observatory on College Hill. The planetarium was opened in 1968 with the lively TV astronomer Patrick Moore as its first director, and now houses one of the United Kingdom's finest collections of antique astronomical books. It also houses exhibits from the American space programme. A telescope once owned by King George III was donated to the observatory in 1840 by Queen Victoria. The Hall of Astronomy is open 1400-1645 Mon-Sat; Star Shows take place at 1500 every Sat, and every day except Sun during July and August.

On the west outskirts of Armagh stands **Navan Fort**, an eighteen-acre hillfort that was the chief stronghold of the kings of Ulster until its destruction in AD 332.

Armagh has a **Tourist Information office** at the Palace Demesne (Tel: 524 052) which is open all year round. They can offer information about where to eat and stay in the town, but two suggestions for a good evening meal are: the **Gallery Restaurant** (Tel: 522 103), 147 Railway Street, which offers good European cooking at moderate prices – grills are a speciality; and **McKenna's** (Tel: 522 645), 21 Lower English Street, offering a varied range of inexpensive dishes in an informal setting.

Armagh's only two hotels are both graded 'B' by the Northern Ireland Tourist Board. The **Drumsill Hotel** (Tel: 522 009) in Moy Road has nine bedrooms, including seven doubles, and an inexpensive dinner menu; the **Charlemont Arms** (Tel: 522 028) at 63 English Street has twelve rooms, including four family bedrooms, but only nine have private facilities.

Armagh's only guesthouse is the **Clonhugh** (Tel: 522 693) which has five bedrooms, available all year round; this includes one large family room with private facilities. Two possibilities for bed and breakfast are: **Mrs Sylvia McRoberts** (Tel: 522 387) at 99 Cathedral Road, and **Mr O'Hagan** (Tel: 523 584), Padua House, 63 Cathedral Road.

From Armagh there are a number of excursion possibilities to the southern part of the county. The main road south-east is the A28 which takes you through **MARKETHILL** and back to Newry again. Markethill is a large village and a good starting point from which to venture into the **Gosford Forest Park**. The Park is dominated by an interesting mock-Norman **castle** which was built around 1820 to replace a much older manor house which burnt down in 1805. The other main road south from Armagh continues to the border with the Irish Republic and goes through the peaceful villages of **KEADY** and **NEWTOWNHAMILTON**. **BESSBROOK** is an old mill village close to Newtownhamilton and was founded by the Quaker John Grubb Richardson in the 1840s. Richardson was also responsible for building the **eighteen-arch viaduct** in 1851, and Bessbrook's small station is still a regular stop for the Dublin to Belfast express.

If you leave County Armagh from the south, the last village you pass through is **CROSSMAGLEN**, whose name may already be familiar because of the heavy army presence here and its recent bloody history. The landscape becomes noticeably flatter as you head either south or east from southern Armagh and leave the beautiful Mourne Mountains behind.

County Tyrone is the largest and least-populated of the province's six counties. It is often called the 'Heart of Ulster' because it lies in the middle of the nine counties. It is noted for its music and poetry as well as its beautiful green countryside. This is an ideal part of Ireland for anyone who is looking for an 'away-from-it-all' holiday in a genuinely unspoilt region.

Three main roads come in from County Armagh, including the M1 from Belfast and the A29 from Armagh town. The A29 enters the county at the village of **MOY** which used to supply the British army with its finest chargers and dress horses. One local sight is the ruined **Charlemont Fort**. This distinctive star-shaped fort was built by Lord Mountjoy in 1602 and burnt down during the struggle for independence in 1922.

One of only two towns of any size in County Tyrone is

DUNGANNON, five miles north of Moy. The town has a population of just over 8000 and grew up as a textile manufacturing town in the late eighteenth and nineteenth centuries. Prior to then, Dungannon was the seat of the O'Neill family, one of Ireland's most significant ruling clans in late medieval times, who used to live in a large castle on a hill overlooking the town. Nothing now remains of the castle but you can still enjoy a fine view over the town from the hill.

Dungannon's oldest building is the **Royal School** in Northland Row which was built at the start of the seventeenth century on the direct orders of James VI and I. General John Nicholson is the school's most famous former pupil; he was killed leading British troops into Delhi during the Indian Mutiny in 1857. A **bronze statue** of the General was brought from Delhi in 1960 and stands outside the school.

Dungannon has a reasonable number of restaurants but very few hotels or guesthouses. Two suggestions for eating out are the **Farmhouse Restaurant** (Tel: 40489) at 95 Cookstown Road, which offers a range of grills and light meals, and the **Inn on the Park** (Tel: 25151) in Moy Road which has an impressive menu including house specialities such as lemon pancakes and rainbow trout.

The town's only hotel is the B-graded **Inn on the Park** (Tel: 25151) in Moy Road. The hotel has fifteen bedrooms including one family room and offers a wide range of leisure activities. Two suggestions for approved bed and breakfast accommodation are: **Mr Cyril Kerr**, Belvedere House, 82 Cunninghams Lane (Tel: 22593) and **Mrs Anne Murphy**, Innisfayle, 28 Circular Road (Tel: 24886).

Knockmany Forest lies to the west of Dungannon and an interesting excursion is to the **chambered cairn** there, which is said to be the burial place of Baine, Queen of the old Kingdom of Oriel, who died at nearby CLOGHER in the sixth century AD.

Clogher today is a small village with a population of less than 600. In early medieval times, however, it was the capital of the Kingdom of Oriel and was the seat of the diocese of Clogher, the oldest bishopric in Ireland – the founding bishop was St MacCartan, once a pupil of St Patrick. The village has a small **Anglican Cathedral**, built in distinctive blue/purple stone in the mid-eighteenth century. The surrounding **Clogher Valley** has many more fascinating little villages which together or individually offer a variety of excursion possibilities. Near BALLYGAWLEY, for example, the ancestral home of former United States President Ulysses Grant has been completely rebuilt. Grant's maternal great-grandfather was born here in 1738 and emigrated to America shortly before it won independence. The President visited the cottage in 1878, the year after he left office.

A prehistoric **passage grave** can be seen near Ballygawley, and the much later ruin of a **church** dedicated to St Kieran occupies a commanding position overlooking the valley at **Errigal Keerogue**. The village of FIVEMILETOWN, as its name implies, lies exactly five Irish miles from Clogher, Tempo and Brookeborough. Fivemiletown has an attractive little **parish church** which was built in 1736, and visitors to the village find it hard to believe that the railway line used to run past the church and down the middle of the main street.

Heading north again from Dungannon, the last town before County Londonderry is COOKSTOWN. Its **main street** is more than a mile long and completely straight. This street (which, incidentally, has changed its name nine times since it was built) is a tourist attraction in its own right, and was conceived by an eighteenth-century landlord, William Stewart. The town has a strong nationalist tradition and its most famous daughter is probably the colourful Bernadette Devlin who sat, briefly, as Britain's youngest MP in the early 1970s.

Two places of interest in the town are the **Holy Trinity Catholic Church**, on the west side of the main street, and an early nineteenth-century **mock-Norman castle** whose vast grounds incorporate the local golf course.

The best of Cookstown's many restaurants are the B-graded hotel the **Glenavon House** (Tel: 63462) at 52 Drum Road, or the **Greenvale Hotel** (Tel: 62243), 57 Drum Road. A couple of relatively inexpensive restaurants are the **Otter Lodge** (Tel: 65427) in Dungannon Road, and the **Raja Indian Restaurant** (Tel: 63911), 86 Chapel Street.

The hill of **TULLAHOGUE**, a few miles to the south of Cookstown, was the ceremonial 'coronation' place for the O'Neill family between the twelfth and seventeenth centuries. When the site was eventually surrendered to the British army in 1602, Lord Mountjoy ordered the great stone throne to be smashed. The O'Hagan family, who provided Tyrone with most of its Chief Justices, was also based at Tullahogue. The last prominent legal officer from this family was the first British Lord O'Hagan (1812–85) who was Ireland's Chancellor towards the end of his life.

The A505 crosses the **Black Bog** which makes up the undulating heart of the county until you reach **OMAGH**, the main town in Tyrone. With a population of nearly 15,000, Omagh is a prosperous market town and a central base for holidaymakers who wish to explore this beautiful county. Although the town's origins go back several hundred years, all the local landmarks date from the nineteenth and twentieth centuries.

Omagh's skyline is dominated by the twin spires of the **Sacred Heart Catholic Church**. It was built in the late 1890s, and, curiously, the spires are unequal in height. Another sight is the town's distinctive classical **courthouse** which was built in 1814 by John Hargrave.

Omagh is a popular holiday spot for fishing enthusiasts who may be keen to try their luck with the local salmon, trout, roach or pike. The town is also frequented by those with an interest in wildfowl. One of the nearest villages to Omagh is tiny Drumquin, which is best known as the birthplace of Jimmy Kennedy (1903–84) who wrote the classic children's song, 'The Teddy Bears' Picnic'.

Places to eat out in Omagh include **McGirr's** (Tel: 2462) at Mountjoy East, who offer an excellent *à la carte* menu on Friday and Saturday, and either the **Bridge Tavern** (Tel: Fintona 841 005) at Eskra, or the **Good Evening Restaurant** (Tel: 47500) in Derry Road, for a more informal meal.

Omagh's two best hotels are the B-grade **Royal Arms** (Tel: 24 3262) at 51 High Street which has twenty-one bedrooms, all but two with private facilities, and the B-grade **Silverbirch Hotel**

(Tel: 242520) at 5 Gortin Road with thirty-one bedrooms, ten of which have bathrooms.

One of Ireland's major tourist attractions is located at CAMPHILL, halfway between Omagh and Newtownstewart. The **Ulster-American Folk Park** allows you the opportunity to follow in the footsteps of the emigrant Irish who sailed from here to the New World. An emigrant ship, complete with dockside buildings and authentically costumed interpreters, transports you back to the early 1800s, when emigration was the order of the day in Ireland. An exhibition gallery gives excellent detail on the conditions of emigration and the whole exhibit is well worth a visit. The museum is open Easter–early Sept Mon–Sat 1100–1830; Sun and public holidays 1130–1900; mid-Sept–Easter, Mon–Fri 1030–1700; closed weekends (Tel: 243 292).

The village of PLUMBRIDGE nestles at the bottom of the valley and from here it is only a short drive to another local beauty spot – **Barnes Gap**. The two largest peaks in view here are **Mount Sawel** (680 metres) and **Mount Dart** (625 metres), which can each be climbed in less than a couple of hours – start early, though, and make sure you are adequately prepared for weather changes.

The A5 continues north towards County Londonderry and passes through the last two towns of any size – Newtownstewart and Strabane. NEWTOWNSTEWART has a population of around 1200, roughly half that of its namesake just across the Irish Sea in south-west Scotland. The town has little to merit a special visit apart from the ruin of **Harry Avery's Castle** half a mile to the west. This was one of Ireland's very few Gaelic stone castles and visitors can still see the unusual D-shaped twin towers, dating from the fourteenth century.

STRABANE is a much larger town with a population of 11,000, and lies right on the border with the Irish Republic. In recent years it has suffered a number of isolated incidents as part of the 'troubles' in the province and is considered an unemployment blackspot in official European Community figures. It is, however, a lively town with a number of points of interest – a good base for exploring the counties of Tyrone, Londonderry, and Donegal over the border.

A town or village of some sort has stood here since early medieval times; the rivers Finn and Mourne converge at Strabane and the strategic importance of this was recognized by James II who made his base-camp here before going on to attack Derry in 1688/9. In the late eighteenth century Strabane was an important printing and publishing centre although the only surviving evidence of this is a tiny Georgian shop in the main street – **Gray's Printing Shop** – which is now looked after by the National Trust. The town's most famous printer was John Dunlop (1747–1812) who copied and published the American Declaration of Independence. He went on to publish the *Pennsylvania Packet* which subsequently became the United States' first daily newspaper.

Two miles outside Strabane is the **Wilson ancestral home**. One James Wilson was born and brought up in this modest cottage. He served his apprenticeship as a printer and emigrated to the United States in 1807; 106 years later, his grandson Woodrow Wilson became President of the United States, subsequently taking America into the First World War a few months before the start of his second term in office in 1917. The National Trust has responsibility for the cottage and it is open all year round.

There are only a few restaurants in Strabane, mostly offering traditional Irish cuisine and a selection of international dishes. Two suggestions are the **Buttery Tavern** (Tel: 884 466) at 30 Market Street, which is open until 2300 Mon–Sat, and **Fir Trees Lodge** (Tel: 382 382) in Melmount Road for a good selection of *à la carte* dishes – last orders at 2130.

There is very little accommodation from which to choose in the town. The only hotel is the B-grade **Fir Trees Lodge** (Tel: 382 382) in Melmount Road which has twenty-six double bedrooms, all with private facilities. Bed and breakfast accommodation is available with **Mr and Mrs McGinley** (Tel: 2687) at Danreen, Curlyhill Road. Inexpensive country house bed and breakfast is offered by **William and Marion Doherty** (Tel: Sion Mills 58526) at Mourne Fox Grove, 30 Liskey Road, Bearney.

West of County Tyrone lies County Fermanagh, one of Ireland's smallest counties with perhaps less to attract visitors than the other regions. Much of the county is lakeland: the area is almost bisected by **Lower Lough Erne**, and the slightly smaller **Upper Lough Erne** to the south. There are 154 islands on the Lough. Fishing enthusiasts will enjoy the uncrowded river and lake banks, and the county is popular with those looking for an away-from-it-all holiday. The **Marble Arch Caves**, also located in Fermanagh, are a great tourist attraction. Tours of the subterranean caverns in the limestone are available to the public. Boat journeys operate through formations of stalactites and stalagmites, past flowstones and other geological features.

The only town of any size is **ENNISKILLEN**, built on a spur of land which divides the county's two great lakes. The town has a population of around 10,000 and was expanded during a period of English occupation in the seventeenth century.

In more recent times, Enniskillen has experienced more tragedy as a result of the 'troubles'. The most shocking example was the IRA's Remembrance Day Bombing in 1987, which left thirteen civilians dead and many more injured. A permanent memorial to those who died stands near the War Memorial where the outrage took place.

Points of interest in Enniskillen include the large **Victorian park**, with a cast-iron bandstand and a large statue to Sir Galbraith Cole who was one of Wellington's leading generals during the Peninsular War. The town's main street also has a small **Anglican Cathedral** featuring a seventeenth-century tower and the original colours of the Inniskillin regiments.

There is a **Tourist Information office** (Tel: 23110) which is open all year round at the Lakeland Visitor Centre in Shore Road. The town's best hotel is the B★ graded **Killyhevlin** (Tel: 323 481) in Dublin Road, with five double and seventeen family rooms. Two suggestions for bed and breakfast accommodation are: the **Willoughby Guesthouse** (Tel: 25275) at 24 Willoughby Place, and the **Interlaken Guesthouse** (Tel: 22274) at 54 Forthill Street.

Here you are well placed to explore the surrounding lakelands and castles. This section offers only a brief introduction to what you can expect to see, and anyone planning more than a day-trip to this part of the province should visit the Tourist office in Enniskillen for information on all the attractions of this often-overlooked part of Ireland.

A good starting point is the ring of castles of which Enniskillen's example is part. The others include the ruined **Portora**, built round the lake shore in 1613 and now in the grounds of the Royal High School – a disastrous chemistry experiment destroyed a large part of the castle in 1859. Portora Royal School's famous former pupils include Oscar Wilde, Samuel Beckett and the composer of 'Abide With Me'.

Two of the most impressive islands on the lower lake are **Devenish** and **White Island**. Devenish is the more extensive and lies two miles south of Enniskillen. A monastery was built here in the sixth century AD by St Molaise, regarded as one of early Christian Ireland's twelve 'apostles'. Among the surviving remains are a thirteenth-century parish church, with a fine south window and twenty-five-metre round tower, and a fifteenth-century Augustinian priory.

The southern lake is better known for its wildlife and fishing than for historical remains. However, two interesting sights in the Upper Lough are **Inishkeen**, with its old St Fergus' cemetery and medieval monastery; and **Cleenish**, which is recognized throughout the world for its unusual carved gravestones. **Crom Castle**, ancestral home of the Earls of Erne, stands on a long headland to the west of **Galloon**.

Cruises on Lough Erne are available throughout the summer. Tourists can take a two-hour tour on a waterbus along the Lough, calling for half an hour at Devenish Island, Lower Lough Erne. Embarkation is at Round 0 pier, Enniskillen. For further details, telephone 0365 22882. A covered motor yacht also cruises Upper Lough Erne, passing **Crom Old Castle** and **Crichton's Tower**. Tours last forty-five minutes. Embarkation is at Crom Estate, Newtownbutler (off the A34). For further details, telephone 03655 21221.

Visitors can also take a one-and-a-half-hour cruise on Upper Lough Erne in a powered longship, past Crom Castle, Gad Island, Innis Rath and many other islands. Sailings commence at the

Share Centre, Smith's Strand four miles south of Lisnaskea on the B127 (Tel: 03657 22122).

North of County Fermanagh and Strabane lies County Londonderry. James VI and I granted vast areas of land to gentry and trading companies who were prepared to settle in this part of Ireland. Many came from London, and the greatest lasting influence of this settlement is the word 'London' which is still reflected in the name – the county is still officially recognized as County Londonderry, but visitors should note that in 1984 the council in Londonderry changed its name to Derry City Council, so that the city itself is now often referred to as Derry. Many maps and guidebooks, however, still refer to the province's second city by its more familiar name, Londonderry.

Most of County Londonderry is rugged terrain, dominated by the beautiful Sperrin Mountains and acres of peat bog for which Ireland is justly famous.

MONEYMORE is one of few villages in the southern half of the county with more than a handful of houses. It was the first village in Ireland to have a piped water supply (in 1615) and both it and nearby **DRAPERSTOWN** grew up as linen plantation towns in the seventeenth century.

Another local village, **MAGHERA**, dates back many hundreds of years to before the birth of the Irish linen industry, and it was here that St Lurach founded a monastery in the sixth century. **Maghera Old Church** stands on the site of the monastery although the oldest surviving part of the building is the finely sculpted west door which dates from the twelfth century.

Visitors with an interest in Ireland's turbulent medieval history may wish to visit the **tomb** of the Derry chieftain Cooey ná Gall O'Cahan (died 1385). The tomb stands amid the ruins of an Augustinian priory a few miles outside the small town of **DUNGIVEN**, on the A6. There is a ruined early **twelfth-century church** on Banagher Hill, two miles south-west of Dungiven.

Northern Ireland's most famous contemporary literary figure, Seamus Heaney, was born in a small farmhouse near the village of **TOOMEBRIDGE** in 1939. A rewarding drive takes one across the Bishop's Road to **Bishop's View**, where there is a spectacular vantage point overlooking **Magilligan Point** and the approach to **Lough Foyle**. The Ulster Gliding Club is based locally and the graceful aircraft have been known to reach altitudes of 15–20,000 feet around this part of the country.

Rolling moorland and undulating acres of peat bog cover most of the rest of County Londonderry until you reach the coast. The A6 heads north-west towards Derry and the border with County Donegal.

DERRY is Northern Ireland's second city and has a population of around 65,000. It stands on a wide hill overlooking the estuary of the River Foyle. St Columba founded the city when he established a monastery on the hill in the sixth century. Columba's monastery flourished long after he left around AD 564 to found a more permanent home for himself on the Scottish island of Iona.

In 1613 Derry was given its formal charter by King James VI and I. This meant that the town could elect a mayor and, such was the extent of London's influence over the new corporation, the prefix 'London' was added. Nothing at all survives from before this period, not even the fragments of the medieval **Cathedral** which was replaced by St Columba's, the present Anglican Cathedral, in 1633. Derry's long history, and its close links with London, are represented in the artwork of many of the Cathedral's fine stained-glass windows.

The Cathedral's chapterhouse has an interesting collection of artefacts associated with the city's history, including several of the original seventeenth-century locks and keys to the city gates, and Lord Macaulay's original handwritten account of the siege of 1689. It is open most days throughout the year.

Derry's second cathedral is **St Eugene's Roman Catholic Cathedral**, which was finished in 1873. The seventy-eight-metre spire was added thirty years later. St Eugene's enormous east window depicts the crucifixion and seven of Ireland's saints. The window is dedicated to Bishop Francis Kelly, who was responsible for the Cathedral's construction. Before St Eugene's was built, the main place of worship for Derry's Catholic population was the **Long Tower Church**, erected in the 1780s.

In earlier times, worship took place in a great medieval cathedral, Templemore, which was built in 1164 and destroyed by fire in 1567. The present Long Tower Church stands on the site of a tenth-century Long Tower which survived the explosion although it, too, was subsequently destroyed.

The most striking relic of the early seventeenth-century English settlers are the **Walls of Derry**, approximately a mile of stone ramparts which form the boundary of the old city centre. At their highest, the walls tower almost eight metres above the pavements and, in places, are more than ten metres thick. Guided tours are available during the summer months, starting from the **Guildhall**. Double Bastion was the most heavily fortified part of the walls, where Roaring Meg, a huge eighteen-pound cannon, is still positioned. The dozens of stained-glass windows illustrate the city's history.

One of the most tragic stories from Ireland's history concerns the siege of Londonderry by James II in March 1689. The townspeople supported William of Orange's claim to the British throne, and in an attempt to starve them into submission, James II personally supervised the investment of the town. The gates were locked and the townspeople thought themselves able to withstand any military attack, but they had not reckoned on a food blockade and, after a few weeks, even rats were being sold in butcher's shops. More than 7000 people died of disease and starvation, but the people refused to give in, and four months later William's forces relieved the town.

Derry's imposing Guildhall is just one of a number of large public buildings in the city centre. Two of the oldest are the Irish Society House and the Court House which date from 1764 and 1813 respectively. From Derry Quay behind the Guildhall thousands of Irish emigrants sailed to the New World. South of Derry lie the Sperrin Mountains – where large deposits of gold have recently been found. The shortest route to the Sperrins is up the pleasant valley of the River Faughan. The route passes Ness Wood, where the Burntollet River plunges thirty feet over Ulster's highest waterfall. The **Tourist Information office** (Tel: 267 284) is directly opposite the Guildhall. It is open all year round (but not Sundays outside the summer months) and can provide you with a free map of the city walls.

There is a reasonable range of good restaurants, hotels and officially 'approved' accommodation. What follows is a selection of hotels and guesthouses, and eating-out suggestions, in three categories.

First Class

Everglades Hotel, Prehen Road (Tel: 46722) – An attractive hotel with thirty-eight bedrooms, mostly singles, but there are six family rooms and the provision for children is excellent. All rooms are well appointed and have private facilities.

Business Class

White Horse Inn, 68 Clooney Road, Campsie (Tel: 860 606) – Forty-four bedrooms available, all with private bathrooms, and a range of both indoor and outdoor leisure facilities; excellent *à la carte* dinner menu.

Economy Class

Broomhill House, Limavady Road (Tel: 44854) – A comfortable guesthouse with twenty-one bedrooms, including four family rooms; none with private facilities.

Clarence House, 15 Northland Road (Tel: 265 342) – Seven bedrooms in this smart B-graded guesthouse.

Mr and Mrs Collins, Inishfoyle, 52 Gleneagles, Culmore Road (Tel: 53800) – Six bedrooms available including two doubles and two family rooms.

Where to eat out in Derry:

First Class

Everglades, Prehen Road (Tel: 46722) – An intimate first-class restaurant; impeccable service and superb *à la carte* menu offering many fine Irish specialities. Open daily throughout the year.

Business Class

Browns, 1 Victoria Road (Tel: 45180) – A cheerful restaurant in the town centre; specialities include enormous Caesar salads and rack of ribs.
Vintage, 67 Strand Road (Tel: 267 302) – Open daily; house specialities include French dishes, fresh mussels in garlic sauce and steak in wine sauce.

Economy Class

Capistans, Richmond Centre (Tel: 264 661) – The best of several city-centre fast-food establishments; large, filling baked potatoes are a speciality.
Acorn, 3 Pump Street (no telephone) – Delightfully informal and the best place in town for large helpings of wholesome Irish cooking – including soup, stew and baked potatoes.
Pancho's, 77 Victoria Road, Newbuildings (Tel: 45589) – Fast and friendly; a varied menu including locally caught fish and sizzling steaks. Open until 2300 Mon–Sat.

Derry's small civilian airport is four miles east of the city, near the village of EGLINTON. **Ballykelly Bridge** is a nearby beauty spot and stands close to the splendour of the eighteenth-century **Walworth House**. The house is not open to the public but visitors can see the remains of a seventeenth-century church, founded by a London fishmongers' company, directly opposite.

The main road passes through **LIMAVADY**, a market town with a population of roughly 8000. A famous old **inn** used to stand in the town's main street, and it was here in 1842 that the English writer Thackeray stopped overnight and composed 'Sweet Peg of Limavady'.

Jane Ross lived in the main street during the last century. She achieved little of lasting significance herself, but she did befriend a musical traveller and took down the pleasant tune he was constantly singing. The song turned out to be 'Danny Boy', now regarded as Ireland's unofficial National Anthem.

There are no sights of note in Limavady, nor much choice of accommodation other than 'approved' bed and breakfast establishments. One interesting detour from the town is the **Roe Valley Country Park** with a large camp site, range of outdoor sporting pursuits, and a host of wildlife in an area of forest carefully restored by the developers of a hydro-electric power plant.

A local beauty spot is **Magilligan Point**, dominated by an early eighteenth-century Martello tower, with superb views across Lough Foyle and beyond. There are one or two good beaches around here, although their exposed position means that it is seldom warm enough for bathing. Ornithologists regularly come to the Point to admire the variety of seabirds which can be seen here.

DOWNHILL is the last settlement of any size before Coleraine. It was originally part of an enormous country estate, and visitors can see the roofless ruin of **Downhill Palace** which was built between 1770 and 1785. One other point of interest is **Mussenden Temple**, a domed rotunda which the local bishop occupied as his library until the last century; it is now in the care of the National Trust.

COLERAINE has a population of 16,000 and is the largest town in the north of the province after Derry and Ballymena. It stands on the estuary of the River Bann and in the early seventeenth century it expanded as a market town as a result of the settlement of traders previously based in London. There are no public buildings of note in Coleraine apart from the old **Town Hall** in the city centre. The **River Bann** is probably the town's most attractive feature and there is a beautiful weir and collection of locks a little way upstream at 'The Cutts'. Visitors can also relax and enjoy the **Guy L. Wilson Memorial Garden**, on the University of Ulster campus. The garden is best seen in spring when hundreds of varieties of daffodils flower, many grown from bulbs descended from those planted by Wilson himself. **Ulsterbus** and the **Old Bushmills Distillery** operate an open-top bus, weather permitting, July–Sept, from Coleraine to the Giant's Causeway, via Portstewart, Portrush, Portballintrae, Bushmills and return.

The town has only a limited selection of restaurants and none at all in the first-class category. Both the B★ hotels we recommend have good restaurants, but two other quality eating places are **Macduff's** (Tel: Aghadowey 433), 112 Killeague Road, Blackhill, which is a little way out of the town and specializes in game and seafood; and **Salmon Leap** (Tel: 2992), 53 Castleroe Road, offering a mouthwatering variety of roasts, game and smoked fish.

Coleraine's only superior hotel accommodation is offered by the B★ graded **Lodge Hotel** (Tel: 4848), Lodge Road, with twenty double bedrooms, and the B★ **Bohill Auto Inn** (Tel: 4406), Bushmills Road, with twenty-six bedrooms including fifteen family rooms. Two suggestions for bed and breakfast accommodation are: **Mr and Mrs Eyre**, Cairndhu, 4 Cairn Court (Tel: 2854), and the student halls at the **University of Ulster** (Tel: 4141) which are available between July and September.

PORTSTEWART is the last village in County Londonderry before the crossing into County Antrim. It is a busy little seaside resort during the summer months, with a small harbour, promenade and three-mile-long beach. Motorcycling enthusiasts flock to Portstewart in May each year to watch one of the principal races in the British calendar.

There is a wide selection of accommodation available in Portstewart, ranging from the B★ **Edgewater Hotel** (Tel: 583 3314) in 88 Strand Road to more than thirty approved bed and breakfast establishments. A couple of guesthouses worth considering are: **Oregon** (Tel: 2826), 118 Station Road, which is open all year, and **Mulroy Guest House** (Tel: 2293), 8 Atlantic Circle, which is open from April until October.

Four miles east along the coast takes you into the province's sixth county, Antrim, and the beautiful little town of **PORTRUSH** which is approximately the same size as Portstewart. Portrush stands on the **Ramore Head** peninsula where visitors can enjoy some of Northern Ireland's finest beaches. A steep cliff marks the end of the peninsula and this is a favourite spot for ornithologists.

The East Strand is the best beach around Portrush and its two-mile length is backed by the Royal Portrush Golf Course, where the British Open has been held on a number of occasions. Many fine walks can be enjoyed along the beach and it is worth investigating the natural caves which have formed in the limestone at one end of the strand. The fifty-five-metre-high **Cathedral Cave** is considered to be the most spectacular.

One of the most beautiful castles in Ireland is the crumbling remains of **Dunluce Castle** which stands on an isolated cliff-edge. After a colourful military history, it fell into disuse in the seventeenth century. Part of it actually fell into the sea in 1639 but what remains is reasonably safe, as long as you do not climb on the old walls or stray too close to the edge of the cliff. The views are breathtaking and there are few more romantic spots to visit in this part of Ireland.

There are a large number of hotels, guesthouses, and bed and breakfast places in Portrush. The **Tourist Information office** (Tel: 823 333), in the Town Hall, is open between April and September and can provide you with a full list of approved accommodation in the town.

Portrush's two best hotels are the B-graded **Eglinton Hotel** (Tel: 822 371), at 49 Eglinton Street, and the **Northern Counties Hotel** (Tel: 823 755), in Main Street, with eighty-eight bedrooms. Three ideas for bed and breakfast are: **Castle Erin Guesthouse** (Tel: 822 744) in Castle Erin Road, the superior-grade **Carrick Dhu Guesthouse** (Tel: 823 666) at 6 Ballyreagh Road, and the

Windsor Guesthouse (Tel: 823 793) with twenty-four bedrooms at 67 Main Street.

The remainder of the north-east coast of County Antrim is considered to be among the most attractive areas in Ireland. Two more villages worth visiting within easy reach of Portrush are **BUSHMILLS**, with its solid Victorian buildings and famous whiskey distillery, and **PORTBALLINTRAE** which is well placed to explore the Causeway beaches.

The most famous sight in Ireland, the **Giant's Causeway**, is a short distance down the coast from here. Tourists have poured into Northern Ireland for generations to see this remarkable geological phenomenon, and few are disappointed. Tens of thousands of columns of cooling volcanic rock formed the Giant's Causeway, and such is its importance to geologists, that UNESCO added it to their list of 'World Heritage' sites in 1986. The Causeway is made up of more than 40,000 volcanic basalt columns packed tightly together along the coastline before finally disappearing under the sea. Most of the columns are hexagonal in shape and some reach more than thirteen metres in height. Before you admire the Causeway itself, spend some time in the impressive **Visitor Centre** and this will give you an idea of the history and legend of the rocks. The Centre is open daily 1000-1700 Oct-May, and 1000-2000 June-Sept.

Continuing round the north-east coastline, two more places of interest are **BALLINTOY** and **BALLYCASTLE**. Ballintoy has a peaceful little harbour, and for a small 'donation' local fishermen will take you a little way along the coast or over to Sheep Island, renowned for its cormorant and puffin population.

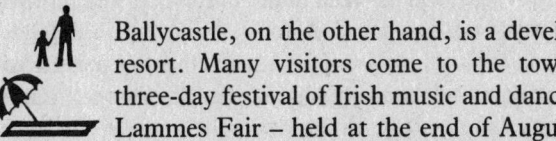

Ballycastle, on the other hand, is a developed seaside resort. Many visitors come to the town during its three-day festival of Irish music and dance – the Ould Lammes Fair – held at the end of August each year. Others come to admire the eighteenth-century **parish church** with its distinctive octagonal tower and enormous clock face. The founders of Ballycastle, the first Earls of Antrim, are buried in the vaults of a **ruined friary** at Bonamargy, about three-quarters of a mile east of the town. This is the departure point for **Rathlin Island**. Ferries operate from Ballycastle to Rathlin Island from Easter to September every day, weather permitting. The trip lasts fifty minutes. Mini-buses meet ferries and are available for trips around the island. Only one hundred people live on the island today. Bird-watchers, geologists, botanists and sea-anglers as well as those who just want to get away from it all, seek refuge in Rathlin Island. Sir Francis Drake landed guns here in 1575. It was also a favourite haunt for pirates and smugglers. Passage to Rathlin Island is by arrangement with the Tourist office, Ballycastle (Tel: 02657 62024/62225), or contact the boatman direct.

Carrick-a-rede rope bridge, also found at Ballycastle, is well worth the visit. The rope bridge hangs eighty feet above the sea and joins a cliff to a precipitous island.

Round the coast a little further visitors can drive through the picturesque coastal villages of CUSHENDUN and CUSHENDALL which lie about four miles apart. Cushendun is the smaller of the two, with a population of less than one hundred, and it sprang up only this century under the supervision of the first ane last Lord Cushendun. **Craighagh Wood**, a little way west of the village, was where Catholics gathered to celebrate Mass during the religious persecution of the eighteenth century.

Cushendun was the home of Moira O'Neill, poetess of the Glens. John Masefield, the English Laureate, met his wife here. Cushendun is preserved by the National Trust for its Cornish-style cottages and unspoiled beauty.

Cushendall has about 800 residents and was founded a century earlier than Cushendun. The village has a fine golf course overlooking the sea, and a sandstone **curfew tower** in Mill Street which was built by the East India Company in 1809 for the 'containment' of local rioters. Just outside the village is **Layde Old Church**, traditional burial place for the MacDonnell family and site of a large stone cross which marks the grave of Dr James MacDonnell, a pioneer of chloroform for surgical operations.

The coast road continues down to another delightful village, GLENARIFF – sometimes known by its old name, Waterfoot. Glenariff host the *Feis na nGleann*, an annual festival of sport and culture held every summer, but visitors at any time of the year can enjoy the **Glenariff Forest Park**. This is one of the most beautiful of all the Antrim Glens and its fine views make it well worth a visit.

Further down the coast you will pass CARNLOUGH which had a number of major limestone quarries until they were exhausted in the 1960s. The white railway bridge which crosses the main road, the nearby clock tower and courthouse, and many private houses were built from local limestone. Earlier this century, the Marquis and Marchioness of Londonderry were responsible for having many of the village's public buildings erected, including the Londonderry Arms Hotel (Tel: 85255) in Harbour Road which was once owned by Sir Winston Churchill.

The neighbouring village of GLENARM still exports some limestone from the small harbour, built in the early years of the seventeenth century. **Glenarm Castle** became the seat of the Earls of Antrim after they left the isolated and crumbling Dunluce Castle. The Castle can be visited throughout the year. Its entrance is through a wide stone arch which dominates one end of the village's main street.

The whole route from Ballycastle to Larne encompasses the **Nine Glens of Antrim**. The names of the nine glens from south to north, are: Glenarm, Glencloy, Glenariff, Glenballyeamon, Glenaan, Glencorp, Glendun, Glenshek and Glentaisie. A final coastal landmark, before you reach Larne once more, is Slemish, a small, long-extinct **volcano** which stands near BROUGHSHANE. Sketchy documentary evidence about St Patrick's early life indicates that it was probably near here that he herded pigs during his childhood, having been brought to Ireland from the coast of Britain by pirates in the late fourth century. Slemish is one of several places in Ireland which is regarded as a place of pilgrimage on St Patrick's Day, 17 March.

Before you leave County Antrim there are one or two places of interest inland – north of the county town of Antrim itself which was covered near the start of the chapter – which you may consider visiting. BALLYMONEY, for instance, is the focal point of an agricultural community and has four-weekly livestock markets and a weekly 'general' market which has been going strong since 1626. At the **Causeway Safari Park** off the Ballymoney–Portrush road (B62) at Ballybogey, motorists can drive through the beautiful wooded reserve where lions roam freely with their cubs. There is also a mini–zoo.

BALLYMENA, with a population of nearly 30,000, is the province's third largest town after Belfast and Derry. It expanded considerably during the seventeenth century with settlers coming from south-west Scotland. One of its most famous sons was David Herbison, better known as the Bard of Dunclug, whose lilting poetry captured the fusion of Scottish and Irish cultures.

Ballymena is overlooked by steep Slemish mountain where St Patrick was a slave boy after being kidnapped from England by Irish pirates in the fifth century.

Ballymena is the centre of a wide agricultural community, and large crowds regularly attend the thrice-weekly livestock markets. A more general town market is held every Saturday and this has been going strong since Charles I gave the Adair family permission to hold such a market. The Adair family later gave the **People's Park**, in the centre of town, to the people of Ballymena.

One interesting excursion from Ballymena is to the **ancestral home of Chester Arthur**, just past the village of Cullybackey on the A96. Chester Arthur was President of the United States between 1881 and 1885 and his ancestors lived here until 1816 when his father decided to emigrate to the 'New World'. The ancestral home is open every afternoon between Easter and September, except Sundays, for a small admission charge.

Further information about what to do and see in and around Ballymena is available from the **Tourist Information office** (Tel: 44111) at 2 Ballymoney Road. Two good hotels are the A-grade **Adair Arms** (Tel: 653 674) with forty-one bedrooms, in Ballymoney Road; and the B-grade **Leighinmohr House** (Tel: 2313) with eighteen rooms, including thirteen doubles, in Leighinmohr Avenue. Relatively inexpensive accommodation is available at the **Clarence Guesthouse** (Tel: 56671) at 84 Lower Mill Street.

Index

Abbeyfeale, 248
Abbeyleix, 307
Accommodation,
  Bed and Breakfast, 8, 30–2, 44, 71, 93, 148, 166, 205, 213, 265, 288, 299, 331, 333, 338, 342–3, 351–2
  Farmhouses/town and country houses, 31, 61, 68, 72, 218, 247, 261, 266, 320, 342
  Guesthouses, 8, 31, 72, 126, 143, 145, 166, 205, 227, 257, 277, 297, 299, 303, 305, 309, 322–3, 326, 331, 336, 348, 351, 356
  Hotels, 8, 31–2, 71–2, 124–6, 139–41, 143, 145, 148, 154, 159, 163, 166–7, 177, 179–80, 182, 189, 198, 204–5, 209, 213–14, 216, 218, 221, 225–6, 229, 232, 242–3, 247, 251, 253–4, 257, 260–2, 264, 266, 269, 276, 278, 281, 283, 286, 288, 297–9, 301–6, 308–9, 322, 326, 329–31, 333, 336, 338–40, 342–3, 348, 351–2, 354–5
  Self-catering, 30–1, 34, 44, 58–9, 73, 92, 245, 260
  Youth hostels, 8, 74
  see also Camping holidays *and* Caravan holidays
Activity holidays, 64, 68
Adare, 246
Aghavannagh, 153
Air travel, 9, 50, 75–6, 119, 156–7, 192, 235, 273, 314, 349
Annacotty, 243
Annalong, 332
Annestown, 179
Antrim, 327
Aran Islands, 18, 254–5
Ardara, 15, 30, 280

Ardee, 144
Ardmore, 14, 186
Arklow, 13, 158
Armagh, 317, 334–6
Askeaton, 248–9
Athenry, 257
Athlone, 295, 302
Athy, 305

Babies, catering for, 31–2
Baggage, *see* Luggage
Balbriggan, 124, 141
Ballaghisheen, 231
Ballina, 265–6
Ballinacurra, 196
Ballinamuck, 299–300
Ballinasloe, 259
Ballincollig, 206
Ballintoy, 353
Ballintra, 277
Ballybay, 296
Ballybunion, 14, 22, 31, 33
Ballycastle, 265, 353
Ballyduff, 186
Ballygawley, 339
Ballyhack, 169–70
Ballyhalbert, 330
Ballyliffin, 290
Ballymahon, 300
Ballymena, 355
Ballymoney, 159, 355
Ballynahinch, 261
Ballyporeen, 184
Ballyshannon, 276–7
Baltimore, 28, 213
Banagher, 294, 303
Bandon Bridge, 210
Bangor, 328
Banks, 39
Bantry, 215

Bed and Breakfast,
  see Accommodation
Belfast, 21, 317–25
  Crown Bar, 320
  Stormont Castle, 322
  Queens University, 320
Belturbet, 298
Bettystown, 142
Bird sanctuaries, 28, 259
Birr, 294, 303
Blackrock, 145
Blackwater, 160
Blarney Castle, 205–6
Boyle, 267
Bray, 13, 149
Budgeting, 8, 30, 43–6
  accommodation, 44
  food and drink, 44–5
  students, 45
  travel, 45
Bunbeg, 284
Bunclody, 162–3
Buncrana, 290
Bundoran, 15, 31, 33, 276
Bunmahon, 33, 179
Bunratty, 252
  Castle, 17, 252
Burtonport, 281
Bus travel, 8, 27, 30, 45, 78–9, 96, 99–100

Caherdaniel, 229
Cahir, 310
Callan, 308
Camping holidays, 73–4, 286
Cappoquin, 184
Car/campervan, see Independent travel
Car-hire, 45, 63–4, 96–7
Caravan holidays, 32–3, 51, 73–4, 100, 286
  horse-drawn, 67, 100
Carlingford, 144
Carnlough, 354
Carraroe, 24, 260
Carrick, 280
Carrickfergus, 326
Carrickmacross, 295
Carrick-on-Shannon, 270–1
Carrigaholt, 253
Carrigart, 286

Carrig-on-Bannow, 168
Carrowmore, 269
Cashel, 244, 261, 310
Cashel Bay, 30
Castlebary, 262
Castleblayney, 295–6
Castleconnell, 243
Castlepollard, 301
Castletown, 159
Castletown Bere, 216
Cavan, 29, 297
Celbridge, 123, 304
Clara, 33, 155
Clarinbridge, 258
Cleggan, 261
Clifden, 30, 261
Climate, 121–2, 157, 193, 236, 274, 294, 316–17
  rainfall, 10–11, 121–2
  temperature, 11, 121, 157, 193, 236, 274, 294, 316–17
Climbing, see Mountain climbing
Clonakilty, 211
Clonea, 14
Clones, 296
Clonfert, 259
Clonmacnois, 294–5, 303
Clonmany, 290
Clonmel, 24, 181–2
Cloyne, 196
Coach travel, 45, 51, 61–2, 68, 96, 192
Cobh, 197
Coleraine, 350–1
Comber, 329
Communications, 94–6
  post offices, 94–5
  poste restante, 95
  telephones, 3, 95–6
Connemara, 260
Cork, 19–21, 93–4, 198–205
  Red Abbey, 201
  St Finbar's Cathedral, 201
Corofin, 251
Cost-conscious holidays, 59–60
Courtown, 160
Craggaunowen, 251
Craughwell, 258
Credit cards, 38
Creeslough,

Crookhaven, 214
Crosshaven, 207
Crossmaglen, 337
Crossmolina, 265
Cruises, 34, 51, 67
Culinary specialities, *see* Food and drink
Curragh, 20
Currency, 37–9
Customs,
  duty-free goods, 36
  regulations, 36–7
Cycling, 23–4, 66, 124, 165, 202, 263, 295

Dalkey, 148
Delvin, 301–2
Derry, 317, 346–9
Dingle, 231
Dingle Bay, 14
Dingle Peninsula, 26, 231
Donaghadee, 329
Donegal, 277–8
  medieval castle, 278
Doolin, 31, 254
Downhill, 350
Downpatrick, 331
Draperstown, 345
Driving holidays, 63–4
Drogheda, 142–3
Dromahair, 271
Drumcollogher, 247
Drumlish, 299
Dublin, 16, 19–21, 26, 93–4, 116–37
  General Post Office, 17, 127
  'Literary Pub Crawl', 135–6
  Phoenix Park, 128–9, 132
  Trinity College, 17, 128
Dun Aengus, 18
Duncannon, 170
Duncormick, 168
Dundalk, 145
Dunfanaghy, 285
Dungannon, 327–8
Dungarvan, 33, 180
Dungloe, 281
Dun Laoghaire, 26, 123–4, 146
Dunmore East, 14, 178

Easkey, 15

Edenderry, 300
Edgesworthstown, 300
Eglinton, 349
Electricity, 82
Embassy and Consulate addresses, 35, 102
Emergencies, *see* Problems/Emergencies
Ennis, 249–50
Enniscorthy, 24, 161–2
Enniscrone, 15
Enniskerry, 149
Enniskillen, 343–4
Ennistymon, 284
Excursions, 131, 137–8, 325

Fahan, 232, 290
Fairyhouse, 21
Falcarragh, 284
Fallmore, 264
Family holidays, 31–4, 124, 141, 155, 158, 236–7, 262, 274–6, 330, 353
Farmhouses/town and country houses, *see* Accommodation
Fermoy, 218–19
Ferns, 160
Ferries, 10, 18, 34, 51, 76–7, 157, 314–15, 325–6
Festivals, 20–2, 91, 122, 165, 167, 178, 224, 237
Fishing, 24–5, 64–6, 124, 141, 147, 170, 182, 184, 211, 221, 227, 237, 243, 251, 264–6, 275, 281–2, 284, 294, 297–8, 301–2, 310, 330, 340, 342
  see also Sporting holidays
Fivemiletown, 339
Fly/drive holidays, 51, 69–70
Food and drink, 88–91
  cost of, 89–90
  culinary specialities, 90–1, 122–3
  drinks, 91–2
  pubs, 134–6, 203
  restaurants/eating out, 89–90, 133–4, 142, 166, 177, 182, 189, 203–4, 209, 221, 225–6, 250, 256–7, 279, 283, 288, 323–5, 326, 338–40, 342, 347–9, 351
Fore, 301

Forest parks, 25, 33, 259, 317, 331, 337, 355
Forest walks and nature trails, 171–3, 194–5, 219–20, 237–9, 275–6
Foxford, 237
Foynes, 248

Galway, 16, 19–22, 238–9, 255–7
   Collegiate Church of St Nicholas, 256
   Irish Crystal Visitor Centre, 257
   'Oyster Country', 258
Garretstown, 210
Garryvoe, 195
Gartan, 289
Geography of Ireland, 5–6
Giant's Causeway, 317, 353
Glanmore, 222
Glenariff, 354
Glenarm, 355
Glenbeigh, 227
Glencolumbkille, 24, 30, 280
Glendalough, 16, 27
   monastery, 27
Glengarriff, 216
Glenties, 280–1
Glenveagh, 28
Glin, 248
Golf, 22–3, 33, 64–5, 124, 139, 147, 221, 261, 263–4, 286, 297, 352
   see also Sporting holidays
Good Tourist, The, 113–14
Gorey, 158
Gort, 251, 258
Gortahork, 284
Gorteen, 187
Granard, 300
Grange, 187
Groomsport, 329
Guest houses, see Accommodation
Gweedore, 282

Health, 41–2
   formalities, 36
   hygiene standards, 41
   medical treatment, 42
   medicines, 48
Healthy holidays, see Sporting holidays
Hillsborough, 328
Hilltown, 332

Hill walking, see Walking
History of Ireland, 103–11, 117–19, 164–5, 173, 184–5, 190–1, 198–201, 208, 234–5, 272–3, 292–3, 312–14
Hitch-hiking, 81–2
Holiday insurance, see Insurance
Holywood, 328
Horse-drawn caravan holidays, see Caravan holidays
Horse-riding, 25, 124, 140, 142, 158
   see also Sporting holidays
Hotels, see Accommodation
Howth, 120, 138

Inch, 14, 159
Independent travel, 51–2, 96
   accommodation, 71–5
   air travel, 75–6, 119–20
   bus travel, 8, 27, 30, 45, 78–9, 96, 99–100, 120
      cost of, 99–100
   camping holidays, 73
   car/campervan, 8, 45, 79–81, 96–9, 120
      documentation, 98
      hire, 45, 96–9, 120–1, 318
      petrol grades and prices, 98
   caravan, 32–4, 73, 96
      hire, 34
   coach travel, 96
   cruiser, 34
   cycle, 23–4, 66, 124, 165, 202, 295
      hire, 23–4, 165, 202
   ferries, 10, 18, 34, 51, 76–7, 157, 314–15, 325–6
      booking, 10, 51
   hitch-hiking, 81–2
   horse-drawn caravans, 67, 100
      cost of, 100
   rail, 8, 27, 30, 45, 77–8, 96, 99, 119–20, 157, 192, 236, 293, 315
      cost of, 99
   self-catering, 73
   taxis, 101, 120, 318–19
      costs of, 101
Information, see Pre-planning and information *and* Tourist Information
Inishkeen, 295

Innishannon, 210
Insurance
  holiday, 39–41
  medical, 42
Irish National Heritage Park, 17, 33, 166

Keadue, 267
Kells, 145
Kenmare, 220–1
Kerryheel, 287
Kilcar, 279
Kildare, 123–4, 305
Kilfenora, 27, 254
Kilfinane, 245
Kilkee, 236, 253
Kilkeel, 332
Kilkenny, 307–8
  Black Abbey, 307
Killala, 265
Killaloe, 243
Killanne, 163
Killarney, 16, 18–19, 22, 28, 94, 223–6
  Muckross Friary, 225
  Torc waterfall, 226
Killary Harbour, 262
Killimer, 252
Killiney, 148
Killmallock, 245
Killorglin, 227–8
Killybegs, 30, 279
Kilmacrennan, 288
Kilmacthomas, 181
Kilrush, 252
Kiltyclogher, 271
Kinsale, 208–9
Kinvara, 237, 258
Knock, 263–4
  Shrine, 18, 264
Knockpatrick, 248
Kylemore, 24

Laghey, 277
Lahinch, 254
Lanesborough, 300
Larne, 325–6
Leixlip, 123
Leopardstown, 20
Letterkenny, 282–3

Limavady, 338–9
Limerick, 16, 19, 20, 22, 94, 237–8, 239–42
  King John's Castle, 240–1
  St Mary's Cathedral, 240
Lisburn, 328
Lisdoonvarna, 237, 255
Lismore, 184–5
Longford, 299–300
Loughrea, 258–9
Louisburgh, 24
Luggage, what to take, 46–8
Lurgan, 333

Macroom, 218
Malahide, 124, 139–40
Malin, 290–1
Mallow, 218
Manorcunningham, 289
Manorhamilton, 271
Marfield, 182
Markethill, 337
Maynooth, 304
Medical insurance, *see* Insurance
Midleton, 196
Milford, 286
Milltown, 259
Miltown Malbay, 254
Monaghan, 296–7
Money, 36–9
  banking hours, 39
  credit cards, 39
  currency, 36–7
  Eurocheques, 37–8
  exchange of, 38–9
  traveller's cheques, 38
Moneymore, 345
Mountain climbing, 180, 193, 216, 263, 269, 284
  see also Walking *and* Sporting holidays
Mountcharles, 278
Mullaghmore, 15, 270
Mullingar, 29, 301
Mulroy Bay, 15
Murroe, 244

Naas, 123–4, 305
National Parks, 27, 30, 289

Nature lover, The, 27–9, 123, 149–50, 158, 167–8, 172–3, 180, 190, 194–5, 198, 213, 219–20, 230–1, 237–9, 245, 259–60, 271, 289, 317, 331, 340, 351
Nature reserves, 331
Nature trails, *see* Forest walks and nature trails
Navan, 20
Nenagh, 309
Newbridge, 305
Newcastle, 330
Newcastle West, 247
Newport, 244
New Ross, 168–9
Newry, 332–3
Newtonards, 328–9
Newtowncashel, 300
Newtownstewart, 341
Nightlife, *see* Socialite, The

Omagh, 317, 340
Oughterard, 260
Out-of-season holidays, 9–10, 34

Package holidays, 9, 51–2
　activity holidays, 64, 68
　caravan, 51, 67–8
　checklist before booking, 69–70
　coach tours, 51, 68
　cost-conscious, 59–60
　cruises, 51
　cycling, 66
　driving holidays, 63–4
　farmhouses/town and country houses, 61, 68
　fishing, 64–5, 68
　fly/drive, 51, 69–70
　golf, 51, 64–5, 68
　horse-drawn caravans, 67–8
　self-catering, 58–9
　short breaks, 60–1
　tour operators, 52–6
　walking, 51, 66–8
Passports, 35
Petrol grades and prices, 98
Plumbridge, 341
Portadown, 333
Portaferry, 330

Portarlington, 306
Portballintrae, 352
Portinard, 248
Port Laoise, 306
Portlaw, 183–4
Portmarnock, 22, 124, 139
Portrush, 351–2
Portstewart, 351
Post offices, *see* Communications
Potted history of Ireland, 103–13
Poulaphouca, 153
Pre-planning and information, 42–3
　accommodation lists, 42
　free information, 42–3
　guide books, 43
　maps, 48
　tourist information, 42–3
Problems/Emergencies, 101–2
　Embassy and Consulate addresses, 102
　medical, 101
　police, 101
　women, 102
　work, 102
Public holidays, 3
Pubs, *see* Food and drink

Rail travel, 8, 27, 30, 45, 77–8, 96, 99, 119–20, 157, 192, 236, 293, 315
Ramelton, 288
Rathkeale, 247
Rathmullan, 287
Recluse, The, 29–31, 123, 151, 190, 194, 213, 219, 272, 285, 289, 317
Religion, 7–8
Restaurants/Eating out, *see* Food and drink
Ringaskiddy, 207
Ring of Kerry, 17–18, 27, 226
Rosapenna, 286–7
Roscommon, 20, 266–7
Roscrea, 309
Rosscarbery, 212
Rosses Point, 15, 268
Rosslare, 14, 26, 31, 93, 166–7
Rossnowlagh, 277
Roundstone, 30, 261
Rush, 124, 141

Sailing, 124, 141, 147, 207, 288, 290, 298, 302, 330
 see also Sporting holidays
Salthill, 15, 31
Scariff, 252
Self-catering holidays,
 see accommodation
Shannonbridge, 303
Shopping, 87–8, 132–2
Short-break holidays, 60–1
Sightseer, The, 15–19, 86–7, 123, 126–31, 138–41, 158, 165–6, 173–4, 179, 193, 200, 205–6, 208–9, 224, 227, 237, 240–1, 243–4, 248, 251, 255–6, 263–4, 268, 277–8, 285, 294–5, 307–8, 317, 331, 334, 343–4, 346, 352
Skerries, 124, 141
Skibbereen, 214
Sligo Town, 267–8
Socialite, The, 19–22, 93–4, 123, 136–7, 148, 157, 176, 179
Special interest holiday, 64–7
Sporting holidays, 24–7, 64–6, 124, 139, 141, 147, 179, 190, 193, 213, 221, 237, 243, 263, 281, 286, 296, 302, 305, 340
 see also under individual sports
Strabane, 341–2
Stradbally, 306
Strandhill, 15, 269
Strokestown, 267
Sun worshipper, The, 13–15, 141, 158–60, 195, 215, 261, 274, 276, 279, 330, 353
Swords, 140

Tallow, 186
Taxis, 101, 120, 318–19
Telephone, *see* Communications
Tennis, 124, 147, 182, 261, 288
 see also Sporting holidays
Termonbarry, 300
Thomastown, 308
Thurles, 310
Time difference, 82
Tipperary, 310

Toomebridge, 345
Tory Island, 285
Tour operators, 52–6
Tourist information, 32, 42, 85–6, 121, 143, 145, 159, 162, 178–80, 182, 188, 202, 216, 219, 221, 232, 236, 247, 249, 253, 255, 262, 266, 269, 274, 276, 278, 282, 293–4, 297, 299, 301, 304, 308, 316, 318, 326, 332, 336, 343, 347, 353, 355
Tourmakeady, 263
Trabolgan Holiday Centre, 33
Tralee, 20, 27, 94, 224
Tramore, 14, 21, 26, 31–2, 93, 178–9
Traveller's cheques, 38
Tuan, 259
Tulla, 251
Tullamore, 303
Tully, 305

Ulster-American Folk Park, 341
Useful information, 82

Virginia, 29, 299

Walking, 25, 51, 66, 68, 243, 262, 282, 285, 294–5, 298
 see also Sporting holidays
Warrenport, 333
Water, 82
Waterford, 173–7
 Crystal factory, 176
 Reginald's Tower, 174–5
Watersports, 25–6, 124, 138–9, 147, 207, 262–3, 286, 302
 see also Sporting holidays
Waterville, 22, 228–9
Westport, 262–3
Wexford, 28, 164–6
 Selskar Abbey, 165
Wicklow, 153–4
Wildlife parks, 28
Woodford, 259

Yeats country (Sligo), 268–70
Youghal, 14, 187–8, 195
Youth hostels, *see* Accommodation

Cheap Sleep Guide to Europe 1992

Katie Wood

The essential companion to *Europe by Train* – and every other cost-conscious travel book.

A constant preoccupation for all budget travellers is where to find cheap accommodation. Most guidebooks offer a few recommendations, but more often than not these places are fully booked *because* they are listed.

Cheap Sleep Guide to Europe has an almost inexhaustible supply of accommodation ideas in over 150 towns and cities in 25 countries, including the former Eastern bloc.

- thousands of hotels, hostels, private lettings, campsites, pensiones, B&Bs, sleep-ins – and where to sleep rough if it comes to it
- full details on cheapest prices available
- streetwise advice on trouble spots
- foolproof directions to accommodation from main train terminals
- tips on how and when to book a bed ahead

The first and only extensive directory to places to stay in Europe for around £10 or less.

No more sleepless nights!

Fontana

Round the World Air Guide 1992

Katie Wood and George McDonald

Round the World Air Guide is for the new breed of serious traveller, whether on a round-the-world ticket or using conventional long-haul options.

Everyone from business men and women combining trips with holidays and visits to the great cities of the world to back-packing students working their way round the world will find this book an essential source of information.

No other guide provides practical up-to-date airline and ticket information and acts as a guidebook to the world's fifty major destinations.

Consult this book before buying any long-haul ticket and discover:

- How to cut costs and get the most out of your ticket
- Stop-off possibilities and side trips
- Airport facilities around the world
- Where to go and what to see
- Where to sleep and what to eat
- Dining out and nightlife

NO FREQUENT TRAVELLER CAN AFFORD TO TAKE OFF WITHOUT IT!

Fontana

European City Breaks
'Weekend' Escapes to 23 of Europe's Major Cities

Katie Wood

As flight times decrease and air fares tumble, and with the approaching reality of the Channel Tunnel, the cities of Europe are becoming as accessible for short breaks – of three or four days, or maybe even a week – as those of Britain. Now, within a matter of hours you can escape the rigours of everyday life and find yourself strolling up the Champs-Elysées or dining in Budapest, rapt in the Rijksmuseum, shopping in Munich or having a drink in St Mark's Square.

Full of advice on how to get there, which tour operators to use, where to stay and eat and what there is to see and do, this is an invaluable handbook for every enthusiastic traveller. Whether you want to wander in your own way, cram in culture, arrange a romantic weekend or visit two cities in a week, *European City Breaks* – the result of several years of research – will help you decide where to go and when, and tells you all you need to know both before you go and when you're there.

Covers every city break operator for:

Austria – Innsbruck, Salzburg, Vienna; **Belgium** – Bruges, Brussels; **Czechoslovakia** – Prague; **Denmark** – Copenhagen; **France** – Nice, Paris; **Germany** – Munich, Berlin; **Great Britain** – London; **Hungary** – Budapest; **Ireland** – Dublin; **Italy** – Florence, Milan, Rome, Venice; **Netherlands** – Amsterdam; **Portugal** – Lisbon; **Soviet Union** – Moscow; **Spain** – Barcelona, Madrid.

Fontana

Europe by Train 1992

Katie Wood and George McDonald

The bestselling classic, recommended by *EUROTRAIN*

Europe by Train is the only guide designed specifically for the eurorailer's needs. It contains all the essential, practical information required by students and those on a tight budget:

- Maximizing the benefits of rail passes
- Train networks and station facilities
- The best routes
- Local transport
- What to see
- Where to sleep
- What to eat
- Where the nightlife is

In addition to being fully revised and updated for 1992, this year's new edition of *Europe by Train* includes even more information on eastern Europe, hostels, pensiones and excursions.

'Excellent . . . a reliable guide to the systems of all European countries' *Independent*

Fontana